AF564680

CORPORATE COLONIALISM

Designs of MNCs in India

yatra yogeshvarah krsno
yatra partho dhanur-dharah
tatra stir vijayo bhutir,
Dhurva nitir matir mama

DEDICATED TO MY
WORTHY TEACHERS ESPECIALLY
DR. JAI NARAIN SHARMA

Contents

Dr. Jai Narain Sharma
Professor and Hony. Director
Gandhi Bhawan,
Department of Gandhian Studies
Panjab University, Chandigarh-14

Foreword

We are all familiar with colonialism. The dates may have varied; the colonising country may have been different; but the main features of our common colonial experience were basically the same.

Using superior military technology, the colonising power forcibly imposed its rule over the peoples, at great cost to us in terms of human lives and suffering and in terms of human and natural ecology.

Military conquest was very often preceded—and most certainly followed—by the imposition of new religions and cultures, which facilitated subjugation by dulling the impulse to resist the clutches. The effects of such cultural implantation on our minds have lingered on and continued to do their damage, keeping us in mental bondage long after the last colonising soldier had left our soil. Soon, the colonial mind started to take for real the masks worn by the colonizers and the words they used to deceive their victims, such as "we bring you civilisation", "we will teach you democracy";, etc. As soon as resistance was quelled, the colonising power set-up a colonial administration, run at lower levels by people culled from local elites, many of whom decided to work hand-in-hand with their colonial masters to preserve their wealth and privileges.

As the colonial bureaucracy was put in place, the process of drawing out our wealth then began. Over the centuries, the colonising powers enriched themselves immeasurably by drawing human and natural resources from our lands—human slaves, indentured labour, tributes, precious metal and other mineral, colonial crops cultivated on seized indigenous land, and so on. At the very foundations of the richest countries of today, are the broken remains of our own ancestors and the wealth plundered from their communities.

The colonizers brought with them the practices of plantation agriculture, large-scale logging, large-scale mining, and unsustainable technologies, which were meant for plunder and for maximising exploitation and profits. These unsustainable practices replaced the sustainable indigenous practices our pre-colonial peoples had relied on for centuries.

The impact on the people and their communities was grievous. We lost our right to self-determination and our freedom. We lost our wealth through colonial plunder. Our best lands were seized for colonial tillage. Indigenous communities lost their rights to their lands. The impact on the people and their communities was grievous. The impact on nature was equally disastrous. Colonial occupation was invariably marked with plunder of our natural resources and the introduction of monoculture in direct contrast to the much more sustainable and ecological practices of our pre-colonial past.

During this period, the colonial powers that took over the globe were mercantilist and, later, early industrial powers. Often operating their own State monopoly corporations, they scoured the globe in search of slaves, tradeable goods or raw materials, and bases for their colonial operations. This period of colonialism may be called the first wave of Globalisation.

Where independence was won by arms in China, for example—the colonial economic and political interests had to beat a full retreat. They lost their territorial rights and their businesses, their properties confiscated and nationalised. Where independence was gained through non-violent means, the nationalists made efforts to regain control of their economy. These took the form of foreign ownership limits, profit remittances restrictions, local content requirements, exports quotas, and other attempts to regulate foreign businesses.

During this post-colonial period, the role of global capital expanded, partly due to internal developments in their home countries, and partly as a counter-response to independence movements and economic nationalism. Having lost direct control over their colonies, global capital sought and became better at indirect control; military aggression was replaced by cultural aggression and economic control. By this time, internal developments within the colonising powers themselves had prepared their economies for this shift: many of them had reached the late industrial stage development. Huge private corporations in partnership with governments had accumulated vast amounts of financial wealth, turning money itself into a major commodity. These corporations needed new markets and investment areas, rather than colonial territories that were becoming more and more difficult and costly to retain politically and militarily.

We are also familiar with these post-colonial developments. Again, they masked their real intention of drawing wealth from our lands and communities with such pretexts as: "we bring jobs"; "we bring technology"; "we will lend you money for development"; "we will protect you from communism"; and so on. Instead of relying on military conquest, these global corporations worked closely with elite-led governments, particularly those local classes whose economic interests coincided closely with their former masters. Often, the local police and armed forces were flooded with aid, to win their loyalty and service.

The post-colonial bottom line was no different: the extraction of wealth. This occurred through: unequal trade (depressed prices for our agricultural commodities, monopolistic prices for their industrial manufactures); high interest rates on foreign loans; using loan conditionalities to exact further concessions, quick and massive profit repatriation; and low wages. By retaining post-colonial dominance and control in the economic and cultural spheres, post-colonial wealth extraction could proceed unabated.

Chemical agriculture was introduced to intensify the production of export crops, widespread poisoning and damage in the countryside. Exploitation of our natural resources intensified, and energy generation projects such as huge dams, coal and oil plants, and nuclear plants in some cases ravaged the countryside.

The development of a nationwide mass media infrastructure served to further strengthen the colonial hold on local minds, to create and expand markets, and to ensure a friendly environment for foreign investments and foreign products.

This post-colonial wave may be called the second wave of Globalisation, where industrial countries and global corporations would range across the globe for investment areas, industrial markets, trading partners, and sources of cheap labour and raw materials.

This wave has gone through several phases, reflecting the progress of an unequal contest between powerful countries strengthened by the immense wealth they had drawn from colonial victims on the one hand, and the newly-independent nations weakened by centuries of plunder and exploitation on the other hand.

The early-independence phase was often marked by intense economic nationalism, as local economic interests tried to mobilize their government to enhance their economic sovereignty while global corporate interest fought to retain their colonial privileges. This phase saw the adoption of economic protectionist measures meant to strengthen local capital *vis-a-vis* foreign capital.

The second phase saw a succession of crises that included the oil shocks of the 70s, the debt crises of the 80s, the socialist crisis of the early 90s, and the financial crisis of the late 90s, which is still going on. Socialism had earlier provided a counter-balance to global corporations and their governments, as well as a possible alternative path for independence movements. These crises weakened the capacity, the will, and the overall position of the former colonies and enabled global corporations to launch major counter-attacks in order to regain much of the colonial power and privileges they had lost during the economic-nationalist phase.

The post-colonial counter-attacks by global corporations mark the third phase of this second wave. Many countries, despite having freed themselves from centuries of colonial rule, then lost much of their economic sovereignty to corporate-controlled international institutions such as the International Monetary Fund (IMF), the World Bank (WB) and the World Trade Organisation (WTO). Through loan conditional ties, structural adjustment programs, and other means, many nationalist laws and provisions gained by earlier anti-colonial independence movements were undermined and dismantled. Some authors Chakravarty Raghavan, for example have called this phase a process of "recolonisation", a return of colonial privileges for global corporations.

The impacts of this wave of Globalisation are no less destructive than the colonialism that preceded it. Our agricultural products consistently suffer from low prices; our workers from low wages. We are losing much of our capital due to profit repatriation and the debt crisis; chemical farming is taking away our food security and putting it in the hands of global chemical and seed conglomerates. We enjoy national sovereignty in name only. We are suffering from widespread ecological disasters, triggered by intensive resource extraction, disruptive energy projects, and toxic pollution. Our forests, mines and quarries are being quickly depleted; our air, water and soil heavily contaminated; and pervasive monoculture is seriously threatening our biodiversity.

This part of our history and current events should also be familiar to most of us.

We are still in the midst of the second wave of Globalisation, yet a third one has already emerged. The third wave of Globalisation began to be felt worldwide in the last half of the 1990s and is expressing its overwhelming presence in full force at the dawn of the 21st century. This looming third wave is the global information economy.

Like the first two waves, the third Globalisation wave arose from internal developments within the hearts of the global powers. It is important to look at these internal developments, because they will, as in the past, eventually impinge or the rest of the world—including our own—often shaping our destinies and steering our development in directions we never wanted to take.

The colonial powers were mercantilist and, later, industrial countries in their early expansionist stages. The post-colonial powers were industrial countries in their late stage, when capitalism had developed further, combining industrial and finance capital into huge monopolistic conglomerates in continual search for new acquisitions, sources of cheap raw materials and labour, and markets. The third wave of Globalisation is marked by the emergence and eventual dominance, within the most advanced industrial countries, of the information sector the sector that produces, manipulates, processes, distributes and markets information products.

The increasing dominance of the information sector in what had been industrial economies is turning them into information economies. These emerging information economics—principally the U.S. and to lesser extent some countries of Europe—are at the core of the third wave of Globalisation. Because of the way these economies are so closely interconnected, they are better seen as a single emerging global information economy. The internet is perhaps the most visible portion of this economy—and certainly the one which has received the most media attention. This emerging global information economy includes the global infrastructure for telecommunications, data exchange, media and entertainment; the knowledge industries; the publishing industries; the computer hardware and software industries; the emerging financial systems that will support online transaction; the emerging global legal infrastructure based on the WTO, including the GATT and the agreements in information technology, telecommunications and financial services; and the biotechnology and genetic engineering industries.

Unlike the first two waves, the implications and consequences of the global information economy are an unfamiliar phenomenon to most of us there are so many new things, so many new possibilities, that it is quite difficult to separate the chaff from the grain, the hype from the substance.

The cost of reproducing information what the economist calls its marginal cost—is very low and oftentimes approaches zero. In the last analysis, this feature is due to the very essence of information itself. Information is non-material in its essence—a numeric measure of the uncertainty which it resolves. The non-materiality of information is the basis of its low reproduction cost, which may be driven lower and lower by adopting representations that can be manipulated at lower cost. With today's digital representations, the costs of reproducing and distributing information have reached historic lows—as low as the cost of copying a diskette or downloading a file from an online server.

The low marginal cost of information has two major implications: one for those who use it and another for those who sell it. For users, it encourages sharing. Many cultures, in fact, see knowledge as social wealth a collective asset that is meant to be shared.

These cultures—including most Third World and indigenous cultures—are therefore in close harmony with the very nature of information. When we share software, for example, we are only being true to the nature of information and to our own cultures.

But there are other cultures, where private property concepts have become more absolute and where almost everything may be commodified. In these cultures—often with capitalism at their core—information has become an object of commodification and privatisation. Culture itself has become commodified, together with knowledge and life. They have become vehicles for profit-making.

Let us look more closely at the mechanism of profit-making through information. First, the seller turns information from a collective asset into private property. Then, copies are sold on the market, at prices set by the "owner"/seller. The near zero marginal cost of reproducing information now makes its selling price nearly pure profit. A diskette of software that may be copied for cents is sold for fifty dollars. A CDROM that may be reproduced for three dollars is sold for three hundred.

To realize these extremely high profit margins made possible by the low marginal cost of information products, however, the seller must create an artificial scarcity of the product. We have seen that information can now be easily copied by users themselves at practically no cost, creating a natural abundance which drives prices down. To keep prices and profit margins high, this natural abundance that proceeds from the essence of information itself must be prevented. The seller does it by essentially prohibiting sharing among users and acquiring from the State a monopoly in using and making copies of the information product. This creates the artificial scarcity that drives prices up and realizes for the seller the potential profits from high margins.

It is monopoly that creates the scarcity. Such monopolies are euphemistically known as intellectual property rights (IPR), the main form of ownership in an information economy. They are the mechanism for maintaining the high profit margins of those who control and sell information products. IPRs have two major forms: copyrights (historically, limited monopolies covering literary materials), and patents (historically, limited monopolies covering inventions). In recent years, as the information sector gained and increased their political and economic power, IPRs have been strengthened and extended to new areas.

IPRs are, in reality, statutory monopolies. They are monopolies over information granted through statutes by the State. Those who control information through IPR are basically rentiers: they make money by charging monopoly rents from users, who are threatened by State action should they continue to practice information sharing.

Still, enforcing information monopolies is not simple. After all, information monopolies are incompatible with the social nature of information. The deeply ingrained cultural habits of information sharing and exchange continue to assert themselves, regardless of the will of monopolists and their State protectors.

This is the dilemma within the emerging global information economy. On the one hand, information itself is a highly social good; on the other hand, the forms of ownership are highly monopolistic. On the one hand, users tend to share information goods; on the other hand, IPR holders insist on their monopolies. On the one hand, developing countries need the widest access to various technology options at the least cost; on the other hand, rich and powerful information economies control almost 90% of all the IPRs in the world today, and want to increase their control further.

The basic conflict within the information sector is the

incompatibility between the highly monopolistic forms of information ownership and the social nature of information. This conflict is also expressed between users who want to share information freely and monopoly claimants who want to prevent free sharing of information. It is further reflected in the conflict between developing countries who need low-cost access to major bodies of information and information economies which have established virtual monopolies over information. Historically, these information economies are basically the same colonial powers that have exploited developing countries over the centuries.

The socialising tendency emanates from the nature of information itself, and can therefore never be suppressed. The monopolising tendency emanates from the potentially high profit margins in selling information and the economic and political power concentrated in information monopolies. The conflicts arising from these two opposing tendencies will drive the historical development of the third wave of Globalisation.

Within the U.S., the high profit margins in the information sector is attracting more investment capital towards this sector, away from the agricultural and industrial sectors. This is the internal engine that is slowly transforming the U.S. economy into an information economy.

Within the emerging global information economy itself, monopoly concepts are already well-established and are even expanding their coverage. One item, for instance, is always non-negotiable in the U.S. diplomatic agenda: intellectual property rights (IPR). These concepts are increasingly dominating international legal system through bilateral negotiations with the U.S. and through the World Trade Organisation (WTO). Thus, worldwide, pressure is increasing on countries with non-monopolistic attitudes towards information to adopt the same U.S. legal system that strictly protects IPRs.

However, the social nature of information continually asserts itself. Information abundance created through user sharing and exchange keeps breaking through the artificial scarcity created by information monopolies. The latest releases of population software, songs or video immediately find themselves being copied in every corner of the globe. In effect, information automatically globalizes itself regardless of the will of those who insist in monopolising them. Ironically, information monopolists find their products better distributed in those parts of the globe where they could not enforce their monopoly. They therefore insist on imposing monopolistic legal systems upon the rest of the globe, so they can realize the same profit margins they enjoy in their monopoly areas. Even one country that refuses to be part of this global legal system will pose a threat to their global monopoly, thus they will exert every effort to bring it in. These monopolists will never leave any country or any community alone. They are the real engines of Globalisation's Third Wave.

This is also what makes the information sector qualitatively different from the industrial and agricultural sectors. It justifies why the emergence of the global information economy must be considered a distinct wave in itself, instead of simply a part of the second wave of Globalisation.

Information monopolies may be established not only by staking monopoly claims over information content through IPR, but also by controlling the hardware infrastructure for manipulating or distributing information. This infrastructure includes computer centers, voice and data switching centers, communication lines, television and radio stations, satellite networks, cable networks, cellular networks, printing presses, movie houses, etc. Like their software counterparts, the owners of the hardware infrastructure make money through monopoly rents, in the form of subscription fees or per-use charges.

Because they earn their incomes from monopoly rents, the propertied classes of the information sectors are rentier classes. They are the landlords, of cyberspace, or cyberlords. The content monopolies are owned by information cyberfords, and the infrastructure monopolies are knowned by industrial cyberlords.

The richest man in the world, as was several others among the ten richest is a cyberlord. The economic powers of cyberlords are immense, and these powers are increasingly being felt in the political and diplomatic arena. Among U.S.

negotiators, for instance, IPR—the mechanism which gives software cyberlords their power—is invariably a non-negotiable item in their agenda. It is the partnership between information cyberlords, industrial cyberlords, and Finance capitalists which is at the core, the third, wave of Globalisation.

Thus an information economy is one whose information sector has become the main source of wealth, eclipsing its industrial and agricultural sectors. The products of industrial and agricultural economies are material goods; the products of an information economy, however, are non-material goods. The reproduction cost of information goods is very low. This has led to the widespread social practice of freely sharing and exchanging information. On the other hand, it also promises extremely high profit margins, if the seller can monopolize information. Information monopolies have become the main form of ownership in the information sector. The high profit margins that they realize have led to a continuous movement of investment capital towards the information sector, eventually making it the dominant sector of the economy and transforming the economy into an information economy. The products of this information economy spread worldwide, as people freely share and exchange information goods.

Thus as information economy needs a global system for enforcing its monopolies as well as for gathering information materials, tapping intellectuals and of course collecting payments worldwide. This leads to the Globalisation of the information economy and is the engine of the third wave of Globalisation. The main propertied classes within the information cyberlords, who control information content, industrial cyberlords, who control information infrastructures, and finance capitalists, who control investment funds.

The present situation of economic imbalance is generally due to evolution of institutions, which are one-sided because these institutions had been the brain child of developed countries. The developed countries, because of their edge over the developing nations, played an important role in international scene. The countries hailing from the South were kept at a low profile as they were considered late comers on the international fora. And this leads to Economic Darwinism.

Economic Darwinism is both a new form of international order and a threat to the poor nations. What we call Darwinism is nearer to Galbraith's 'Second Imperialism', which deals with the core nations behaviour *vis-a-vis* others. The will to national independence according to him, is the most powerful force in modern times. Therefore, its antithesis is not mere imperialism but, to use Kautsky's phrase, 'Ultra Imperialism' if the national leadership is strong, effective and well regarded, it will not tolerate foreign domination. If the leadership is weak, ineffective, unpopular, corrupt and oppressive, it may accept foreign guidance, support and a measure of domination, to be ultimately marginalised. But then it may not be tolerated by its own people. This is the eroding effect of new imperialism.

It is universally recognised that the present international system is in some kind of crisis. Capitalism is in crisis, Communism is in crisis, the Third World is in crisis and so on. But talking about crisis has become an international industry. Those who control the international system or its sub-system and who enjoy its fruits, living in great luxury are most vocal about it. One of the techniques they have developed is to talk continuously about the urgency to help the poor. International organisation such as the UN, NAM and the commonwealth produce mountains of documents. This exercise creates the illusion that somebody is concerned about the world and its people. In reality, this is a fraudulent exercise.

Since this exercise is conducted through top world leaders of the great powers, it becomes difficult to expose its real meaning in order to understand what is really happening behind the scene, and why the present highly exploitative and inequitrous international order as well as national orders are continuing.

No matter how one looks at its opponents or critics, the system is nothing but a well designed international dictatorship: political, economic and military. International economic monopolies buttress this dictatorship. Paradoxically this dictatorship is internally democratic and externally authoritarian. It has come to loom large in the perceptions of policy-makers, and adjustment to it in the form of economic liberalisation and the shrinking of the state has moved to the forefront of their economic agenda, even when not imposed on them. The phenomenon of economic globalisation provides the widest possible context for the examination of economic policy reform. However, as a concept in contemporary social science, it appears in many variants. In one strong version, globalisation refers to the presumed emergence of a 'supra-national', borderless global economy with its own laws of motion, encompassing and subordinating the various local economics in a single worldwide division of labour, rendering national governments into municipalities. A softer version of the concept treats globalisation less as an end-stage and more as a process in which the 'international' economy becomes more closely integrated, with domestic economic agents increasingly oriented to the global market rather than to particular national markets, even as the state continues to remain central to national economic advancement. Regardless, economic globalisation represents only one part of the equation. Equally necessary to the understanding of economic policy reform is the opposing social force in the form of economic nationalism. While diverse meanings go with the term, economic nationalism's core is constituted by the paramountcy of national economic interest against the claims of other nations.

Economic globalisation and economic nationalism are, then, the two fundamental forces that have been shaping the world's economic terrain over the last several decades. The two forces are obviously related to each other, with globalisation opposing and provoking economic nationalism as well as transforming and transcending it, even as its own apparently inexorable path of expansion and possible eventual triumph has been continually interrupted and redirected by nationalism. Both contending forces are integrally linked with markets and states, for both have been fundamentally rooted in the rise of markets and states in the modern era. Indeed, economic globalisation is simply a fuller expression of the expansion of one or more markets to world scale, while economic nationalism is nothing but the manifestation in the economic arena of the consolidation of states in the international system. They thus simply represent another level of the working of markets and states. At the same time, each by itself as well as in interaction with the other generates pressures for economic policy reform, which, in turn, has principally to do with the roles of states and markets in economic affairs. One of the vital questions for the developing world at the dawn of a new century, therefore, becomes precisely the relationship of globalisation and nationalism to economic policy reform.

'Good economics is bad politics' as the saying goes, is an erroneously conceived garbling. Some spontaneous adverse responses may emerge as misplaced reactions to a good policy regime that may be aimed at long-range structural corrections of the growth path as well as the developmental course of the economy. These policy alternates are like a minor, and sometimes major, surgery that may be painful for a while. Yet if these pains persist too long and turn out to be too severe, the well intended surgical operation may ricochet to spell disaster. An effective and rational economic policy regime entails sensitive balancing process and amounts to walking on a tight rope of trade-offs between economic logic and political sensitivities of affected sections of society. Characteristically, in the context of political economics, if good economics is not viewed as good politics, it is no economics at all. It is the violation of logical politic-economic parameters that generate antipathy to the ruling authority.

In such a scenario we can learn a lesson or two from Mahatma Gandhi in a speech delivered before the Missionary Conference, Madras on 14 February 1916, Gandhi defined swadeshi (self-reliance) in the following terms, "After much thinking I have arrived at a definition of swadeshi that, perhaps, best illustrate my meaning. Swadeshi is the spirit in us, which restrict us to use of the service of our immediate surroundings to the exclusion of more remote. I should use things that are produced by my immediate neighbours and serve these industries by making them efficient and complete where they might be found wanting."

While it is true, we have duties to all humankind, but the duties we own to all segments of it are not of equal importance. There is a hierarchy of duties based on the degree of proximity: Proximity is the decisive elements in forming ties in terms of both closeness of feelings and knowledge of circumstances. Accordingly we must start with service to neighbours. An individual service to his country and humanity consists in serving his neighbours. One could not starve one's neighbours and claim to serve one distant cousin in Antarctica, for one must not serve one's distant neighour at the expense of the nearest. This is not only the teaching of all the religions in the world but also the foundation of true and human economics.

Asked if a man can serve the immediate neighbours and yet serve the whole of humanity. Gandhi replied that he can, provided the service of neighbours was not itself exploitative of others. The neighbours would in turn serve his neighbours and in this way the chain of service would be expanded to include the world, rather than shut it out. Gandhi was neither metaphysical nor too philosophical for comprehension but just, good common sense, for it you love your neighbour as thyself, he will do likewise with you, and both would gain thereby.

There is no denying of the fact that Gandhi's doctrine of buying local products have some protectionist implications. In response to an interviewer's comment that no country was free from foreign competition. Gandhi observed that on contrary each sovereign nation tried to protect its infant industries by bounties and tariffs. However, the exercise of ethical preference by consumer was, he claimed a better solution, because it was voluntary and hence was in correspondence with the principle of non-violence and was more likely to benefit the poor. Consumption behaviour that corresponds to the principle of ethical preference, far from destroying the economic benefits flowing from foreign trade would be conductive to the healthy growth of nations and so promote both material and moral progress.

If India is to emerge as a nation whose global relevance is commensurate with its image, it must establish its credentials by further multilateral economic and political relationship all around, and not remain hostage to the western global interests. In fact, the linkage of India's economy with the global economy is such that India has no option but to grapple with the dynamics of globalisation. Whether to globalise India or not is not the question now because globalisation of the world financial system is a historical process. India is already hooked on to both the world financial economy and the ballooning flow of world information. It can not hope to remain half pregnant, and it can't abort it also but have to go all the way.

Economic revival is an exciting proposition. It has to be invigorating, self-generating and mass-based. Herein lies the test for the nation nerves. Indeed India's future depends upon the rational choices made today and those to be made from now onward. History is full of examples of countries, which got crushed under their own follies just by ignoring the basic human values and cultural roots. Every economic gains or losses its credibility by its conduct and approach to human beings especially the havenots. The liberalisation and globalisation have to address themselves to the liberation of millions from the clutches of poverty and deprivation globally. Swami Ramakrishna Paramhansa once remarked: "While seeing goods in all persons and all things do look for the holes in the pot you purchase", while embracing the new creed of globalisation we should not overlook the holes in the foreign pot and discard the time tested swadeshi pitcher.

I welcome this study by Dr. Anil Arora, a Chartered Accountant. It is based upon his Ph.D. thesis completed under my supervision and guidance. Dr. Arora is a serious scholar. He makes out a strong case against the multinationals and their evil designs and produces an indigenous solution for the problems and needs of India's teeming millions, while, at the same time, keeping his mind open to whatever fresh ideas and ideals, ways and means, are available from anywhere in the world. I hope that he will continue his pursuits further in his chosen field of interest. I wish him all the best in his future endeavours.

Chandigarh

DR. JAI NARAIN SHARMA

Preface

Preoccupation with the corporate world has become one of the emblematic feature of our time. The immediacy and longer term impact of major forces of change are enormously enhanced by the growing interconnections between all parts of the world. The most significant development in the world economy during the past few decades has been the increasing internationalisation—and arguably, the increasing globalisation—of economic activities. The internationalisation of economic activities is nothing new. Some commodities have had an international character for centuries; an obvious example being the long established trading pattern in spices and other exotic goods. Such internationalisation was much enhanced by the spread of industrialisation from eighteenth century onwards in Europe. Nevertheless until very recently the production process itself was primarily organised within national economies or parts of international trade developed primarily as an exchange of raw materials and food stuffs with products manufactured and finished in single national economies ... In terms of production, plant, firm and industry were essentially national phenomena.

The nature of the world economy has changed dramatically, however, especially since the 1950s National boundaries no longer act as 'watertight' containers of the production process. Rather, they are more like sieves through which extensive leakage occurs. The implications are far reaching. Each one of us is now more fully involved in a global economic system than were our parents and grand parents. Few, if any, industries now have much 'natural production' from international competition whereas in the past, of course, geographical distance created a strong insulating effect. Today, in contrast, fewer and fewer industries are oriented towards local, regional or even national markets. A growing number of economic activities have meaning only in a global context. Thus, whereas a hundred or more years ago only rare and exotic products and some basic raw materials were involved in truly international trade, today virtually everything one can think of is involved in long distance movement. And because of the increasingly complex ways in which production is organised across national boundaries, rather than contained within them, the actual origin of individual products may be very difficult to ascertain.

Although the nation of a globalised world has become pervasive there are strong opponents who argue, in effect, that globalisation is a mirage. According to this view the 'newness' of the current situation has been grossly exaggerated.

So on the one hand; we have the view that we do, indeed, live in a new-globalised-world economy in which our lives are dominated by global forces. On the other hand, we have the view that no all that much has changed; that we still inhabit an international, rather than a globalised, world economy in which national forces remain highly significant. The truth lies in neither of these two polarised positions. Although in quantitative terms the world economy was perhaps at least as integrated economically before as it is today—in some respects, even more so—the nature of that integration was qualitatively very different.

Typologies or classifications of the prevailing global system, based on one theory or the other, are bewilderingly complex and unamendable to comprehension by the common man. The global system itself remains imprecisely defined. Broadly it means the whole structure of nation-states, international institutions, processes and relations that influence or determine the behaviour and fate of people and states. One cannot be concerned with all these, no matter in what order they are organised. Besides the superpowers, there are dozen or so middle powers that do not interact with one another as middle powers in any significant way. Then there are a large number of nations, small powers, which are victims of aggression, exploitation and blackmail.

The various models of the world order are almost extensions of a set of analytical theories and ideologies based on a single paradigm, be it capitalist, socialist or any other, and aim at the survival of the existing international world economy, which is or marginal significance for the welfare of the majority of the people. Even where the models or their typologies have strong explanatory powers, they are not necessarily valid or relevant for having an equitable order. This is because one man's or nation's order is another's disorder.

While earlier there was British Colonialism which dominated the world. In the second half of the last century its place was taken over by Dollar Colonialism and now it is the Corporate Colonialism which is emerging and has started dominating the world.

The study of corporate colonialism is important, both in itself and because of its far reaching influence in the making of the contemporary world. To understand colonialism and its impact is to understand today's world, as also to contribute to the making of a better world tomorrow.

The analysis of colonialism and its impact is also closely linked to the choice of strategies and policies of development followed in a post-colonial society. Development strategies and policies are crucially determined by the historical roots and causes of backwardness, the inherited pattern of underdevelopment, and the consequent obstacles to development.

Colonies underwent a fundamental transformation or modernisation under colonialism. But this transformation or modernisation did not convert them into carbon copies of the metropolitan societies. The colonies, instead of undergoing a process of development leading to the constant revolutionisation of their productive forces, experienced underdevelopment. The colonies did undergo modernisation, but it was not capitalist modernisation that they underwent, as in the metropolis. A colony was moulded as an image of the metropolitan capitalist society, but as its negative image. This also meant that the initial conditions from which a newly liberated colony started its development process were not those of its pre-colonial past but those created during the colonial period.

(i) The efforts to make complete integration of the colony with the corporate world leads to its subordinate or subservient position.

(ii) Unequal exchange between a colony and the multinational may pave the way of internal disarticulated parts through the world market and imperialist hegemony with the metropolitan economy. (Expressed another way, a particular international division of labour exists by which the metropolitan countries produce high-technology, high-productivity, high-wage, and capital-intensive goods, while the colony produces low technology, low productivity, low wage, and labour intensive goods).

(iii) The problem is the appropriation of the colony's economic surplus, reflected in the drain of wealth or the unilateral transfer of surplus to the developed world through unrequited or uncompensated exports. This is important because the heart of the process of economic development is the amount and pattern of utilisation of the economic surplus generated in an economy for extended reproduction. Then the danger of foreign political domination as the corporations plays a crucial role in the colonial structure and so on.

Going along the path that he had chalked out, Gandhi arrived at a philosophy which could be categorised as synthesis between the needs, urges and aspirations of the individual and the society of which individual is inseparable and indivisible part.

Since he was sensitive to the feeling and needs of masses he could never stand apart from his people. Satisfaction of needs and moral elevation of individual were not antithetical.

The study becomes more relevant and urgent when an attempt is made to review some of the existing literature on the subject. Though considerable work has been done on globalisation, there is hardly any serious study on corporate colonialism.

Chandigarh ANIL ARORA

1

Introduction

Colonies as fragmentarian settlements of a people beyond their hereditary boundaries, must have come into being shortly after the dawn of civilisation. Colony is a populated area held by subjugation and governed by an outside country. Thus a colony is a subject territory under the sovereignty (complete control) of the outside country, which rules it either with or without allowing some measure of local self-government. Colony also means a group of people who migrate from their homes to another land but remain under the rule of their native country. As individuals, these people are called colonists or colonials.

The word 'Colony' according to the Oxford English Dictionary is derived from the Latin word for farmer, cultivator, planter, or settler in a new country (colon-us).[1] Some people have a conventional conception of colonies. The word colony comes through from an Indo-European root. Colere meant "to inhabit, to cultivate"; it was applied to the gods in the sense of "to protect." Colonia had thus the senses of "farm", "landed estate", "settlement" and was especially the proper term for a public settlement of Roman citizens in a hostile or newly conquered country, where they, retaining their roman citizenship, received lands, and acted as a garrison, being mostly formed for veteran soldiers who had served their time; hence it was applied to the place so occupied, or to towns which were raised to the same rank and privileges. Colonus meant "a holder of land" and later referred to as a "colonist." The Greeks used to speak of apoikia, emigration. Among the nine Roman coloniae in Britain were London, Bath Chester, Lincoln. The Roman writers further used their word colonia to translate German apoikia a settlement of apoikoi, literally as, "people from home", i.e. a body of emigrants who settled abroad as an independent self-governed polity or state, unconnected with the mother city save by religious ties. Its modern application to the planting of settlements, after Roman or Greek precedents, in newly discovered lands, was made, in the 16th century, by Latin and Italian writers, whose works were rendered into English by Richard Eden. The related term Colonial is explained by Oxford English Dictionary as, "Of, belonging to, or relating to a colony, or (specially) the British colonies; in American history, of or belonging to the thirteen British colonies which became the United States, or the time while they were still colonies. Now frequently derogatory."[2]

People hold the belief that colonisation is the only form of conquest, that is to say the subjection of others by armed forces, that the founding and expanding of colonies is only one form of aggression. In this belief, they have coined the words "Imperialism" and "Colonialism." The rule of an area and its people by another country is called colonialism. The philosophy that underlies the acquisition of colonies is known as imperialism.[3] According to the Oxford English Dictionary, it means (1) "The practice or manner of things colonial" and often serves as a synonym for "provincial;" (2) "The colonial system or principle. Now frequently used in the derogatory sense of an alleged policy or exploitation of backward or weak peoples by a large power."[4]

By the word, colony, Edward Gibbon Wakefield[5] did not mean such a country as either British India, which is a great dependency, or the Mauritius, which was a colony of France, but is only a dependency of England: still less would term Malta or the Ionian Islands a colony. Nor does the process by which these places became dependencies of England, partake in any degree of the character of colonisation. Of colonisation, the principal elements are emigration and the permanent settlement of the emigrants on unoccupied land. A colony, therefore, is a country wholly or partially unoccupied, which receives emigrants from a distance; and it is a colony of the country from which the emigrants proceed, which is, therefore, called the mother-country. To the process by which the colony is peopled and settled, and to nothing else, would be given the name of colonisation.... Is the subordination of the colony to the mother-country, as respects government, an essential condition of colonisation? He says not. The independent sovereign states which we term colonies of ancient Greece, shall suppose to be properly so-called. To his view, the United States of America, formed by emigration from this country, and still receiving a large annual increase of people by emigration from this country, are still colonies of England. He divided colonies into two classes; the dependent and the independent, like Canada and Massachussetts.

The fact that colonialism is fundamentally based upon stressing absolute difference between colonizer and colonised, rests often in terms of "race." This stark fact undermines any attempts to "reform" colonialism to achieve a modern regime of power.

Colonies were established for a variety of reasons:

(a) Settlement so that the dependencies could absorb the surplus population of the European people; this worked effectively only in North America, Australia, and the New Zealand where colonialism ended in the nineteenth century;
(b) Strategic importance—military colonies helped to control other dependent territories or to secure strategically important sea routes;
(c) Economic purposes—this has been regarded as the primary motivation for colonialism. The economic motive was considered quite legitimate by the colonizers. Private capital was most frequently the main force behind the establishment of colonial rule (for example, the East India Companies of England and Holland), even though in the case of

France, the mercantilist state was economically most active.[6]

(d) Colonies of exploitation.

(e) Missionary Colonies—i.e. occupations or settlements in South America by the Spanish.

(f) Protectorates—A relationship between two states in which the stronger state guarantees to protect the weaker one from external aggression or internal disturbance in return for full or partial control over its foreign and domestic affairs.

(g) Mandates.

(h) Trusteeship system.

The main types of colonies were the settle-ment colony and the exploitation, or trading, colony. A settlement colony was an area in which large numbers of people came to live permanently. The land from which they came was called the mother country. Because the colonists sought to develop their territory, a settlement colony tended to become self-supporting. The British portions of North America were settlement colonies. An exploitation colony was established primarily to add to the wealth of the colonial power. Usually, it had a semi-military government and a few permanent settlers from the colonising country. Most European colonies in Africa were of this type.

EXPANSION OF COLONIES

From 1492 until 1807, the European expansion was directed to America, India (including Indonesia) and Siberia (mercantilist colonial empires). From 1878 to 1914 the Middle-East, East Asia, and particularly Africa were the objects of the European powers. Colonialism commenced with the Emerging European nation-states: England, France, Portugal, Spain, and the Low countries. After the opening of a sea route around Southern Africa in 1488 and the discovery of America in 1492, voyages of colonisation and conquest were sent out by most nations of Atlantic Europe. Portugal led the way in discovery. The Portuguese expanded westward to Brazil and eastward to the Indian Ocean, where they traded without competition until other nations began to move on their monopoly.

After Christopher Columbus discovered Cuba, the Bahamas, and Hispaniola for Spain in 1492, other Spanish voyagers staked claims to Brazil and the Isthmus of Panama. Spanish conquest of the Americas began with the occupation of the larger West Indian Islands. Later, encouraged by the occupation of Aztec, Mexico by Hernan Cortes, which yielded much gold and silver, the Spanish established an American empire stretching from Chile in the South to Mexico and California in the north and including present day Florida.

Early in the 16th century, the Dutch became the leading European naval and commercial power, with an Asian empire that developed rapidly after the chartering of the Dutch East India Company in 1602 and the company's founding of Batavia (now Jakarta), Java, as the centre of trade with China, Japan, India, Ceylon (now Sri Lanka), and Persia.[7]

France, beset by problems on the European continent, was a weak administrator of its overseas empire. The French New World settlements began after Giovanni da Verrazano's trip in 1524 and the exploration of the St. Lawrence River. Samuel de Champlain went to New France (Canada) in 1603 and founded Quebec in 1608, but, despite the status of royal province granted in 1663, the colony grew slowly, numbering by 1754 only some 55,000 souls.·

England's East India Company (Chartered in 1600) led the acquisition of India, an achievement largely due to Robert Clive. The 13 colonies that England founded (1607-1732) on the Eastern Seaboard of North America became the nucleus of the future United States. Further British gains in North America resulted from the colonial wars of the 18th century. By Queen Anne's War with Spain ending in 1713, England won Newfoundland, Nova Scotia, and part of northern Canada. The successful conclusion of the French and Indian War in 1763 gained for Britain all of North America east of the Mississippi River. The first great colonial era ended with the British Empire as the most wealthy of all European colonial systems. British sea power propelled the empire to the South Pacific East Asia, the South Atlantic, and the

African Coast. The loss of the American colonies in 1783 was a blow, although offset by the consolidation of India after the defeat of the Maratha opposition in 1803 and by settlement of Australia and the Caribbean.

In contrast, Spain's and Portugal's colonial growth suffered during the Napoleonic Wars, French occupation of the Liberian Peninsulas in 1807 led to estrangement between South American colonies and their mother countries, both of which were too preoccupied to intervene effectively in nationalistic movement, civil wars and revolutions. By 1825, Brazil had freed itself from Portugal, and Spain had lost all its colonies but Cuba and Pureto Rico.

Many motivations pushed Europeans towards colonising foreign lands. Primarily, nations established colonies to gain economic profits. In the early 1800's, the Industrial Revolution was beginning in such places as Great Britain, and new markets and raw materials were needed to uphold the new industries. Nations depended on their colonies for raw materials to be used in their factories so that they could produce a growing number of manufactured goods. They then hoped to sell the manufactured goods to consumers in their colonies, which served as new markets.

In addition to a desire for economic profit, nationalism also served as a reason for colonisation. After the French Revolution, European nations had a strong sense of national pride, and felt that in order to prove themselves as strong world power, they would need to gain control of other countries. By obtaining power over foreign lands, nations were also able to strengthen their military. This further increased their status as a world Power.

The Europeans used the ideas of the "White Man's Burden" to help justify their colonisation of foreign lands. The White Man's Burden was the idea that as supreme beings, it was the job of the white people to spread their superior ways of living to the inferior people of other places. An Englishman, Cecil Rhodes stated, "I contend that we Britons are the first race in the world, and the more of the world we inhabit, the better it is for the human race. I believe it is my duty to God, my Queen, and my Country..."[8] In keeping with the ideas of white supremacy, the Europeans also colonised to spread their religion to nations that they felt were inferior.

Colonisation brought to the original inhabitants of a colony, the technological advances of a more developed society and, in some cases, a higher standard of living. New institutions—such as the Christian religion and Western legal systems—often were introduced. These changes, however, proved frequently detrimental to the indigenous culture. Sometimes, the original inhabitants were deprived of their land or their freedom. In some instances, highly developed civilisations (such as that of the Incas) were destroyed.[9]

Colonisation was the cause of many wars, waged for a variety of reasons. In some, settlers fought against the indigenous population; in others, colonial powers contended over territory. Ultimately, many colonies fought wars of independence.

According to Osterhammed, Colonisation is a phenomenon of colossal vagueness because it covers large and different parts of the world and its history.[10] Colonisation has to do with migration, because it describes the movement of people from one part of the world to another to establish a settlement, quite often an agrarian one. In this sense, the term has a neutral connotation. In contrast, colonialism has become a general invective against western policy, especially since the Bandung Conference of decolonised Asian countries in 1955. In the nineteenth century, however, it was used more or less neutrally to characterize the condition of colonies and the (speech) habits of colonials.[11]

COLONIALISM AND IMPERIALISM

Colonialism is not a modern phenomenon. World history is full of examples of one society gradually expanding by incorporating adjacent territory and settling its people on newly conquered territory. The ancient Greeks set-up colonies as did the Romans, the Moors, and the Ottomans, to name just a few of the most notorious examples. Colonialism, then, is not restricted to a specific time or place. Nevertheless, in the sixteenth century, colonialism changed decisively because of technological developments in navigation that began to connect more remote parts of the world. Fast sailing ships made it possible to reach distant ports while sustaining closer ties between the centre and colonies. Thus, the modern European colonial expansion as project emerged when it became possible to move large numbers of people across the ocean and to maintain political sovereignty in spite of geographical dispersion. This entry of people uses the term colonialism to describe the process of European settlement and political control over the rest of the world, including Americas, Australia, and parts of Africa and Asia.

The difficulty of defining colonialism stems from the fact that the term is often used as a synonym for imperialism. Both colonialism and imperialism were forms of conquest that were expected to benefit Europe economically and strategically. The term 'colonialism' is frequently used to describe the settlement of places such as North America, Australia, New Zealand, Algeria, and Brazil that were controlled by a large population of permanent European residents. The term 'imperialism' often describes cases in which a foreign government administers a territory without significant settlement; typical examples include the scramble for Africa in the late nineteenth century and the American domination of the Philippines and Puerto Rico. The distinction between the two, however, is not entirely consistent in the literature. Some scholars distinguish between colonies for settlement and colonies for economic exploitation. Others use the term colonialism to describe dependencies that are directly governed by a foreign nation and contrast this with imperialism, which involves indirect forms of domination.[12]

The confusion about the meaning of the term imperialism reflects the way that the concept has changed over time. Although the English word imperialism was not commonly used before the nineteenth century, Elizabethans already described the United Kingdom as "the British Empire." As Britain began to acquire overseas dependencies, the concept of empire was employed more frequently. Thus, the traditional understanding of imperialism was a system of military domination and sovereignty over territories. The day-to-day work of government might be exercised indirectly through local assemblies or indigenous rulers who paid tribute but sovereignty rested with the British. The shift away from this traditional understanding of empire was influenced by the Leninist analysis of imperialism as a system-oriented towards economic exploitation. According to Lenin, imperialism was the necessary and inevitable result of the logic of accumulation in late capitalism. Thus, for Lenin and subsequent Marxists, imperialism described a historical stage of capitalism rather than a trans-historical practice of political and military domination. The lasting impact of the Marxist approach is apparent in contemporary debates about American imperialism, a term which usually means American economic hegemony, regardless of whether such power is exercised directly or indirectly.[13]

Given the difficulty of consistently distinguishing between the two terms, this entry will use colonialism as a broad concept that refers to the project of European political domination from the sixteenth to the twentieth centuries that ended with the national liberation movements of the 1960s. Post-colonialism will be used to describe the political and theoretical struggles of societies that experienced the transition from political dependence to sovereignty. This entry will use imperialism as a broad term that refers to economic, military, political domination that is achieved without significant permanent European settlement.

Colonialism is a practice of domination, which involves the subjugation of one people by another. One of the difficulties in defining colonialism is that it is difficult to distinguish it from imperialism. Frequently, the two concepts are treated as synonyms. Like colonialism, imperialism also involves political and economic control over a dependent territory. Turning to the etymology of the two terms, however, provides some suggestion about how they differ. The term colony comes from the Latin word colonus, meaning farmer. This root reminds us that the practice of colonialism usually involved the transfer of population to a new territory, where the new arrivals lived as permanent settlers while maintaining political allegiance to their country of origin. Imperialism, on the other hand, comes from the Latin term imperium, meaning to command. Thus, the term imperialism draws attention to the way that one country exercises power over another, whether through settlement, sovereignty, or indirect mechanisms of control.

The legitimacy of colonialism has been a long standing concern for political and moral philosophers in the Western tradition. At least since the Crusades and the conquest of the Americas, political theorists have struggled with the difficulty of reconciling ideas about justice and natural law with the practice of European sovereignty over non-Western peoples. In the nineteenth century, the tension between liberal thought and colonial practice became particularly acute, as dominion of Europe over the rest of the world reached its zenith. Ironically, in the same period when most political philosophers began to defend the principles of universalism and equality, the same individuals still defended the legitimacy of colonialism and imperialism. One way of reconciling those apparently opposed principles was the argument known as the "civilising mission," which suggested that a temporary period of political dependence or tutelage was necessary in order for "uncivilised" societies to advance to the point where they were capable of sustaining liberal institutions and self-government.

The goal of this entry is to analyze the relationship between Western political theory and the project of colonialism. After providing a more thorough discussion of the concept of colonialism, the third and forth sections of the entry will address the question how European thinkers justified, legitimised, and challenged political domination. The fifth section briefly discusses the Marxist tradition, including Marx's own defense of British colonialism in India and Lenin's anti-imperialist writings. The final section provides an introduction to contemporary "post-colonial theory." This approach has been particularly influential in literary studies because it draws attention to the diverse ways that post-colonial subjectivities are constituted and resisted through discursive practices. The goal of the entry is to provide an overview of the vast and complex literature that explores the theoretical issues emerging out of the experience of European colonisation.

In this sense, colonialism can be defined as the control

of one people by another, culturally different one, an unequal relationship which exploits differences of economic, political, and ideological development between the two.[14]

Colonialism in the English language originally indicated a practice or idiom associated with British colonies (e.g., the phrase 'the place was going ahead' was described in 1887 as a 'colonialism'). Colonialism defies simple definition, for its usage has tended to reflect changing moral judgments. In the late 1800's, the term was applied only to colonies of the white settlers and was used in either of the two ways, both morally neutral: (1) a trait characteristic of such colonies, and (2) the political status of a dependency as distinct from the metropolis (parent state) or another sovereign state.

Actually, the term colonialism was rarely used in the sense of a colonial system. Its later usage resulted from its adoption as part of the verbal ammunition of the age of decolonisation. In this, it suffered the fate of "imperialism", which, after 1900, was adopted by the critics of European expansion to serve ideological purposes and used imprecisely to suggest both the annexation of territories and their subsequent state of subordination in each case to serve the economic interests of the capitalist powers of Europe and North America.

CLASSIFICATION OF COLONIES

The colonies are classified into the forms that they assume according to time and place. To arrive at a classification, let us consider the variations of their two essential elements: emigration and domination. Therefore, work out a classification of the *de facto* position and then of *de jure* position; or to put it in other words, first the economic classification, and secondly, the legal or political classification.

Emigration

The aspect of emigration varies according to duration, degree and motive. As regards duration, we must distinguish intermittent and permanent colonisation; the full importance of this distinction lies in its bearing on race contact. Accordingly, as penetration is intermittent or permanent,

CHART 1.1

Classification of Colonies

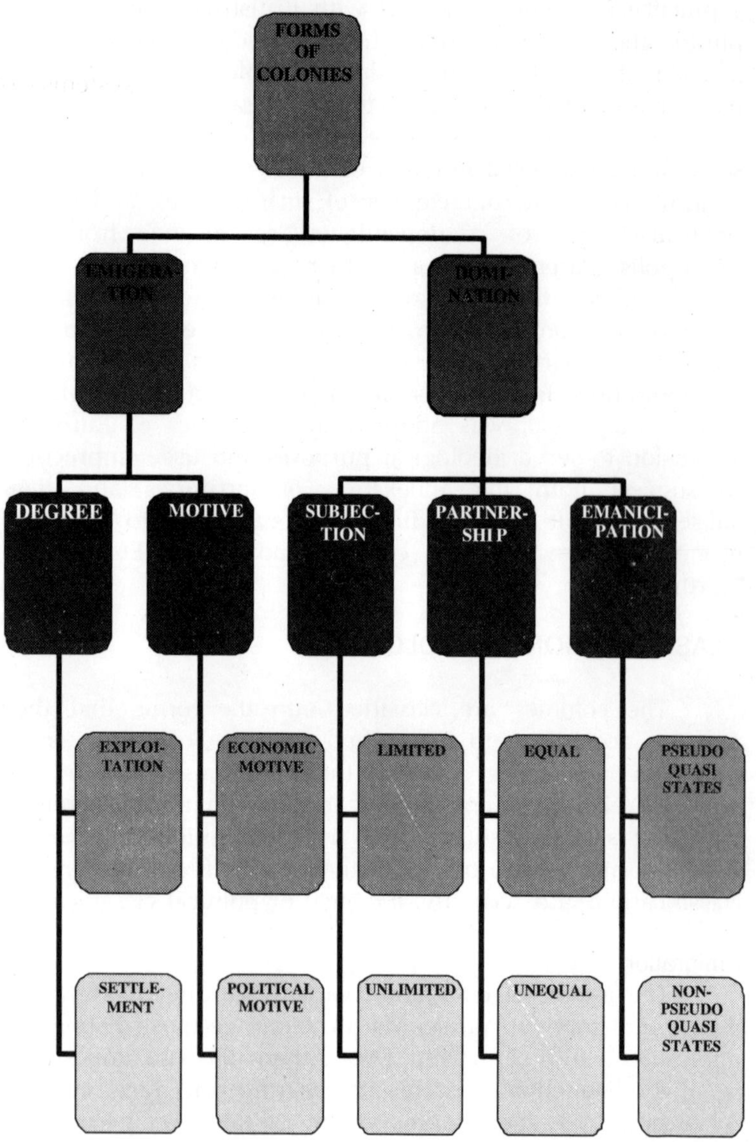

colonisation displays less or more activity and intercommunication—a lesser or greater degree of intimacy. Markets and fairs set-up in a new country are the beginnings of colonisation from which warehouses and cities may develop. French centres of commerce and industry had their birth from colonies, which, in their early days, were precarious; their first white inhabitants came from abroad and were only transitory travelers. Again and again, in the French colonies, the temporary laid the basis of the enduring; offices, missions, cultural and industrial undertakings, are emigrations which began by being temporary, and ended by becoming permanent.

Regarding degree, we must distinguish between exploitation colonies and settlement colonies; the latter are more commonly called resident colonies. Exploitation colonies are those where Europeans live in small numbers; in many cases, in very small numbers, mainly because the climate forbids residence. Residential colonies are those where Europeans have made their home and increased in number both by further immigration and by natural reproduction. There are colonies which have been wholly peopled by Europeans. Canada and Australia, for instance, consisted of forests and deserts before the coming of the first colonists who have since increased to millions. But in exploitation colonies, the Europeans are counted merely by thousands, sometimes by hundreds only. In Indo-China, the French population totaled 20,000.

As regards motive, we must distinguish three principal cases in the order in which they occurred, for the logical classification here coincides roughly with the chronological. There is the political motive, the theological motive and, finally, last but not least, the economic motive, which nowadays predominates.

In ancient times colonies were often founded for political reasons. Expansion towards the Mediterranean in particular, was inspired by the founding of Empires that brought greatness with it; it was also inspired by ambition, the desire to be more powerful and better equipped for defence against the foreigners. The "will to power" revealed itself already in olden days; imperialism, in the proper sense of the term, is the desire for greatness. Later, towards the end of the Roman Empire, arose the fear of invasion; for the Barbarian was already threatening the frontiers, and colonies were the defence outposts of civilisation. The Byzantine Empire was primarily[15] an instrument of self-protection.

So, one can see that the spirit or conquest was frequently responsible for the foundation of Empires often of excessive extent—the Hittite, Assyrian and Roman Empires for instance—the focus of which in course of time might be displaced. Towards the close of the Roman Empire, the capital was transferred to Arles, a town with a population of 100,000, in an ancient colony on the frontier of the Empire. Here Constantine took up his residence as Julian took his at Lutetia (the ancient name of the city that we now call Paris).

Similar transfers of the centre of power have taken place in other Empires. Who knows whether Delhi, or perhaps Canberra, may one day figure instead of London as the capital of the British Empire.

The political motive, a motive essentially imperial, the lust of pacific or warlike conquest, is by no means a thing of the past. There are colonies in the French Empire which have, to date, no economic value, but which are of extreme political importance; they have called them "Junction Colonies", for they serve to link the scattered fragments of the French Empire. The Sahara desert, or the river Shari in Equatorial Africa, contribute at the moment nothing to the prosperity of the French Empire, but much to its unity and its security. These territories are liaison colonies which serve to unite colonies otherwise separated.

The theological or proselytising motive for emigration is of quite a different order. It was the desire to convert the heathen which first lured the colonisers of modern times to seek to conquer a universal empire. Sometimes, this was the chief motive. The explorers who set out by sea to find a North-West passage to Asia in the course of which America was rediscovered—were, at least in part, inspired by the idea of spreading the Christian faith. This was religious imperialism, the imperialism of the theologian who sought, by persuasion or compulsion, to convert to Christianity all the peoples "without the pale." Spaniards and Portuguese at one time colonised as much for proselytising purposes as for territorial ambition or economic greed. Even the great role missions have played in colonial history can't be undermined. It was the preachers, no less than the conquerors and the traders, who pushed penetration forward and opened up communications. In the 17th century, they had completed the exploration of New France, or Canada; it was they who laid the foundation of our knowledge of "the savage." In the 18th century, they opened the gates of China; it was through them that European influence gained a footing at the court of Peking. In the 19th century they assisted in the exploration and the penetration of African countries. Roman Catholics or Protestants, they built in forest and desert; often they were the first to get into touch with the native inhabitants.

These missionary centres led to other establishments. Under the missionaries' wings, late comers were able to make peaceful contact; it was often the missions which made occupation possible. Exploitation, the opening of business and of concessions, sprang up and flourished in the shade of the mission. There were even missions which, on their own initiative, organised plantations in new countries. The colonies of Paraguay and Peru administered and organised by the Jesuits, were the first attempt of this kind and were extolled by Montesquieu and even by Voltaire. Their founders set out, not like the Spanish pioneers, to seek gold and silver, but to promote the profitable development of new territories.[16]

So, pass directly from the proselytising to the economic motive. Political and religious imperialism have both led, sooner or later, to industrial imperialism, which now takes the centre of the stage. Colonies are business, people say; their aim is profit, not ambition. The desire to get rich has superseded both the desire to become great, and the desire to convert. The economic motive itself, however, is complex; material interests take many and changing forms.

The Colonies have aimed, and still aim, at the export, or alternatively at the import of supplies and produce. In the past, this was the main interest people had in founding colonies. The motive was predominantly commercial: the export to the colonies of the mother-country's produce; the import into the mother-country of the produce of the colonies. Colonial possessions were primarily markets, secondarily sources of supply; outlets for European manufactures, storehouses of raw materials, food-stuffs and exotic produce for European consumption. Even today, the possession of colonies has in certain cases this over-riding use. If Germany passionately coveted colonies, her first-desire was to use them, as did the ancient Greeks, to absorb the excessive increase of her population; also, sometimes, primarily, to provide her industry with markets and with supplies of raw materials. But in earlier days, the commercial aim was the over-riding one. It was in order to secure precious metals that the Spaniards made such great sacrifice of men and wealth in their colonies. Later, it was the quest for spices—as of old in the East, the quest for perfumes—that so grievously embittered the struggle between French, English and Dutch for possession of the "Spice Islands." An adventurous expedition was necessary as Jean-Baptiste Say has said, to enable that great man of action, "the respectable" Pierre Poivre to secure one clove plant from the Sunda Islands! That was in 1755.

But during the 19th century, the cause of battles is neither metal nor spice but raw materials. What the producing nations henceforth covert is fodder for their industries, to make them independent of the foreigner. This craving has a special name: it is called "economic autarky" that is to say the need which the great States have discovered of being self-sufficing in peace ... and in war. They fully understand that they cannot be independent without the aid of their colonies from which they hope to draw food supplies and raw materials of "vital" importance. Here, the political and the economic motives are fused. The mother-country looks to her Empire to guarantee her economic and political autonomy. There is no longer the hope that flourished in the distant days of "mercantile" doctrine, that the Nation, the Little Nation could live for and by itself; but a whole Empire, a great universal Empire, constitutes as it were a closed circle: a hitherto unknown type of economic imperialism, manifest in the British Empire with its plans for unity. England, if she were cut-off, would have food enough for two or three weeks only. She, therefore, suffers more than any other nation from colonial or imperial anxiety.

This was where another economic motive was "on the agenda." "Interest" in the possession of colonies henceforth centres less on export and import than on exploitation or, as say, profitable development (la mise en valeur). Sacrifices of men and money are made in the colonies to promote cultural and industrial undertakings. When we speak of "profitable development", it means that the colonies are, no longer, as they formerly were, simply and solely the means of finding an outlet for manufactures, or even the sole and obvious means of supplying consumer needs, but the means of greatly increasing resources and prosperity by the methodical and systematic development of the soil and the subsoil. Profitable agriculture and industrial development are now major preoccupations.

DOMINATION

The various facets of domination can be distinguished, according as it is weighty or light: first, 'subjection; secondly, partnership; thirdly, separation or emancipation of the colonies. These three methods of colonising are in logical orders which are more or less combined.

Subjection, or colonisation properly so-called in the legal sense, is the most extreme case we have defined. There is subjection in the passive sense or domination in the active sense when the colony is subject to the authority of the mother-country, when it is ruled and administered by a metropolis, of which it is an appurtenance; the colony being then merely the "accessory" which "follows the principal."

Even subjection, however, has its degrees; it may be unlimited or limited. We meet unlimited subjection in every "possession" properly so-called, and more especially in what the English have styled "Crown Colonies." Such colonies, and the majority of French colonies are of this type: these are wholly dependent on the metropolis with no reservation whatever. Legislative, executive and administrative powers are exercised in the name of the mother-country. If there exist in such a colony consultative bodies, or—more rarely—representative bodies, they exist solely as a concession granted by the grace of the colonising State. This is the state of affairs which has persisted in the French and almost wholly disappeared in the British Empire, with the exception of some Crown Colonies[17] which are predominantly islands possessing strategic importance. The British Colonies are not subject colonies. They were such in olden days under the system their historian Seeley has called "The Old Colonial System",[18] the system namely of "Mercantile States" which were wont, if necessary, to sacrifice the colony to the mother-country. This was the system which operated in France under the Ancient Monarchy in virtue of the commercial monopoly known as "The Exclusive", where trade with the colonies was confined to Privileged Companies or even, as with the Spaniards, to the State itself. This was paradoxically called the "Colonial Pact", whose aim was to exclude the "interloper", that is to say the contraband trader.

In other cases, subjection is limited, not unlimited. This is particularly the case of Protectorates and even of Mandates. If we use the term for colonial or pseudo-colonial regimes, it is a fictional not a genuine partnership. Both in law and in fact there is subjection in these cases: tempered subjection in the Protectorate and controlled subjection in the Mandate: but subjection none the less. The dominant State, as principal, exercises the power; in case of divergence; it carries the day, and the protected or mandated State is not truly independent.

In the second place, one finds the germ of partnership between colonisers and the colonised. In this case, the legislation and administration of a new country are not the unilateral work of the metropolitan power, but of two conjoined powers on a basis of equality. In the commercial sphere, it is the liberal economic doctrine which has paved the way for such a contractual system.[19] This system, which belongs rather to the future than to the present, but towards which we seem to be making progress, is based on two ideas. On the one hand, there is the equality of the two countries, the two States; their full and complete legal assimilation. On the other hand, there is solidarity, the reciprocity of their interests, weighed and balanced in free discussion.

Thus Mandate has more affinity with partnership than with subjection, for under it there exists certain, if imperfect, equality between the mandatory power and the people under mandate. One may, if one will, conceive a Mandate as enjoying a status between subjection and partnership, the latter position being still incompletely realised. The Mandatory state is a guardian rather than a ruler; it is his duty to act solely in the interests of the people under mandate, and to be prepared to accord them ultimate liberty.

Lastly, there is what one may call separation or emancipation. This is the legal status which has begun to evolve in the British Empire: separation but not secession, the preservation of at least a moral bond between the colony and the mother-country, for if this tie should chance to be broken, the dominions or the British overseas Nations would become independent states. In speaking of a separation or, more exactly of a quasi-separation, it means a separation that remains uncompleted. This is not complete autonomy, in the Greek sense of the word, for it does not prevent certain laws being "suggested" to the colonies by central power. Such is the position of Australia, Canada and South Africa, which are not absolutely independent States, but pseudo- or quasi-States; States, much more than half-sovereign States—as are the French Protectorates and perhaps the French Mandates—free, but not separated States. The Greek colonies at a certain period, similarly became quasi-independent of their metropolis, to which they remained linked only by their worship and the payment of tribute; in the same way as the "Nations" of the British Empire are quasi-independent. It is chiefly their loyalty to the King, reinforced by a moral and religious bond, which made the British Empire. This is the separation, not domination: a separation which does not exclude free voluntary partnership.

Unquestionably this is the road by which colonies, starting from domination or subjection, will be able to progress towards emancipation. Perhaps, it is also the means by which it will be possible to avoid a snapping of the tie between a colony and its distant metropolis, and by which the venerable term "mother-country" may retain its meaning.

COLONIALISM: A FUNDAMENTAL TRANSFORMATION OF PRE-CAPITALIST ECONOMY

Many Marxists and other radical writers have tended to follow a more anti-colonial version of the duality model which may be described as the "partial modernity" or "arrested growth" model. According to this view, imperialism partially modernised the colony but failed to carry out the task fully. Thus, the restrictive, inhibitive, feudal or semi-feudal features of the colonial economy are seen to be remnants of the past which imperialism failed to, or did not desire to, uproot. For example, these writers accuse colonialism of "preserving" feudal exploitation and of "deforming the evolution of Indian feudalism." A recent Marxist writer has criticised colonialism for "preservation in many instances of pre-capitalist relations and classes in the interests of metropolitan capital"; and asserted that colonialism "did not require the destruction of existing pre-capitalist foundations."[20]

The development of agrarian relations in the colonies—namely, India, Indonesia, Egypt, Latin America—provides an interesting example of such transformation by colonialism. In colonial India, for example, the semi-feudal structure of agrarian relations was not a carry-over or perpetuation from the Mughal period. It was the result of two serious and massive efforts to transform pre-colonial agriculture into capitalist agriculture. But since this was done under colonial conditions, the result was a semi-feudal, semi-colonial agriculture dominated by the colonial state, world capitalist market, landlords, merchants, and moneylenders, and exhibiting many capitalist features—bourgeois property relations, commercialisation and other elements of capitalist agriculture.[21]

This effort to change pre-colonial agriculture into capitalist agriculture and the coming into being of a different agrarian structure was perceived quite early and clearly by Karl Marx who wrote in *Das Capital*, Vol. 3:

"If any nation's history, then the history of the English in India—is a string of futile and really absurd (in practice infamous) economic experiments, in Bengal they created a caricature of large-scale English landed estates; in south-eastern India a caricature of small parcelled property; in the north-west they did all they could to transform the Indian economic community with common ownership of the soil into a caricature of itself."[22]

Thus, it can be said that the colonies underwent a fundamental transformation under colonialism which led to their becoming structured colonial societies. Moreover, colonialism did make the colony an integral part of the world capitalist system. But did this integration lead to the development of a capitalist economy and structure? Let us take the example of India.

During the nineteenth century, John Strachey, a brilliant Indian Civil Service Officer in the second half of the nineteenth century pointed out that the colonial transformation of colonies, especially India, was carried out under the slogan of making them capitalist, and the task, it said, was getting established the elements of capitalist development in agriculture, trade and industry. This view has been the staple of imperialist writers since the days of John Strachey. It is very much in vogue even today. The manifest deficiencies of capitalist development in the colonies are then ascribed to the poverty of the initial conditions from which colonialism had to initiate the task and to the density of the social, economic, geographical, demographic, and cultural conditions in the colonies—which capitalism found difficult to penetrate and overcome, except very slowly.

Among some Marxists, this notion tends to find acceptance because of the classical economists' view—which Marx and Engels, and early Indian intellectuals such as Raja Rammohan Roy tended to accept that the colonising of capitalist society would reproduce its capitalist character in the colony. As Marx and Engels put it "In the Communist Manifesto",[23] capitalism, being a world system, compels all nations, on pain of extinction, to adopt the bourgeois mode of production .... to become bourgeois themselves. In one word, it creates a world after its own image. In other words, despite "blood, sweat and tears" and "swinishness", a colony would be transformed into an image of the metropolitan country, that is, into a full-fledged industrial, capitalist society.

It is, however, to be noted that Marx was only seeing the potential of the colonial societies; he had neither studied the colonial reality in depth, nor had the contradictions of societies dominated by industrial capitalist metropolises come to the surface yet.[24] Marx was quite right in pointing to the universal character of capitalism, to the fact that it would not—indeed could not, because of its very character—remain confined to a single country or region. Capitalism must engulf, penetrate and transform the entire world. It is, in other words, a world system.

What Marx failed to see was that while capitalism is a single world system and colonies become its basic constituents, colonies do not become capitalist in the same way as the metropolis do. Capitalism is a world system, but it has 'one' face in the metropolis and another in the colony. Nor is it that imperialism does not attempt to transform and develop the colonies in a capitalist direction and around the capitalist principle of extended reproduction. It does, as Marx saw clearly. But because it does so under colonial conditions, imperialism neither transforms colonies into spitting images of the metropolises nor does it succeed in developing them. It underdevelops them and transforms them into colonial societies.[25]

Imperialism introduces capitalism, capitalist production and capitalist property relations in the colonies but not capitalist development. It uproots and transforms the old economy, social formation and structures, but the new colonial economy and social formation were not more conducive to development. Rather, they were quite regressive. The colony was integrated into world capitalism without enjoying any of the basic benefits of capitalist development and, in particular, without taking part in the industrial revolution. Colonialism does mean the introduction of capitalist relations of production or capitalist structure into trade, industry, agriculture and banking; the introduction of bourgeois state structure, legal and property relations, but not the development of capitalist production or of "productive powers."

After all, the capitalist mode of production involves not only capitalist relations of production but also the development of productive forces in agriculture and industry. There is no capitalist development when the social forces of production are not developed nor constantly revolutionised. This is where lies the superiority of capitalism over all previous modes of production. Thus, capitalism means, above all, the development of productive forces.

In the colonies, there was no constant revolutionisation of the forces of production. While there was no breakthrough in industry, in agriculture there was in most colonies—except where the foreign controlled plantation system was introduced—constant growth of semi-feudalism as well as stagnation in productivity. Thus, colonialism was not, unlike capitalism, an advanced stage of social development.[26]

COLONIALISM: NOT A DISTINCT MODE OF PRODUCTION

Hamza Alavi describes colonialism as "colonial capitalism", that is, "a capitalist mode of production that has a specifically colonial structure." The two specific features of colonialism as mode of production, according to him, are "the internal disarticulation and external integration of the rural economy" and the realisation of "the extended reproduction of capital" not in the colony but "in the imperialist metropolis."[27]

Colonialism, in the long course of its history since the eighteenth century, does not represent a mode of production, its basic feature is the appropriation of the social surplus produced in the colony by varied modes of production. Colonial appropriation of surplus is not crucially linked to the metropolitan bourgeoisie's ownership means of production, or to the form of appropriation of surplus at the point of production, or to the level of the development of productive modes except very partially during the third or final imperialism stage of colonialism. In this respect, colonialism differs in a basic manner from capitalism in which the surplus is appropriated by means of ownership or control over the means and conditions of production. For example, colonialism in its long history in India did not introduce new relations of exploitation or modes of production of social surplus for nearly hundred years. Further, it did not promote or rather impeded their development, once new relations were introduced during the second half of the nineteenth century.[28]

FEATURES OF COLONIAL STRUCTURE

Colonialism is best seen as a totality or a unified structure. All the changes and the newly formed institutions and structures form a network, mutually interconnected and reinforcing each other, which subserve and bring into being the colonial structure. To see colonialism as a structure is also to realize that it will go on reproducing itself unless it is shattered.

Despite attempts by a long series of writers from the 1920s, we are not yet in a position to fully understand the colonial structure in the manner in which the structure of capitalism was illuminated by Marx. What Bipin Chandra Pal wrote in 1976 still hold good: "The intellectual resources do not yet exist to understand this colonial structure fully and to trace the multifarious channels and ties the veins and arteries through which this structure is articulated."[29]

The four basic features of the colonial structure as described by the nineteenth-century Indian nationalists as well as the more recent writers are.

CHART 1.2

Features of Colonial Structure

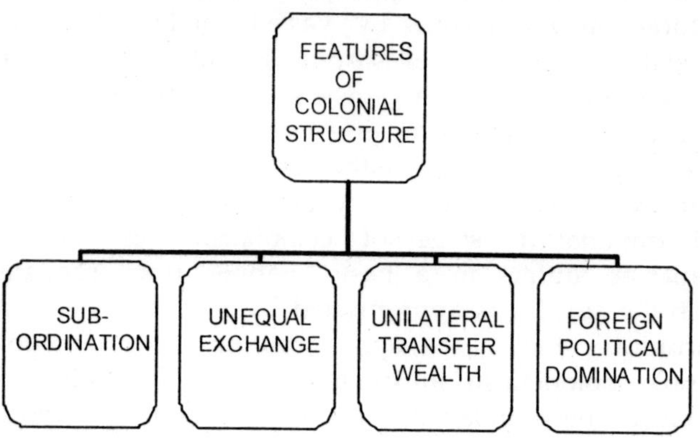

The first basic feature is the complete but complex integration and enmeshing of the colony with the world capitalist system in a subordinate or subservient position. Subordination means that the fundamental aspects of the colony's economy and society are not determined by its own needs or the needs and interests of its dominant social classes but by the needs and interests of the metropolitan economy and its capitalist class. It is important to note that subordination of the colony's economy and society is the crucial or determining aspect, and not mere linkage or integration with world capitalism or the world market. The latter aspect, i.e. linkage and integration with the world market, is true even of independent capitalist economies; nor does such linkage automatically lead to colonialism or semi-colonialism. (This aspect is often missed, leading to newly independent capitalist countries being branded as neo-colonies. This also leads to a failure to theorize the difference between Manchu China after 1840 and Japan after 1868. One of the many sources of this error is the failure to take into account the role and nature of the state—weak or strong, dependent or independent.)[30]

The second feature of colonialism is encompassed by the twin notions of unequal exchange and internal disarticulation of the colonial economy and the articulation of its different disarticulated parts, through the world market and imperialist hegemony, with the metropolitan economy.[31] For example, the colony's agriculture does not directly relate to the colony's industrial sector; it does not articulate internally. Rather it articulates with the world capitalist market and is linked to the metropolitan market which buys its products. The industrial products of the metropolitan economy are imported into the colony and sold in the rural market thus closing the circuit of commodity circulation. The colony thus experiences "a disarticulated generalised commodity production."[32]

Marx and Engels and early Indian nationalists brought out the same features by pointing to several aspects—a specifically colonial structure of production whereby the colony specialised in the production of raw materials and the metropolis in manufactured goods; the role of railways as subserving the interests not of Indian industry and trade but the needs of British production; a particular international division of labour brought about by colonialism, by which the metropolis produced high-technology, high-productivity, high-wage goods while the colony produced low-technology, low-productivity, low-wage goods (thus making international trade an instrument of exploitation and underdevelopment). They also criticised the fact that iron and steel and other capital-goods industries were confined to the metropolis.[33]

The third feature of colonialism is the drain of wealth or unilateral transfer of social surplus to the metropolis through unrequited exports. This aspect was the heart of the early Indian nationalists' critique of colonialism and their explanation of the economic underdevelopment and poverty of India. Marx's rethinking on the role of colonialism in India was also strongly influenced by this aspect. In the 1950s, through the writings of Paul Baran, once again the question of the utilisation of social surplus became centre stage in the discussion of colonial underdevelopment. Early Indian nationalists, as also recent writers, also pointed to the fact that a great deal of the colonial state expenditure on the army and civil services in the colony represented a similar external drain of surplus.[34]

This aspect has been recently rephrased from the pattern of accumulation of capital on a world scale to that while surplus is produced in the colony, it is however accumulated abroad. Or, "a substantial part of the surplus generated" in the colony "enters into expanded reproduction not directly within the colonial economy but rather at the imperialist centre." Consequently, "the attendant rise in the organic composition of capital" also occurs in the metropolis. Thus, "the colonial form was a deformed extended reproduction."[35]

The fourth basic feature of colonialism is foreign political domination or the existence and role of the colonial-state which plays a crucial role in the colonial structure. While this feature was recognised by most of the nineteenth-century Indian nationalists only after bitter political experience, and was given full place in their analysis by the Marxists, the fuller historical role of the colonial state still awaits analysis. In fact, there is an urgent need for a theory of the colonial state and for a historical study of the nature of the colonial state and in its relation to colonial society. Such a study would not only enable a better understanding of colonialism but would also facilitate a superior analysis and understanding of post-colonial states and societies.

NATURE OF COLONIAL STATE

The colonial state is a basic part of the colonial structure. At the same time, the subordination of the colony to the metropolis and other features of the colonial structure evolve and are enforced through the colonial state. The parameters of the colonial structure are constructed through, and determined and maintained by, the colonial state.

The colonial state differs from the capitalist state in important aspects. It does not "reflect" economic power but creates and enforces it. It is not a superstructure erected on the economic base. It helps create the economic base; it is a part of the economic base of colonialism. It not only enables the ruling classes to extract surplus, it is itself a major channel for surplus appropriation. Under capitalism, the ruling class is that which, to quote Ralph Miliband "owns and controls the means of production and which is able, by virtue of the economic power thus conferred upon it, to use the state as its instrument for the domination of society."[36] Reverse is the case under colonialism. It is because of its control over the colonial state that the metropolitan ruling class is able to control, subordinate and exploit the colonial society. In other words, the metropolitan ruling class does not control state power and the social surplus, in the colony mainly because of its ownership of the means of production in the colony. Rather, because the ruling class controls state power in the colony, it controls its social surplus and is able to subordinate its producers. The metropolitan capitalist class may not own the means of production in the colony to any significant extent—as for instance, it did not in India to any significant extent till the 1920s and subsequently not even predominantly.

Furthermore, while the capitalist state is the instrument for enforcing the rule and domination of one class over another, the colonial state is the organised power of the metropolitan ruling class for dominating the entire colonial society. Also, while in the metropolis, the state is a relation between classes, in the colony it is a relation between the foreign ruling class and the colonial people as a whole. This virtually amounts to a truism, but it still has to be stressed because nearly all historians and other social scientists of the imperialist school ignore or obscure this aspect and its implications.

The colonial state, thus, does not represent any of the indigenous social classes of the colony. It subordinates all of them to the metropolitan capitalist class. It dominates all of them. None of the indigenous upper classes shares state power in the colony, none of them is a part of the ruling class. They are not even its subordinated or junior partners. The metropolitan ruling class may share the social surplus in the colony with the indigenous upper classes, but it does not share power with them. Not even princes, regents and landlords have a share in colonial state power. It is, of course, true that the economic class position of the landlords and capitalists in the colony is "articulated through, and by, the colonial state." But they are not part of the ruling class. Their interests are freely sacrificed to the interests of the metropolitan bourgeoisie.

This also enables the colonial state to introduce certain reforms at the cost of the indigenous upper classes such as factory legislation, tenancy and anti-usury legislation, support to minority communities, and so on. (This explains the paradox of the ease with which Irish landlords talk of tenant interests when they administer India, or the Lancashire spokespersons urge labour legislation in India, or anti-Semites become champions of minority rights.) The colonial state is thus able, for a certain period and in certain situations, to play against each other—landlords and tenants, capitalists and workers, and higher and lower castes. It is also able to play all sorts of majorities against minorities.[37]

STAGES OF COLONIALISM AND THEIR INNER CONTRADICTIONS

It is to be noted that colonialism goes through several stages during which the fact of subordination is constant, but the forms or patterns of subordination undergo changes over time according to changes in the historical development of capitalism as a world system, the place of the individual metropolis within this system and the development of colonialism in the colony itself. Similarly, while the appropriation of the colony's surplus by the metropolis is a constant feature, the forms of this appropriation undergo changes from one stage to another. Stages of colonialism are thus basically differentiated by these two features—patterns of subordination and patterns of surplus appropriation.

Marx was the first to notice this fact, though by the very nature of things, he conceptualised only two stages—the stage of monopoly trade and direct appropriation of surplus, and of free trade or unequal exchange.[38] Basing himself on Lenin, R. Palme Dutt added a third stage, that of finance imperialism.[39] Unfortunately, later writers have tended to ignore wholly or partially this distinction. Thus, Samir Amin and many others theorize as if only the third stage constituted colonialism.[40] (Lenin who emphasised the third stage never ignored the first two.)

Basic to colonialism is economic exploitation or the appropriation of the colony's social surplus. Forms of surplus appropriation or the manner in which the colonial economy and society is to be subordinated and put at the service of the metropolis undergo changes over time. And as these forms change, so do the colonial policy and the colonial state (and its institutions, culture, ideas and ideologies).

Colonialism, thus, is not to be seen as one continuous, unchanging structure; it goes through distinct stages which are linked to the forms of surplus appropriation.

Historically, colonialism developed through three distinct stages, each stage representing two different patterns of subordination of the colonial economy, society and polity, and, consequently, different colonial policies, ideologies, impact and response of the colonial people. The change from one stage to the other was partially the consequence of the changing patterns of the metropolitan's social, economic and political development, and of its changing position in the world economy and polity.

Stages of colonialism, as given by Bipin Chandra, in different colonies are not bound by the same time horizons; but the basic content of the different stages is broadly the same in all the colonies. Moreover, the stages do not exist in pure forms; in a sense, each stage is an abstraction. Nor is there a sharp break between one stage and another. Forms of surplus appropriation and other features of colonialism in earlier stages persist in later ones. Each stage, however, is marked by distinct, dominant, qualitative features which demarcate it from the other stages. It is also to be noted that a particular form of surplus appropriation may become atrophied in a particular colony because of distinct historical factors. Thus the third stage of colonialism, finance imperialism, was atrophied in India; the second, free-trade stage, in Indonesia, and the second stages, mercantilist and free trade, in Egypt.[41]

First Stage: Monopoly Trade and Revenue Appropriation

During the first stage of colonialism, the basic objectives of colonialism were: (1) the monopoly of trade with the colony *vis-à-vis* other European merchants and the colony

CHART 1.3

Stages of Colonialism

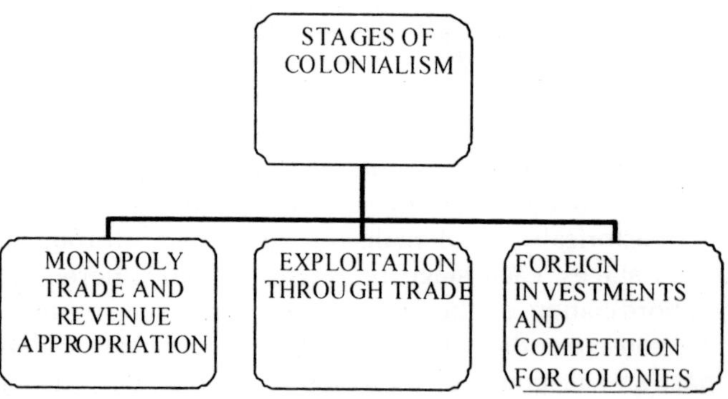

traders and producers, and (2) the direct appropriation of the revenue and surplus through the use of state power. Whenever craftsmen or other producers were employed on account of the colonial state, corporation or merchants, their surplus was directly seized, not in the manner of industrial capitalists, but that of merchant-usurers.

The colonial state or corporations required large financial resources to wage wars in the colony and on the seas, and to maintain naval forces, forts, armies and trading posts. Direct appropriation of the colony's surplus was also needed to finance the purchase of colonial products since the colonies did not import sufficient quantities of metropolitan products. Directly appropriated surplus also served as a source of profit to the merchants, corporations and the exchequer of the metropolis. The large number of Europeans employed in the colony also appropriated a large part of the colony's surplus directly, through extortion, corruption and high salaries.

It is to be noted that during the first stage of colonialism, (1) the element of plunder and direct seizure of surplus was very strong, and (2) there was no significant import of metropolitan manufactures into the colony.

A basic feature of colonial rule during this period was that no basic changes were introduced in the colony in administration, the judicial system, transport and communication, methods of agricultural or industrial production, forms of business management or economic organisation (except the putting-out system and plantations in some colonies), education, culture and social organisation. The only changes made were in military organisation and technology which contemporary independent chieftains and rulers in the colonies were also trying to introduce—and in the upper tiers of the revenue-collection structure to make it more efficient.

Why was this so? Because the colonial mode of surplus appropriation via purchase of the colony's urban handicrafts and plantation and other products, through a buyer's monopoly and control over its revenues, did not require basic socio-economic and administrative changes in the colony. Such a mode of surplus appropriation could be superimposed over its existing economic, social, cultural, ideological and political structures. Also, the colonial power did not feel the need to penetrate the villages in the colony further than their (indigenous) predecessors had done, as long as their economic surplus was successfully sucked out.

This lack of need for change was also reflected in the ideology of the rulers. There was, for one, no ideology of development. Not a changed colonial economy but the existing economy of the colony was to be the basis of economic exploitation. There was also, therefore, not much need to criticize the colony's civilisation, religions, laws and so on, for they were not seen as obstacles to the then current modes of surplus appropriation. The need was to understand them so that the wheels of administration might move smoothly. Criticism was confined to the missionaries.

Second Stage: Exploitation through Trade

The newly developing industrial and commercial interests in the metropolis, and their ideologies, began in time to attack the existing mode of exploitation of the colony with a view to making it serve their interests. Moreover, as it became clear that colonial control was to be a long-term phenomenon, the metropolitan capitalist class as a whole demanded forms of surplus appropriation which would not destroy the golden goose. It realised that the plundering form of surplus appropriation is less capable of reproducing the conditions for its own reproduction than other forms. This is the secret of the critique of the colony's exploitation which is often made during the first stage by the liberals and 'radical' democrats of the metropolis. In the end, sooner or later, the administrative policies and economic structure of the colony came to be determined by the interests of the industrial bourgeoisie of the metropolis.

The industrial bourgeoisie's interest in the colony lay in finding outlets for their ever-increasing output of manufactured goods. Linked with this was the need to promote the colony's exports for several reasons:

1. The colony could buy more imports only if it increased its exports—which could only be of

agricultural and mineral products—to pay for them. The colony's exports had also to pay for the 'drain' or in other words had to earn foreign exchange to provide for the export of business profits and the savings and pensions of Europeans working there.

2. The metropolis desired to lessen the dependence on non-empire sources of raw materials and foodstuffs. Hence the need to promote the production of raw materials in the colony, which the colonial rulers must enable the colony to do so. The colony had to be developed as a reproductive colony in the agricultural and mineral spheres.
3. As the subordinated compliment of a capitalist economy, the use of the colony both as a market for goods and as a supplier of raw material had to occur within the perspective of extended reproduction.

Thus emerged the essence of the second stage of colonialism war; the making of the colony into a subordinate trading partner which would export raw materials and import manufactures. The colonies' social surplus was to be appropriated through trade on the basis of selling cheap and buying cheap. This stage of colonialism could even embrace countries which retained political freedom.

A question that still awaits solution is the mechanism through which the colony's surplus is appropriated under conditions of metropolis buying and selling at competitive prices. The dominant school of European economists has, for nearly two centuries, denied that "any exploitation is involved in this particular relationship; rather, it has maintained through the theory of comparative costs and international division of labour that both sides of the economic relationship benefit. Many of the critics of this stage of colonialism have argued that the exploitation of the colony occurs through the terms of trade which on the whole move against primary products. This is not always true. Export prices of the metropolis may fall faster than import prices, reflecting falling costs due to technological improvement and greater and better use of machinery, partly made possible by expanding trade and widening markets. Rising import prices and falling export prices may expand exports fast enough to lead to rising productivity in the industrialising metropolis and retarded productivity in the raw material producing colony. Hence, the basic question regarding this stage of colonialism is what happens to productivity in the metropolis and the colony

The question of the mechanism of surplus appropriation in this stage of colonialism has been reopened in recent years in the works of Arghiri Emmanuel and Samir Amin. The colony could not be exploited to meet the new requirements within its existing economic, political, administrative, social, cultural and ideological setting; this setting had to be shattered and transformed all along the line. This transformation was actively undertaken under the slogan of development and modernisation. In the economic field, this meant integration of the colonial economy with the world capitalist economy and, above all, the metropolitan economy. The chief instrument of this integration was the freeing of foreign trade in the colony of all restrictions and tariffs especially in so far as its trade with that metropolis was concerned. For most of this period, the colony was to be far more of a free trading country than the metropolis itself. Free entry was now given to the capitalists of the metropolis to develop plantations, trade, transport, mining and, in some cases, industries in the colony. The colonial state gave active financial and other help to these capitalists, even when the doctrine of *laissez-faire* reigned supreme at home. The agrarian structure of the colony was sought to be transformed with the purpose of making it a reproductive colony, by initiating capitalist agriculture. Similarly, a major effort to improve the system of transport and communications was made.

Major changes occurred in the administrative field. Colonial administration became more detailed and comprehensive as well as to permeate deeper if metropolitan products were to penetrate the interior towns and villages and the agricultural produce was to be drawn out of them. The legal structure in the colony had to be overhauled, as now the sanctity of contract and its enforcement were essential if the millions of transactions needed to promote imports and exports were to become viable. It was during this stage that the Western capitalist, legal and judicial system was introduced in the colonies and semi-colonies. The changes, however, often related only to criminal law, the law of contract, and the civil law procedure; personal law, including that of marriage and inheritance, was often left untouched. Modern education was now introduced, to a lesser or greater extent, basically with a view to adequately man the new, vastly expanded administrative machinery, but also as an aspect of the transformation of the colony's society and culture. In other words, modern education was promoted both with a view to making the colony reproductive and promoting the culture of loyalty among the colonial people. Many intellectuals in the colonies also picked up the banner of social and cultural modernisation, but for opposite reasons.

The second stage of colonialism generated a liberal imperialist political ideology among sections of the imperialist statesmen and administrators, who talked of training the colonial people in the arts of democracy and self-government. It was believed that if the colonial people learn the virtues of law and order, sanctity of business contract, free trade and economic development, the economic relationship lying at the heart of this stage of colonialism could be perpetuated even if the metropolitan power was to withdraw direct political and administrative control.

The effort at transformation of the colony's socio-economic structure inevitably required that its existing culture and society be declared inadequate and decadent, and they were now subjected to sharp criticism. This stage also witnessed the birth and flowering of the ideology of development. Because of the emergence of development economics after the Second World War, following the success of the national liberation movements, it is often forgotten that the colonisation of the economies of most of the colonies occurred under the banner of the earlier ideology of development. Moreover, in many ways the two theories of economic development, that of the early nineteenth century and that of the post-Second World War, are similar, even though separated by entire epochs. The earlier theory of economic development emphasised (1) law and order, (2) private property in land, (3) investment of foreign capital to compensate for the lack of capital in the colony and to act as an example to domestic enterprise, (4) development of means of transport, (5) promotion of foreign trade, (6) modern education which would enable the colonial people to understand these theories of development, and (7) modern culture which would promote habits of thrift (savings) and enterprise.

One point needs to be stressed in this connection: the colonial authorities did not deliberately set out to develop the underdeveloped colony. On the contrary, their entire effort was to develop it so that it could complement, though in a subordinate position, the metropolitan economy and society. Underdevelopment was not the desired but the inevitable consequence of the inexorable workings of colonialism, free trade, i.e. colonialism, during its second stage, and of its inner contradictions. For the same reason, there was no imperialist theory of underdevelopment—which was the result of the practice of particular theories of development.

The earlier forms of surplus extraction continued during this stage and became a drag on the full working out of this stage. Moreover, since the colony had also to pay the costs of its own transformation, the burden on the colonial peasant rose sharply.

In practice, the transformational effort was limited in many sectors and above all in the agricultural sector because of the inner contradictions of colonialism. For example, it was during this stage that most of the colonies acquired what came to be known as the semi-feudal features of their agricultural sectors.

Third Stage: Foreign Investments and Competition for Colonies

A new stage of colonialism was ushered in as a result of several major changes in the world economy due to industrialisation of Europe, North America, Japan; intensification of industrialisation as a result of the application of scientific knowledge to industry; and further unification of the world market due to a revolution in the means of international transport. There now occurred an intense struggle for new, secure and exclusive markets, and sources of agricultural and mineral raw materials and foodstuffs. Moreover, expanded reproduction at home and extended exploitation of colonies and semi-colonies abroad produced large accumulations of capital in the developed capitalist countries. There occurred simultaneously the concentration of capital and merger of banking capital with industrial capital in several countries. This led to large-scale export of capital and search for fields and areas where the imperialist countries could have a monopoly in capital investment.

All the three aspects, namely, markets, sources of raw materials, and capital export, were interlinked, and none of them should be overemphasised at the cost of the others. For example, investment abroad would sustain the rate of profit at home (metropolis), which provided impetus to aid for the production of raw materials and to create a market for home industrial products directly or indirectly. As the struggle for the division and re-division of the world among the imperialist countries was intensified, fresh use was found for the older colonies. Their social surpluses and manpower could be used as counters in this struggle. Colonialism at this stage also served an important political and ideological purpose in the metropolis. Nationalism or chauvinism, adventure, and the glorification of empire could be used to tone down the growing social divisions at home, by stressing the common interests in the empire. More specifically, the ideology of empire and glory were used to counter the growth of popular democracy and the introduction of adult franchise, which could have posed a danger to the political domination of the capitalist class and which increased the importance of the ideological instruments of hegemony over society. The idea of empire played an increasingly important role in constituting this hegemony.

Where colonies had been acquired in the earlier stages, vigorous efforts were made to consolidate metropolitan control. Reactionary imperialist policies now replaced liberal imperialist policies. Preservation of direct colonial rule on a permanent basis was now essential on all counts, but especially to attract metropolitan capital to the colony and to provide it security. In this respect, it must, however, be noted that with regard to most colonies, it was their being perceived as potential absorbers of Metropolitan capital—rather than they actually attracting such capital—that motivated Imperialist policy. As a motive for metropolitan control, the role of the colonies as potential absorbers of capital was very powerful and important. In reality, many of the first and second-stage colonies and semi-colonies failed to absorb large quantities of metropolitan capital, and in nearly all cases, they were net 'exporters' of capital—that is, the social surpluses exported from them far outweighed the imports of capital into them. Often, even the limited extent of foreign capital invested in the colonies amounted to a small percentage of the social surplus appropriated by the metropolis.

The major reason why metropolitan capital was not invested in these colonies to a significant extent was that their economies had been wrecked or underdeveloped during the second stage of colonialism. If foreign capital was to be invested in the colonies, the resulting products had to be in the main sold in the colony; but the failure to make them reproductive colonies during the second stage now stood in the way. More than capitalism at home, it was capitalism in the colonies that was in a Moribund stage! Consequently, even the limited foreign capital was invested in only those agricultural or industrial enterprises whose products had a ready market outside the colony, or invested in providing infrastructure for such exports. The colonial market was of little use to the foreign capitalists, for it had already been captured, squeezed to the maximum, and wrecked. It must, however, be again stressed that as potential absorbers of foreign capital, these colonies continued to remain eldorados—powerfully affecting colonial policy.

Once again, the earlier forms of surplus appropriation continued into this stage. In fact, in some of the colonies, for example, India, the earlier two forms of surplus extraction remained more important than the third one.

Politically and administratively, the third stage of colonialism meant renewed and more intensive control over the colony. Moreover, it was now even more important that colonial administration should permeate every pore of colonial society and that every port, town and village be linked with the world economy. The administration now also became more bureaucratic, detailed and efficient.

A major change now occurred in the ideology of colonialism. The talk of training the colonial people for independence died out and was revived later only under the pressure of anti-imperialist movements. Instead, now there was talk of benevolent despotism, of the colonial people being a permanently immature or 'child' people over whom permanent trusteeship would have to be exercised. Geography, race, climate, history, social organisation, culture and religion of the colonial people were cited as factors which made them permanently unfit for self-government. This was in stark contrast to the earlier belief, during the second stage, that colonial people were capable of being educated and trained into becoming carbon copies of the advanced European people and therefore self-governing nations.[42]

Efforts at the transformation of the colony's economy, society and culture continued during this stage though, once again, with paltry results. However, now there developed a tendency to abandon social and cultural modernisation, especially as the anti-imperialist forces began to take up the task. Colonial administration increasingly assumed a neutral stance on social and cultural questions, and then began to support social and cultural reaction in the name of preserving indigenous institutions.

Therefore, Colonialism was originally a morally neutral term; in the twentieth century, it acquired a negative connotation as democracy, and the striving for self-determination signaled its end. Former possessions became independent.

INNER CONTRADICTIONS TO EACH STAGE OF COLONIALISM

As a structure or social formation, colonialism is from the beginning ripe with inner contradictions whose characteristics change from stage to stage. The colonial state evolves its policies in part as the effort to resolve these inner contradictions at each stage of colonialism. It may be said that colonialism and the colonial state, and its policies, are best illuminated through a study of the numerous inner contradictions of colonialism.

A historiographic point may be made here. Any system or structure "opens" itself to scientific study only when its inner contradictions emerge or can be discerned. It was the surfacing of real-life class contradictions of capitalism in the 1840s and 1850s that enabled Marx to scientifically study capitalism. The inner contradictions of first stage of colonialism in India surfaced by the end of the 1760s. This enabled both Adam Smith and Karl Marx to understand its basic features. On the other hand, the inner contradictions of second-stage colonialism—"free trade" colonialism had not surfaced in India by the 1850s when Marx wrote about India. He could, therefore, not fully grasp its character or impact except for the impact on handicrafts and agriculture. He did so later in the case of Ireland and very sporadically in the case of India. What enabled early Indian nationalists to grasp the basic features of colonialism was the fact that from 1870 onward, they came face to face with the inner contradictions of colonialism.

This aspect of colonialism may be illustrated by bringing out some of the contradictions which characterised colonialism in India. The following were some of the contradictions in the first stage of colonialism (the list is purely illustrative):

1. Plundering form of exploitation *vs.* reproduction of the conditions of exploitation.
2. Exploitation of Bengal *vs.* reproduction of Bengal's economy.
3. Gains by the East India Company's servants *vs.* gains by the Company.
4. Exploitation of India in the interests of the Company and its allied interests vs. exploitation of India in the interests of developing industrial economy of the metropolis and the rising industrial bourgeoisie.

5. The Company's dividends and solvency *vs.* territorial expansion in India, promising future gain, and defence of the existing empire.
6. Short-term exploitation *vs.* long-term exploitation—that is not killing the goose that lays the golden eggs.

During the second and third stages of colonialism, the contradictions assumed a different form.

It was necessary to modernize and transform India in basic aspects so that its economy could become reproductive on an extended scale and subserve industrial and, later, finance capital of Britain—thus Imperial Britain's need to develop India. This came up against the financial constraint. The revenues of India were growing marginally in a stagnant economy. This contradiction made the entire development effort limited and petty. It made the colony less useful than desired. It also made Indian people discontented, further limiting the possibilities of taxing the peasantry and other sections of Indian society.

Similar was the contradiction between civil and military expenditure and development expenditure, that is, between the need to develop India and the need for Imperial control.

There was the need to develop agriculture. The peasants had to be helped to save so that they could become buyers of British goods, invest in agriculture, produce the needed raw materials and in general develop agriculture on an extended scale. There was the counter need to make them pay for the defence and expansion, of the empire, for its administration—and development, and the need in general for the peasants to provide the social surplus for export. In other words, was the peasant to provide the mainstay of the colonial state or the base of a reproductive colony? The end result of this contradiction was that all the schemes for capitalist development of agriculture led to its feudalisation; and the more British officials abused the moneylender, the more both the government and the peasant depended on him for revenue payment, and the peasant for even physical survival.

There was the contradiction between de-industrialisation (and pressure on land) and development of agriculture, leading to rack-renting and feudalisation.

There was the contradiction of balance of payments. Should Indian export surpluses be used for expanding the Indian market for British goods or for remitting home the profits?

There was the crucial contradiction between the need for economic development (making India a reproductive colony) and the objective consequences of colonialism which produced the opposite result. This gave rise to the basic contradiction between colonialism and the Indian people, leading to the struggle for national liberation.

Similarly, even the limited transformation necessary to make India a "useful" colony led to the rise of social forces which began to oppose, colonialism and organize a struggle against it.

COLONIALISM AS A SOCIAL FORMATION

Quite often, the underdevelopment, and the economic obstacles to development, in the colonies during the colonial period have been seen as expressions of their pre-capitalist or traditional backwardness, or at least as the remnants of the pre-colonial past. Even when they are seen in—'a historical perspective', an understanding of the role of colonialism is drained out. Others have seen colonialism as an effort at modernisation, which did not fully succeed in some cases as, for example, in India, because of the weight of the past backwardness, and which thus led to a dual society, part modern and part traditional. This was the dominant view among the metropolitan writers during the nineteenth century, though they were convinced that modernisation would be accomplished in, at the most, a few decades. Several twentieth-century writers have also seen colonialism as a transitional stage, though they do not ask the question: transition to what? Would the colony have developed, however slowly or gradually, into a "modern" or industrial capitalist society, i.e. the spitting image of the metropolis, if colonialism had continued to develop 'naturally' for a sufficient period, that is, without its overthrow?

In reality, colonies underwent a fundamental transformation under colonialism. They were gradually integrated into the world of modern capitalism. The conditions of economic, social, cultural and political backwardness in the colonies and former colonies—the initial conditions from which they started the development process after political freedom—are not those of their pre-colonial past. They are the creation of the colonial period, the era in which there occurred "the onslaught of modernisation from outside." Far from being traditional, these conditions signify the evolution of the 'traditional pre-colonial societies into colonial societies. Thus, for example, India under the Britain was not basically similar to Mughal India; nor was it pre-industrial, for it had felt the full impact of industrial capitalism. In fact, colonialism, in India was as modern as historical phenomenon of industrial capitalism in Britain; the two developed together. As J.S. Furnivall put it: "Modern India grew up with modern Europe."[43] And, interestingly enough, the basic integration of India, as also of other colonies, with the world capitalist economy and its transformation into a classic colony occurred during the nineteenth century, precisely under the banner of modernisation, economic development and transportation of capitalism. It is this colonial pattern of modernisation which inevitably led to "the development of underdevelopment" to use the apt phrase of Andre Gunder Frank.[44] The same social, political and economic processes which produced social development in the metropolis produced and maintained underdevelopment and backwardness in the colony. The two countries were organically linked and participated for decades and centuries in a common, integrated world economic system, though with opposite consequences. The colony was thus modernised and underdeveloped at the same time.[45]

Traditionally, colonialism is seen as the result of the ideology or personality of colonial administrators or, at the most, of colonial policy which is itself guided by the first two. Thus, if different colonial administrators can be shown to have different personal motives, ideas and policies, it is concluded that there is no such thing as colonialism in any meaningful sense, except as foreign political rule. Similarly, many economists dealing with development theory, today, criticize the role of colonialism, but they consider merely the political domination aspect of colonialism

As pointed out earlier, the recent tendency is to see colonialism as a structure. The intellectual resources do not yet exist to understand this structure fully and to trace the multifarious channels and ties—the veins and arteries---through which this structure is articulated. But we can certainly assert that colonialism is something much more than political control or colonial policy.

The colonial-state was undoubtedly a part of the colonial system; it was the instrument through which the system was best enforced; and colonial policies helped evolve and maintain the colonial structure. But the colonial state and colonial policies did not constitute the essence of colonialism. Colonialism was the complete but complex integration and enmeshing of India's economy and society with world capitalism carried out by stages over a period lasting nearly two centuries.[46]

Thus when we say that colonialism is to be seen as a structure, we mean that colonial interests, policies, states and its institutions, culture and society, ideas and ideologies, and personalities are to be seen as functioning within the parameters of the colonial structure, which is itself to be defined by their interrelationships as a whole.

Colonialism is structured from the moment of contact between the capitalist metropolis and the colony, whose economy and society are subordinated to the metropolis from the beginning, though the patterns of subordination undergo changes over time. Consequently, colonialism has led to underdevelopment from the beginning. This view is contrary not only to the traditional capitalist-colonial view that colonialism develops and modernizes the colony—or at least tries to do so—but also to the traditional Marxist view that colonialism went through two stages, one positive and the other negative, with the positive belonging to the first period and the negative to the second. According to this view, during the first pre-imperialist stage, the character and impact of colonialism was on the whole positive despite many crimes and much oppression, while it turned negative once modern imperialism (finance imperialism) entered the stage between 1870 and 1914.[47]

In fact, both aspects and consequences of colonialism operated simultaneously. The so-called positive aspect was as integral a part of, and contributed effectively to the structure of, colonialism as was the negative aspect. The positive and negative stages of colonialism were rather stages in the cognition and understanding of the colonial phenomenon by its victims. Thus many colonial and metropolitan intellectuals, including Marx before 1859, failed to grasp the basic features of colonial societies in the early years of their structuring and accordingly had a certain positive image of colonialism. Later, as the reality surfaced, they were able to see its essentially negative features. Instead of seeing this change as an aspect of intellectual and political history linked to the early stages of colonialism, these intellectuals assumed that the reality had undergone a drastic reversal. Hobson's and Lenin's writings regarding a new stage of imperialism in the last quarter of the nineteenth century added fuel to this misunderstanding.

THE COLONIAL EXPERIENCE

Several aspects of a country and its colonial experience affect the prospects of democracy. The first, often neglected, is the nature of the pre-existing society. Except where the native population was virtually eliminated, as in certain settler colonies of the Americas, indigenous cultural traditions survive. These have complex, sometimes contradictory, and often still potent implications for the development of democracy. In Latin America, for example, authoritarian cultural legacies often attributed to the colonizers had roots in the pre-colonial societies, such as those of the Aztecs and the Incas.[48]

Even within a single country, groups with different indigenous cultural legacies absorbed and reflected the colonial experience in politically divergent ways; this divergence was particularly so among the constituent nations of the British Empire, which emphasised "indirect rule." Thus, in the politically centralised, culturally authoritarian emirates of Nigeria's Islamic north, British rule actually reinforced the power of the emir as absolute ruler, while British administration of the more decentralised, participatory, and constitutional societies of southern Nigeria allowed for the emergence of their more democratic tendencies in modern politics. The other English-speaking foreign rulers—Australia (in Papua New Guinea) and the United States (in the Philippines and Puerto Rico)—and the Dutch (in Indonesia) apart, the imperial powers exercised "direct rule"—control by repre-sentatives of the overseas government. Hence the subject population usually lacked experience in self-government before obtaining independence.

Furthermore, the same colonizer could administer different societies differently, depending on what the prospective colony had to offer. Burma, unlike India, was governed directly by the British and has been more authoritarian since independence. Where mineral resources were particularly abundant and indigenous populations large, as in Peru and Mexico, or where slaves were imported for plantation agriculture, as in Brazil or the Dominican Republic, colonial rule by the Spanish and Portuguese was particularly intrusive and exploitative. In parts of the New World where both of these features were lacking, as in Uruguay, Argentina, or especially Costa Rica, Spanish control was less penetrating and authoritarian.[49]

The timing of foreign invasion also affected what potential colonizers wanted and could use from their colonies, which in turn affected their legacy. The British pattern established in the 1600s and 1700s in India and the Americas differed from Britain's mode of operation in nineteenth-century Africa and in Burma. The later instances of colonisation, which occurred after the beginning of the Industrial Revolution, concentrated much more on the control of production than did early colonisation, which had focused on the control of trade.

More significant perhaps for democracy, the early British colonisation of Asia and the Caribbean, along with certain other islands such as Mauritius, gave these countries much longer and deeper contact with British values and institutions as well as more time for the gradual emergence of indigenous representative institutions. With the British colonial presence dating back to the seventeenth century, both India and Jamaica, for example, had several centuries of contact with the British and many decades of experience with their own representative institutions, which gradually expanded to incorporate much of the population. By contrast, because Britain's colonisation of Africa and Burma occurred later, and its withdrawal was more hurried, the colonizer's influence on post-colonial governments was weaker.

Finally, the most important aspect of colonialism and its legacy is the identity of the colonizer. One of the most widely recognised and powerful determinants of the likelihood of democracy among the new nations of the developing world is a simple, dichotomous, historical variable: whether or not the nation has been ruled by Britain. By no means have all of Britain's former colonies become stable democracies, but the developing countries with the most successful democratic experience since independence are, by and large, former British colonies—whether in Asia, Africa, or the Caribbean. Even in Africa, where experiences with democracy have generally been unsuccessful, the four countries where multiparty democracy has managed to persist—Botswana, Gambia, Mauritius, and (in its limited way) South Africa—all have experienced British domination. The reasons behind this striking pattern require closer examination.[50]

BRITISH COLONIAL PRACTICES VIS-A-VIS OTHER NATIONS

The imperial powers affected the subsequent democratic prospects of their dependencies in different ways. The positive impact of the British legacy can be seen among the older overseas colonies, as a comparison of the post-independence histories of Australia and British America with that of Spanish and Portuguese America indicates. The minor imperial powers—Australia and the United States—can roughly be classed with Britain (if the short-lived interventions in and occupations of Haiti, Nicaragua, Mexico, and other countries in Latin America by the United States are excluded).

French colonisation gave rise to democratic traditions and values in some countries, but not to the same extent as British colonisation. Quebec, as Pierre Trudeau noted in 1958, was much less democratic than English-speaking Canada until its "quiet revolution" of the 1960s. In Africa and Asia, Belgian, Dutch, and Portuguese rule (not to mention Japan's later entry into colonial domination) were almost completely devoid of any democratic legacy.

The Spanish and Portuguese legacy in Latin America is more difficult to assess, as nearly two centuries of independence have seen the colonial heritage recede in importance. Certainly, however, the newly independent states of Central and South America were notable mainly for their lack of democracy and political stability in the nineteenth century. The most significant, if limited, democratic ventures emerged in those states—Chile, Uruguay, and Costa Rica—where the Spanish colonial presence and influence had been the weakest.[51]

What accounts for the relative success of democracy after British colonial rule? Political scientist, Myron Weiner, cites two components of the British colonial model: the establishment of the rule of law through effective (and increasingly indigenous) bureaucratic and judicial institutions and the provision for some system of representation and election, which gave educated native elites experience in political leadership and limited governance. The resulting legacy, Weiner maintains, was not simply the presence of more effective political institutions at independence (in terms of both government administration and political party mobilisation and competition), but also an enduring cultural commitment to the procedures of democratic politics and governance and to the rule of law as a constraint on government.[52]

Where the British ruled for a long time, democratic institutions emerged gradually and expanded over time to incorporate larger segments of the population and to assume increasingly significant responsibilities. During its last eighty years under the British, India went through several phases of constitutional reforms that opened government to indigenous representation and public scrutiny while successively broadening the basis of participation. The dramatic reforms vide the Government of India Act of 1935, extended the franchise to only one-sixth of the population, but provisions for self-government in the provinces along with widespread electoral competition were to prove invaluable in preparing Indians and the Indian National Congress for the rigours of democratic politics. Of course, one cannot overemphasize the importance of the existence and growth of the Congress for Indian democracy. For six decades preceding independence in 1947, the Congress acted not just as a nationalist organisation but as a political party, democratic in its procedures and goals, conciliatory in its approach to conflict, and increasingly incorporative of rural and urban mass groups. The contrast with Pakistan, where political parties were less active and where the process of obtaining separation from India stunted the development of party competition, suggests the usefulness of pre-independence development of democratic political institutions.

India was perhaps unique in the depth and complexity of its pre-independence democratic experience, though not in the fact of it. Indeed, Sri Lanka was the first country in the colonial world to win universal suffrage (in 1931), and its impressive democratic success in the decades following independence in 1948 had been prepared by seventeen years of limited self-government, during which the island colony held three general elections. In Malaysia under the British, the Philippines under the United States, and Papua New Guinea under the Australians, pre-independence electoral competition permitted the development of political parties and coalitions and the acquisition of democratic experience that clearly enhanced the capacity of democratic institutions after independence.[53]

Jamaica—one of the most stable post-colonial democracies in recent decades—is another instructive example of the effect of long British control. During the nineteenth century, the island evolved a very limited, exclusive parliamentary structure. Although Jamaica was long dominated by aristocratic-white settlers and endured periods of revolt and repression, its governmental institutions gradually broadened to incorporate middle-class groups between 1884 and 1944, when the British granted the country universal adult suffrage and considerable self-governance. There followed eighteen years of two-party competition and gradual colonial withdrawal, leading to independence in 1962. The British handed over the administration of the colony to indigenous ministers in 1953 and granted full internal self-government in 1959. This staging was perhaps the ultimate expression of British colonial democratic design. Political scientist, Carl Stone, observes that the slow movement from British supervision to local leadership ensured that post-independence political structures would resemble the parliamentary democracy established in Great Britain.[54]

A related strategy guided the British colonial project in Africa. Africanists, Lewis Gann and Peter Duignan, note that British-ruled Africans were more likely than black people in any other part of colonial Africa to have exercised executive power, and that power was transferred from London to local African governments by a constitutional machinery. The phased development of indigenous capacities for self-rule was a hallmark of the philosophy of indirect rule, which derived from a domestic political culture in Britain that distrusted rapid change and emphasised gradualism.[55]

The Legacy of British Values: So far, the distinctive (although delayed, ambivalent, and paternalistic) British commitment to the transfer and development of representative institutions in the colonies have been stressed. But other elements also made British rule more conducive than the rule of other colonial powers to the development of democracy.

Perhaps because of their own commitment to liberal, pluralist values, the British, as rulers, permitted significantly more free expression and open, autonomous associational life than did the other European colonizers (especially the Portuguese, Spanish, and Belgians). At the same time, the spread of education, transportation, and communication—although generally limited to urban elites among the native population—made possible higher levels of political consciousness and organisation than ever before.

Decades of practice in the arts of independent reporting and political organisation—even within the overall context of a generally undemocratic state that had become the target of nationalist demands—gave rise in many British colonies to a spirited civil society. Many of the lawyers, teachers, journalists, intellectuals, trade unionists, activists, entrepreneurs, and politicians in the making who composed this civil society internalised (sometimes directly from study in Britain) the democratic values of Great Britain. In addition, the domestic elites revealed and synthesised numerous continuities between British democratic principles and their own cultural traditions, thus giving democracy a deeper basis of legitimacy.

Again, the experience of India—the "jewel in the crown" and still in many ways the most important and surprising postcolonial democracy—is instructive. By the late nineteenth century, hundreds of newspapers and periodicals were in circulation, reporting on British and European politics as well as on the debates within the colonial administration in India. These media sources had an educational and unifying effect on the various regions of India as activities and matters of public interest were reported and reviewed.

The British commitment to constitutional procedures and forms (as reflected in the successions of constitutional reforms and conferences) and to the rule of law was no doubt influential in the post-colonial governments. Ironically, a surviving concern with legalism has been apparent not only in the strength of the judiciary, the legal culture, and the legal profession in many former colonies, such as India, but even in actions that have temporarily curtailed free expression and choice. The suspension of democracy under the National Operations Council in Malaysia (1969-71) followed appropriate legal and constitutional procedures; the council emphasised the temporary nature of the emergency, implying a return to democratic rights upon the restoration of law and order. Indira Gandhi's curtailment of democracy in India (1975-77) was pursued and justified through the use of emergency powers in the constitution and was entrenched by laws and constitutional amendments duly passed in the parliament. One may speculate that the institutional and cultural legacies left by former rulers were important factors in limiting the duration and scope of these abridgments of democracy.

Along with a respect for constitutional law, the British conveyed a cultural commitment to democracy. Even in many of the former British dependencies that have not shown great success in maintaining democracy—such as Pakistan, Nigeria, and Ghana—a strong commitment to liberal principles, and to the eventual adoption of democracy, has persisted among segments of the political elite and general public. These values have preserved some space for political pluralism and autonomous organisations even during authoritarian regimes, while motivating citizens to press for a return to democracy.

The Australian and American experiences as colonizers in New Guinea and the Philippines, respectively, fit broadly with the British pattern. Even more explicitly and extensively than the British perhaps, American colonial rule in the Philippines during the first decades of the twentieth century set out to school the people in democratic citizenship. The United States left behind some important developmental and institutional legacies including universal education, a high literacy rate, a politically active elite, and a free press. Unfortunately, these democratic legacies had to contend with the deeply rooted legacies of four centuries of autocratic Spanish colonial rule. The earlier background, Karl Jackson, a student of Filipino politics, suggests, may help to account for the stubborn persistence of oligarchical control and corrupt, clientelistic politics beneath the veneer of democratic commitment.[56]

THE FRENCH COLONIAL LEGACY

Many of the characteristic differences between the British and other colonial administrations resulted from governing arrangements. The French and most other colonizers chose to govern directly from their own capital; the British favoured indirect rule and allowed the colonies some autonomy. In Africa, French administration was highly centralised, and local colonial officials were closely directed from Paris or from the regional headquarters at Daka or French West Africa and Brazzaville for French Equatorial Africa. Traditional rulers were typically undermined rather than cultivated and incorporated into colonial government, and they were often replaced by "straw chiefs" who served at the bottom of the colonial administrative hierarchy.

In every respect, the French colonies were much more strongly tied to France than the British colonies were to England. French colonial policy until the 1950s, according to Africanist J. Gus Liebenow, was to form "black Frenchmen" and to develop a French-speaking political community led by the French Republic and encompassing the African areas. Economically and politically, the local population remained dependent on France, and little attention was paid to the development of indigenous political and administrative abilities. Close economic links between the colonies and France were encouraged through practices such as direct subsidies from the French treasury and the establishment of common currency backed by the Bank of France. The British, in contrast, enforced as much budgetary independence as possible in individual colonies even before relinquishing political authority over them.[57]

For the most part, the French waited longer than the British to initiate indigenous political representation. Although the four communes in Dakar began electing a deputy to the French National Assembly in 1948, and a little later started electing members of municipal councils, the French did not introduce broadly elected indigenous assemblies into their African territories until reforms in 1956.

Britain and France often left behind political institutions that reflected their own constitutional models, an inheritance that led to differing democratic prospects in their colonies. The British transferred their parliamentary system; the French transferred the presidentialism, of the Fifth Republic. The British embedded in their colonial constitutions emphasis on dispersed power and autonomous local government, which in some cases took the form of explicit federalism. France gave its colonies centralist and unitary constitutions. The stronger executives, weaker parliaments, and much more centralised governments of the former French colonies were more conducive to authoritarianism. This may be one reason why several former British colonies—Ghana, Tanzania (Tanganyika), Uganda—switched over to presidential systems upon establishing dictatorial governments.[58]

The British exported their electoral system of single member districts (constituencies), while the French provided for election of assembly members from party lists. In British colonies, the emphasis was more likely to be on the individual candidates in the district (with the ballot, as in Britain, sometimes lacking party identifications). Independents or small or local parties could win seats and survive politically. In the French colonies, where the multi-member candidate lists were identified by party name, voters had to choose a party rather than an individual candidate, and the leading party claimed all the district seats on a winner-take-all basis. As David Collier noted, the French system favoured the emergence of a dominant party.

Thus, even within Africa, with its generally dismal record with regard to democracy, it may be suggested that the variations in colonial legacies have been of great significance in accounting for the more extended and frequent (if not ultimately much more successful) experimentation with democracy among former British as opposed to former French colonies, and for the greater level of electoral competition within dominant-party systems in English-speaking, as opposed to French-speaking, countries. Even setting aside the three former British colonies in Africa that have remained democratic, the countries that have made the most renewed attempts at democracy in the post-colonial period—such as Ghana, Nigeria, Sudan, and Uganda—have all been former British colonies.[59]

When we turn to the other colonial legacies in Africa, however, we can appreciate the elements of democratic concern and potential for free institutions in the French colonial practice that were virtually absent in the rule of the Belgians and Portuguese. The French, in contrast to the Portuguese, Spanish, and Belgians, allowed some scope for the emergence of autonomous organisations. One former French African colony, Senegal, today has a functioning and relatively liberal semi-democracy, which can be traced in part to the lengthy exposure of the elite to political debate, organisation, and competition. As Christian Coulan emphasizes, this exposure has made it difficult to restrict the activities of a people with more than a century of political experience.

OTHER COLONIAL LEGACIES IN AFRICA AND ASIA

It is not by coincidence that the former African colonies of Belgium (Zaire, Burundi, and Rwanda) and of Portugal (Angola, Mozambique, and Guinea-Bissau) have experienced some of the greatest repression, ethnic turmoil, instability, and bloodshed of all independent countries in Africa. The Belgian Congo, which later become Zaire, was intensely exploited by King Leopold and later by the Belgian state for its extraordinary mineral resources. Belgium expected to hold on to the colony indefinitely, in contrast to the British goal of self-government and the French ideal of incorporation. Thus, although Belgium created a class of Westernised evalues (assimilated persons), who had education and training, they were prevented from developing associations, from obtaining post-secondary education (except for priests), and from holding responsible administrative positions. Representative institutions were not introduced in the Congo until 1957; even these consisted largely of a few indirectly elected urban councils on which Europeans were guaranteed parity. Subsequent reforms hastily enlarged the scope of elections, but these remained indirect, complex, and ineffectual. The 1959 inaugural elections for a territorial assembly were widely boycotted. After popular pressure and the experiences of other African states forced Belgium to grant independence in 1960, the Congo was left with virtually no preparation for self-government.

Portugal had the longest history of direct colonial domination in Africa, but it was the most repressive of all the European powers in Africa and did the least to prepare its colonies for independence. As a result of Portugal's intransigence, it alone experienced armed revolt in all its territories; ultimately, it had to be forced to withdraw, following a coup in April 1974 that ended dictatorship in Portugal itself.

Colonial experiences have shaped the subsequent democratic histories of nations in important ways, affecting cleavage structures (that is, class, ethic, religious, and comparable groupings), economic patterns, and institutional development. These factors, in turn, continue to influence the opportunities and obstacles for stable democracy. Any effort to understand the variations in postcolonial political systems, therefore, must deal with the colonial past.

Notes and References

1. Simpson John and Edmund Weiner (eds.), Oxford English Dictionary (Oxford: Oxford University Press), 1976, pp. 12-13.
2. *Ibid.*
3. The Encyclopedia Americana International Educational (Conneciticut: Grolier Incorporated), 1981, p. 298.
4. Marie-Bénédicte Dembour,Recalling the Belgian Congo: Conversations and Introspection, Berghahn Books; 2nd edition, 2001 pp. 1-5.
5. Wakefield, Edward Gibbon, A View of the Art of Colonisation in Present Reference to the British Empire in Letters between a Statesman and a Colonist (London: John W. Parker), 1849. (Rpt. by NY: Augustus M. Kelley, 1969), pp. 14-20.
6. Pauling Linus, World Encyclopedia of Peace (Oxford: Pergamon Press), Vol. 1, p. 151.
7. The New Encyclopaedia Britanncia (Chicago: Encyclopaedia Britannica Inc.), Vol. 3, 2002, p. 464.
8. Sills, David, L. (ed.), International Encyclopedia of the Social Sciences (London: Collier-Macmillan Publishers), Vols. 3 and 4, n.d., pp. 2-3.
9. New Standards Encyclopedia (Chicago: Standard Educational Corporation), Vol. 3, n.d., pp. C458c.
10. Osterhammel, J., Colonialism: A Theoretical Overview (New Jersy: M. Wiener), 1997, pp. 4-5.
11. Fieldhouse, D. K., Colonialism 1870-1945: An Introduction (London : Weidenfeld and Nicholson), 1981, p. 6.
12. http://plato.stanford.edu/entries/colonialism
13. Young, Robert, Postcolonialism: A Historical Introduction (Oxford: Blackwell), 2001, pp. 490-512.
14. Reinhard, W., Kleine Geschichte des Kolonialismus (trns.) (Stuttgart: Kroner), 1996, p. 1.
15. René Maunier, "The sociology of colonies: an introduction to the study of race contact", Part 1, Routledge, 2002, London, pp. 18-24.
16. Muratori, Relations des missions du Paraguai, (French trans) J. Marmaduke, 1759. (Paris), pp. 52-62.
17. Kingsley, Mary, West African Studies (London: Oxford Press), 1901, Chaps. XII to XV.
18. Beer, G.L., The Old Colonial System (1660-1754), (New York), 1912. pp. 20-28.
19. Smith, Adam, Wealth of Nations (New York: Modern Library), 1776, pp. 1-43.

20. Patnaik, Prabhat, A synoptic View of Underdevelopment. Review of The Political Economy of Underdevelopment, by A.K. Bagchi, *Economic and Political Weekly*, Vol. 19, No. 28, 14 July 1984, p. 1086.

21. *Ibid.*

22. Ian Cummins, "Marx, Engels, and National Movements", Redwood Burn Ltd., London, 1980, pp. 76-178.

23. Marx, Karl and Engels, Communist Manifesto, Foreign Languages Publishing House, Moscow, 1962, pp. 34-39.

24. Chandra, Bipin, Sociological Theories: Race and Colonialism, UNESCO, Paris: 1980, p. 430.

25. Chandra, Bipin, Nationalism and Colonialism in Modern India (New Delhi: Orient Longman), 1979, pp. 5-10.

26. Chandra, Bipin, Sociological Theories: Race and Colonialism, (UNESCO), *op. cit.*, p. 435.

27. Alavi, Hamaza, *et. al.*, Capitalism and Colonial Production (London: Oxford University Press), 1982, pp. 63-78

28. Chandra, Bipin, Essays on Colonialism (New Delhi: Orient Longman), 2000, pp. 5-10.

29. *Ibid.*

30. Alvai, Hamza, "India and the Colonial Mode of Production", in Miliband R. and J. Saville (ed.), Socialist Register, London, 1975, pp. 167-187.

31. Chandra, Bipin, Essays on Colonialism (New Delhi: Orient Longman), 2000, pp. 202-06.

32. *Ibid.*

33. Marx, Karl and F. Engels, Collected Works (Moscow), Vol. 6, 1976.

34. Chandra, Bipin, Essays on Colonialism (New Delhi: Orient Longman), 2000, pp. 10-12.

35. Alavi, Hamzai, *et. al.*, Capitalism and Colonial Production, Routledge, 1982 *op. cit.*, p. 63.

36. Miliband Ralph, The State in Capitalist Society, Oxford University Press (London:), 1969, pp. 20-24.

37. Raj Kumar, "Essays on modern India?", Discovery Publishing House, New Delhi, 2003, p. 212.

38. *Ibid.*

39. *Ibid.*

40. *Ibid.*

41. Chandra, Bipin, Essays on Colonialism, Orient Longman Ltd., New Delhi, 1999, pp. 62-72.

42. B. Sheikh Ali, H.V. Sreenivasa Murthy, "Essays on Indian history and culture: Felicitation volume in honour of Professor B. Sheik Ali", Mittal Publications; 1st edition, New Delhi (1990), pp. 150-56.

43. Furnivall, J.S., Colonial Policy and Practice, New York University Press, (New York), 1956, p. 537.

44. B. Sheikh Ali, H.V. Sreenivasa Murthy, "Essays on Indian history and culture: Felicitation volume in honour of Professor B. Sheik Ali", Mittal Publications; New Delhi (1990), pp. 140-46.

45. *Economic and Political Weekly*, Volume 21, 1986, pp. 1417-18
46. Anesty, Vera, The Economic Development of India, Arno Press, (New York), 1977, pp. 433-70.
47. B. Sheikh Ali, H.V. Sreenivasa Murthy, "Essays on Indian history and culture: Felicitation volume in honour of Professor B. Sheik Ali", Mittal Publications; 1st edition, New Delhi (1990), pp. 140-46.
48. Lipset, Symour Martin, The Encyclopedia of Democracy (London: Roultege), Vol. I, 1995, p. 264.
49. *Ibid.*, p. 265.
50. *Ibid.*, p. 263.
51. By Krister Lundell, Contextual determinants of electoral system choice: a macro, Abo Akademis forlag (the University of Michigan), Michigan, 2005, pp. 102-12.
52. Weiner, Myron, "Empirical Democratic Theory", in Competitive Elections in Developing Countries (ed.) Myron Weiner and Ergun Ozbunduu (Durham, N.C.: Duke University Press), 1987, pp. 56-58.
53. Lipset, Seymour Martin, Kyoung-Ryung Seong and John Charles Torres, "A Comparative Analysis of the Social Requisites of Democracy", *International Social Science Journal*, Vol. 45, 1993, pp. 155-75.
54. Seymour Martin Lipset, Jason M. Lakin, The democratic century, University of Oklahoma Press, Oklahoma, 2004, pp. 170-82
55. http://afraf.oxfordjournals.org/cgi/reprint/68/272/269.pdf
56. *Ibid.*
57. Gus Liebenow African politics: crises and challenges, Indiana University Press, Indiana, 1986, pp. 24-35.
58. *Ibid.*
59. Smith, Tony, "A Comparative Study of French and British De-Colonisation", Comparative Studies in Society and History, Vol. 20, 1978, pp. 70-102.

2

Public Sector in India

At the time of independence in 1947, India was a typically backward economy. Owing to poor technological and scientific capabilities, industrialisation was limited and lopsided. Agricultural sector exhibited features of feudal and semi-feudal institutions, resulting into low productivity. Means of transport and communications were underdeveloped, educational and health facilities inadequate, and social security measures virtually non-existent. In brief, poverty was rampant and unemployment widespread, both making for low general standard of living.

These were the socio-economic settings under which the leadership had to chart out a programme of nation-building. In their collective wisdom, they adopted the middle course of a mixed economy, assigning a pivotal role to public sector and economic planning. This new approach to economic and social development was set within a framework of parliamentary democracy guaranteeing universal franchise. India began the process of planned economic development with the start of the First Five Year Plan in April 1951. Since then, the country has completed ten Five Year Plans and the implementation of the Eleventh Five Year Plan (2007-12) is underway. The economic history of post-independence India is a mixed experience of achievements and failures. After more than 60 years of development efforts, India is presently one of the world's fastest growing economies. In the last few years, it has emerged as a global economic power, the leading outsourcing destination and a favourite of international investors.

The immediate task before an underdeveloped country is not merely to get better results within the existing framework of economic and social institutions. It has to mould and recondition these institutions so that they contribute effectively to the realisation of wider and deeper social values. The Directive Principles of state policy are fundamental in the governance of the country. It shall be the duty of the State to apply these principles in making laws. The State shall try to promote the welfare of the people by securing and making as effectively as it may a social order in which justice, social, economic and political, shall inform all the institutions of national life (Art. 38). It shall, in particular, direct its policy towards securing:

(a) that the citizens, men and women, equally, have the right to an adequate means of livelihood;
(b) that the ownership and control of the material resources of the community are so distributed as best to subserve the common good; and
(c) that the operation of the economic system does not result in the concentration of wealth and means of production to the common detriment. (Art. 39)

Articles 38 and 39 further directed the state to make policies and strategies to minimize the inequalities of income. The question that arises is as to why this type of direction is given to the state when, as Myrdal points out, "Western economists for the most part assume a conflict between economic and egalitarian reforms."[1]

According to western economists, inequalities in income contribute to the growth of the economy.[2] Thus, the alms of the Constitution-makers were quite clear. They were keen to establish a welfare state based on social and economic justice because income disparity produces range of inequalities, which pervade more than one generation in a poor family.[3] The main reason for adopting the Soviet model of development with high state intervening policy was to secure the double ends of social welfare and economic development.

P.C. Mahalanobis, the great visionary, in the early phases of planning, gave the development model, which strengthens the infrastructure of the country. But sooner, it was found that excessive government intervention and license raj proved a stumbling block on the way of industrial development of the country. This hurdle proved detrimental. In the words of P. C. Mahalanobis: "We have failed to raise the living standards of the people to the extent required for a steady and harmonious growth. This is a failure at home. We are now looking westwards but have hopes in eastern magic as well. When the Americans, the Europeans, and Japanese come what will they do to our economy and to our people?[4] As because we are at half way house a convenient halting place between stages of journey. Presently, India is at the crossroads either to keep moving forward or stepping backward. Such a situation is described by American dictionary as 'half house', a place where persons are aided in readjustment to society following imprisonment, etc. For describing the condition of the Indian poor, one has to accept the American version of a halfway house, but with some modification. Our poor have always been in prison, they are aided not for readjustment but for adjusted survival. The adjustments are being made by the bosses, as the American says, at the top.[5]

The term "public enterprises" has come to be associated mainly with what is called the "commercial undertakings" of the Government, which have been formed, or registered, in the form of companies. But it is important to remember that "public enterprise" in India is a much wider term than the "public sector undertaking." Manorama Year Book prefers to call public sector as omnibus term.[6] In France, Public Enterprises mean industrial and commercial undertakings of the Government. In U.S.A., public sector means all government agencies which are engaged in providing specific goods and services. In U.K., public corporations are the public enterprises. In Italy, public enterprises are those which are run either by local bodies or by State Government. So, industries run, owned and controlled by the state are generally called public sector.[7] A.H. Hanson defines "public enterprises" to mean state ownership and operation of industrial, agricultural, financial and commercial undertakings."[8] The Encyclopedia Britannica depicts—"public enterprise may be defined as an undertaking that is owned by a national, state (provincial) or local government, supplies services or goods at a price, and is operated on a more or less self-supporting basis. Such enterprises may also be international, interstate or inter-municipal in character, i.e. owned and operated jointly by two or more national, state or local governments."[9] A more comprehensive definition has been provided by International Development Research Centre of Canada which runs as "Public enterprise is a productive entity/organisation which is owned and or controlled by public authorities and whose output is marketed."[10]

Public enterprises are an offshoot of the philosophy enshrined in the Indian Constitution. Public enterprises were set-up after independence. Of course, many of our public enterprises were in existence before independence. The only instances worthy of mention were: (a) the Railways, (b) the Posts and Telegraphs Department, (c) the Port Trusts, (d) the Reserve Bank of India, (e) the Ordnance and Aircraft factories, and (f) a few state-managed undertakings like the Government Salt factories, Quinine factories, etc. This was so because of historical reasons. Although the East India Company had encouraged the development of a few indigenous industries in its own interest, the policy was later reversed for the benefit of industries in Great Britain. Even after the Crown had assumed responsibility in 1857 for the management and good governance of the country, the policy followed was one of *laissez faire*. In 1904, during Lord Curzon's regime, an Industries Department was set-up by the Government of India (this was followed by the setting up of corresponding Industries Departments in some of the Provinces as well), but the then Secretary of State for India did not approve of Government taking even these comparatively innocuous steps. Then came the World War I and a realisation by the British Government that an industrially developed India could have been a greater use to them even from the limited objective of winning the war. Attention was, therefore, given to the development of industries and an Industrial Commission was appointed in 1916 to conduct a comprehensive survey of resources and industrial possibilities. The Indian Munitions Board was set-up in 1917 to foster the development of certain types of industries. As a result of all these and other measures, several new industries were started and many existing ones were further developed and extended.

The sustained growth of public enterprises in India dates from the early years of planning following national independence. The 1956 Industrial Policy Resolution affirmed the objective of a socialist pattern of society and the concomitant need for planned and rapid industrial development to achieve this objective. It proposed that all basic and strategic industries, and public utilities, should be located in the public sector. Public ownership, part or complete, was especially required in those fields where technological considerations fostered the concentration of economic power and wealth. Public enterprises thus came to establish their dominance in basic and strategic industries such as steel, minerals, metals, coal, power, petroleum, chemicals, fertilizers, Pharmaceuticals, heavy engineering, and a substantial presence in industries such as transportation services, agricultural-based products, trading and marketing, and financial services.

Over the last thirty years or more, the growth of public enterprises in India has been phenomenal in terms of investment, production and range of activities. Under the central government, from only 5 enterprises in 1951, public enterprises had grown to 226 (excluding departmental undertakings, insurance, banking and financial institutions) by 1987, employing more than 2 million people. The public sector has spread over all parts of India. Its coverage has extended beyond the basic and heavy industries into light manufacturing, a variety of consumer goods, electronics, high-technology products, construction, consultancy services, and even tourism and hotel industries. The share of the public sector, in terms of gross domestic product, rose from 14.9 per cent in 1970-71 to 25 per cent in 1984-85.

These public enterprises, as instruments of national development, supplement government efforts to promote the social and economic objectives laid down in the national plans. They provide greater flexibility in implementing programmes such as expansion of employment opportunities, balanced regional development, acceleration of the rate of growth of agricultural and industrial production, prevention of concentration of economic power and technological self-sufficiency. Public enterprises have thus become principal instruments of planning in India, occupying commanding heights of the economy, and controlling and directing in a large measure the entire course of national development.

OBJECTIVES OF PUBLIC SECTOR ENTERPRISES

The objectives of setting up public enterprises in India are:

- (i) To promote rapid economic development through creation and expansion of infrastructure;
- (ii) To generate financial resources for development;
- (iii) To promote redistribution of income and wealth;
- (iv) To create employment opportunities;
- (v) To promote balanced regional growth;
- (vi) To encourage the development of small scale and ancillary industries; and
- (vii) To promote exports on the one side and import substitution, on the other.

TYPES OF PUBLIC ENTERPRISES

In India, there are four categories of public enterprises, as listed below:

- (i) Departmental undertakings (e.g. railways, posts and telecommunications) are an integral part of government departments. Such bodies operate both at the central and state government levels. They perform service-oriented, trading or manufacturing functions and are expected to function profitably. The operating results of these business-type undertakings are kept separately in accordance with normal commercial principles, but are integrated with the accounts of their parent departments for government accounting purposes.

(ii) Statutory corporations both at the Central Government level (e.g. Oil and Natural Gas Commission, Indian Oil Corporation, and Food Corporation of India) and state government levels (e.g. state warehousing corporations) are established by the statutes of the respective legislatures.

(iii) Some autonomous bodies are set-up as registered societies (e.g. Council of Scientific and Industrial Research, Indian Council of Agricultural Research) under government resolutions. They are established both at the central and state government levels and are either substantially or partly funded by the respective governments.

(iv) Government owned or controlled companies outnumber any other form of public enterprises by far. These companies are established under the Companies Act in common with companies in the private sector, and comprise companies in which not less than 51 per cent of the paid up share capital is held by the central government or by any state government—or partly or wholly by both. Included in this fourth category are holding companies (e.g. State Trading Corporation of India, Minerals and Metals Trading Corportion of India) which own more than 50 per cent of the share capital of their subsidiaries.

This form of enterprise was started immediately after independence. The Government entered business for a variety of reasons. Sometimes, it might have been because the order of investment was very high and at that time the private sector was not in a position to raise that amount of money. Sometimes, it might have been because the gestation period involved was so long that the private sector would not like to wait for that length of time. Sometimes, it might have been because of the deliberate effort to develop certain backward areas where no private entrepreneur would go. Sometimes, it might have been because of technological grounds: the technology was such that either it was available only to the public sector, or the Government desired that it should be available through the public sector. Or, it might have been also because of strategic considerations. There were then a variety of considerations for which the Government decided to enter business.

Later on, other compulsions also developed. In certain cases, on policy considerations, on expediency, certain enterprises were nationalised. For example, non-ferrous metals, zinc and copper were nationalised. Banks were nationalised. Insurance was nationalised.

The third category of public enterprises are the sick units. The companies in the private sector, for a variety of reasons, sometimes deliberately, sometimes maybe because of reasons beyond their control, fell sick, and the Government had to take over in order to protect employment and also to ensure the availability of essential services and products.

While setting up these enterprises, the Government deliberately chose the company form of management. It was open to the Government to set-up these enterprises as departmental undertakings or to adopt some other form, but it chose to set-up all these organisations as companies, because here was a statute, a system which was already available which, could be straightaway made use of, and the company form of management gave a fair amount of freedom which was necessary for good and efficient management of enterprises, be they public enterprises or private enterprises.

To enter a particular area of business or industry is a policy decision. It might be largely a political decision that has been taken. Once it is decided to enter a particular area, it is necessary to ensure that the management is efficient, that the activity undertaken is performed well, operated well, that the enterprise works well. The company form of management did provide the necessary base which could be used for efficient management of public enterprises.

The close of the first half of the 20th century witnessed

tremendous changes, both in political as well as in economic fields. Emergence of government as a giant industrial producer is one such development. The Industrial Policy Resolutions of 1948 (Annexure I) and of 1956 (Annexure II) envisaged a pivotal role to the public sector as an instrument of socio-economic development in the country. In other words, they made government a major partner. It was given the role of a big brother in the industrial development of the country. A large number of public enterprises came into being under the control and supervision of the government sector, i.e. the public sector. The overall purpose of such enterprises, set-up either at the Central or State level, was the economic welfare of the people.

The policy-makers under the leadership of Jawaharlal Nehru had the conviction that the State had to assume a major economic role in order to break the structural bottlenecks and achieve rapid economic and social transformation.

Many economists have expressed the view that the Indian development strategy was based on the Soviet planning model. This does not seem to be a correct perception. There has, in fact, been a continuity in Indian economic thinking right from the early years of the twentieth century, highlighting the role of the State, particularly in the process of rapid industrialisation. Mahadev Govind Ranade, as early as in 1906, advocated the State promotion of industrialisation through protection.[11] Later, Visvesvarayya presented in 1931, a ten-year plan for rapid industrialisation of the country initiated by the State.[12] This was followed by the constitution of a National Planning Committee by the Indian National Congress in 1938. The Committee appointed a number of sub-committees which consisted of members from all walks of life, such as academics, scientists, professionals, trade unionists and political leaders subscribing to different ideologies. The various sub-committees prepared their reports during the period 1938-40 which were published together with the report of the National Planning Committee in 1949.

It may also be noted in this context that Indian industrialists like J.R.D. Tata, G.D. Birla, Shri Ram and Kasturbhai Lalbhai also prepared a plan for India's economic development in 1944 which came to be popularly known as the "Bombay Plan." This Plan highlighted the need for constituting a Central Planning Authority and developing domestic capital goods industries. It is important to note that both the Reports of the National Planning Committee and the Bombay Plan explicitly put forward two developmental concepts, namely, central planning and the role of the public sector. Thus, Indian economic thinking has always emphasised the strategic role of the public sector in national economic development, taking a broader view of the development process.

Jawahar Lal Nehru carried forward this line of economic thinking and translated it into action when the development process was launched in the 1950s. He was, no doubt, convinced of the appropriateness of this tenor of thinking due to the influence of the idea of contemporary Fabian socialism as well as the emergence of central planning in the Soviet Union. While Nehru recognised the crucial role that the State had to play in formulating a programme of structural transformation, he never displayed a liking for "Statism" as such (as in the case of the Soviet Union) because of his firm conviction that planning must be carried out in a democratic environment.[13]

The economic rationale for the establishment of basic industries in the public sector was explained by Nehru as follows: "In planning the under-developed economics, it becomes essential that the limited resources are used to the best advantage and that the strategic points of the economy are controlled. Among the strategic points are basic industries. We, therefore, come to the establishment of public enterprises."[14]

It is also important to note that the concept of mixed economy, with a dominant public sector, enjoyed almost universal acceptance during the fifties and sixties. The very first U.N. Report dealing with the problems of development of underdeveloped countries, prepared by Arthur Lewis, D.R. Gadgil and others, clearly indicated that the living standards of the people in economically backward countries could be raised through deliberate policies of State action.[15] While it is true that the economic and political philosophy that in India during the 1950s favoured the reservation of basic industries for the public sector, it is also important to note that private investment in basic industries and infrastructure was not forthcoming for various reasons such as long gestation periods, lumpy investment and low returns. Under such circumstances, the establishment of basic industries in the public sector did not remain merely a matter of choice, but turned out to be an economic necessity as well.

While the economic rationale for the creation of basic industries and infrastructure in the public sector in India in the early stages of development was clearly enunciated, one cannot find a convincing argument for the subsequent expansion of the public sector in the areas of many consumer good industries. There is no gainsaying the fact that the growth of PEs, since the early 1970s was not necessarily planned. In other words, the expansion of PEs in diverse economic areas was the result of attempts at finding out *ad hoc* solutions for economic problems as well as due to reasons of political expediency. However, there were also a number of other reasons for the establishment of PEs in different fields. It would be useful to put them all in one place.

Firstly, the operation of market forces was not likely to produce a satisfactory outcome in all spheres of economic activity. Increasing returns, positive externalities, and indivisibilities fall into this category. The process of industrialisation greatly depends on the expansion of infrastructural facilities and public utilities, especially power, transport and communication networks which are also considered as natural monopolies. For example, transport is not a single homogeneous commodity, but can be provided by a number of modes which can be both competitors as well as complements. However, each mode requires its own dedicated infrastructure, such as rail tracks, roads, ports and airports. The development of these infrastructures, which have come to be more commonly known as "ground facilities", involve lumpy investments and, hence, represent "sunk capital." Since these investments display considerable economies of scale, the transport infrastructure had become a classic example of natural monopoly in the economics literature. It was for this reason that the State came to be actively involved in the development of these infrastructural facilities. The establishment of PEs in these areas was justified in view of their strategic importance and high social value, although their expected commercial returns were known to be poor.

Secondly, PEs were established in certain areas to produce goods and services (e.g., machine tools and similar engineering industries) which the private sector was not willing to undertake. The establishment of PEs like Food Corporation of India was sought to be justified on grounds of meeting social and equity objectives.

Thirdly, the involvement of the public sector was further reinforced by the need to address social and political concerns. The take-over of sick industrial units in the private sector by the public sector with a view to protect employment and thereby avoid social tension illustrates the social concern. This policy extended the domain of the public sector into a large number of consumer goods industries (e.g. sick textile units) which proved to be unprofitable and thereby increased the fiscal burden.

Lastly, the PEs (e.g., developmental agencies) were often used by the political elite to promote their own self-interests or those of their political parties and this aspect provided further momentum for the expansion of PEs into areas which did not provide any social benefits.

As a result of the above factors, the size of the PEs has considerably grown, so as to constitute a significant share of the national output. The number of PEs under the Central Government rose from 5 to 245 between 1951 and 1993 while the total investment in these enterprises increased from Rs. 29 crore to Rs. 146,971 crore during the same period. The PEs today provide not only basic inputs and infrastructural facilities that affect the entire economy, but also their operations have extended to a wide spectrum of activities ranging from agriculture, industry, trade, transport and commerce to finance, insurance and banking as well as personal services like hotels and tourism. Thus, one finds that the expansion of the public sector has been brought about by different rationales and considerations in respect of various public enterprises. In this context, Jawaharlal Nehru said, "the public sector represents a dynamic urge to go towards the socialist society which we are seeking to build up. The public sector has to grow. It has a strategic importance."

ORGANISATIONAL STRUCTURE

Departmental undertakings come under the jurisdiction of their respective ministries and operate within the administrative framework in the same way as other government departments. They are controlled by chief executives who are government officials. Their tenure of office and administrative independence are much the same as those of other governmental heads.

The management of corporations and companies is controlled by their boards of directors. Each board has a chief executive assisted in most cases by two or more functional directors, one of whom is generally in charge of finance, and part-time directors. The boards are responsible to administrative ministries and their members are appointed and removed by the government. They function independently but are required to submit performance reports to their parent ministries from time to time. They also cannot incur capital expenditure beyond certain limits, without the concurrence of their respective ministries.

Staffing and Training

The personnel in departmental undertakings are civil servants recruited on a permanent basis by the Union or State Public Service Commission/Staff Selection Commission. In the case of other public enterprises, posts are either filled by direct recruitment from the open market or by promotions within the undertaking itself or by taking officers from government departments or other public enterprise on secondment. In some specialist areas, recruitment is by contract. Board level appointments to central corporations and companies are made by government on the recommendations of the Public Enterprises Selection Board; all other appointments are considered either at board or management levels.

The salaries and allowances of the officers and staff in

public enterprises do not compare favourably with those prevailing in the private sector. Although this disparity has not resulted in any perceptible attrition of qualified staff to the private sector, the public sector has not always been able to attract the best talent. Despite these negative factors, public enterprises have by and large been able to obtain qualified staff at all levels. Various institutions in India offer managerial development programmes and some of the major enterprises such as those in the field of insurance, banking, trading, heavy engineering, petroleum and textiles have their own establishments for meeting training requirements of their officers and staff.

As public enterprises play a crucial role in national development, considerable attention is given to recruitment, training and manpower planning. Emphasis is given to corporate planning, both long-term and short-term, in order to plan the quantity and quality of personnel needed for achieving the objectives of various segments of each enterprise. To ensure that key management posts do not remain vacant for long, a monitoring system exists whereby the managements/boards/ministries keep themselves informed about progress in filling vacancies which fall within their respective authorities.

Financing

Departmental undertakings form an integral part of government activities and as such their expenditure is met from the government budget. In contrast, the main source of finance for public sector corporations and government companies, apart from their own income derived from rates, fees and sales, are equity capital, loans and subsidies from the government. Pricing in some vital areas such as steel, fertilizers, and cement, require government approval. Where there is a deficit in operating costs, or where funds are required for development programmes or other specific purposes such as rural electrification or housing, grants or subsidies are obtained from the government in the absence of internal funding.

Departmental undertakings are not permitted to borrow, but other public enterprises may obtain loans from domestic and foreign sources. Government loans may be given to some public enterprises for approved purposes and are required to be repaid within a stipulated time. The government at times allows waiver of interest or sets out soft terms and conditions for repayment of loans, having regard to the nature of the business of the enterprise and the long gestation period of the schemes financed by such loans. Where public enterprises are unable to meet their loan obligations despite rescheduling efforts, governments sometimes have to accept their capital restructuring by conversion of the government loan into equity, because they cannot afford to close down such enterprises.

Surplus funds accumulated by departmental undertakings form part of government funds. With corporations and government companies these surpluses are partly returned to government in the form of dividends and partly retained to meet their future expansion programmes. Though rare, public enterprises which continue to make losses risk being wound up by the Cabinet on the recommendation of their respective ministries.

Efficiency of Public Sector

The working of the public enterprises for more than a quarter of a century has brought out an important fact into limelight that these enterprises can succeed in achieving their basic objectives through efficiency alone, the efficiency with which the top executives and the management run the affairs of the enterprises. In the ultimate analysis, it is the qualitative manpower resources which act as a decisive factor bringing success or failure to them. Therefore, it becomes a moot question how the good human qualities like ability, honesty, dedication and fearlessness can be generated and harnessed for the betterment of the working results of the enterprises. In other words, it will be a useful exercise to analyse the concept of efficiency and economy at this stage. What does the term "Efficiency" connote and what is it that needs to be done to achieve efficiency? The answer to the above question lies in an enquiry into types of efficiency with which we are familiar at present. Efficiency is of three kinds.[16]

(a) Physical efficiency (or Engineering efficiency),
(b) Business efficiency (or pecuniary efficiency), and
(c) Human Efficiency (or Social efficiency).

Physical Efficiency: Physical efficiency is a direct concern of Engineers. They measure efficiency in quantitative and qualitative terms. They go by specifications of machines and materials. They are production and productivity-oriented. They concern themselves with what is to be done by whom and how. They speak of process specification, layouts, jigs and tools, designs and drawings, output per man-hour, machine hour, capacity utilisation, maintenance of machines and training of personnel.

On the side of physical efficiency, it is the utilisation of Physical resources, largely the plants and machines which are important. The maximum utilisation of machine for a longer period with higher productivity depends upon their proper maintenance. Truly speaking, well maintained machines play an important role in raising the overall productivity of an undertaking. The maintenance schedules and the timely repairs, and avoidance of mishandling and negligence are important for maintaining them in good health. Public Enterperises have been victims of frequent plant breakdown. They have lost millions of machine hours. The case of burning out of the connector, the smashing of roller by an old block, the cracking of the blast furnace of Hindustan Steel, the corrosion of pipes and machines in oil refineries, etc., all reveal the lack of timely attention to maintenance and mishandling of costly machines and equipment.

Business Efficiency: Business efficiency, on the other hand, is concerned with financial results mostly reflected through profit or loss. This involves question of financial discipline and use of management technique, cost control, flexible yet firm budgetary control as well as effective decision-making technique and their timely implementation.

Human Efficiency: Human efficiency is indicative of the utilisation of manpower resources. How far the physical and mental faculties of manpower resources engaged in enterprises are being utilised is an important question. It is partly a function of organisation and partly personnel management. A well drafted organisational chart is a guarantee for optimum utilisation of manpower resources. Similarly appropriate personnel management also goes a long way in making best out of the existing human force. Such policy would provide for human satisfaction—economic, social and psychological, etc.[17]

Importance of the Public Sector

The Public Sector assumes a very important role in the development of the whole economy. In this connection, three important trends are observed in many countries.

First, there is a growing trend of public expenditure as a percentage of GNR in the United States, public expenditure as a proportion of GNP increased from 21 per cent in 1940 to nearly 40 per cent in 1996. In the same way, for the UK, it was 29 per cent in 1932 which increased to 55 per cent in 1985.

Second, employment in the Public Sector has been constantly growing in many countries (at least before the period of large-scale privatisation). For instance, in the USA, 4 per cent of the working population was employed in the Public Sector, and the figure went up to 12 per cent after the Second World War. In Norway, the corresponding figure was 5 per cent in 1900, which escalated to 16 per cent in 1960.

Third, public revenue as a percentage of GNP has been increasing almost in every type of country; and larger and larger percentage of public revenue has been transferred to the private sector in the form of subsidies, insurance, interest and so on. Inter-country studies also reveal considerable increase in the share of the disposable revenue for public consumption and saving. Adolph Wanger was right in propounding the law of increasing expansion of public activity in 1880.

Public Sector Economics (PSE) studies the economic rationales and effects of the activities of the Public Sector. In a sense, PSE is the study of the macroeconomic effects of the changing economic activities of the Public Sector. A study of such effects is important at least for the following reasons:

(i) The Public Sector (PS) is often the largest employer;

(ii) It is the controller of the economy: prices, output and so on;

(iii) In terms of its number of enterprises and its expansion, its importance is often overwhelming;

(iv) The government is often an important capitalist, and its assets and investments in the market are pretty large;

(v) It is also of considerable significance as a provider of social reproduction (like public health, education) and public utilities.

Distinguishing Features of the Public Sector

(i) As a large sector which is directed from the central authority, the Public Sector does exert influence over the whole economy.

(ii) Unlike the private sector, the Public Sector is not guided by the motive of profit maximisation. It has some important motives, e.g., Social Welfare Maximisation, national interest, and so on.

(iii) The Public Sector has some distinct types of power and means of action for directing and regulating its activities and to correct the distortions in the economy through taxation and subsidies.

(iv) The Public Sector has financially much better and free scope than the private sector. Income is guided by expenditure and not the other way round as in the case of the private sector.

(v) The Public Sector can be regarded as a system of collective action helpful for solving socio-economic problems, which is not possible for the disintegrated individual units of the Private Sector.

Role of Public Sector in Developing Economies

The public sector occupies a vital role in India's economic strategy. For a long time, it was hoped that investments in that sector would generate further resources for rapid economic growth. Heavy investment was, therefore, made in public enterprises (PEs) to: (i) build infrastructure, (ii) promote rapid economic growth and industrialisation,

(iii) secure balanced regional development, (iv) create job opportunities, where persons belonging to socially-disadvantaged communities could have their due share, (v) prevent concentration of economic power, and (vi) reduce disparities in income and wealth.

There are persons who distinguish between underdevelopment and developing ones. The economy which has less potentiality of development is termed as underdeveloped economy and the economy having greater or smaller potentialities of development is called developing nations. Whatever may be the actual position, developing nations are possessed with vast natural resources but yet to be exploited. First Five Year Plan of India reveals that an underdeveloped country is one which is characterised by the coexistence, in greater or smaller degree of utilised or unutilised manpower on the one hand and of unexploited natural resources on the other. In this sense, India is a developing nation.

The role of public enterprise differs from economy to economy. The philosophy of the public sector enterprises in the developing economies is different from that of developed countries. "In recent times, in most of the developing economies, public sector is emerging not for the ideological caprice of some indoctrinated individuals but from a realistic assessment of the prevailing economic situation and circumstances. Exigency rather than ideology is influencing the emergence and growth of Public enterprises these days. Of late, for most of the newly emerging nations public enterprises are more a matter of necessity than of choice."[18] Thus, the public sector has become a necessity for developing economies. Prof. A.H. Hanson opined—"Whatever the ultimate perspective may be, the country anxious to develop economically has no alternative but to use public enterprise on a considerable scale, at the very least in order to get things doing." A.H. Hanson went on saying in this regard—"Public Enterprise without a plan can achieve something, a plan without public enterprise is likely to remain on paper."[19] It is clear from the above discussion that public sector has become necessary in developing nations. The necessity will explain the role of public sector in developing economies some of the most striking logical arguments about the role of public sector in developing economics. Examples will be cited from Indian context the relevance or role of public sector is the same, which are following:

The First and formost desire of the developing economy would be to start the process of economic development and break the vicious circle of stagnation. It would only be feasible when state directly takes part in economic development. State would come forward with the weapon of public sector only.

Secondly, the state has to perform the task of a bold and courageous entrepreneur; because private enterprise remains shy in regard to capital, and cherishes maximum profit. The economic development rests on the construction of key infrastructure in which cost goes high whereas profit becomes negative or negligible. Here the role of public sector becomes imperative.

Thirdly, higher rate of capital formation is required for higher rate of industrialisation and thus economic development. Public Sector plays its role in increasing savings in chanelising their proper direction and best use. As the grip of public sector increases, the capital formation enhances and thus the pace of industrialisation goes up. It helps in providing maximum goods and services for the masses.

Fourthly, public sector properly utilises the foreign capital assistance; because developing nations lack indigenous capital. This foreign assistance is used in two ways, one by purchasing machines and capital intensive machine-making machines and the other, by borrowing foreign technology for industrialisation of the economy. India has seen this process while erecting Rourkela or Bokaro Plants.

Fifthly, public sector is favoured to make balanced development and minimize regional disparities. The regional disparities have to be removed mainly by the help of suitable public policies and a network of necessary and relevant public undertakings. State only can think of setting up enterprises in underdeveloped or less developed regions.[20] Private capital will normally shy away from making ventures in such areas. This preferred to set-up enterprises in areas having well developed infrastructure facilities. Therefore, public enterprises are asked to fulfil this national goal.

Further, public sectors are stated to serve the interests of the consumers as well as of labourers. They provide proper impetus and direction to economic development of the society. Consumers want maximum goods and services for them and labourers want a model employer where there is no exploitation. These twin-aims can be fulfilled only by public enterprises.

Lastly, developing economies aspire to achieve socialistic pattern of society. For this, they have to set-up a number of public enterprises for rapid establishment of basic and key as well as capital good industries. To achieve this goal no one can rely on private enterprises. These areas are earmarked for gaining commanding heights and be owned, operated and controlled by the state through public sector. Here the role of public sector is obvious.

Besides these, Public enterprises are entrusted with developing economies to remove economic disparities, to lesson the effect of uncertainties of marketing, to collect financial resources and to increase employment opportunities. The Economic Committee of UNO observed—public enterprise plays an important and vital role in developing countries inasmuch as it helps in capital formation, in fuller utilisation of natural resources and in achieving a more equitable distribution of income and wealth."[21] A. H. Hanson rightly observed—"There is not royal road to economic development, no single or specific way for the disease of poverty. Public enterprise—with which we are primarily concerned—has its part to play, but only as one of the varied collection of expedients."[22]

SIZE AND GROWTH OF PUBLIC SECTOR

Share in Gross Domestic Product

The public sector in the Indian economy includes, apart from public administration and defence, various Central and State Government undertakings operating in different branches of the economy, such as railways, post and telegraph, communications, transport, power and several other manufacturing, trade and service activities. Departmental enterprises include the railways and its production establishments, posts, telecommunications and production establishments under the Ministry of Defence. Non-departmental enterprises cover all establishments set-up by the government either as statutory corporations or as companies producing and selling goods and services. The term "public enterprises" in the present study relates only to "non-departmental enterprises."

The share of the public sector in the total Gross Domestic Product (GDP) at factor cost at constant (1999-2000) prices in 2005-06 at 8.1 per cent was up to 0.6 percentage points over the 7.5 per cent growth recorded in 2004-05. The

CHART 2.1

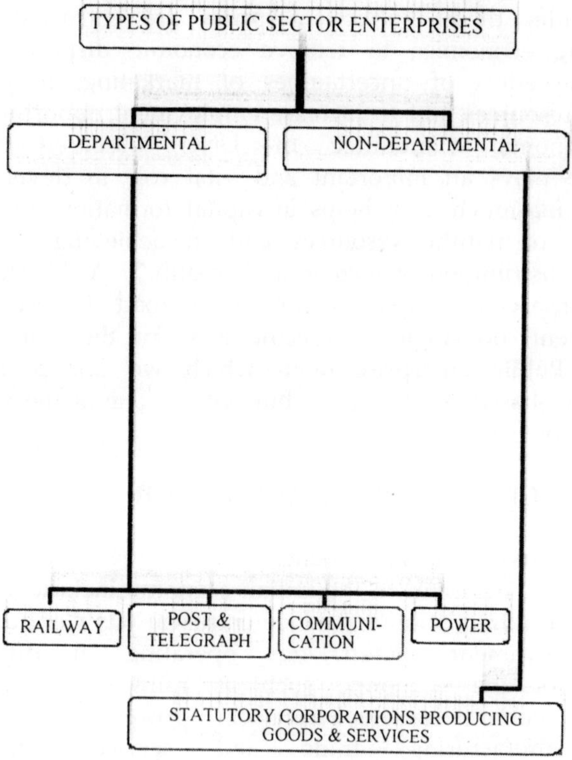

Source: Chart drawn on the basis of Shares in Gross Domestic Product.

projected economic growth of 8.7 per cent for 2007-08 is fully in line with this trend. There was an acceleration in domestic investment and saving rates to drive growth and provide the resources for meeting the 9 per cent (average) growth target of the Eleventh Five-Year Plan. Macroeconomic fundamentals continue to inspire confidence and the investment climate is full of optimism. Buoyant growth of government revenues made it possible to maintain fiscal consolidation as mandated under the Fiscal Responsibility and Budget Management Act (FRBMA). The decisive change in growth trend also means that the economy was, perhaps, not fully prepared for the different sets of challenges that accompany fast growth. Inflation flared up in the last half of 2006-07 and was successfully contained during the current year, despite a global hardening of commodity prices and an upsurge in capital inflows. An appreciation of the rupee, a slowdown in the consumer goods segment of industry and infrastructure (both physical and social) constraints, remained of concern. Raising growth to double digit will, therefore, require additional reforms.

Growth is of interest not for its own sake but for the improvement in public welfare that it brings about. Economic growth, and in particular the growth in per capita income, is a broad quantitative indicator of the progress made in improving public welfare. Per capita consumption is another quantitative indicator that is useful for judging welfare improvement. It is, therefore, appropriate to start by looking at the changes in real (i.e. at constant prices) per capita income and consumption.

The pace of economic improvement has moved up considerably during the last five years (including 2007-08). The rate of growth of per capita income as measured by per capita GDP at market prices (constant 1999-2000 prices) grew by an annual average rate of 3.1 per cent during the 12-year period, 1980-81 to 1991-92. It accelerated marginally to 3.7 per cent per annum during the next 11 years, 1992-93 to 2002-03. Since then, there has been a sharp acceleration in the growth of per capita income, almost doubling to an average of 7.2 per cent per annum (2003-04 to 2007-08). This means that average income would now double in a decade, well within

TABLE 2.1

Per Capita Income and Consumption

(in 1999-2000 prices)

	Income		Consumption	
	Rs. Growth	*(%)*	*Rs. Growth*	*(%)*
Xth Plan Avg.	19245	3.4	12392	3.0
Xth Plan Avg.	24156	6.2	14677	4.3
2002-03	20996	2.2	13352	1.1
2003-04	22413	6.8	13918	4.2
2004-05	23890	6.6	14413	3.6
2005-06	25696	7.6	15422	7.0
2006-07	27784	8.1	16279	5.6
2007-08	29786	7.2	17145	5.3

Income is taken as GDP at market prices.
Consumption is PFCE.
Per capita is obtained by dividing these by population.

one generation, instead of after a generation (two decades). The growth rate of per capita income in 2007-08 is projected to be 7.2 per cent, the same as the average of the five years to the current year.

Vigorous growth with strong macroeconomic fundamentals has characterised developments in the Indian economy in 2006-07 so far. However, there are some genuine concerns on the inflation front. Growth of 9.0 per cent and 9.2 per cent in 2005-06 and 2006-07, respectively, by most accounts, surpassed expectations (Table 2.2). While the up-and-down pattern in agriculture continued with growth estimated at 6.0 per cent and 2.6 per cent in the two recent years, and services maintained its vigorous growth performance, there were distinct signs of sustained improvements on the industrial front (Table 2.3). Entrenchment of the higher growth trends, particularly in manufacturing, has boosted sentiments, both within the country and abroad. The overall macroeconornic fundamentals are robust, particularly with tangible progress towards fiscal consolidation and a strong balance of payments position. With an upsurge in investment, the outlook is distinctly upbeat.

TABLE 2.2

Key Indicators

Items	2003-04	2004-05	2005-06	2006-07	2007-08	2003-04	2004-05	2005-06	2006-07	2007-08
	Absolute values					percentage change over previous period				
1	2	3	4	5	6	7	8	9	10	11
Gross domestic product (at factor cost) (Rs. thousand crore)										
At Current prices	2538	2878	3276	3790 Q	4283 A	13.4	12.0	13.8	15.7 Q	13.0 A
At 1999-2000 prices	2223	2388	2613	2864 Q	3114 A	8.5	7.5	9.	4 9.6 Q	8.7 A
GDP at market prices (Rs. thousand crore) (at Current prices)	2755	3149	3580	4146 Q	4694 A	12.3	13.1	13.7	15.8 Q	13.2 A
Gross national product (at factor cost) (Rs. thousand crore)										
At Current prices	2520	2855	3250	3760 Q	4263 A	12.6	11.9	13.8	15.7 Q	13.4 A
At 1999-2000 prices	2205	2367	2593	2845Q	3102 A	8.7	7.4	9.6	9.7 Q	9.0 A
Foodgrains production (million tonnes)	213.2	198.4	208.6	217.3	219.3a	22.0	-6.9	5.2	4.2	0.9a
Index of industrial production	189.0	204.8	221.5	247.1	261.4b	7.0	8.4	8.2	11.68	9.0b
Electricity generated (in billion kwh)	558.3	587.4	617.5	662.4	525.9b	5.0	5.2	5.2	7.3	6.6b
Wholesale price index	180.3	189.5	197.2	210.4	217.4e	5.0	5.1	4.1	5.9	4.1e

(Contd.)

TABLE 2.2 (CONTD.)

1	2	3	4	5	6	7	8	9	10	11
Consumer price index for industrial workers	504	525	551	588	620g	4.2	4.2	4.9	6.7	5.5g
Money supply (M3) (Rs. thousand crore)	2005.7	2251.4	2729.5	3310.3	3750.3l	16.8	12.3	17.0	21.1(j)	22.4 j
Imports at current prices										
(in Rs. crore)	3,59,108	5,01,065	6,60,409	8,40,506	68,20,88k	20.8	39.5	31.8	27.3	11.5p
(in US $ million)	78,150	1,11,518	1,49,166	1,85,747	1,68,803k	27.3	42.7	33.8	24.5	25.9p
Exports at current prices										
(in Rs. crore)	2,93,367	3,75,340	4,56,418	5,71,779	4,48,377k	15.0	27.9	21.6	25.3	7.7p
(in US $ million)	63,843	83,536	1,03,091	1,26,360	1,10,965k	21.1	30.8	23.4	22.6	21.6p
Foreign Currency assets										
(in Rs. crore)	4,66,215	5,93,121	6,47,327	8,36,597	11,12,080m	36.5	27.2	9.1	29.2	41.7m
(in US $ million)	1,07,448	1,35,571	1,45,108	1,91,924	2,81,183m	49.5	26.2	7.0	29.4	57.9m
Exchange rate (Re./US $)	45.95	44.93	44.27	45.25	40.41o	5.3	2.3	1.5	-2.2	12.0o

Note: Gross domestic product and Gross national product figures are at factor cost (new series base 1999-2000). Q-Quick estimates; a Advance estimates 2007-08; i Average exchange rate for April-January, 2006-07.

j Computed over comparable data, i.e. April 1, 2005 due to 27 fortnights during 2005-06.

b April-December, 2007 g As on December 2007.

p April-December, 2006 on provisional over provisional basis.

c Index of industrial production: (base 1993-94=100). d. Index (with base 1993-94 = 100) at the end of fiscal year.

3, Index (with base 1982 =100) at the end of fiscal year. l. Outstanding at the end of financial year. e. As on February 2, 2008, i. As on January 4, 2008, year-on-year growth. h. Outstanding at the end of financial year. n. Percent change indicates the rate of appreciation (+)/depreciation (-) of the Rupee *vis-a-vis* the US Dollar. m. at the end of February 8, 2008.

TABLE 2.3

Sectoral Real Growth Rates in GDP at Factor Cost

(at 1999-2000 prices)

Item	Percentage change over the previous year							
	2000-01	2001-02	2002-03	2003-04	2004-05	2005-06	2006-07	2007-08
(i) Agriculture and allied	-0.2	6.3	-7.2	10.0	0.0	6.0	3.8	2.67
(ii) Industry	6.4	2.7	7.1	7.4	9.8	9.6	10.0	-
Mining and quarrying	2.4	1.8	8.8	3.1	7.5	3.6	5.7	3.4
Manufacturing	7.7	2.5	6.8	6.6	8.7	9.1	12.0	9.4
Electricity, gas and	2.1	1.7	4.7	4.8	7.5	5.3	6.0	7.8
Water supply construction	6.2	4.0	7.9	110	14.1	14.2	12.0	9.6
(iii) Services	-5.7	7.2	7.4	8.5	9.6	9.8	8.5	12.1
trade, hotels, transport and communication	7.3	9.2	9.2	12.1	10.9	10.4	16.6	-
Financial services	4.1	7.3	8.0	5.6	8.7	10.9	13.9	11.7
Community, social and personnel services	4.8	4.1	3.9	5.4	7.9	7.7	6.9	7.0
(iv) Total GDP at factor cost	4.4	5.8	3.8	8.5	7.5	9.0	9.6	8.7

Source: Central Statistical Organisation.

The declaration of growth in 2007-08 is generally spread across most of the sectors except electricity, community services and the composite category "trade, hotels, transport and communications."

In contrast to the sharp fluctuations in agriculture, industry and services have continued to expand steadily. Indeed, since the beginning of the Tenth Plan in 2002-03, with annual growth of 7.0 per cent or more, industry and services have acted as the twin engines propelling overall growth of the economy. Over a somewhat longer horizon, in the six years between 2000-01 and 2005-06, on average, services with a share of 52.0 per cent of GDP, contributed 65.0 per cent of GDP growth, and increased its share in GDP from 49.8 per cent to 54.1 per cent. During the same reference period, on average, with a share of 25.8 per cent of GDP, industry, by contributing 28.0 per cent of GDP growth, increased its share in GDP from 25.9 per cent to 26.2 per cent.

The ratcheting up of growth observed in recent years is reflected in the Eleventh Five Year Plan target of an average annual growth of 9 per cent relative to 8 percent targeted by the Tenth Plan (2002-03 to 2006-07). The shortfall in the annual average growth of 7.6 percent from the target of 8 percent in the five years of the Tenth Plan is attributable to the disappointing 3.8 per cent growth in the first year of the Plan and its subsequent surge to 8.6 per cent, on average, in the last four years. A notable feature of growth during the Tenth Five Year Plan was resurgence of manufacturing.

Overall industrial recovery that commenced from the second quarter of 2002-03 continues. After an acceleration of growth of industrial GDP at factor cost at constant 1999-2000 prices from 7.0 per cent in 2002-03 to 7.6 per cent and 8.6 per cent in the next two years, the industrial resurgence is manifest in the projected step up in its growth to 9.0 per cent in the current year (2007-08). In the current year, industrial growth is driven by robust performances from manufacturing and construction sectors. Within industry, white manufacturing growth has accelerated steadily from 7.1 per cent in 2003-04 to 9.4 per cent in 2007-08, construction growth has been in double digits in each of the last three years. Substantive commercial bank credit flows to the housing and

TABLE 2.4

Savings and Investment

(New series base 1999-2000)

	Ave. IXth Plan	2001-02	2002-03	2003-04	2004-05	2005-06	2006-07	Ave. Xth Plan
		(as per cent of GDP at current market prices)						
Gross, Domestic Savings	23.6	23.4	23.5	26.4	31.8	34.3	32.4	34.8
(a) Public	-0.7	-1.9	-2.0	-0.6	1.2	2.4	2.0	3.2
(b) Private	24.3	25.3	25.5	27.0	28.5	28.7	30.4	31.6
(i) Household	20.3	21.0	21.8	22.7	23.8	21.6	22.3	23.8
Financial	10.3	10.2	10.8	10.3	11.3	10.2	11.7	11.3
Physical	10.0	10.8	10.9	12.4	12.4	11A	10.7	12.5
(ii) Private Corporate	4.0	4.3	3.7	4.2	4.7	7.1	8.1	7.8
Gross Domestic Investment	25.9	24.0	22.9	25.2	28.0	31.5	33.8	35.9
Public	7.4	6.9	6.9	6.1	6.3	7.1	7.4	7.8
Private	17.9	16.5	16.3	18.4	19.4	21.3	23.6	27.0
Valuables	0.8	0.7	0.6	0.6	0.9	1.3	1.2	-
Gross Fixed Capital Formation	23.4	22.8	23.0	23.8	24.8	26.3	28.1	32.5
Change in stocks	1.9	0.6	0.2	0.7	0.8	2.0	2.9	2.3
Valuables	0.8	0.7	0.6	0.6	0.9	1.3	1.2	1.2
Saving-Investment Gap @	-1.1	-0.6	0.6	1.2	1.6	-0.4	-1.3	-1.1
Public	-8.2	-8.6	-8.9	-6.6	-5.2	-4.7	-5.4	4.5
Private	7.7	8.8	9.2	8.6	9.2	7.4	6.9	-4.5

Note: (i) Gross Domestic investment denotes gross domestic capital formation (GDCF); (ii) Figures may not add up due to round off. @: Difference between the rate of savings and the rate of investment.

Source: Central Statistical Organisation

real estate and retail sectors continue to provide support to the boom in construction and consumer durables. On the negative side, a deceleration in the growth of mining and quarrying, partly due to a fall in the levels of crude oil production as a result of a fire accident in July 2005 at Mumbai High North Platform, has had a dampening impact on overall industrial growth.

Services sector growth continued to be broad-based. Among the three sub-sectors of services, "trade, hotels, transport and communication services' continued to lead by growing at double-digit rates for the fourth successive year (Table 2.2). It has been the fastest growing with growth averaging 15.3 per cent per annum during the Tenth Five Year Plan period followed by 'construction'. Impressive progress in expanding railway passenger network and production of commercial vehicles, and fast addition to existing stock of telephone connections, particularly mobiles, played key roles in such growth. Growth in financial services (comprising banking, insurance and real estate services), which after dipping in 2003-04 had bounced back in the following year, maintained the momentum with progressive maturing of Indian financial markets and the ongoing construction boom. Besides manufacturing, the two other sectors whose contribution to growth has increased over the two plans are construction and communication. Growth in financial services (comprising banking, insurance, real estate and business services), after clipping to 5.6 percent in 2003-04 bounced back to 8.7 percent in 2004-05 and 10.9 per cent in 2005-06. The momentum has been maintained with a growth of 11.1 per cent in 2006-07 and 11.7 per cent in 2007-08.

SHARE IN CAPITAL FORMATION AND CAPITAL STOCK

Share of Public Sector in Saving and Capital Formation

The increasing trend in gross domestic savings as a proportion of GDP observed since 2001-02 has continued with the savings ratio rising from 26.4 per cent in 2002-03 to 29.7 per cent in 2003-04, 31.1 per cent in 2004-05, 34.3 per cent in 2005-06 and 34.8 per cent in 2006-07 (Table 2.4). The rise in the savings rate in 2006-07 was contributed by two of its three components: private corporate and the household sector, which as proportion of GDP, increased by 1.0 percentage point and 0.7 percentage point, respectively. The third component, namely public savings, declined by 0.4 percentage points and made a negative contribution to the overall savings rate. However, a redeeming feature of recent years is that the savings of the public sector, which had been negative until 2003-04, was positive for the fourth successive year in 2007-08.

A notable feature of the recent GDP growth has been a sharply rising trend in gross domestic investment and saving, with the former rising by 13.1 per cent of GDP and the latter by 11.3 per cent of GDP over five years till 2006-07. The average investment ratio for the Tenth Five Year Plan at 31.4 per cent was higher than that for the Ninth Five Year Plan, while the average saving rate was also 31.4 per cent of GDP higher than the average ratio of 23.6 per cent during the Ninth Five Year Plan.

The 1990s reforms transformed the investment climate, improved business confidence and generated a wave of entrepreneurial optimism. This has led to a gradual improvement in competitiveness of the entire corporate sector, a resurgence in the manufacturing sector and an acceleration in the rate of investment. The FRBMA mandated fiscal correction path, was also helpful in raising the credibility of the Government with respect to fiscal deficits, in which India was at the bottom of global rankings. This has improved perceptions about the long-term macroeconomic stability of the economy. Moderate tax rates, coupled with buoyant sales growth, increased the internal accruals of the corporate sector. The improved investment climate and strong macro-fundamentals also led to an upsurge in foreign direct investment. The combined effect of these factors was reflected in an increase in the investment rate from 25.2 per cent of GDP in the first year of the Tenth Five Year Plan to 35.9 per cent of GDP in the last year. The higher investment was able to absorb the domestic savings and also generated an appetite for absorption of capital inflows from abroad.

Gross domestic savings as a proportion of GDP continued to improve, rising from 26.4 per cent in 2002-03 to

34.8 per cent in 2006-07 with an average of 31.4 per cent during the Tenth Five Year Plan. The savings-investment gap which remained positive during 2001-04 became negative thereafter. In a modern economy, the excess of domestic saving over domestic investment suggests a deflationary situation in which demand has not kept pace with increased capacity. Thus the reversal of the saving-investment balance should be viewed as a correction of the domestic supply-demand balance, occurring through above normal (and welcome) increase in demand during 2005-06 and 2006-07.

Savings

Both private and public savings have contributed to higher overall savings. Private savings have risen by 6.1 per cent points of GDP over the Tenth Five Year Plan period while public sector savings increased by 5.2 per cent of GDP. Both have increased steadily over this period, though private savings appear to have reached a plateau in 2005-06 (Table 2.4). The savings from the private corporate sector were particularly buoyant, while the turnaround in public sector savings from negative to positive from 2003-04 onwards is heartening. The increase in private savings is due to a (more than) doubling of the rate of corporate saving over the plan period. Savings of the household sector were stable at 23 to 24 per cent of GDP, averaging 23.7 per cent during the Tenth Five Year Plan. The physical and financial components of the household savings also remained stable. With the upsurge in private corporate and public sector savings, the share of the household sector in gross domestic savings declined from 94.3 per cent in 2001-02 to 68.4 per cent in 2006-07.

Investment

In contrast to the increase in savings, the increase in investment has been driven by private investment, which went up by 10.3 per cent of GDP over the five years of the Tenth Five Year Plan. This improvement was in turn driven by private corporate investment, which increased by 9.1 per cent of GDP over these five years. Private corporate sector investment improved from 5.4 per cent of GDP in 2001-02 to 14.5 per cent in 2006-07. The upsurge in private corporate investment has been visible even to the public as a "Capex" boom, and that is still continuing. Household investment remained close to the plan average of 12.7 per cent of GDP throughout the period, while the public sector investment increased by less than 1 per cent of GDP over the plan period.

The National Accounts provide the data of the gross domestic capital formation at constant 1999-2000 prices also. In terms of constant prices, the ratio of gross investment to GDP is estimated to have increased from 25 per cent in 2002-03 to 33.8 per cent in 2006-07. The gross fixed capital formation accounted for more than 90 per cent of the investment. The ratio of fixed capital formation to GDP is estimated to have increased to 30.6 per cent in 2006-07.

TABLE 2.5

Real Gross Domestic Capital Formation

(as percent of GDP at constant 1999-2000 market prices)

	1999-00	*2000-01*	*2001-02*	*2002-03*	*2003-04*	*2004-05*	*2005-06*
GDCF	25.9	23.8	22.2	25.0	27.4	30.2	32.2
Public	7.4	6.9	6.8	6.1	6.0	6.5	6.9
Private	17.9	16.3	15.8	18.1	19.1	20.6	22.6
Corporate Sector	7.4	5.6	5.2	5.8	6.7	9.5	12.2
Household Sector	10.5	10.6	10.6	12.3	12.4	11.1	10.3
Valuables	0.8	0.7	0.6	0.6	0.9	1.3	1.2
GFCF	23.4	22.5	22.4	23.5	24.5	25.3	26.7
Public	6.6	6.5	6.4	6.2	6.4	6.2	6.5
Private	16.8	16.1	16.0	17.2	18.1	19.0	20.2
Change in Stocks	1.9	0.6	0.1	0.7	0.6	1.8	2.8
Public	0.8	0.4	0.4	-0.2	0.4		
Private	1.1	0.2	-0.2	0.9	0.9	1.5	2.4
Valuables	0.8	0.7	0.6	0.6	0.9	1.3	1.2

Note: GDCF: Gross domestic capital formation
GFCF: Gross domestic fixed capital formation
Figures may not add up due to rounding

Source: Central Statistical Organisation

Of the two components of GDCF, namely gross fixed capital formation (GFCF) and changes in stocks, the contribution of GFCF (consisting of items such as plant and machinery) to growth of GDFC was lower than the corresponding contribution of changes in stocks between 2003-04 and 2004-05. While GFCF continued to lag behind changes in stocks in terms of contribution, the difference between the two contributions narrowed. This may indicate a recent pick up in fresh investment for creating additional capacity through fixed capital formation, particularly in the private sector. From the demand-side perspective, unlike countries of East Asia during their high-growth phase or China in more recent times, GDP growth in India in the post-reform period was driven mostly by private final consumption expenditure or PFCE growth. PFCE contributed more than one half of the growth every year until 2001-02. After falling below one half in 2002-03, it had again dominated GDP growth in 2003-04. But this pattern appears to have undergone a virtuous transformation with investment rather than private consumption being the main source of GDP growth in the latest two years of 2004-05 and 2005-06 (Table 2.4). Data on consumption and investment in the national accounts available till 2004-05 show that the 6.8 percentage point contribution of investment to 13.1 per cent growth in GDP at current market prices in 2004-05 exceeded the corresponding contribution of private final consumption expenditure at 6.1 percentage point for the first time in recent years. In terms of contribution to growth of GDP at current market prices, from the demand side, investment continued to provide the lead during 2004-05 and 2005-06. The percentage point contribution of investment in the growth of GDP at current market prices of 13.1 per cent and 14.1 per cent in 2004-05 and 2005-06, respectively, were 7.6 per cent and 7.0 per cent, respectively. With imports growing faster than exports, the external balance continued to have a negative contribution to GDP growth in recent years.

GDCF at constant prices (base: 1999-2000) as a proportion of GDP (Table 2.4) is consistently lower than the corresponding proportion at current prices (Table 2.3). This differential may reflect the greater increase in the prices of capital goods relative to the general price level, with growing technological sophistication of the production processes in the economy in general and manufacturing in particular. But, irrespective of the choice of constant or current prices as the weights, the direction of change from year to year remains unaltered. The lower values of the change in GDCF as a proportion of GDP at constant prices, particularly in more recent years, may reflect the higher prices of capital goods relative to the general price level, with growing technological sophistication of the production processes in the economy in general and manufacturing in particular.

At constant 1999-2000 prices, the composition of GDCF for 2003-04 and 2004-05 reveals a faster growth in the public component than in the private. Furthermore, there is a faster growth in inventories and valuables in the latest two years, with gross fixed capital formation (GFCF) growing at a lower rate than gross domestic capital formation. This may partly reflect a process of adjustment to the rapid decline in the change in stocks as a proportion of GDP from 2.0 per cent in 1999-2000 to a low of 0.5 per cent in 2001-02 and the progressive liberalisation of gold and silver imports.

In terms of contribution to growth of GDP at current market prices, from the demand side, there was a change in the pattern of PFCE providing the lead (Table 2.5). PFCE contributed as much as 54.5 per cent of the growth in GDP at current market prices between 2000-01 and 2003-04. The percentage point contribution of private final consumption expenditure was as much as 7.4 percent out of the overall growth of 12.7 per cent in GDP in 2003-04. In the same year, the corresponding contribution of investment was 5.4. In an encouraging development, the percentage point contribution of investment at 6.8 out of 13.1 per cent growth in GDP in 2004-05 exceeded the corresponding contribution of private final consumption expenditure at 6.1 for the first time in recent years. Reflecting the higher growth of imports relative to exports, the negative contribution of external balance increased in 2004-05.

Three basic causes for the decline of the share of the public sector in total savings are:

TABLE 2.6

Disposition of Gross Domestic Product (GDP)

	(Percentage change over previous year)											
	(at current prices)						(at 1999-2000 prices)					
	2001-02	*2002-03*	*2003-04*	*2004-05*	*2005-06*	*2006-07*	*2001-02*	*2002-03*	*2003-04*	*2004-05*	*2005-06*	*2006-07*
Total final consumption expenditure	6.7	8.5	5.0	10.2	9.5	11.7	1.7	5.9	1.7	6.2	5.7	7.4
Govt. final consumption expenditure	5.0	6.3	3.3	6.6	10.3	18.1	-3.6	6.3	-0.4	2.5	5.4	9.8
Private Final consumption expenditure	7.1	8.9	5.4	10.9	9.4	10.6	2.8	5.8	2.1	6.9	5.7	7.0
Gross domestic capital formation	-0.3	3.3	19.0	24.9	27.3	22.1	-4.5	-1.8	16.6	19.1	19.0	16.5
Of which												
Gross fixed capital formation	4.8	9.9	11.2	17.6	19.7	21.6	0.3	4.5	8.7	13.1	11.8	15.3
Exports of goods and services	22.1	4.5	22.3	14.7	39.5	27.4	18.2	5.7	21.8	5.8	28.1	22.0
Less Imports of goods and services	12.0	4.5	22.2	16.7	41.2	32.7	3.5	3.4	10.4	7.2	22.3	7.1
GDP at market prices	7.7	8.5	7.8	12.5	13.1	14.1	4.0	5.2	3.7	8.4	8.3	9.2

Source: Central Statistical Organisation.

(i) Rapid increase in state expenditure at a rate higher than increase in state revenues.

(ii) The inefficiency of the government and the public sector enterprises and their consequent failure to generate internal surplus commensurate with the increase in their capital stock.

(iii) The self-defeating efforts of the government to make up the shortfall in resources through excessive borrowings from the banking sector (better known as deficit financing).

Accordingly, the savings of the private sector had to be diverted to the public sector so that it could meet its expanding obligation in the process of development, this fact, however, does not absolve the public sector to generate adequate internal surplus by improving its efficiency.

Share of the Public Sector in Gross Fixed Capital Formation

Among the many factors that influence the economic growth of a nation, capital stock is all important one. The term "capital stock" represents the stock of physical productive assets, such as machinery, transport equipment, buildings and other construction structures like irrigation works, roads, railway track, etc. and other capital goods available at a point of time for further production. Any increase in the capital stock leads to expansion in productive capacity. The addition to capital stock during a specified period, usually a year, is known as capital formation or investment, Capital stock relates to a particular point of time, i.e. end of the accounting period say, 31st March (financial year) or 31st December (calendar year) depending on the method of compilation of information. On the other hand, capital formation (investment) is a "flow", measured in terms of a specified period, i.e. financial or calendar year. Gross Capital formation refers partly to meet the needs of depreciation of the capital stock and partly to increase the size of the total capital stock on a net basis. Both capital stock and capital formation are important for economic growth and, as such, they are extensively used in economic analysis.

But the amount of capital employed per unit of output

in the public sector is far greater than in the private sector. This is largely due to the differences in the nature of investment in the public sector. The important differences are:

(i) A good part of the public sector investment goes into economic infrastructure (roads, buildings, irrigation works, bridges, etc.) which is essential for economic development but does not contribute to output in the normal sense of the term.

(ii) Public sector has played a significant role in developing the key sectors of the economy e.g., railways, iron and steel, power, oil exploration, irrigation, etc. By their very nature they are areas of high capital intensity.

(iii) The projects in the public sector have longer gestation periods. Partly this is due to the technological nature of investment in heavy and basic Industries and partly it is due to the inefficiencies in public agencies in the implementation of these projects.

(iv) There is lower utilisation of capacities in the public sector and this is also responsible to an extent to lower capital output ratios.

(v) Areas of higher capital-output ratios fall largely or wholly in the private sector. This includes consumer goods industries, small scale and cottage enterprises and agriculture.

Share of Public Sector in Employment

There are two important categories of public sector employment: (a) Government administration and defence and other government services like health, education, research and various activities to promote economic development; and (b) public sector proper, i.e. economic enterprises owned by the Centre, State and Local Government

Table 2.6 shows the size and growth of employment in the organised sectors since 1990. The total number of workers employed in the public and private sectors in 1990 was 264.53 lakhs, but by March 2005, their number grew to about 264.58 lakhs.

TABLE 2.7

Estimates of Employment in Organised Public and Private Sectors

(Lakh persons as on March 31)

Years	*Public Sector*			*Private Sector*			*Public and Private Sector (Total)*		
	Male	*Female*	*Total*	*Male*	*Female*	*Total*	*Male*	*Female*	*Total*
1990	165.22	22.50	187.72	61.88	13.94	75.82	227.09	36.44	263.53
1991	167.10	23.47	190.57	62.42	1434	76.76	229.52	37.81	267. 33
1992	167.81	24.29	192.10	63.67	14.79	78.46	231.48	39.08	270.56
1993	168.49	24.77	193.26	63.01	15.50	78.51	231.51	40.26	271.77
1994	168.80	25.65	194.45	63.41	15.89	7930	232.21	41.54	273.75
2000	168.66	26.00	194.66	64.31	16.28	80.59	232.97	42.28	275.25
1996	168.31	27.28	195.59	67.77	19.09	86.86	236.08	46.37	282.45
1998	166.55	27.63	194.18	67.37	20.11	87.48	233.92	47.74	281.66
1999	166.04	28.11	194.15	66.80	20.18	86.98	232.84	48.29	281.13
2000	164.57	28.57	193.14	65.80	20.66	86.46	230.37	49.23	279.60
2001	162.79	28.59	19138	65.62	20.90	86.52	228.40	49.49	277.89
2002	158.86	28.87	187.73	63.83	20.49	84.32	222.71	49.35	272.06
2003	156.75	29.05	185.8	63.57	20.64	84.21	220.32	49.68	270.00
2004	153.07	28.90	181.97	62.02	20.44	82.46	215.09	49.34	264.43
2005	150.86	29.21	180.07	63.57	20.95	84.52	214.42	50.16	264.58

Note: (i) Includes all establishments in the Public Sector irrespective of size of employment and non-agricultural establishments in the Private Sector employing 10 or more persons.

(ii) Excludes Sikkim, Arunachal Pradesh, Dadra and Nagar Haveli and Lakshadweep as these are not yet covered under the programme.

Source: Ministry of Labour and Employment (DGE&T).

TABLE 2.8

Employment in the Public Sector by Industry

(Lakh persons as on 31 March)

	1998	*1999*	*2000*	*2001*	*2002*	*2003*	*2004*	*2007*
A. By branch								
1. Central Government	32.53	33.13	32.73	32.61	31.95	31.33	30.27	29.38
2. State Governments	74.58	74.58	74.60	74.25	74.84	73.67	73.22	72.02
3. Quasi-Governments	64.61	63.85	63.26	61.92	60.20	59.01	58.22	57.48
4. Local bodies	22.46	22.59	22.55	22.61	21.75	21.79	21.26	21.18
Total	194.18	194.15	193.14	191.38	187.73	185.80	181.97	180.07
B. By industry								
0. Agriculture, hunting, etc.	5.30	5.15	5.14	5.02	4.83	5.06	4.93	4.96
1. Mining and quarrying	9.37	9.26	9.24	8.75	8.61	8.47	10.30	10.14
2&3. Manufacturing	16.16	15.69	15.31	14.30	13.50	12.60	11.89	11.30
4. Electricity, gas and water	9.54	9.62	9.46	9.35	9.23	9.13	8.74	8.60
5. Construction	11.09	11.07	10.92	10.81	10.26	9.48	9.32	9.11
6. Wholesale and retail trade	1.64	1.63	1.63	1.63	1.57	1.82	1.81	1.84
7. Transport, storage and communications	30.84	30.84	30.77	30.42	30.09	29.39	28.15	27.51

8. Finance, insurance, real estate, etc.	12.88	12.95	12. 96	12.81	12.30	13.77	14.08	14.08
9. Community, Social and personal services	97.37	97.94	97.71	98.30	97.35	96.09	92.76	92.52
Total	194.18	194.15	193.14	191.38	187.73	185.80	181.97	180.07

Note: Totals in A and. B differ due to rounding off.

Source: Ministry of Labour and Employment (DGE&T).

The trends in employment in the organised sector of the Indian economy show that total employment in public sector registered a relatively high growth rate of 2.4 per cent per annum between 1976 and 1991 as compared to a very low growth rate of 0.8 per cent in the organised private sector during the same period (Table 2.7). It may be noticed that employment in manufacturing industries in the public sector increased by 3.5 per cent per annum during 1976-91 whereas it was merely 0.5 per cent in the organised private sector. Administrative services, employment in trade and services in the public sector showed high growth rate of 6.8 per cent followed by banking and services with a growth rate of 6.1 per cent. Thus, expansion of public sector in the above branches of the economy has been helpful for expanding employment opportunities.

The share of public sector in total employment in the organised sector increased from 66 per cent in 1976 to 71 per cent in 1991. The faster growth in public sector can partly be attributed to over manning in many PEs, as a result they are now finding it difficult to shed the excess labour force.

Share in Production

The second advance estimates of crop production released by the Directorate of Economics and Statistics, Department of Agriculture and Cooperation on February 5, 2007 has placed total foodgrains production in 2006-07 at 209.2 million tonnes, which is marginally higher than the production of 208.6 million tonnes in 2005-06. Production of wheat and pulses is expected to increase by 4.5 per cent and 8.2 per cent respectively. Production of commercial crops is expected to be significantly higher. Production of cotton expected at 21.0 million bales is not only up 13.5 per cent from 2005-06, but also an all-time record. Similarly, sugarcane production projected at 315.5 million tonnes is up 16.8 per cent from total output of 270.0 million tonnes in 2005-06. Output of coarse grains and oilseeds is likely to be lower than their levels in 2005-06 by 6.2 per cent and 15.7 per cent, respectively. Production is expected to improve in plantation crops (coffee, tea and rubber), livestock and poultry products; horticulture products; and dairy and fisheries.

TABLE 2.9

Employment in the Private Sector by Industry

(Lakh persons as on March 31)

	1998	1999	2000	2001	2002	2003	2004	2007
0. Agriculture, hunting, etc.	9.04	8.71	9.04	9.31	8.55	8.95	9.17	9.83
1. Mining and quarrying	0.91	0.87	0.81	0.79	0.68	0.66	0.65	0.79
2&3. Manufacturing	52.33	51.78	50.85	50.13	48.67	47.44	44.89	44.89
4. Electricity, gas and water	0.42	0.41	0.41	0.52	0.42	0.50	0.47	0.49
5. Construction	0.74	0.71	0.57	0.57	0.56	0.44	0.45	0.49
6. Wholesale and retail trade	3.21	33.23	1.10	1.19	3 35	3.60	3.51	3.75
7. Transport, storage communications	0.65	0.69	0.70	0.76	0.76	0.79	0.81	0.85
8. Finance, insurance, real 9. Community, social and personal services	16.77	17.00	17.23	17.34	17.42	17.56	17.92	18.2
Total	87.48	86.98	86.46	86.52	84.32	84.21	82.46	84.52

Note: Coverage in construction, particularly on private account, is known to be inadequate

Source: Ministry of Labour and Employment (DGE&T).

Production of crops, particularly wheat and pulses, has plateaued for some time now. Wheat production reached its peak of 76.4 million tonnes in 1999-2000, which has not been achieved again. In case of pulses, production reached 14.9 million tonnes in 1998-99 and again in 2003-04, but has remained significantly below that level in the last three years. There has not been any varietal breakthrough in pulses. Though pulses were brought within the ambit of Technology Mission on Oilseeds in 1990 and the centrally sponsored scheme of Integrated Scheme of Oilseeds, Pulses, Oilpalm and Maize (ISPPOM) is being implemented in major pulses-growing States with effect from April 2004, productivity of pulses has remained stagnant. Since pulses are genetically low-yielding, and are grown on marginal and sub-marginal lands under rain-fed conditions, focus needs to shift to micro-irrigation, micro-nutrients, improved production practices and development of improved/better yielding seeds. With overseas availability being limited, reduction in price volatility of pulses will depend on steady growth of domestic production. In case of wheat, there is need for the development of area-specific varieties, particularly to suit the water-abundant eastern region.

The year 2006-07 not only witnessed sustained growth in manufacturing, but also a distinct improvement in the growth of electricity. With a year-on-year growth of 11.4 per cent during April-December 2006 compared to a growth of 9.0 per cent in the corresponding period of 2005, manufacturing contributed over 91 per cent to the overall industrial growth measured in terms of IIP. Within manufacturing, chemicals, basic metals, machinery and equipments and transport equipments, with a weight of 35.0 per cent in IIP, contributed 55.2 per cent to its growth. All these industries are skill-intensive and produce relatively high value-added products. Growth in cotton textiles and textile products was also in double digits. Poor performance of the sub-sectors of' food products and leather, however, continues to be a cause of concern. Both these industries are not only local resource-based, but also employment-intensive. In terms of use-based classification, in the current year, higher growth rates were observed in basic goods, capital goods and intermediates. These sectors are expected to sustain these higher growth rates with nearly 85 per cent of the respondents of a Survey conducted by the Confederation of Indian Industry indicating their intentions of making additional investments. Notwithstanding a recovery in the growth in the mining sector to 4.0 per cent in April-December 2006 from 0.4 per cent in April-December 2005, performance of the sector continues to be below par.

The expansion of the PEs has also enabled the public sector make a significant contribution to the total production in some basic sectors, such as fuel, basic metals, non-ferrous metals and communication equipment, while the entire production of coal and petroleum products comes from the public sector, a substantial share in the production of basic metals and non-ferrous metals is also accounted for by the public sector. An important point to note in this context is that public investment in these sectors, which are characterised by lumpy investment, long gestation lags and low returns, they have contributed in a large measure towards savings in foreign exchange resources and reduction in dependence. As is well-known, the private sector had neither adequate resources nor willingness to invest in these sectors till the late 1980s even if these areas had been opened up earlier for the private sector.

Infrastructure Development by the Public Sector

Rapid industrialisation of a backward but developing country like India depends upon the creation of infrastructure or economic overheads such as transportation, communication, power development, basic and key industries, etc. Unless the infrastructure is created, it is not possible for other industries to come into existence or to develop fast enough. But the development of basic and capital goods industries and creation of infrastructure involves heavy investment, low yield and long gestation period. These investments were, therefore, not attractive to the private sector nor could the private sector raise such huge resources in the fifties and sixties. Naturally, it was left to the Government to develop them and most of the public enterprises were set-up in these industries. The private sector welcomed government investment in developing these industries as it stood to gain directly from them.

In fact, the basic rationale of public enterprises, soon after India launched ambitious economic plans, was to create and expand the infrastructure and this they have done quite successfully, by and large. Their contribution to the Indian economy should therefore, be judged from this angle and not from the point of view of profit alone.

STRONG INDUSTRIAL BASE IN INDIA

Despite many criticisms against the public sector enterprises, there is no denying the fact that rapid industrialisation in the first three decades after independence was mainly due to the public sector. The Industrial Policy Resolutions reserved certain industries—atomic energy, ammunition and armaments, aircraft, etc.—with the government in the interest of national security. The state also took the responsibility for the development of key industries such as coal, iron and steel, aircraft, shipbuilding, etc. The rest of the industries were left to the private sector. But the experience of the first three Plans showed clearly that the private sector had inherent handicaps and that it was not suitable for rapid industrial development. At the same time, the Planning Commission realised that a much more diversified development in the field of industries was necessary if Indian economy had to become self-generating. Naturally, the government had to come in a big way to undertake the development of basic and strategic industries, capital goods industries and even some consumer goods industries. A strong industrial base has been laid, though there are still many weaknesses and gaps in the industrial structure of the country. Credit has to be given to the public sector for this achievement. Even after the introduction of economic reforms, private sector investment has not increased as expected and it is being suggested that the public sector should take up the responsibility of infrastructure development.

Dominance of Public Sector in Critical Areas

Public sector has entered into a wide spectrum of industries and products. Its operations extend from basic and capital goods like steel, coal, copper, zinc and other minerals; heavy machinery on the one hand, and on the other, we find drugs and chemicals, fertilizers, consumer goods like textiles, hotel services, watches, confectionery, etc. Most of these industries have a strategic importance in the Indian economy since they have high linkages.

In highly critical areas such as copper, lead, coal, petroleum products, hydro and steam turbines the share of public sector is 100 per cent. In quite a large number of products, it ranges between 50 to 95 per cent.

Role of Public Sector in Export Promotion

Most of the public sector enterprises have been started keeping in mind the requirements of the Indian economy, in the fields of production and distribution. However, some public enterprises have done much to promote India's exports. The State Trading Corporation (STC) and the Minerals and Metals Trading Corporation (MMTC) have done a wonderful job of' export promotion in all parts of the world, especially in the East European countries. That metal ores have become the second largest single item on our list of exports, has been due to the pioneering efforts of these organisations. Considerable success has been achieved in pushing up the exports of Indian handicrafts, light engineering goods and many other new items of exports. Hindustan Steel Ltd., the Bharat Electronics Ltd., the Hindustan Machine Tools, etc. are some of the public enterprises which are exporting increasing proportion of their output and earning foreign exchange. For instance, the HSL has made huge strides in the field of exports.

Role of the Public Sector in Import Substitution

Some public sector enterprises were started specifically to produce goods which were formerly imported and thus to save foreign exchange. The entry of Hindustan Antibiotics Ltd. and the Indian Drugs and Pharmaceuticals Ltd. (IDPL) into the manufacture of drugs and pharmaceuticals so as to remove the monopolistic stranglehold of foreign concerns in this field helped India save foreign exchange used for importing these items. Likewise, the Oil and Natural Gas Commission and the Indian Oil Corporation Ltd., are public enterprises which attempt directly to increase self-reliance of the country and reduce our dependence on imports. The Bharat Electronics Ltd. had saved foreign exchange by way of import substitution. Complete self-sufficiency may not be possible at present, but a determined effort should be made to achieve this goal in the shortest possible time.

Role of Public Sector in Raising Internal Resources

The generation of internal resources by the public sector has assumed greater importance because, in addition to financing their own planned expansion and development, they are also expected to generate surplus for financing the needs of other priority sectors. Internal resources consist of depreciation and retained profits. With every five year plan, the public sector was able to mobilise larger internal resources. The Central public enterprises have succeeded in increasing their internal resource generation over the years. This trend should be welcomed.

Contribution to the Exchequer

Apart from generation of Internal resources and payment of dividend public enterprises have been making substantial contribution to the Government exchequer through payment of corporate taxes, excise duty, customs duty and other duties; in this way they help in mobilising funds for financing the needs for the planned development of the country.

Causes for the Expansion of Public Enterprises

In a developing economy like India, some industries had to be brought within public ownership and control for otherwise rapid growth of the economy was thought to be impossible. Nationalising some of the industrial, banking and insurance units and starting new units was expected to help in speeding up the rate of economic growth. Therefore, public enterprises became an essential part of the economic development programme of India. The need for or the rationale of public enterprises in the context of economic planning in India is given below:

(i) Rate of Economic Development and Public Enterprises

the justification for public enterprises in India was based on the fact that the rate of economic development planned by the government was much faster than could achieved by the private sector alone. In other words, the public sector was essential to realise the target of the high rate of development deliberately so fixed by the government.

To fulfil this ambitious plan target, the government had to resort to compulsory saving through taxation. In the words of Professor Ramanadham, "Having gathered the resources, the government and other important policy making bodies like the Planning Commission are under the normal human temptation to use the funds under the government's own aegis and it appears to be an avoidable botheration for the administration to offer the money to private enterprises in the first instance and then go about instituting the necessary checks and balances for the sake of ensuring the safety and proper use of funds. Instead it appeals as preferable to parliament as well as the administrative bodies to launch industrial enterprises in the public sector."[23]

(ii) Pattern of Resource Allocation and Public Enterprises

In Ramanadham's words again, "The main reason for the expansion of the public sector ties in the pattern of resources allocation decided upon under the plans.[24] In the Second Plan the emphasis was shifted to industries and mining, mainly basic and capital goods industries to be developed under the aegis of the public sector. Thus more resources for industrialisation were funnelled through the public sector. Under these circumstances, "It is inevitable that the public sector must grow not only absolutely but also relatively to the private sector."[25]

(iii) Removal of Regional Disparities through Public Enterprises

Another important reason for the extension of the

public sector was the anxiety for balanced development in different parts of the country and to see that there were no serious regional disparities. Public enterprises of the Central Government were set-up in those regions which were underdeveloped and where local resources were not adequate. Good examples are the setting up of the three steel plants at Bhilai, Rourkela and Durgapur and the Neyveli Project in Tamil Nadu which were meant to help industrialise the regions surrounding the projects. In certain cases, the State Governments were unable to raise adequate resources for development of its regions. The only alternative available was the setting up of projects by the Central Government or to start enterprises which were financed by the Centre.

(iv) Sources of Funds for Economic Development

Initially, state was all important source of funds for development. The surplus of government enterprises could be re-invested in the same industries or used for the establishment and expansion of other industries. It may be noted that private sector industries can also plough back whole or substantial amounts of their profits for expansion. However, profits in private enterprises are declared as dividends among shareholders. This would only create inequalities among people. But profits of public sector industries can be directly used for capital formation.

(v) Socialistic Pattern of Society

The socialistic pattern of society calls for extension of public sector in two ways. For one thing, production will have to be centrally planned as regards the type of goods to be produced, the volume of output and the timing of their production. It may be comparatively easy to achieve this through the public sector rather than through private sector. We may quote the Second Five-Year Plan here: "The adoption of the socialistic pattern of society as the national objective, as well as the need for planned and rapid development require that all industries of basic and strategic importance, or in the nature of public utility services, should be in the public sector. Other industries which are essential and require investment on scale which only the state, in present circumstances, would provide, have also to be in the public sector."[26]

Besides, one of the objectives of the Directive Principles of state policy of the Indian Constitution is to bring about reduction of the inequalities of income and wealth and establish an egalitarian society. The Five-Year Plans have taken this up as a major objective of planning. The public enterprises were used as major instruments for the reduction of inequalities of income and to bring about more equitable distribution of income in several lays: (a) The profits of public enterprises would go to the government unlike those of private enterprises which go to enrich private pockets; (b) There could be effective regulation of income of top executives in public enterprises, taking, of course, steps to maintain high managerial efficiency; (c) The public enterprises could be asked to adopt discriminatory price policies which would benefit the low-income consumers; and (d) They generally make it easy to raise wage income of the low-paid staff.

Explaining the importance of the public sector in a mixed economy and its role in the establishment of socialist pattern of society, Professor V.K.R.V. Rao opined, "Sectors of economic activity which involve either monopoly conditions of strategic economic power or possession of large resources in private hands should be publicly owned and operated as public enterprises. It also means that public enterprise should make itself responsible for the building of the economic overheads on the external economies like transport, power, fuel, and basic capital goods without which increase in the production of consumption goods and services either on the required scale or necessary economic basis will not be possible, irrespective of whether it is to be in the private or public sector. It also means that the extension of the public sector, in economic enterprise, will be followed by a substantial growth in the volume of national saving and investment as well as the funds available for government outlay on social services. . . . Without public enterprise, there can be no private enterprise. In fact, it is the former that enables the full growth of the latter."[27]

(vi) Limitations and Abuses of the Private Sector

The behaviour and attitude of the private sector itself was an important factor responsible for the expansion of the public sector in the country. When the Americans insisted on the Bokaro Project to be set-up in the private sector, J.R.D. Tata openly confessed that the private sector was not in a position to mobilise resources to the tune of Rs. 700 crores. Thus, the private sector did not want to move into certain sectors or if it wanted to move in, it did not have the necessary resources. This was understandable but the private sector was unwilling to take even the normal risks of business. During the Second Plan period and later, many of the licences issued to the private sector for setting up fertiliser units were surrendered when the need for fertiliser production was paramount for the country to push an agricultural breakthrough. To give another example, the business recession of 1966-67 frightened the private sector cement industry from expansion, even though it had given an undertaking to the Government to expand. To safeguard the long-term prospects of the economy, the Government had to set-up the Cement Corporation of India to boost the production of cement. The failure of the private sector drug industry to manufacture antibiotics and at the same, its tremendous exploitation of the consumers—to the extent of holding them practically to ransom—was responsible for the entry of the Government in drugs and pharmaceuticals industry.

In a number of cases, the Government was forced to take over a private sector industry or industrial units either in the interest of workers or to prevent excessive exploitation of consumers. The private sector Life Insurance companies were taken over by the Government to protect the interest of the insured from the shortsighted and rapacious private exploiters. The top 20 commercial banks were nationalised, among other things, to prevent bank funds being used for building up private industrial and commercial empires. The takeover of sick cotton mills was due to the failure of the private sector. The point to note here is that often the private sector did not function as it should have and did not carry out its social responsibilities. Accordingly, the Government was forced to takeover or nationalise the private sector units.

Performance of Public Sector Undertakings

While the Government has been pushing ahead with more and more public sector undertakings, there has been considerable criticism about the poor performance and in some cases utter failure of government undertakings in the country. Some economists have argued that profit should not be used as a criterion for judging the performance of public enterprise. According to them, public enterprises are guided by a variety of considerations in determining prices and it would not be appropriate to use profit as a criterion of their efficiency. This is particularly so in social utility services, like railways, posts and telegraphs, supply of water, electric energy, etc. The state should not raise the prices of these services, even though costs may have risen. Similarly, the public enterprises have a bulk of their investment in heavy and basic enterprises. Such enterprises have long gestation (work-in progress) period and a part of the investment may be under construction. It would, therefore, be appropriate to calculate the rate of return on effective capital employed and thus not include the capital employed in undertakings under construction or in the process of expansion or capital work-in-progress. In other words, "profitability" of the running concerns alone should be the index of their performance.

Besides, the term 'profitability' should not always be used in a business or a pure commercial sense with reference to public enterprises which are not permitted to manipulate depreciation or other payments to show higher rate of return. Moreover, PSUs offer much better reward for labour in terms of wages and salaries and other perquisites in comparison with small and medium enterprises in the private sector. To judge their performance, an adjustment should, therefore, be made for a higher social rate of return. The concept of total surplus generated in the form of declared profits, retained profits and depreciation becomes more relevant in the case of private sector enterprises and not for PSUs. This is not to suggest that profitability should not be considered as an index of efficiency, but to emphasize that the problem should be viewed in a proper perspective.

Although profit maximisation (or in the case of public enterprises, the generation of surplus) may not be the sole criterion to Judge their performance, yet it cannot be denied that it would be a folly to ignore it altogether. It has been aptly pointed out that profit maximisation may not he treated as a positive virtue but it may well be a 'good whip' to prevent the public enterprises from misbehaving. Thus the principle of profit maximisation has a negative virtue that it impels enterprises to reduce wastes of resources and inefficiency arising therefrom. From this point of view, the argument for generation of surplus by public enterprises to be used for economic development has a great force.

Financing of the Eleventh Plan

The National Development Council at its 52nd meeting on December 9, 2006 adopted the Approach Paper to the Eleventh Plan setting a "faster, more broad-based and inclusive" growth at the average annual rate of 9 per cent for the five years starting from 2007-08. This, as the Approach Paper points out, 'requires a substantial increase in the allocation of public resources for plan programmes in critical areas', including education, health, agriculture and infrastructure; an improvement in government savings from around -1.5 per cent of gross domestic product (GDP) in 2005-06 to at least + 1.0 per cent to support—without a balance of payments problem—an increase in the total investment rate (as a proportion of GDP) from 30.1 per cent in 2005-06 to an average of 35.1 per cent on average during the Eleventh Plan; and 'call for additional (Public Sector) plan expenditure above current levels, of about 1 percentage point of GDP in 2007-08, rising to about 2.5 percentage points of GDP in 2011-12. The Approach Paper points out that "The final picture on the size of the 11th Plan will only emerge after further consultations with the States and Central Ministries, and taking account of the reports of the various working groups on Plan resources."

Employees' Welfare in Public Enterprises

While evaluating the performance of the public sector, it is necessary to refer to the gains to the employees in the form of a steady improvement in their emoluments, provision for housing, medical care and educational facilities.

TABLE 2.10

Central Government Finances

	Budget estimates 2006-07	April-December		Col. 4 as per centre of BE 2006-07	Percentage change over 2005-06 (Col. 4/3)
		2005-06	2006-07		
1	2	3	4	5	6
			(Rs. crore)		
1. Revenue receipts(net to Centre)	403,465	216,746	280,915	69.6 2	9.6
Gross tax revenue	442,153	230,839	306,527	69.3	32.8
Tax (net to Centre)	327,205	168,715	232,171	71.0	37.6
Non-tax	76,260	48,031	48,744	63.9	1.5
2. Capital receipts	160,526	115,753	101,806	64.0	-11.2
Of which:					
Recovery of loans	8,000	7,408	7,952	99.4	7.3
Other receipts	3,840	11	0	0.0	-100.0
Borrowings and other liabilities	148,686	108,334	94,854	63.8	-12.4
3. Total receipts (1+2)	563,991	332,499	383,721	68.0	15.4

(Contd.)

TABLE 2.10 *(CONTD.)*

1	*2*	*3*	*4*	*5*	*6*
4. Non-plan expenditure (a)+(b)	391,263	237,904	272,203	69.6	14.4
(a) Revenue account	344,430	221,552	253,791	73.7	14.6
Of which:	0	0	0	0.0	0.0
Interest payments	139,823	80,972	92,634	663	14.4
Major subsidies	44,532	33,230	40,225	90.3	21.1
Pensions	19,542	14,621	15,050	77.0	2.9
(b) Capital account	46,833	16,352	18,412	39.3	12.6
5. Plan expenditure (i)+(ii)	172,728	94,595	111,518	64.6	17.9
(i) Revenue account	143,762	74,875	93,901	65.3	25.4
(ii) Capital account	28,966	19,720	17,617	60.8	-10.7
6. Total expenditure (4)+(_5)=(a)+(b)	563,991	332,499	383,721	68.0	15.4
(a) Revenue expenditure	488,192	296,427	347,692	71.2	17.3
(b) Capital expenditure	75,799	36,072	36,029	47.5	-0.1
7. Revenue deficit	84,727	79,681	66,777	78.8	-16.2
8. Fiscal deficit	148,686	108,334	94,854	63.8	-12.4
9. Primary deficit	8,863	27,362	2,220	25.0	91.9

Source: Controller General of Accounts

Shortcomings of the Public Sector

It would be unreasonable to argue that all is well in the public Undertakings. There is much scope for improving the efficiency and working of public sector enterprises. The main points which merit consideration are:

(i) *Mounting Losses*: as review of the working of public sector enterprises reveals that either the profits in them have been deplorably low or that they have been making losses. As compared with the performance of the Central Government, however, the State Governments are having perennial loss-makers like irrigation works, State Electricity Boards and State Road Transport. The biggest losses are made by SEBs.

The losses of State Road Transport Undertakings (STRUs) were of the order of Rs. 1,282 crores. The situation has been summed up ably by CMIE in the following words: "It is the losses of the Central Government enterprises which have generally received maximum publicity. It is not realised, however, that the worst culprits in this respect are to be found among state governments. There, the State Electricity Boards, the irrigation works, the Road Transport Corporations and other State Government-owned enterprises have the most scandalous record of making losses."

So far as the Central Government is concerned, the public sector enterprises have shown a net profit. This indicates overall improvement. But 46 per cent of the total profit is contributed by petroleum enterprises only by raising the price of oil. The Government should, therefore, make case-by-case study of the loss incurring enterprises and take remedial action.

(ii) *Political factors influence decision about location*: It has been noted that in many situations, political factors influence decisions about location of projects. Powerful ministers in the ruling party make promises about the future location of projects in a state irrespective of the results of the feasibility study about costs. This approach leads to a considerable wastage of capital resources. A classic instance of this political but irrational approach, is the decision of the Central Government to break-up the MIG aircraft project into two parts to be located in two separate states. These two locations—Nasik and Koraput--are over 900 kms apart. This was done to satisfy two powerful political bosses from two states.

(iii) *Delays in completion and increase in costs of construction*: many reports on the working of public sector projects have pointed out that many of the projects took longer time to complete than was initially envisaged. Not only that, the cost of the projects was also revised upwards. For instance, in the case of Trombay Fertilizer Project, it took 6-7 years to complete against the original estimate of 3 years. Similarly, the original estimate of cost and the final cost varies. Most of the delay in construction time-schedule and increase in costs can be traced to poor and inadequate project planning. It is very necessary to prepare comprehensive construction plans so that the avoidable delays and increases in costs should not put additional burden on the scarce resources.

(iv) *Over-capitalisation*: Public sector projects are charged with over-capitalisation. In other words, the input-output ratio obtaining in many projects was unfavourable. The Study Team found several undertakings, viz., Heavy Engineering Corporation, Hindustan Aeronautics, Fertilizers Corporation (Trombay Project), etc. over-capitalised. In this connection, the Study Team mentioned: "The causes leading to over-capitalisation can be traced to inadequate planning, delays and avoidable expenditure during construction, surplus machine capacity, tied aid resulting in the compulsion to purchase imported equipment on a non-competitive basis, expensive turn-key contracts, bad location of projects and the provision of housing and other amenities on liberal scale."[28]

(v) *Price Policy*: The pricing policies of the public sector undertakings are not guided solely by the profit maximisation principle, but are under the regulation and control of the Government. Most of the public enterprises produce products which serve as inputs for other sectors of the economy. It would be suicidal from the point of view of the overall growth of the economy if the prices of steel, oil, fertilisers or coal are fixed very high. The public sector has to keep in mind the social implications of its price policy. In this connection, it is important to remember that in many cases. under public pressure, prices are kept low even when costs and prices have been rising. This naturally affects commercial profitability.

In most public sector enterprises, pricing policies are not rational. They have no declared price policy, except perhaps that they have some departmental directives and ad hoc piecemeal orders. It is being gradually realised in the country that profit should be recognised as an index of efficiency and that the profit motive is not inconsistent with the broad objective of the socialist pattern of society. There can, however, be no hard and fast rule on the question of price policy for public sector undertaking. There are some enterprises which are run by the Government mainly to protect the interests of consumers and considerations of profit should be the least important. But there are some public enterprises which are basic to others and public operations can help in all-round economic development only when prices are fixed without regard to high profits. There is yet a third group of public enterprises in which high profit policy can safely be adopted. It is necessary that the Government classifies its enterprises under these three groups and acts accordingly.

(vi) *Use of man-power resources in excess of actual requirements*: It has been brought out that in most public enterprises, man-power is in excess of' actual requirements. There is poor manpower planning and this is clearly reflected in the inadequate arrangements for training and education of workers. The unsatisfactory salary and wage rates and the absence of incentives to staff have resulted in the flight of personnel from the public sector to the private sector. It has been suggested that top position in a public sector undertaking should also be opened to its employees. Besides, professional and technical persons of an undertaking should be trained and induced into management.

Labour indiscipline was one of the causes for the poor performance of the public sector enterprises in recent years. Indiscipline among the workers and poor management-labour relations plagued many of the large government enterprises. Supervision was also difficult in giant undertakings. The situation is not very happy. Government should make a determined bid to improve industrial relations.

(vii) *Capacity utilisation*: During 2007-08, 87 units or 52 per cent of all manufacturing/producing units had recorded capacity utilisation of more than 75 percent. On the other hand, 32 public sector enterprises operated in the capacity utilisation range of 50 to 75 per cent and 47 functioned below 50 per cent utilisation of rated capacity. This is certainly not an optimum situation. It is very necessary to find the causes of low capacity utilisation and thus remedy the situation by appropriate measures.

(viii) *Faulty controls*: The poor performance of public sector enterprises is often ascribed to faulty controls, financial and otherwise, exercised over them. At present, control is exercised by the Finance Ministry and the Minister-in-Charge of the undertaking and the Parliament. The Ministry of Finance exercises excessive financial control over the operations of public enterprises in India which have to submit to all the budgetary controls applicable to Government departments. The audit of the Auditor-General tends to be inhibitive of all initiative by the enterprises. Parliamentary control over the operations and capital development plans of public enterprises tend to become quite rigid. There is, therefore, the need to provide greater functional autonomy to the management of public enterprises.

(ix) *Inefficient management*: Managerial effectiveness and efficiency are crucial factors in improving the overall performance of the public enterprises. For efficiency in business and industrial enterprises, it is necessary that operational decisions are prompt. This necessitates a large measure of autonomy and flexibility of operations in the Government enterprises. Again, delegation of authority and elasticity in working are needed in a high degree. Within the enterprise itself, the delegation of authority from the top management to lower levels is another essential condition for efficiency in operation. Every officer should know what he is required to do and what result he is expected to produce. Unfortunately, there has been general failure to define responsibilities and duties in public sector enterprises in India. Finally, the successful operation of public enterprises is dependent upon the availability of experienced persons to fill up top positions. Public enterprises are sarcastically referred to as 'colonies for bureaucrats'. In the initial stages, the officers of the ministry who provided funds, for the projects, also pre-empted the right of management. In this way they infused 'bureaucratic blood' in the system. An unfortunate practice has been to use bureaucrats as chairmen, managing directors and managers of public enterprises. Many of them are

> not really qualified to run industrial enterprises. The government should progressively shift to professionalised management in these enterprises. As a consequence of all these factors, the element of subsidisation of the public sector assumed intolerable proportions. As a reaction to the inefficient working of the state-owned enterprises, the wave of privatisation spread all over the world. The disequilibrium in the macro-economic balance of the socialist economies as well as the developing countries led to disequilibrium in their balance of payments. The dependence of these economies on the advanced capitalist economies of the West, especially USA, hastened the process of economic reform. The unrelenting pressure from the USA and other capitalist economies on the World Bank, IMF and other international financial institutions to bail them out of economic crisis also forced them to accept privatisation as the new philosophy for regeneration.

Thus, the operation of the public sector resulted in a number of state failures. These failures were highlighted by a number of committees and economists. Principal failures were over manning and low work ethics leading to low capacity utilisation over-capitalisation due to substantial time and cost overruns, political and bureaucratic interference stifling the ability to innovate take quick and timely decision, burden of taken-over private sector sick units, excessive social welfare expenditure, absence of rational pricing policy based on economic calculus. All these factors resulted in a low rate of return which tarnished the image of public sector

A serious charge against the operation of the public enterprises is that they were used for private purposes, deliberately ignoring the objectives for which they were established. One would have expected that when new plants were set-up and existing plants were expanded in the public sector, the PE's would buy the available capital goods and technology from the sister PE's. In reality, however, imports of capital goods and technology continued despite the domestic availability. Secondly, in cases when foreign companies are appointed as contractors for public sector projects, they often chose international suppliers of plants, equipment, and technology, ignoring domestic sources. "There are reasons to believe that some of top level decision makers in the government have also used the PE's to further their own interest Imports provide one such opportunity; foreign manufacturers are naturally interested in pushing their products in India. Reportedly, it is common for them to bribe the influential persons to secure the order. Once this is realised, it may not be difficult to understand why the capabilities of PE's are not recognised or further developed, why indigenous efforts were often opposed and imports were preferred."[29] Among the glaring examples are import of shipping vessels by Shipping Corporation of India, rather than buying them from Cochin shipyard, of former price was higher. In case of foreign aid agencies, power equipment was imported in the bilaterally aided projects, depriving BHEL the opportunity to supply it. Global tendering was resorted to either on the insistences of World Bank or that of the financiers. Economic reasoning was not on many occasions the basis; but price factors such as delivery time, quality reliability were advanced as arguments to defend imports.

Lack of autonomy in decision-making, use of PE's for furthering private interest, absence of a comprehensive policy for public enterprises sector in decision-making, use of PEs by ministers and bureaucrats to siphon-off funds, low work ethics resulting in low efficiency all these factors conspired to create an environment of low or, in some cases, negative rates of return for public enterprises. Consequently, the movement for liberalisation got legitimacy and this prompted the late Prime Minister, Rajiv Gandhi, in his first broadcast to nation in 1984, to declare in unambiguous terms: "The public sector has spread in to too many areas where it should not be. We will be developing our public sectors to undertake jobs that the private sectors can not do but we will be opening up more to private sectors so that it can expand and economy can grow more freely."[30]

Notes and References

1. Gunnar Myrdal, Challenge of World Poverty (Pelican Books), p. 64.
2. *Ibid.*, p. 65.
3. Mohammad Ghosh, Poverty Structural Change and the Indian Constitution", in M. Mehmood (ed.), Social Justice and Social Process in India, p. 38.
4. Krishnaji, N., Halfway House (New York: New York Press), 1980, p. 29.
5. *Ibid.*, p. 30.
6. Manorma Year Book (Kerela: Manorama Publishing House), 1982, p. 491.
7. Farooqi, I.H., Macro Structure of Public Enterprises in India (Bombay: Asia Publishing House), 1979, p. 5.
8. Hanson, A.H., Public Enterprises and Economic Development (London: Routledge and Kegan Paul Ltd.), 1960, p. 115.
9. Encyclopedia Britanica (London: Encyclopaedia Britanica Inc.), 2002, p. 819.
10. Performance of Indian Public Enterprises—Scope, New Delhi, 1978, p. 22 (Qtd)
11. Ranade, M.G., Essays in Indian Economics (Madras: G.A. Natesan & Co.), 1906.
12. Visvesvarayya, M., Planned Economy for India (Bangalore: Bangalaore Press), 1934.
13. Chakravarty, "Development of Development Thinking" in R.R. Kale Memorial Lecture delievered at the Gokhakle Institute of Politics and Economics, Pune, reprinted in "Selected Economic Writings (Delhi: Oxford University Press), 1989, pp. 204-33.
14. Nehru, Jawaharlal, "The State's Role in Industrialisation", Inaugural address to the U.N. Seminar on Management of Public Industrial Enterprises in the ECAFE region, in "Jawaharlal Nehru's Speeches, 1957-63" (New Delhi: Publications Division, Government of India), 1959, pp. 131-33.
15. United Nations, "Measures for Economic Development of Underdeveloped Countries", New York, 1951.
16. Mallya, M.N., Public Enterprise in India (New Delhi: National Publishing House), 1971, p. 176.
17. Koontz, Harold and O'Donnell Cyril, Essentials of Management (New Delhi: Tata Mc-Graw Hil), 1978, pp. 418-19.
18. Singh, K.P.R., "Relevance of Public Enterprises" in Developing Economics (Bangalore: *Southern Economists*), 1986, p. 27.
19. Hanson, A.H., Public Enterprises and Economic Development, *op. cit.*, p. 183.
20. Singh, K.R.P., "Relevance of Public Enterprises—Developing Economics, *op. cit.*, p. 26.
21. Gupta, K.L., Bharat Men Lokudyog, Navyug Sahitya Sadan (Agra), 1984, p. 73.

22. Hanson, A.H., Public Enterprises and Economic Development, *op. cit.*, p. 183.
23. Ramanadham, V.V., The Stucture of Public Enterprises in India, p. 56.
24. *Ibid.*, p. 57.
25. Second Five Year Plan, p. 231.
26. *Ibid.*, p. 45.
27. Rao, V.K.R.V., "The Public Sector in Indian Socialism", Indian Economic Development and Policy, P.R. Brahmananda and Others (eds.), 1979, pp. 26-27.
28. Report of the Study Team on Public Sector Undetakings, 1967, p. 200.
29. Chaudhri, Sudip, Public Enterprises and Private Purposes, *Economic and Political Weekly*, Vol. XXIX, No. 22, May 28, 1994, p. 1345.
30. Datt and Sundharam, Indian Economy, 1988, p. 233.

3

Liberalisation, Privatisation and Globalisation

The end of the twentieth century has witnessed a wave of economic policy reforms in the developing world, with one country after another taking the liberalisation course, often imposed by the international financial institutions. This wave of reforms had been preceded by a quarter-century of state-directed effort at economic development, during which time the goals of economic self-reliance and import substitution industrialisation (ISI) were the hallmarks of development strategies in the less developed countries. These goals seemed particularly justified, given the long experience of these countries with colonialism and the agricultural nature of their economies. There was, besides, intellectual support for them from Keynesianism and the new discipline of development economics, especially in view of the historical memories of the massive market failures of the Depression years. However, all this seemed designed to be overtaken by the subsequent surge of liberalisation.

Economic liberalisation covers many aspects of policy, but the central issue at stake is the relative role of the state and market in the operation and management of the national economy. The contemporary movement in economic policy reform has involved the retreat of the state and the shedding of many of its economic functions in favour of the market, which has been accorded a wider and increasingly important role.

The recent wave of economic policy reform in the developing world has been seen as a necessary consequence of a changed world economic system. The key feature of the changed word economy is the element of heightened economic globalisation, which provides new external challenges as well as opportunities for development. As globalisation has accelerated, it has come to loom large in the perceptions of policy-makers, and adjustment to it in the form of economic liberalisation and the shrinking of the state has

CHART 3.1

GLPC

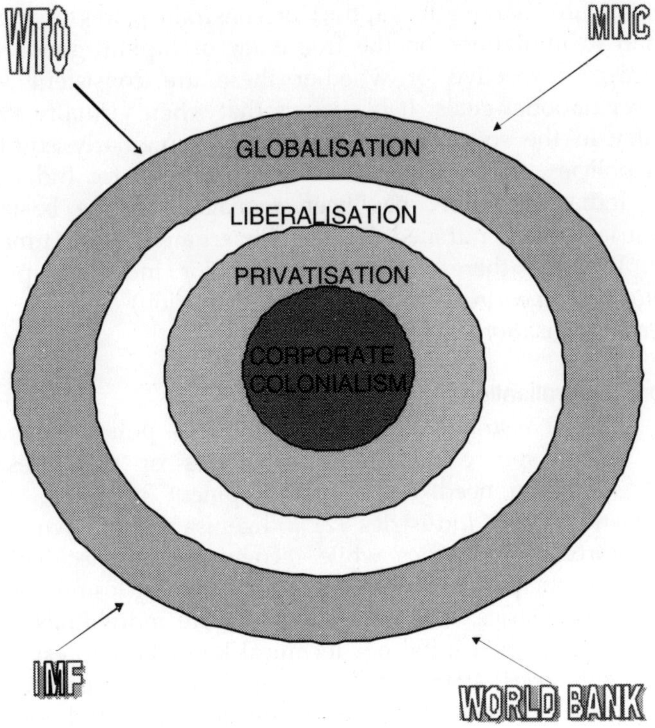

moved to *the forefront of their economic agenda, even when not imposed on them. The phenomenon of economic globalisation provides the widest possible context for the examination of economic policy reform. However, as a concept in a contemporary social science, it appears in many variants. In one strong version, globalisation refers to the presumed emergence of a 'supra-national', borderless global economy with its own laws of motion, encompassing and subordinating the various local economies in a single world wide division of labour, rendering national governments into municipalities.*[1]

LIBERALISATION

Liberalisation means abandoning the right and responsibility of the state to make choices about what form of enterprises best suits the needs of the public at large. It also means abandoning the right and responsibility of Government to enter into markets to support or constrain prices. It means an end to limitations on the free entry of capital, goods and services, irrespective of whether these are consistent with broader national goals. It is curious that when virtually every country in the so-called developed world regularly employs such policies, they are somehow inappropriate for India.

Indian Economy has been managed on the basis of industrial policy pursued by the Government from time to time. Broadly, there are only two major industrial policy resolutions., i.e. in 1956 (before liberalisation) and in 1991 (after liberalisation).

Before Liberalisation

1956 Industrial Policy Resolution—This policy extended Government sphere into more categories of industries. It emphasised the need for (1) development of small scale, khadi and village industries (2) indigenisation of ownership and control of industries while recognising the necessity of securing participation of foreign capital without losing control over the industries. It is a fact that private individuals were neither having the capital nor technical know-how to establish heavy industries after independence. Within a span of 35 years, these influential groups which acquired black money demanded to remove all restrictions on industries so that private investment would go up. So, the question is how all of a sudden some people would be able to organise so much capital. Perusal of an official statistics on black money will make the picture clear. The black money, which was around Rs. 650 crores in 1962 jumped to Rs. 80,000 crores in 1990 as estimated by Finance Ministry and Wanchoo Committee appointed by Government of India on Taxation. The National Institute of Public Finance and Policy estimated that Rs. 40,000 crores were being generated every year by the parallel economy. This money requires an outlet and hence led to the demand by the black money holders to open the economy so that this could be converted into white money through the investment route.

After Liberalisation

1991 Industrial Policy Resolution—India's financial condition was in bad shape as Government had no control over expenditure, balance of payment position was worse, and there was no enhancement of revenue. Government had no option other than to approach the IMF and World Bank to come to its rescue. Finally, IMF and World Bank came to India's rescue and advised India to liberalise the economy. Accordingly, in 1991 The Government of India reversed its economic policy.

The Broad Aspects of this Policy on:

1. To remove all control of the Government on industry.
2. To restructure the public sector, it meant to privatise public sector.
3. To allow free entry of domestic industry to all major categories of goods and services barring a few for reasons of country's security and strategic importance.
4. To allow foreign capital to flow without any restriction.
5. To integrate and transform the Indian economy into the world economy.

"Liberalisation" is not just some policy option that the government chooses, like choosing a particular tariff rate or a particular price policy. It is a major episode in the history of class struggle. It corresponds to a new phase of world capitalism with new class configurations. To discuss the effects of "liberalisation" without taking into account this entire class context, in terms exclusively of text book propositions about the benefits of trade is both naive and banal. The thrust of the present wave of "liberalisation" which is sweeping the entire third world is three-fold: to shift the balance away from the workers, peasants, petty producers and even small capitalists towards large capitalists—both domestic and foreign; to shift the balance away from domestic capital in general towards foreign capital; and to shift the balance away from capital-in-production towards capital-as-finance. To be sure, different countries are at different stages in this process, which is carried forward by a combination of forces driven by international finance capital whose chief spokesmen are the Bretton Woods institutions.

A country travelling down the path of "liberalisation" cannot even pause to provide a "human face" to the process. To provide even a mere "human face" it has to abandon that path altogether which in turn can become possible only with the widest mobilisation of classes against those promoting "liberalisation."

In so far as "liberalisation" is not a mere policy option but a process driven by international finance capital in the current stage of imperialism, it follows that the nation-State that is carrying forward this process is trapped willy-nilly into defending the interests of international finance capital even against its own population. This gives rise to a major contradiction: since the State exists on the domestic civil society, and, in conditions of bourgeois democracy, has to respond to pressures from the latter, its pursuit of the path of "liberalisation" comes into conflict with the legitimacy which it would like to surround itself with. This contradiction is typically sought to be overcome in two ways: first through an explicit attenuation of domestic sovereignty by tying the domestic State into international agreements like the WTO; and secondly through a host of measures that "roll back" democracy at home and the exercise of the democratic rights of the people.

The defenders of "liberalisation", despite being on the defensive as regards the recent growth performance, argue nonetheless that it has ushered in a remarkable acceleration in the growth rate of the economy over the period as a whole, that the 3-3.5 percent growth rate at which we had been stuck for decades after independence (which was sometimes facetiously called the "Hindu rate of growth") has finally given way to more impressive figures. As a matter of fact, however, the acceleration in growth began much before the "liberalisation" of 1991. The average annual rates of growth of GDP at constant prices (1993-4=100) for the three decades 1971-80, 1981-90 and 1991-2000 were 3.66 percent, 5.60 percent and 6.45 percent, respectively. It is the 1980s in other words that saw an acceleration in the growth rate. The 1990s appear merely to have continued along the higher growth trajectory. Even this appearance, however, is erroneous. Decadal comparisons hide important shifts within the decade.

Compared to the peak growth rate experienced during the second half of the 1980s, there has actually been a steady deceleration of the growth rate of the economy. Apologists might claim that the process of "liberalisation" itself began in the late eighties, so that the earlier acceleration must still be attributed to "liberalisation." But even the first half of the eighties witnessed a significant acceleration in growth which suggests that its genesis lay elsewhere. And this was the increase in the investment ratio.

In any economy, as long as demand constraints do not become more pronounced, the growth rate is determined essentially by the ratio of investment to GDP. Through the eighties, this ratio climbed up steadily in the economy, reaching the figure of 25 percent by the end of the decade. During the nineties, while this ratio has remained unchanged and lower on average than the end-eighties peak, demand constraints have become more pronounced; the growth rate, far from accelerating has, therefore, tended to come down compared to the late 1980s. "Liberalisation" in short has not raised the investment ratio; on the other hand, it has made the demand constraint on the economy more pronounced.

The collapse in the growth rate of the primary sector is continuous, while that of the secondary sector occurs mainly in the latter half of the nineties. Taking both sectors together, i.e. the entire sphere of material commodity production, both quinquennia in the nineties witnessed growth rates that were distinctly lower than in the latter half of the eighties.

Why India's growth rate suddenly picked up in the eighties and why it has been going down from the late-eighties peak deserves discussion. The reason for the sudden pick-up in growth as we have seen lies not in some magic of "liberalisation" but in the increase in the investment ratio. This latter increase in turn was not because the Indian rich suddenly became more frugal, so that investment ratios which earlier would have precipitated severe inflationary crises now became accessible to the economy. The reason lies in the fact that in the post-oil shock period when multinational banks were flush with petro-dollars and were actually pushing loans to third world countries, the Rajiv Gandhi government went in for larger foreign borrowings to jack up the investment ratio. It is this debt-overhang that precipitated the 1991 crisis by engendering sudden capital outflows, and the "confidence" of the renters had to be restored by enacting these so-called "reforms." The Rajiv Gandhi regime, in other words, did not resolve the earlier crisis of the Indian economy; it passed over it by picking up easy foreign loans and this in turn produced an even bigger crisis, of a different genre, in 1991.

In the "reform" era, a whole range of commodities which were hitherto inaccessible to the Indian upper classes suddenly became accessible, and soon their domestic production began. In certain other areas too, e.g. agri-export, profitable opportunities of investment opened up. While these opportunities held up the investment ratio, the rise in the rate of surplus value that was taking place through cuts in subsidies and the social wage, and through higher administered prices impinging on the working people, together with the curtailment of public investment, ensured a degree of demand compression that prevented any excess-demand-caused inflation (inflation in this period was administered rather than excess-demand-caused). This demand compression, however, has now pushed the economy into a recession, and the investment ratio itself started coming down.

Tendency Towards Generalised Over-production

The imminent tendency of a "liberalised" economy in the contemporary context is to be beset by acute and generalised demand constraints; it is intrinsically characterised by a perennial crisis of generalised over-production owing to the jacking up of the rate of surplus value in the economy and the deflationary policies imposed by the State. The Indian economy escaped this fate temporarily because of the pent-up demand that existed for a variety of hitherto-inaccessible goods under the dirigiste regime, and because of certain unused investment opportunities that existed in its interstices owing to the controls it imposed. But these demand stimuli are essentially transitory and evanescent. Once their effect is exhausted, the economy is back to its state of a perennial over-production crisis, which is exactly what it is experiencing now.

The reasons why a contemporary "liberalised economy" tends to be perennially demand-constrained are: The rise in the rate of surplus value that such an economy necessarily brings about restricts the growth of consumption of the working masses. This could be offset only if the investment demand rises sufficiently. But public investment in such an economy gets curtailed, since a retreat of the State from its role as a producer and investor (and its increasing reorientation as an entity serving directly and exclusively the needs of capital including international finance capital) is a hall-mark of "liberalisation." Investment by capitalists, both domestic and foreign, which is supposed to come forth in large quantities as the so-called fetters imposed upon them by the dirigiste regime are withdrawn, is constrained by three factors: the first is the shrinking of the mass market that the rise in the rate of surplus value brings about; the second is the rise in the real interest rate which is a necessary fall-out of financial "liberalisation", since exposure to the free flow of finance into and out of the country necessitates that rentiers have to be "bribed" through a higher real interest rate to prevent them from taking their funds to the "safe haven" provided by the metropolitan countries; and thirdly, the very curtailment of public investment has a dampening effect on private investment both by aggravating infrastructural constraints, and also because the growth of markets caused by the former autonomous growth, which is a stimulant for the latter (i.e. public investment "crowds in" rather than "crowds out" private investment), is no longer available.

This, of course, still leaves the possibility of larger exports offsetting demand constraints. But contemporary "liberalisation" is occurring within the context of the ascendancy of a new form of international finance capital whose effect is to slow down the rate of growth of the world capitalist economy as a whole, by rolling back Keynesian "demand management" policies, and by privileging speculation over "enterprise" everywhere. This in turn adversely affects export prospects of "liberalised" third world economies (the fact that a country like China continues to experience a successful export drive, far from constituting a counter-example to this argument, indicates on the contrary that China is not an example of a "liberalised" third world economy).

It may, of course, be argued that precisely in a period when the world capitalist economy is slowing down, competition among capitals to lower costs to grab a larger share of the shrinking market would take the form inter alia of investing in low-wage third world countries to meet world demand. This, however, never occurs (except possibly in the geographical fringes of the metropolis itself, such as parts of Northern Mexico), because of the infrastructural constraints in most third world countries, aggravated by declining public investment, and of the general uncertainty that metropolitan capital experiences in operating in the third world (which it overcomes only when its object is to capture third world markets themselves through local production). It follows then that the era of "globalisation" is an era of "globalisation" of finance and not of productive facilities. And precisely because "globalisation" of finance entails a slowing down of the world capitalist economy, economies that are drawn into the vortex of "liberalisation" and "globalisation" have an imminent tendency towards generalised over-production, which manifests itself through recession, unutilised industrial capacity, and unsold food-stocks, i.e. through the fact that everywhere it is demand that limits what is produced and sold. (The exception of course is the infrastructural sector, but the shortages here are a reflection of the same phenomenon, and coexist with unutilised capacity in sectors producing equipment for this sector).

This tendency can only be temporarily masked by the upsurge in elite consumption that occurs in the immediate aftermath of "liberalisation" when all restrictions on the availability of consumption goods are done away with. But once this transition phase is over, the basic tendency towards over-production manifests itself, as it is doing now.

Fiscal Policy

The need for enticing multinational corporations, for liberalising capital flows, for privatising public sector enterprises and for restricting public investment is argued typically by citing the fiscal crisis of the State. The State, it is argued, has inadequate fiscal resources; it has very little prospects for raising additional fiscal resources, hence it must step back and allow private, including foreign, capital to undertake the task of investing, for which it has to create a conducive environment. Now, there is no doubt that the contradictions of the dirigiste regime have come to a head through the fiscal crisis of the State, as the attempt of the ruling classes to enrich themselves through budgetary transfers and tax evasion denudes the State exchequer. But this fiscal crisis is vastly compounded under the "liberal" regime. The scale of transfers, especially to private, including foreign, capital, increases many-fold. If primitive accumulation through the instrumentality of the State budget underlay the crisis of dirigisme, this primitive accumulation reaches massive proportions in the "liberal" regime, with large chunks of State property grabbed "for a song", and with subsidies (to capital), transfers and tax cuts scaling new heights. The argument for rolling back the State from its producing and investing role, therefore, becomes a self-justifying one. While it invokes the fiscal crisis for its justification, this fiscal crisis itself, to a very significant extent, is its own contribution.[2]

PRIVATISATION

The term 'privatisation' connotes a wide range of ideas. It would, therefore, be appropriate to understand the meaning of the term.

In a narrow sense, privatisation implies the induction of private ownership in publicly owned enterprises, but in a broader sense, it connotes besides private ownership (or even without change of ownership), the induction of private management and control in the public sector enterprises. Barbara Lee and John Nellis define the concept in this manner: 'Privatisation is the general process of involving the private sector in the ownership or operation of a state owned enterprise. Thus the term refers to private purchase of all or part of a company. It covers 'contracting out' and the privatisation of management—through management contracts, leases, or franchise arrangements.'[3] Thus privatisation covers three sets of measures: (a) Ownership measures, (b) Organisational measures, and (c) Operational measures.

(a) *Ownership measures*: the set of measures which transfer ownership of public enterprises, fully or partially, lead to privatisation. The higher the proportion of transfer of ownership to the individual, cooperative or corporate sector, the greater is the degree of privatisation. This can take three forms :

(i) Total denationalisation implies a complete transfer of ownership of a public enterprise to private hand.

(ii) Joint venture implies partial introduction of private ownership. The range of private ownership can vary from 25 to 50 per cent or even more, depending upon the nature of the enterprise and state policy in this regard.

(iii) Liquidation implies a sale of assets to someone who may use them for the same purpose or some other purpose depending upon the preference of the buyer.

(iv) Management buy-out is a special version of denationalisation. It implies sale of assets to the employees. For this purpose, appropriate provision of loans from banks is also made to enable employees to take over ownership. The employees may form a cooperative to run the enterprise. In this case, employees become entitled, besides wages, to ownership dividend.

(b) *Organisational Measures*: A number of organisational measures are conceived to limit state control. They include :

(i) *A holding company structure*: may be so designed that the government limits its control interventions to apex level decisions and leaves the operating companies within the arrangement to a sufficient degree of autonomy in decision-making within the framework of the market forces. Some times, a very big monolithic organisation is split into smaller units without loss of economies of scale. Although the smaller units comprise of a family, but they become independent in certain product lines or regional operations. A big organisation like Bharat Heavy Electricals Ltd. may adopt the holding company status by transferring a number of functions to smaller units, thereby reducing centralised managerial functions.

(ii) *Leasing*: A public enterprise while retaining ownership may lease out to a private bidder for a specific period of use. The Chinese government adopted the Asset Responsibility System (ARS) in which tenderers becomes the general executive of an enterprise for a specified period of say 5 years. But before the appointment of the bidder is finalised, the tenderers have to give an undertaking of the profits they would pass over to the state and also give a convincing set of measures that they propose to undertake in this regard. The government enjoys the right of obtaining profits as per agreement; on the other hand, tenure ownership is expected to lead to improved efficiency or lower costs of operation. In case, a particular bidder fails to come up to the expectations of the government, the latter reserves the right to replace him with a more promising bidder.

(iii) *Restructuring*: To bring public sector enterprises under market discipline, it would be desirable to go in for two forms of restructuring: (a) Financial restructuring can be effected in the sense that accumulated losses are written off and capital composition is rationalised in respect of debt-equity ratio, (b) Basic restructuring may be effected by redefining the set of commercial activities which the enterprise will undertake henceforth. It may shed-off some activities to be taken up by ancillaries or small scale units

(c) *Operational Measures* are intended to improve efficiency of the organisation, even when full denationalisation has not been undertaken. They, infact, inject the spirit of commercialisation in public enterprises. The measures include grant of autonomy to PEs in decision-making, provision of incentives to blue-collar as well as white-collar employees consistent with the increase in efficiency of productivity, freedom to acquire certain inputs from the market by a system of 'contracting' instead of producing them within the enterprise, development of proper investment criteria, permitting PEs to got to the capital markets to raise funds, etc. The basic purpose of these measures of operational privatisation is to bring about a drastic reform to reduce government control over the enterprise.

The upshot of the list of measures enunciated above is that while privatisation is more often equated with transfer of ownership, the critical manifestation of privatisation is the transfer of managerial control to private hand, individual or co-operative. Sometimes, even 'token privatisation' in the sense of 'disinvestiture' has also been mentioned as a measure of privatisation.

The privatisation wave that swept the whole world was bound to have its effect in India. The experience of economic reform in erstwhile Soviet Union and East European countries is not of much benefit for India on account of two reasons:

(a) There was absence of the market mechanism in these countries and the entire pricing system was based on cost plus pricing. The existence of the total monopoly in production gave unbridled power to the state to determine prices of products in an arbitrary manner.

(b) The size of the public sector engulfing the entire economy required the dismantling of one system nurtured for over more than half a century and its replacement by a new economic order. This is a much more difficult process than introducing privatisation in mixed economies like India which worked in an environment of co-existence of the public and private sectors and had the market system as a signaling mechanism in resource allocation

But in India, the wave of privatisation did not have the like of determination that was displayed by Marget Thatcher in U.K. No political party in India belonging to the rightist or centrist ideology has the courage to mention privatisation as an article of faith as was done by the Conservative Party manifesto in 1987 in the U.K. It was claimed that the productivity and profitability has soared in the newly privatised companies; competition had forced the economy to respond to the needs of the consumer; it promoted efficiency and held down costs. To quote Ridley Report (1987) "where nationalised industries have the nation by the jugular vein, the only feasible options is to pray up." Political parties do speak of reform of public sector but do not intend to take a frontal position against the public sector. The New Industrial Policy (1991) only codified the intentions of Congress Party. It limited the priority areas for the public sector in the future to

(a) essential infrastructure goods and services;
(b) exploration and exploitation of oil and mineral resources;
(c) technology development and building of manufacturing capabilities in areas which are crucial in the long-term development of the economy and where private sector investment is inadequate; and
(d) manufacture of products where strategic considerations predominate such as defense equipment.

The role of the public sector which was sought to be enlarged in the Industrial Policy of 1956 would henceforth be limited to essential infrastructure and defense and more and more areas would be opened to the private sector. Besides this, more congenial environment would be built for foreign capital to seek avenues of direct foreign investment.

Although there is a strong case in favour of privatisation, in reality, it is becoming increasingly difficult to push through proposals of privatisation.

Firstly, with the emergence of strong trade unions in India, privatisation in the sense of denationalisation is not considered possible. Feelers have been sent by the Ministers by issuing statements regarding denationalisation of banks, insurance companies, power generation companies, coal mines, unviable public sector units, postal services, etc., but they have aroused spontaneous and violent reactions from trade unions which are highly organised. Even INTUC which is affiliated to Congress (I) had to fall in the line with the CITU, HMS, AITUC and BMS in opposing all moves against denationalisation.

Two attempts were made: First, the Government decided to transfer the ownership of Scooters India—a loss-making public sector concern to Bajaj Auto Ltd. But the intervention of INTUC that such a step would go against the interests of the labour, forced the Government to withdraw the proposal. Second, the BALCO deal selling the profit-making company at a price of Rs. 550 crores came up for sharp criticism. Bhartiya Mazdoor Sangh (BMS) leader Dattopant Thengadi criticising the Government's policy of disinvestment on 16th April 2001 said, 'Modern food was sold at a throw away price and BALCO agreement is a fraud.' He accused the government of 'killing the goose that laid golden eggs.' The trade unions belonging to the left (and even the right) are all set against attempts to privatisation of profit-making PSUs. The government is, therefore, slowing down the pace at which it wanted to go ahead with its policy of disinvestment.

Privatisation in a Democratic Society

In a democratic set-up, it would not be possible to carry out privatisation in blatant disregard of the interests of workers. Secondly, it would be a fraudulent practice on the part of the state to use book value of net assets? Thirdly, is the aim of privatisation to encourage corporatisation to benefit the big industrialists, or is it aimed at exploring the possibilities of other forms of privatisation such as workers' cooperatives? The example of Kamani Tubes—a loss-making private sector corporation shows that the workers' co-operative experiment can lead to recovery and a sick PSE can become a profit-making enterprise under worker's management. Such experiments should be given a fair trial. There should be a right of pre-emption for the workers to run a sick unit as an employees-owned corporation. If the workers refuse, the sick unit may be transferred to the big business. Lastly, there should be complete transparency of transactions of privatisation.

Another major resistance against privatisation is the facile manner in which these proposals indicate retrenchment of workers. Some estimates reveal that there is 25-30 per cent over-staffing in public sector enterprises. So the first axe of privatisation must fall on redundant workers.

Retrenchment of workers with a compensation or

Voluntary Retirement Scheme (VRS) is not considered to be a solution by the workers. The bitter experience of workers in the payment of relief by the Textile Industry has been highlighted by Sanat Mehta who writes: "The workers who lost their job especially through closures have had in almost all cases, nothing to fall back on, not even their legal dues which have not been fully paid to them."[4]

The absence of a social security system in India, as against well-organised social security systems in the developed countries is another potent reason why the trade unions are against schemes of retrenchment or voluntary retirement. The employers consider the payment of compensation to workers as a burden and use all legal and non-legal methods to delay such payments as long as possible. This attitude of the employers and the bureaucratic delays in the State-owned enterprises has not been able to instill confidence among the workers that they would get the promised golden handshake.

Despite all resistance, the Government has been able to transfer the ownership of some public sector units to private sector. Notable among these attempts at privatisation are: Allwyn Nissan—a public sector concern of Andhra Pradesh was handed over to Mahindra; Mangalore Chemicals and Fertilizers—a public sector undertaking of Karnataka was handed over to UB Group and Maharashtra scooters was handed over to Baja Auto (India).

Privatising Loss-making or Profit-making Units

The question arises: Which units should be privatised—profit-making or loss-making units? There does not seem to be enough *raison-d'etre* for privatising a profit-making unit, because the entire argument for privatisation is based on the fiscal health of the unit measured by the rate of return. But the Government offered 20% equity in such units to the public so as to raise resources via the mutual funds/financial institutions to reduce the budget deficit. The Government of India raised Rs. 4,950 crore by the sale of PSU shares till March 2004. Some critics have described it as "Deficit Privatisation" because this is not consistent with the philosophy of privatisation. So far as it goes, it may sound all right. But there is an apprehension in the minds of the Trade Unions that the financial institutions would in turn sell it to the public which implies big business. Thus, this may act as a clever two-stage move to permit backdoor entry for the private sector. This needs to be avoided.

But a relevant question that may be raised is: Why should private sector be willing to take a loss-making sick unit? Private sector is not interested in the sick unit. It is only an excuse to appropriate the real estate attached with these units so that it could make use of the land and other physical assets to start fresh undertakings in the premises available at a very low cost. This implies that the principal objective of privatisation to infuse the commercial spirit in PSU may not be achieved and revival of the sick unit may not be the priority for the private sector. This explains the excessive emphasis on shedding the load of excess labour by making lump sum payment in the form of voluntary retirement schemes or retrenchment. In some situations, the scheme can succeed also if very lucrative sums are paid to the workers as golden handshakes. This provides a safety net for excess labourers who may make an effort to find an alternative job or set-up some small scale unit of production to earn a living.

But there are certain large public sector undertakings like the Delhi Transport Corporation, State Electricity Boards, State Road Transport and State Irrigation Projects which the Government may find very difficult to privatise. The DTC is a perennial loss-maker and part of the explanation is the low tariff and theft of petrol and spare parts. The government should, therefore, raise tariffs on the one hand and reduce the loss due to theft of petrol and spare parts. But the experience of private bus operators has been very nasty, especially due to the heavy incidence of accidents on account of a reckless driving to earn more profit. The common man has, therefore, again felt that DTC was a better alternative since the aspect of security of passengers was being looked after. Thus, all is not well with the policy of privatisation. But these attempts cannot be treated as privatisation, since the essence of privatisation lies in improving the quality of management and operation of enterprises.

Joint Ventures

The Government is also considering transfer of ownership by establishing joint ventures. This can be affected by the sale of equity. Three kinds of proposals, broadly speaking, have been put forward:

(i) 25% ownership by the private sector (banks, mutual funds, corporations or individuals), and of workers also to be included to the extent of 5% (equity to be transferred to them). This creates veto power by the public sector against the private sector ownership

(ii) Government retains 51% equity and sells 49% equity to the private sector. Keeping the essential character of the public enterprises, it introduces a big share for the private sector ownership.

(iii) 74% of equity is transferred to the private sector and the Government retains 26% with the added proviso of Government's veto power and minority control over major corporate decisions.

The three variants of privatisation indicate different degrees of ownership transfer from the public sector to the private sector. The basic assumption of these models is that ownership transfer will generate new forces which will impel joint ventures to improve productivity of the assets and make them more profitable. The first variant of 75% state-ownership, it is suspected, will not achieve the desired results, because despite minority participation by the private parties, which brings in some resources from the private sector, nothing appears to undergo a change in terms of bringing about operational efficiency.

However, since in the second variant, substantial ownership, i.e. 49 per cent is transferred to the private sector, the impact of the private sector in decision-making can become significant.

It is, however, the third variant which brings about a basic restructuring of the enterprises and transfers 74% ownership to the private sector. In other words, it transfers decision-making power in all policy matters and operational control to the private sector, but keeps government veto power in major corporate decisions. In other words, micro-decision-making is totally privatised, but the power to regulate consistent with macro-economic goals of the economy remains with the state.

But a mere change of ownership will not bring about the much-desired increase in productivity. Supporting measures like linking wages to productivity, introducing measures that lead to a more competitive environment so that efficiency pricing becomes a norm, have to be taken.

Privatisation, Roy concludes, is essentially 'the transfer of productive public assets from the state to private companies. Productive assets include natural resources. Earth, forest, water, air. These are the assets that the state holds in trust for the people it represents..... To snatch these away and sell them as stock to private companies is a process of barbaric dispossession on a scale that has no parallel in history."[5]

GLOBALISATION

Globalisation is a misleading concept, since what is described as globalisation has been happening for 500 years. Rather, what is new is that one is entering an "age of transition." One can usefully analyze the current world situation using two time frames: 1945 to the present and circa 1450 to the present.

The period since 1945 has been one long Kondratieff cycle, with an A-phase that ran through 1967-76 and a B-phase ever since. The economic and political developments of the last 52 years are easy to place within this framework. The period from 1450 to the present is the long history of the capitalist form world economy, with its secular trends—all reaching critical points. The period 1945 to this date is that of a typical Kondratieff cycle of the capitalist world economy, which has had as always two parts: an A-phase or upward swing or economic expansion that went from 1945 to 1967-73, and a B-phase or downward swing or economic contraction that has been going from 1967-73 to the present, and probably will continue for several more years. The period

1450 to today, by contrast, marks the life cycle of the capitalist world economy, which had its period of genesis, its period of normal development, and now has entered into its period of terminal crisis. In order to comprehend the present situation, we need to distinguish between these two social times, and the empirical evidence for each of them. The A-period of the present Kondriatieff was what the French aptly called les trente glorieuses. It coincided with the high point of U.S. hegemony in the world system, and occurred within the framework of a world order that the United States established after 1945.

The way the term "Globalisation" is widely used, tends to obfuscate the historical process of which it is a part; and, seems to provide a studied ambiguity, if not a misleading veneer, to its meaning and attributes. To quote from Michel Beaud's 'A History of Capitalism'. plump and round, smooth and slippery, the word "Globalisation" is an all-purpose word. It can be substituted for terms such as "Imperialism", "World Capitalism" or "Dependence", as well as for the whole group of phrases which express forward progress toward a unified and happy humanity.

Globalisation is not a phenomenon, much less the destiny of humanity, as some would like to present the concept. It is also not a moral or social goal to strive for. In these days when it has become fashionable to resurrect ancient concepts or adages, totally out of their context, only to justify certain untenable or unjust propositions, some have tried to discern the message of "Vasudhaiva kutumbakam" in "Globalisation." Others are content with imagining the realisation of the dream of a "global village" in it. Such romantic nonsense need not detain us here. A casual look at the long queues at the consulates of the countries, like USA and UK; the guns and electric fences that guard the borders of USA from Mexico; nearer home, the chauvinism, verging on inhumanity, expressed by the elite and their representatives in the government, in dealing with the alleged immigrants from a neighbouring country, which, only a few decades ago, was part of the one and the same sub-continental entity to which we belonged; and, the overwhelming reality of the "local" and the "national" for the large masses of humanity all over the third world: these are sharp enough reminders to wake up anyone to the reality of a fragmented world.

Globalisation is the effective erasure of national boundaries for economic purposes. National boundaries become totally porous with respect to goods and capital, and increasingly porous with respect to people, viewed in this context as cheap labour, or in some cases cheap human capital. It is the process of integrating various economies of the world without creating any hindrances in the free flow of goods and services, technology, capital and even labour or human capital. It opens the door for India to compete abroad, the fact of the matter is that, indignant protestants of Government notwithstanding, globalisation means hamburgers, pizzas, colas, fancy cloths, new movies and CDs to tillilate our elite. Globalisation can ultimately mean that our wheat farmers labour for a multinational company run by bandicoots in Minnesota while the women who raise and feed our milch animals earn dividends for stockholders in Geneva. The term globalisation has, therefore, four parameters:

(i) Reduction of trade barriers to permit free flow of goods and services among nation-states;
(ii) Creation of environment in which free flow of capital can take place among nation-states;
(iii) Creation of environment, permitting free flow of technology; and
(iv) Last, but not the least, from the point of view of developing countries, creation of environment in which free movement of labour can take place in different countries of the world.

Globalisation, therefore, in the world economy, demanded for regulatory and other barriers in nation states. States, through the rules of WTO, were pressurised to remove these barriers. But at the same time, as there is deregulation at a national level, there is more regulation at a global level. The Uruguay round of the General Agreement on Trade and Tariffs (GATT) and the setting up of the WTO is an illustration to this.

It is the restructuring of colonisation with far more dire consequences. It is the conversion of the vast sector of the human race, living mostly in the so-called Third World, into a global market for exploitation by the neo-capitalists, in the main, the G8 Nations. The decolonised has been re-colonised, this time round, not by "mother countries", but by "mother industries", a few multi-nationals whose sole interest is profit which it pursues licentiously with practically no restraints. After all, the earliest colonisers were trading companies, the Dutch East India and the British East India, not nation-states.

Whereas the first capitalism, or "liberalism", was constrained by governments, neo-liberalism or globalisation subsumes governments and indeed the whole of society. It exploits freely, without any restraints, neither of governments nor of any moral order. The International Monetary Fund and World Bank invented at the end of World War Two to rescue and revive European and Japanese Economies, today prey on "Third World" governments in particular and bend them to their economic policies that are anti-democracy, anti-poor, anti-humanity, focused on securing giant corporations their monopolistic profits.

George Soros, from within the capitalist rank, confirms this when he states; "The protection of the common interest used to be the task of the nation state. But the powers of the state have shrunk as global capital markets have expanded. When capital is free to move around, it will avoid any state that seeks to impose taxes and regulations. Since capital is essential to the creation of social goals, governments must cater to its demands often to the detriment of social goals. This holds true for all governments, even the United States."[6]

So, capital governs, and the global capitalists lay down the policy to exploit and plunder the world regardless of the destruction to nature or humanity. Any government desiring foreign capital has to submit to this policy, which, like colonialism, is a one way traffic of resources plundered and transferred from the poor to the rich; from the south from Africa, Asia and South America, to the North-Europe the UK, the USA, Japan and Canada. It is, in turn, the sale of manufactured goods and machinery to the former colonies, the "Third World", at exorbitant prices, made more exorbitant by the devaluation of indigenous currencies.

Globalisation is reduced to a single component, trade, with its global media that fashions the tastes of the world and manipulates the market. The main orchestrator and beneficiary of this process is the USA which enjoys 50% of the world market in many industries; controls more than half of the world business activity, and two-thirds of advertising and marketing services. Globalisation is essentially Americanisation.

Soros informs us that "capitalism is very successful in creating wealth"[7] and Felix Yurlov expands on this when he reports that the world's per capita income tripled in the last 50 years, that the world GDP grew ten-fold—from $30 million to $30 billion. That revenue from the entertainment and book business grew "from $67 billion in 1970, to $200 billion in 1991, (the USA being the chief beneficiary and the biggest exporter, with fifty percent of the revenue of Hollywood coming from overseas). Cultural products move in a one-way stream, from the rich to the poor."

The advocates of globalisation, more especially from developed countries, limit the definition of globalisation to only three components, unhindered trade flows, capital flows and technology flows. They insist on developing countries to accept their definition of globalisation and conduct the debate on globalisation within the parameters set by them. However, several economists in the developing world believe that this definition is incomplete and in case the ultimate aim of globalisation is to look upon the world as a 'global' village, then the fourth component, unrestricted movement of labour cannot be left out.

Basically, globalisation signifies a process of internationalisation plus liberalisation. According to Stiglitz, "Globalisation is the closer integration of the countries and peoples of the world which has been brought about by the enormous reduction of costs of transportation and communications, and the breaking down of artificial barriers to the flow of goods and services, capital, knowledge, and (to a lesser extent) people across borders."[8] Jagdish Bhagwati defines globalisation in the following words: "Economic globalisation constitutes integration of national economies into the international economy through trade, direct foreign investment (by corporations and multinationals), short-term capital flows, international flows of workers and humanity generally, and flows of technology."[9]

The Two Faces of Globalisation

In the early 1990's globalisation was greeted with euphoria. Capital flows to developing countries had increased six fold in six years, from 1990 to 1996. The establishment of the World Trade Organisation in 1995—a goal that had been sought for half a century—was to bring the semblance of a rule of law to international commerce. Everyone was supposed to be a winner—those in both the developed and the developing world. Globalisation was to bring unprecedented prosperity to all.

No wonder then that the first major protest against globalisation—which took place in Seattle in December 1999, at what was supposed to be the start of a new round of trade negotiations, leading to further liberalisation—came as a surprise to the advocates of open markets.

On 17 December 1999, the WTO secretariat and leadership, and the major trading nations, had reassembled in Geneva at the General Council in a state of shock (almost like shell-shocked soldiers in a war) after the shambles that was the Seattle Ministerial meeting and its collapse. In this state, they set in motion a process of "confidence-building" among the members and in the outside world. But since then they have been undermining it.

At least in retrospect, it is now apparent that the majors and the WTO leadership had in fact no intention of making any serious changes—either to the decision-making process (in the way of real transparency of the process to the members and to the public) or to bring about equity within the system to ensure equitable benefits for all.

The Seattle Ministerial Conference and the preparations before it were given by deep differences among the major trading entities (the Quad countries—Canada, the EC, Japan and the US) and between them and the developing nations, big and small. For a rules-based system and organisation, the meeting itself had been constituted and called to order in disregard of the rules again, and ended even more so—with the final statements of the conference chair recorded in the official summary records in a way that increased the public perception of illegitimacy of the system.

In the post-Seattle meetings of the General Council, first in December 1999 and later in February 2000, it was announced that the organisation was embarking on "confidence-building" measures to improve internal transparency, and democratic decision-making, and to take steps to address the "implementation issues"

This broad rubric of "implementation" covered proposals of developing countries for measures, some immediate and others within a year or so, needed to address the grievances of these countries, their parliaments, enterprises and public, about the WTO system and its failure to deliver on the 'promises' based on which their countries had signed on to the Marrakesh Agreement and its offspring, the WTO.

However, as in the run up to Seattle, since then too the majors and the WTO leadership and secretariat appear to have hoped that the implementation issues could be talked out and rolled on to a new round and buried. However, through the year,. a large number of developing countries, particularly the Like-Minded Group, the African Group and the African, Caribbean and Pacific (ACP) countries, and several others too in varying ways, continued to raise the implementation issues as adamantly as the Cairns Group have on agriculture talks and the US and the EC on services, thus in effect putting the developed world and the WTO leadership on the defensive and forcing them to respond on implementation.[10]

But the major industrialised nations have yielded little ground in terms of actual decisions and commitments, despite the some 800 hours that the General Council chair, Ambassador Kare Bryn of Norway, said he had personally spent in consultations on the implementation questions.

The EC and Canada have used different language to insist that these issues could only be dealt within new negotiations, while the US, at the General Council meeting on 15 December 2000, talked of the need to find a "different process" than the implementation mechanism agreed upon in May.

Even one or two developing-country Members of the Cairns Group have been privately talking of the implementation issue having become a "cancer" in the system that has to be quickly eliminated by getting it off the WTO special mechanism or General Council agenda.

While discussions on the implementation issues were ongoing at the level of trade ambassadors in the General Council and subordinate bodies (although decisions thereon were blocked), efforts were made through regional meetings to sneak in endorsements for the idea of a new round with a "broad-based agenda", where and where alone (it was argued) developing countries, concerns could be addressed.

Talk of a "broad-based" agenda is seemingly neutral language but these are in fact code words for a new round of negotiations of the mandated and built-in agenda of the WTO as well as the issues pushed by the North—investment, competition policy, labour and environment issues, government procurement and trade facilitation (code words for opening up developing-country markets to multinational corporations by removing or diluting procedures that come in the way of transfer pricing and other corporate activities).

In these regional meetings (like the November workshop of African Trade Ministers at Libreville and meetings between ACP countries and the EC, efforts were made to sneak in such formulations to get a new round launched. But these failed. Even the maneuvers at the end of the year concerning the venue of the next Ministerial Qatar or Chile or Geneva (whether a suitable host developing country could use its chairmanship of the meeting to advance the cause of a new round with a broad-based agenda)—seemed related to these.

At the end of the year, while the developing countries barely managed to keep the implementation issues on the table and got a commitment of sorts that these would be pursued in the new year, the majors regrouped and seem set to ensure the developing world in a new round, hoping to sneak in the "new issues" of investment and competition policy as negotiating issues for "plurilateral agreements" and bring labour and environment issues on to the agenda of the WTO "for clarifying" their relation to the WTO system and rules.

The majors, particularly the Europeans and the EU Trade Commissioner, Pascal Lamy, have been saying how they have got the message of the developing countries (at Libreville and the ACP meetings) and were taking steps to meet the concerns of developing countries and win their confidence and support for a new round.

The European Commission itself has formulated its position paper for a new round and submitted it in December to its '133 Committee' in Brussels (so named after the rule in the Rome treaty of the EC, the committee of representatives of the EU members).

Globalisation had succeeded in unifying people from around the world—against globalisation. Factory workers in the United States saw their jobs being threatened by competition from China. Farmers in developing countries saw their jobs being threatened by the highly subsidised corn and other crops from the United States. Workers in Europe saw hard-fought-for job protections being assailed in the name of globalisation. AIDS activists saw new trade agreements raising the prices of drugs to levels that were unaffordable in much of the world. Environmentalists felt that globalisation undermined their decade's long struggle to establish regulations to preserve our natural heritage. Those who wanted to protect and develop their own cultural heritage saw too the intrusions of globalisation.

The current process of globalisation is generating unbalanced outcomes, both between and within countries. Wealth is being created, but too many countries and people are not sharing its benefits. They also have little or no voice in shaping the process. Seen through the eyes of the vast majority of women and men, globalisation has not met their simple and legitimate aspirations for decent jobs and a better future for their children. Many of them live in the limbo of the informal economy without formal rights and in a swathe of poor countries that subsist precariously on the margins of the global economy. Even in economically successful countries, some workers and communities have been adversely affected by globalisation. Meanwhile, the revolution in global communications heightens awareness of these disparities....these global imbalances are morally unacceptable and politically unsustainable.[11]

In short, globalisation may have helped some countries—their GDP, the sum total of the goods and services produced, may have increased—but it had not helped most of the people even in these countries. The worry was that globalisation might be creating rich countries with poor people.

Those who are discontented with economic globalisation generally do not object to the greater access to global markets or to the spread of global knowledge, which allows the developing world to take advantage of the discoveries and innovations made in developed countries. Rather, they raise five concerns:

- The rules of the game that govern globalisation are unfair, specifically designed to benefit the advanced industrial countries. In fact, some countries are actually worse-off.
- Globalisation advances material values over other values, such as a concern for the environment or for life itself.
- The way globalisation has been managed has taken away much of the developing country's sovereignty, and their ability to make decisions themselves in key areas that affect their citizens' well-being. In this sense, it has undermined democracy.
- While the advocates of globalisation have claimed that everyone will benefit economically, there is plenty of evidence from both developing and developed countries that there are many losers in both.
- Perhaps most important, the economic system that has been pressed upon the developing countries—in some cases essentially forced upon them—is inappropriate and often grossly damaging. Globalisation should not mean the Americanisation of either economic policy or culture, but often it does—and that has caused resentment.[12]

There are many forms of market economy—the American model differs from that of the Nordic countries, from the Japanese model, and from the European social model. Even those in developed countries worry the globalisation has been used to advance the "Anglo-American liberal model" over these alternatives—and even if the American model has done well as measured by GDP, it has not done well in many other dimensions, such as the length (and, some would argue, the quality) of life, the eradication of poverty, or even the maintenance of the well-being of those in the middle. Real wages in the United States, especially of those at the bottom, have stagnated for more than a quarter century, and incomes are as high as they are partly because Americans work far longer than their European counterparts. If globalisation is being used to advance the American model of a market economy, many elsewhere are not sure they want it. Those in the developing world have an even stronger complaint—that globalisation has been used to advance a version of market economics that is more extreme, and more reflective of corporate interests, than can be found even in the United States.

IMPACT OF GLOBALISATION ON INDIA

A spectre haunts India, the spectre of stagflation. But if, as appears increasingly true, globalisation has triggered the problem, it also offers a possible consolation: much of the world is perhaps faced with the same fate in the foreseeable future. Certainly, the rest of the South Asia is in the same soup, since food and energy prices world-wide show no signs of falling. Given how much pride we take in India in repeating mistakes of the West and suffering from the same problems, it will perhaps pacify some people to know that "the world" shares our fate.

Stagflation is the name economists give to any economy that is slowing down at a time of rising prices (stagnation plus inflation = stagflation). For the very first time, certainly since 1991, economic growth in India is decelerating just when record inflation is ripping through the budgets of the poor and the salaried classes, giving painful headaches to the ruling coalition in this election year. This is not what economists are typically trained to expect: normally, rising prices with growth and falling unemployment, and fall with recession and rising unemployment. To get both rising inflation and growing unemployment simultaneously was an anomaly even in the West till the oil price shocks of the 1970s.

Galloping inflation in the price of food and energy is a global phenomenon today. As per the latest data released by the Government of India, inflation, according to the wholesale price index, is almost 8% p.a., the highest in four years. (Unlike in other countries the government in India does not ordinarily report the consumer price index.) Retail prices have risen much more. (it is important to remember that services including health and transport are not included in calculations of the inflation rate in India.) More to the point, the rise in price of food is even more serious. The retail price for rice, for instance, has gone up by 20% during the past one year. Certain varieties of pulses have risen by the same proportion. Most disturbingly, edible oils (in which India was self-sufficient decade ago now imports a very large fraction of its need by 40% during the past one year.

Normally, economists confronted with this data on rising prices would expect that the economy was growing rapidly. But of late, the Indian growth engine seems to have slowed down quite dramatically, as well as, raising fears of stagflation. Recently released data indicates that the industrial production increased by 3% between March 2007—and March 2008. (In the corresponding period before March 2007, the rate of industrial growth was as high as 14.8%). The slowdown in the capital goods sector always warning signal since it indicates business expectations most accurately—has been dramatic: from 16.3% during 2006-07 to 2.1% in 2007-08.

Almost equally portentously, the consumer durables sector had been growing at 5.3% in 2007-08. Finally, there is a perceptible fall in the rate of growth of all the key infrastructure industries, including coal, electricity and petroleum refinery products. Little wonder that *The Economic Times* carried the headline recently: "Industrial engine misfires on manufacturing defect."[13] The Finance Minister's repeated reassurances that "the India growth story is here to stay" have an increasingly hollow ring about them.

Food Crisis

(i) The inflation in food prices around the world has been unprecedented in at least a generation. The prices of wheat, rice, corn and other major food items have doubled or even tripled over the past few yeas. What lies behind the food crisis?

(ii) *Significant change in demand*: Firstly, there is significant change in the demand side of the world market. The middle class has grown in emerging economies, especially China and India, adding to the number of people in a position to demand meat. It takes about 700 calories of grain-feed to generate 100 calories of beef. So, the rise in the demand for meat has put pressure on grain supplies. American-style diets are taking their toll. But the global middle class has been growing for at least a decade, whereas most of the rise in prices has transpired only during the past few years.

(iii) *Rapid increase in oil price*: The rapid increase in the price of oil has to be considered in any explanation for the inflation in food prices. This has resulted in pushing up both the cost of production (through costlier inputs such as fertilizer) and the cost of transport.

(iv) *Bad weather*: The third significant factor that has to be noted in an experimentation of the food price rise is the run of bad weather that has come to many parts of the world in a time of rapid climate change. Australia, one of the largest wheat exporters in the world, has had a succession of bad harvests.

(v) *Bio-fuel*: Fourthly, Bush administration's decision to aggressively push bio-fuels since 2006 is seen by many to be perhaps the main trigger for the recent rise in food prices. The US government started giving subsidies to farms for growing corn for the purposes of making ethanol for use in automobiles. The aim was to reduce dependence on West Asian oil as much as to reduce carbon emissions. The side-effect was to raise corn prices, making farmers plant more corn and, as a consequence, less soya and wheat. The final effect was a surge in the price of all grains worldwide, since more than 20% of American corn fields were reallocated for the purpose. Apart from the fact that fuel for the poor, it turns out that producing a gallon of ethanol from corn uses most of the energy that the gallon contains.

(vi) *20 years of mistakes*: "We are paying for 20 years of mistakes. Nothing was done to prevent speculation on raw materials, though it was predictable that investors would turn to these markets following the stock market slowdown."[14]

(vii) *Multinational agri-business*: Moreover, world food prices are being controlled and manipulated more and more by a handful of powerful grain traders operating through centralised institutions like Chicago Board of Trade. A recent UN report has highlighted that thanks to the lobbying efforts of multinational agribusinesses and the aggressive conditionality applied by Washington's IMF and the World Bank on poor countries (including India), "In the last two or three decades, there had been a significant increase in the concentration of power of multinational agro-businesses that had come to dominate not only marketing and consumption, but also the production and supply of food inputs. That problem was being exacerbated because of the strengthening of the intellectual property rights and the extension of those rights to cover agricultural inputs. The consequences had largely been at the expense of small farmers and consumers, especially the poor."

(viii) *Polices of WB, IMF, WTO*: One must notice the method in madness: it is no coincidence that food is being taken away from the plates of the world's poor. It is the natural side-effect of the policy-package imposed on the poor nations by the triumvirate of the IMF, the World Bank and the WTO who have been spearheading corporate globalisation over the past two decades since the end of the Cold War. In order to secure the business and financial interests of Western corporations, they have aggressively pushed a set of policies on poor countries which are inimical to the interests of the latter.

Inequality and Poverty

ILO Report, in a very forthright manner, states: "Income inequality has increased in some industrialised countries, reflected in an increase in the share of the capital in national income as well as an increase in wage inequality between mid-1980s and the mid-1990s."[15]

The widening inequality has been the result of the very high compensation (salaries and perks) paid by MNEs, the development of new businesses with a global reach and global "superstardoms." The public perception is that globalisation has resulted in high degree of concentration of wealth. But all this wealth has not benefited the world because of its globalisation, that is, concentration among a few nations and the abject deprivation of the vast majority.

The peoples of the world have never been as divided in their standards of living in the entire history of the human race as today. Globalisation has produced more inequality than ever before. The assets of the three richest countries in the world today are greater than the combined GNP of the 48 least-developed countries.

The rich countries enjoy 60% of the world's GNP but have only 15% of the world population. The gap between the world's richest and poorest countries has doubled in the last 50 years.

World poverty is escalating, as is too unemployment with one-third of the world's labour force being unemployed or underemployed. Added to this, the southern non-European countries are heavily indebted to the northern European, through loans their leaders were seduced into taking. While the initial capital on the loans have been paid several times over, the interest payment continues ad nauseam and international calls to cancel these unfair debts continue to be ignored, the USA being the main obstacle. In practically every case, there is pressure on the creditors to give priority to servicing their debts at the cost of such primary needs as education, health and welfare.

Poverty is not the problem in the Third World alone; even within rich countries, the poor are getting poorer and the rich richer. In the USA, the income of the poorest 20% has steadily declined since the 1970s while that of the rich 20% has increased by 15% and the top 1% percent by more than 100%. Mikhail Gorbachev sums up this situation as a failure, once again, of world leaders to learn from the errors of the past. "We had indeed a truly big opportunity resulting from the ending of the Cold War and stopping the confrontation between the military blocs... In my assessment, we were not able to use these opportunities in a proper way, and I am using very mild wording here. Resources freed from fuelling the arms race could have been used against poverty, underdevelopment, and diseases in the vast regions of the world where the bulk of the world population is concentrated."[16]

Globalisation continues because of its success at money-making, but even this is not true. George Soros informs us that it is not the wealth-producing factory it is made out to be. He tells us: "Global financial markets are inherently unstable."[17] So, apart from its enormous potential for plaguing the world with every conceivable misery, globalisation is not even the wealth-churning wizard it is made out to be.

Human Rights

Globalisation, far from promoting human rights, actually creates conditions for their violation. Soros states: "Free competition creates and reinforces inequalities both on the national and the international level and collective interests ranging from the preservation of peace to the protection of human rights and the environment receive shot shrift."[18]

He correctly observes "capitalism and political freedom do not necessarily go hand in hand. Capitalism is very successful in creating wealth but it does not assure freedom, social justice and the rule of law; it is not designed to safeguard universal principles" and concludes, "While we can speak of the triumph of capitalism, we cannot yet speak of the triumph of democracy. If we care about universal values such as freedom and democracy, we cannot leave them to the care of market forces."

Nonetheless, he is concerned and asks, "How can the needs of a global society be reconciled with the sovereignty of states?" He correctly observes that the United Nations "is ill-suited to safeguard universal principles because it is subject to the whims of its members."

He proposes the international rule of law which, he states, could work with the help of civil society. "It may be true that States have no principles, but democratic States are responsive to the wishes of their citizens. If the citizens have principles, they can impose them on their governments. That is why we need the active engagement of civil society in support of international law."[19]

This is the Gandhian solution, Satyagraha, of civil society which is already manifesting itself in the campaigns against globalisation. This campaign is becoming internationalised as the poor, joined by the conscience-stricken members of the First World, unite to bring down parasitic globalisation through sheer soul force. Globalisation creates wealth, it does not distribute it. It hoards it, as power, to dominate and destroy those who stand in its path. Our evolution has become warped and appeared to be reverting to the beast. One is barely recognisable as the human as we were in pre-capitalist times.

The USA dominates the global economic process; American foreign policy is committed to maintaining that dominance, and has done so hitherto through violence. What is the difference between an attack by terrorists which leaves death and destruction, and an attack by a well-heeled, uniformed army which leaves death and destruction?

Environmental Destruction

The world's high consumers are also the world's high destroyers of our natural resources. They are responsible for our current environmental crisis, which, apart from the depletion of forests and pollution of rivers, impoverishment of soils through the dumping of pesticides and fertilisers (banned in the West), on the unsuspecting for huge profits, are threatening such calamities as ozone depletion and global warming which threaten to melt the ice caps and submerge coastal cities and cause massive displacements of populations on scales never known before. This in turn can result in new waves of racial, ethnic and political problems worse than anything we have yet experienced; all so that a few may profit.

The neo-liberals are so obsessed with immediate gains that they do not even care if they denude the universe and leave nothing, even for their own biological heirs. It refers to the dominance of some nations over others by means of unequal conditions of economic exchange.

The USA is the most serious global polluter but it refuses to reduce its carbon emissions to the limits set by the Kyoto Protocol and has actually increased it in her greedy pursuit of capital and her determination to be the world's leader regardless of the fact that it is a Satanic leadership.

Domination through Ideas

Ultimately, we are dominated through ideas and ideas emanating from the West have insinuated themselves into the rest of the world in the last one-and-a-half centuries, through colonisation, and now far more massively and intrusively through globalisation.

Humans are not born with instincts, one responds to ideas and the ideas are constituted into material "realities." Like the architect who draws a plan and executes it into a Taj Mahal or the Empire State Building, so ideas are constituted into social, economic and religious institutions. One is susceptible to the ideas of those who have dominion over us. As colonised people, one grew ashamed of one's own ideas, ideas enunciated by one's own seers and philosophers, we suppressed them, devalued them, short of throwing them into the refuse bin, and took on the ideas of our colonisers. In Africa, we suppressed our traditional beliefs that linked us to our fellow-beings and to nature and God. We have become creatures of capitalism and communism. We accepted the notion that these "isms" define the truth of our existence. But basically, we accepted them because they came from our dominators, the successful colonisers, the masters of the First World. We became focused on the here and the now, on the material, the evidential. However, more convincing, more comforting, our own ideas, drawn from our own traditions, our own antiquities, we abandoned them for the foreign and European. We need to retrace our steps and recover our moral systems; we need to resurrect God whom they effectively killed yet again in the 1970's and recover Him/Her, so that our social systems are answerable to the Divine as they are intended to be, and not to vicissitudes of the market.

Justifying Exploitation

The exploiters, on their part, having killed God, have produced their own theodicies to sanctify their exploitation. The Protestant Ethic turned the Gospel upside down and the poor from being celebrated became damned, their poverty a sign of their damnation: the wealthy from being damned became saved, their wealth being a sign of their election to God's grace. The Darwinian thesis of the survival of the fittest, pits humans in a war of destructive competition in which only the best survive (the global gobblers being the best), and merit the fruits of the earth. The rest, the masses, the failures, the poor are the wretched of the earth deserving of their wretchedness.

Both theories justify colonialism and colonial exploitation. They not only salve the conscience of the rich and the powerful, but legitimate their exploitation with "evidence" that they were "naturally" selected or "divinely" selected to dominate and appropriate the resources of the colonised world which were wasted on them since they did not know how to use them. In both theodicies, the poor are the refuse of the earth, unworthy and justifiably marginalised.

Divisions

These theories developed in the west divide humanity and in that division, breed inequality, violence, and the preying of the strong on the weak. Marx contributes his own divisive thesis, the irresolvable conflict between classes, between capital and labour, the dominance of the one depending on the elimination of the other.

Not only do these theories divide people from each other, they also divide the person against him or herself. Capitalism has no use for the soul; it rips it out of the body and discards it as useless, as indeed it is to capitalism. Not being material, it is unexploitable! The body consumes, and it can be manipulated to have an insatiable appetite. It will consume everything the neo-capitalists invent and put on the market. The body is the market. The multi-nationals clothe it, feed it, take it on holidays, inject it with drugs, clean it with ever new brands of soaps, toothpastes and shampoos and seduce it with scents and cosmetics; they tempt it with millions of ever changing newer products—the market is endless.

One tolerates the excesses of the immoral, inhuman, ruthlessly exploitative globalisation because we are bamboozled into believing that there is no alternative. "This is the only way. You can't fight it as if globalisation is a God-given natural truth like the law of gravity and we are inherently controlled by it." One submits to the tyranny of globalisation, despite the fact that one know better, being heirs to the God-inspired truths communicated to him through generations of Prophets. One accepts the Adam Smith doctrine that the human is impelled by self-interest, and is naturally selfish and self-oriented, and society is the construct of selfish interests.[20] One does so despite one's theological teachings that the human being is fashioned in the image of God, that he pursues God and goodness.

EFFECT OF GLOBALISATION ON THIRD WORLD

Globalisation is not divinely ordained but a product of human society and has no *a priori* existence independent of structures human kind has put in place, nor are its basic tenets foreclosed from negotiation, two human rights jurists have said in a progress report to the UN Sub-Commission on the Promotion and Protection of Human Rights.

Globalisation is not simply an issue of economics but very much a political phenomenon, with its process taking place in the context of increased social tension and political discordance, says, Joseph Oloka-Onygano of Uganda, expert member, of the Sub-Commission, and Deepika Udagama, alternate expert from Sri Lanka.

In sum, globalisation is the economic integration of the globe. But exactly what is "integration?." Integration is the act of combining separate albeit related units into a single whole. Since there can be only one whole, it follows that global economic integration logically implies national economic disintegration—parts are torn out of their national context (disintegration), in order to be re-integrated into the new whole, the globalised economy. As the saying goes, to make an omlette you have to break eggs. The disintegration of the national egg is necessary to integrate the global logic as well as the cost of disintegration, is frequently met with denial.

Mr. Wolfensohn, President of the World Bank told the audience at the Aspen Institute's Conference in August 2000 that 'Globalisation is a practical methodology for empowering the poor to improve their lives.'[21] That is a wish, not a definition. It also lies in the face of the real consequences of global economic integration.

A few consequences of globalisation, of the erasure of national boundaries for economic purposes, include the following in brief:

1. Standards, lowering competition to externalize social and environmental costs to achieve a competitive advantage the race to the bottom in terms of both efficiency in cost accounting and equity in income distribution;
2. increased tolerance of mergers and monopoly power in domestic markets in order to be big enough to compete internationally;
3. More intense national specialisation according to the dictates of competitive advantage with the

consequence of reducing the range of choice of ways to earn a livelihood, and increasing dependence on other countries. Free trade negates the freedom not to trade; and

4. world-wide enforcement of a muddled and self-serving doctrine of 'trade-related intellectual property rights.'

Let us look at each of these in a bit more detail—

1. Globalisation undercuts the ability of a nation to internalize environmental and social costs of production into its prices to get a competitive advantage in international trade. More of world production shifts to countries that do the poorest job of counting costs—a sure recipe for reducing the efficiency of global production.
2. Fostering global competitive advantage used as an excuse for tolerance of corporate mergers and monopoly in national markets. It is ironic that this is done in the name of deregulation and the free market.

   More and more resources are allocated by within-firm central planning, and less by between-firm market relationships. And this is hailed as a victory for markets. It is no such thing. It is a victory for corporations relative to national governments.
3. Free trade and free capital mobility increase pressures for specialisation according to competitive (absolute) advantage. Therefore, the range of choice of ways to earn a livelihood becomes greatly narrowed.

   In Uruguay, for example, everyone would have to be either a shepherd or a cowboy in conformity with the dictates of competitive advantage in the global market. Everything else should be imported in exchange for beef, mutton, wool and leather.
4. Of all things, knowledge is that which should be most freely shared, because in sharing it is

> multiplied rather than divided. Yet, our trade theorists, have rejected Thomas Jefferson's dictum that 'Knowledge is the common property of mankind' in exchange for a muddled doctrine of 'trade-related intellectual property rights' by which they are willing to grant private corporations monopoly ownership of the very basis itself patents on seeds and knowledge of basic genetic structures.

Once knowledge exists, its proper allocative price is the marginal opportunity cost of sharing it, which is close to zero, since nothing is lost by sharing it. This is not to say that we should abolish all intellectual property rights—that would create more problems than it would solve. But we should certainly begin restricting the domain and length of patent monopolies rather than increasing them so rapidly and recklessly.

Only, a few years ago, 'globalisation' seemed to be, an inevitable process that no one should challenge, or else risk being labelled old-fashioned reactionary and unrealistic.

There was a consensus at the top levels of the global elite, especially at the secretariats of the international financial agencies (the IMF and World Bank) and the World Trade Organisation (and the governments of rich countries), that globalisation is good for all and that those who did not join in would miss the train.

What they meant by globalisation was a policy prescription that all countries, big or small, rich or poor, should open up their borders to the free flow of money, capital, good and services. Countries should no longer protect their local firms, banks, farms or money markets from the inflow of investment or speculative funds, from cheaper imports or bigger foreign enterprises.

The infusion of foreign money, goods, services and companies, would fuel growth, inject efficiency, and help poor countries take-off, so the argument went. However, most developing countries that undertook this process did not improve. Foreign credit that went in led instead to a debt crisis. Cheaper imports, displaced local goods and industries.

On the export side, the situation was equally bad. Prices of commodities sold by developing countries slumped. And markets of the North remained closed for products (such as textiles and agricultural goods) the poorer countries are good at producing.

The result was a widening trade deficit in many developing countries, leading them into further debt, and curbing their development. Only a few developing countries, mainly of East Asia, seemed to escape this no-growth or low-growth trap. They were held up as models of growth led by exports and foreign investment, two of the instruments of globalisation.

But even some of them succumbed to one aspect of globalisation. The liberalisation of finance and financial markets led to a rapid build-up of short-term private foreign debt. It also enabled speculation of the local currencies and stock markets by foreign financial institutions such as hedge funds.

Rodrik, Professor of International Political Economy at the John F. Kennedy School of Government (Harvard University) and coordinator of the research programme of the Group of 24 (the developing-country group at the IMF/World Bank institutions), decries the perversion of priorities in the remarkable consensus on the imperative of global integration which he calls "the Refurbished Washington Consensus."[22]

Rodrik notes that foreign trade and investment have now become the ultimate yardsticks for evaluating actions of governments, including in relation to crime and violence, and shows the perversion of priorities behind the consensus on imperatives of global integration. Openness to trade and investment is no longer viewed simply as a component of a country's development policies, but has "mutated into the most potent catalyst" for economic growth. This 'faith' has spread from a handful of proselytising academic economists to world leaders and policy-makers of all stripes, and is incessantly repeated by senior officials of the WTO, IMF and other international agencies as the surest way to achieve economic growth and poverty alleviation.

Insertion into the world economy is no longer a matter simply of removing trade and investment barriers, but involves a long list of admission requirements, "ranging from patent rules to banking standards." The apostles of economic integration prescribe institutional reforms that took today's advanced industrial economies "generations to accomplish."

"Global integration," Rodrik comments, "has become, for all practical purposes, a substitute for development strategy," and this is bad news for the world's poor. However, the new agenda is built on "shaky empirical ground" and is seriously distorting the priorities of policy-makers. Compliance with these prescriptions would divert human resources, administrative capabilities and political capital of countries away from the more urgent development priorities such as education, public health, industrial capacity and social cohesion. It also undermines nascent democratic institutions by removing choice of development strategy from public debate.

Globalisation, Rodrik stresses, is not a shortcut to development. Successful development strategies require a judicious blend of imported practices with domestic institutional innovations, and a domestic growth strategy relying on domestic investors and domestic institutions.[23]

The "integrationist faith" is crowding out serious thinking and efforts along these lines. And reality has not been kind to the faith. Despite sharply lowered barriers to trade and investment, scores of Latin American and African countries are stagnating or growing less rapidly than in the heydays of import substitution; the fastest-growing economies are those of East and South-East Asia, mainly China and India, all of whom espoused trade and investment liberalisation but did so in an unorthodox manner gradually and sequentially, and after an initial period of high growth. But the disappointing outcomes of deep liberalisation have been "absorbed into the faith with the aplomb", with global integration presented as requiring more than throwing borders open, with a full complement of institutional reforms being prescribed.

According to the World Bank economists, successful liberalisation requires a whole laundry list: tax reforms, social safety nets, administrative reforms (to bring trade policy into conformity with the WTO), institutional innovations to enhance credibility on permanence of reforms, labour market reforms for labour mobility, technological assistance to upgrade firms hit by imports, and training programmes to ensure availability of skilled workers for export-oriented firms and investors. And if benefits of trade liberalisation fail to materialize, the prerequisites keep expanding; for example, Britain's Development Minister Clare Short recently added "universal provision of health and education" to the list.

In the financial arena, complementary reforms have been pushed with greater fanfare. Viewing the Asian financial crises as caused primarily by weaknesses in prudential regulation, corporate governance and bankruptcy procedures, the Group of Seven (G-7) leading industrial nations are trying to establish international codes and standards on fiscal transparency, monetary and financial policy, banking supervision, data dissemination, corporate governance and accounting standards. Twelve of these standards have been prescribed by the Financial Stability Forum (created by the G-7) as the key for sound financial systems in developing countries—the FSF's own compendium has 52 standards, raising the total to 64—the primary motive being to make integration of developing countries into global markets safe, "safe for themselves and other emerging markets."[24]

Considering how demanding the prerequisites are, one might wonder whether the point of all this "is not to provide easy cover for eventual failure"—blaming 'slippage' in implementation is more convenient than pointing to poorly designed liberalisation. If Bangladesh trade reforms do not produce a large enough spurt in growth, the World Bank concludes it is due to lagging reforms in public administration or political uncertainty. And if Argentina is caught up in a confidence crisis, the IMF blames inadequate structural reforms and advocates deepening them! Most of the institutional reforms, Rodrik agrees, are sensible ones; in a world without financial, administrative or political constraints, there could be little argument on the need to adopt them. But in the real world of scarce resources on all three fronts, choices have to be made and, from the perspective of insertion into the global economy, the choices have real opportunity costs.

In each area of the prerequisites for integration, the "globalisation-above-all" crowds out the "more development-friendly." Many institutional reforms may be desirable, but their priorities do not coincide with priorities for a more full development agenda.

The Asian experience shows that a sound development strategy producing sustained growth over the medium to long-term is far more effective for achieving integration than freeing up trade and investment and waiting for it to work its magic. The frequent incantation that economic salvation lies in greater integration with the world economy is "both misleading and hollow." In any event, integration into the world economy is not something policy-makers control directly. Asking countries to increase their participation in world trade is as meaningful and helpful as asking them to improve their technological capabilities.

The resulting financial crisis of 1997-99, which also spread to Russia, Brazil and other countries, seriously damaged the image and reputation of globalisation.

In the developed countries, meanwhile, increasing numbers of people felt insecure with the intense competition engendered by globalisation. The drive for companies and countries to compete, so intrinsic in the global market economy, meant that social and environmental considerations were sidelined whilst the demands of the big corporations were given top priority.

THE FIRST WAVE OF GLOBALISATION

Our Common Colonial Experience

One is familiar with colonialism. The dates may have varied; the colonising country may have been different; but the main features of common colonial experience were basically the same. Using superior military technology, the colonising power forcibly imposed its rule over the peoples, at great cost to us in terms of human lives and suffering and in terms of human and natural ecology.

Military conquest was very often preceded—and most certainly followed—by the imposition of new religions and cultures, which facilitated subjugation by dulling the impulse to resist the clutches. The effects of such cultural implantation on our minds have lingered on and continued to do their damage, keeping us in mental bondage long after the last colonising soldier had left our soil. Soon, the colonial mind started to take for real the masks worn by the colonizers and the words they used to deceive their victims, such as "we bring you Christianity"; "we bring you civilisation", "we will teach you democracy";, etc. As soon as resistance was quelled, the colonising power set-up a colonial administration, run at lower levels by people culled from local elites, many of whom decided to work hand-in-hand with their colonial masters to preserve their wealth and privileges.

As the colonial bureaucracy was put in place, the process of drawing out our wealth then began. Over the centuries, the colonising powers enriched themselves immeasurably by drawing human and natural resources from our lands—human slaves, indentured labour, tributes, precious metal and other mineral, logs and lumber, colonial crops cultivated on seized indigenous land, and so on. At the very foundations of the richest countries of today, are the broken remains of our own ancestors and the wealth plundered from their communities.[25]

The colonizers brought with them the practices of plantation agriculture, large-scale logging, large-scale mining, and unsustainable technologies, which were meant for plunder and for maximising exploitation and profits. These unsustainable practices replaced the sustainable indigenous practices our pre-colonial peoples had relied on for centuries.

The impact on the people and their communities was grievous. We lost our right to self-determination and our freedom. We lost our wealth through colonial plunder. Our best lands were seized for colonial tillage. Indigenous communities lost their rights to their lands. The impact on the people and their communities was grievous. The impact on nature was equally disastrous. Colonial occupation was invariably marked with plunder of our natural resources and the introduction of monoculture in direct contrast to the much more sustainable culture and ecological practices of our pre-colonial past.

During this period, the colonial powers that took over

the globe were mercantilist and, later, early industrial powers. Often operating their own State monopoly corporations, they scoured the globe in search of slaves, tradable goods or raw materials, and bases for their colonial operations.

This period of colonialism may be called the first wave of Globalisation.

Range of Anti-Colonial Responses

Where independence was won by arms in China, for example- the colonial economic and political interests had to beat a full retreat. They lost their territorial rights and their businesses, their properties confiscated and nationalised. Where independence was 'granted' to a local elite which had been trained by their colonial masters, the latter still had to put up with some nationalist efforts by locals to regain control of their economy. These took the form of foreign ownership limits, profit remittances restrictions, local content requirements, exports quotas, and other attempts to regulate foreign businesses.

The Corporate Counter-response

During this post-colonial period, the role of global capital expanded, partly due to internal developments in their home countries, and partly as a counter-response to independence movements and economic nationalism. Having lost direct control over their colonies, global capital sought and became better at indirect control; military aggression was replaced by cultural aggression and economic control. By this time, internal developments within the colonising powers themselves had prepared their economies for this shift: many of them had reached the late industrial stage development. Huge private corporations in partnership with governments had accumulated vast amounts of financial wealth, turning money itself into a major commodity. These corporations needed new markets and investment areas, rather than colonial territories that were becoming more and more difficult and costly to retain politically and militarily.

We are also familiar with these post-colonial developments.

Again, they masked their real intention of drawing

wealth from our lands and communities with such pretexts as: "we bring jobs"; "we bring technology"; "we will lend you money for development"; we will protect you from communism"; and so on.

Instead of relying on military conquest, these global corporations worked closely with elite-led governments, particularly those local classes whose economic interests coincided closely with their former masters. Often, the local police and armed forces were flooded with aid, to win their loyalty and service.

The post-colonial bottom line was no different: the extraction of wealth. This occurred through unequal trade (depressed prices for our agricultural commodities, monopolistic prices for their industrial manufactures); high interest rates on foreign loans; using loan conditionalities to exact further concessions, quick and massive profit repatriation; and low wages. By retaining post-colonial dominance and control in the economic and cultural spheres, post-colonial wealth extraction could proceed unabated.

Chemical agriculture was introduced to intensify the production of export crops, widespread poisoning and damage in the countryside. Exploitation of our natural resources intensified, and energy generation projects such as huge dams, coal and oil plants, and nuclear plants in some cases ravaged the countryside.

The development of a nationwide mass media infrastructure served to further strengthen the colonial hold on local minds, to create and expand markets, and to ensure a friendly environment for foreign investments and foreign products.

THE SECOND WAVE OF GLOBALISATION

This post-colonial wave may be called the second wave of Globalisation, where industrial countries and global corporations would range across the globe for investment areas, industrial markets, trading partners, and sources of cheap labour and raw materials.

This wave has gone through several phases, reflecting the progress of an unequal contest between powerful countries strengthened by the immense wealth they had drawn from colonial victims on the one hand, and the newly-independent nations weakened by centuries of plunder and exploitation on the other hand.

The early-independence phase was often marked by intense economic nationalism, as local economic interests tried to mobilize their government to enhance their economic sovereignty while global corporate interest sought to retain their colonial privileges. This phase saw the adoption of economic protectionist measures meant to strengthen local capital *vis-a-vis* foreign capital.

The second phase saw a succession of crises—that included the oil shocks of the 70s, the debt crises of the 80s, the socialist crises of the early 90s, and the financial crises of the late 90s,—which is still going on. Socialism had earlier provided a counter-balance to global corporations and their governments, as well as a possible alternative path for independence movements. These crises weakened the capacity, the will, and the overall position of the former colonies and enabled global corporations to launch major counterattacks in order to regain much of the colonial power and privileges they had lost during the economic-nationalist phase.

The post-colonial counterattacks by global corporations mark the third phase of this second wave. Many countries, despite having freed themselves from centuries of colonial rule, lost much of their economic sovereignty to corporate-controlled international institutions such as the International Monetary Fund (IMF), the World Bank (WB) and the World Trade Organisation (WTO). Through loan conditionalities, structural adjustment programmes, and other means, many nationalist laws and provisions gained by earlier anti-colonial independence movements were undermined and dismantled. Some authors, Chakravarty, Raghavan, for example, have called this phase a process of "recolonisation", a return of colonial privileges for global corporations.

The impact of this wave of Globalisation is no less destructive than the colonialism that preceded it. Our agricultural products consistently suffed from low prices; our workers from low wages. We are losing much of our capital due to profit repatriation and the debt crisis; chemical farming is taking away our food security and putting it in the hands of global chemical and seed conglomerates. We enjoy national sovereignty only in name. We are suffering from widespread ecological disasters, triggered by intensive resource extraction, disruptive energy projects, and toxic pollution. Our forests, mines and quarries are being quickly depleted; our air, water and soil got heavily contaminated; and pervasive monoculture is seriously threatening our biodiversity.

This part of our history and current events should also be familiar to most of us.

ALERT: THE THIRD WAVE IS COMING

We are still in the midst of the second wave of Globalisation, yet a third one has already emerged. The third wave of Globalisation began to be felt worldwide in the last half of the 1990s and is expressing its overwhelming presence in full force at the dawn of the 21st century. This looming third wave is the global information economy.

Like the first two waves, the third Globalisation wave arose from internal developments within the hearts of the global powers. It is important to look critically at these internal developments, because they will, as in the past, eventually impinge on the rest of the world, including our own often shaping our destinies and steering our development in directions we never wanted to take.

The colonial power were mercantilist and, later, industrial countries in their early expansionist stages. The postcolonial powers were industrial countries in their late stage, when capitalism had developed further, combining industrial advancement and finance capital into huge monopolistic conglomerates in continual search for new acquisitions, sources of cheap raw materials and labour, and markets. The third wave of Globalisation is marked by the emergence and eventual dominance, within the most advanced industrial countries, of the information sector—the sector that produces, manipulates, processes, distributes and markets information products.

A GLOBAL INFORMATION ECONOMY

The increasing dominance of the information sector in what had been industrial economies is turning them into information economies. These emerging information economics principally the U.S. and to lesser extent some countries of Europe are at the core of the third wave of Globalisation. Because of the way these economies are so closely interconnected, they are better seen as a single emerging global information economy. The Internet is perhaps the most visible portion of this economy and certainly the one which has received the most media attention. This emerging global information economy includes the global infrastructure for telecommunications, data exchange, media and entertainment; the knowledge industries; the publishing industries; the computer hardware and software industries; the emerging financial systems that will support online transaction; the emerging global legal infrastructure based on the WTO, compliances including the GATT and the further agreements in information technology, telecommunications and financial services; and the biotechnology and genetic engineering industries.

Unlike the first two waves, the implications and consequences of the global information economy are an unfamiliar phenomenon to most of us. There are so many new things, so many new possibilities, that it is quite difficult of separating the chaff from the grain, the hype from the substance.

Let us understand it.

Information: A Closer Look

The cost of reproducing information what the economist calls its marginal cost is very low and oftentimes approaches zero. In the last analysis, this feature is due to the very essence of information itself. Information is non-material in its essence—a numeric measure of the uncertainty which it resolves. The non-materiality of information is the basis of its low reproduction cost, which may be driven lower and lower by adopting representations that can be manipulated at lower cost. With today's digital representations, the costs of reproducing and distributing information have reached historic lows as low as the cost of copying a diskette or downloading a file from an online server.

Low Marginal Cost Leads to Sharing

The low marginal cost of information has two major implications: one for those who use it and another for those who sell it. For users, it encourages sharing. Many cultures, in fact, see knowledge as social wealth, a collective asset that is meant to be shared.

These cultures—including most Third World and indigenous cultures—are, therefore, in close harmony with the very nature of information. When we share software, for example, we are only being true to the nature of information and to our own cultures.

But there are other cultures, where private property concepts have become more absolute and where almost everything may be commodified. In these cultures often with capitalism at their core information has become an object of co-modification and privatisation. Culture itself has become co modified, together with knowledge and life. They have become vehicles for profit-making.

Profit-making Mechanism: The Monopoly

Let us look more closely at the mechanism of profit-making through information. First, the seller turns information from a collective asset into private property. Then, copies are sold on the market, at prices set by the "owner"/seller. The near zero marginal cost of reproducing information now makes its selling price nearly pure profit. A diskette of software that may be copied for cents is sold for fifty dollars. A CDROM that my be reproduced for three dollars is sold for three hundred.

To realize these extremely high profit margins made possible by the low marginal cost of information products, however, the seller must create an artificial scarcity of the product. We have seen that information can now be easily copied by users themselves at practically no cost, creating a natural abundance which drives prices down. To keep prices and profit margins high, this natural abundance that proceeds from the essence of information itself must be prevented. The seller does it by essentially prohibiting sharing among users and acquiring from the State a monopoly in using and making copies of the information product. This creates the artificial scarcity that drives prices up and realizes for the seller the potential profits from high margins.

It is monopoly that creates the scarcity. Such monopolies are euphemistically known as Intellectual Property Rights (IPR), the main form of ownership in an information economy. They are the mechanisms for maintaining the high profit margins of those who control and sell information products. IPRs have two major forms: copyrights (historically, limited monopolies covering literary materials), and patents (historically, limited monopolies covering inventions). In recent years, as the information sector gained momentum increased it political and economic power, IPRs have been strengthened and extended to new areas.

IPRs are, in reality, statutory monopolies. They are monopolies over information, granted through statutes, by the State. Those who control information through IPR are basically rentiers: they make money by charging monopoly rents from users, who are threatened by State action should they continue to practice information sharing. (impiniging upon IPR like copy Right)

Conflicts within the Information Economy

Still, enforcing information monopolies is not simple. After all, information monopolies are incompatible with the social nature of information. The deeply-ingrained cultural habits of information sharing and exchange continue to assert themselves, regardless of the will of monopolists and their State protectors.

This is the dilemma within the emerging global information economy. On the one hand, information itself is a highly social good; on the other hand, the forms of ownership are highly monopolistic. On the one hand, users tend to share information goods; on the other hand, IPR holders insist on their monopolies. On the one hand, developing countries need the widest access to various technology options at the least cost; on the other hand, rich and powerful information economies control almost 90% of all the IPRs in the world today, and want to increase or tighten their control further.

The basic conflict within the information sector is the incompatibility between the highly monopolistic forms of information ownership and the social nature of information. This conflict is also expressed between users who want to share information freely and monopoly claimants who want to prevent free sharing of information. It is further reflected in the conflict between developing countries who need low-cost access to major bodies of information and information economies which have established virtual monopolies over information. Historically, these information economies are basically the same colonial powers that have exploited developing countries over the centuries.

The socialising tendency emanates from the nature of information itself, and can, therefore, never be suppressed. The monopolising tendency emanates from the potentially high profit margins in selling information and the economic and political power concentrated in information monopolies. The conflicts arising from these two opposing tendencies will drive the historical development of the third wave of Globalisation.

Internal Engine

Within the U.S., the high profit margins in the information sector is attracting more investment capital towards this sector, away from the agricultural and industrial sectors. This is the internal engine that is slowly transforming the U.S. economy into-an information economy.

Within the emerging global information economy itself, monopoly concepts are already well-established and are even expanding their coverage. One item, for instance, is always non-negotiable in the U.S. diplomatic agenda: Intellectual Property Rights (IPR). These concepts are increasingly dominating international legal system through bilateral negotiations with the U.S. and through the World Trade Organisation (WTO). Thus, worldwide pressure is increasing on countries with non-monopolistic attitudes towards information to adopt the same U.S. legal system that strictly protects IPRs.

However, the social nature of information continually asserts itself. Information abundance created through user sharing and exchange keeps breaking through the artificial scarcity created by information monopolies. The latest releases of population software, songs or video immediately find themselves being copied in every comer of the globe. In effect, information automatically globalizes itself regardless of the will of those who insist in monopolising them. Ironically, information monopolists find their products better distributed in those parts of the globe where they could not enforce their monopoly. They therefore insist on imposing monopolistic legal systems upon the rest of the globe, so they can realize the same profit margins they enjoy in their monopoly areas. Even one country that refuses to be part of this global legal system will pose a threat to their global monopoly, thus they will exert every effort to bring it in. These monopolists will never leave any country or any community alone.

They are the real engines of Globalisation's Third Wave.

This is also what makes the information sector qualitatively different from the industrial and agricultural sectors. It justifies why the emergence of the global information economy must be considered a distinct wave in itself, instead of simply a part of the second wave of Globalisation.

The richest man in the world, as were several others among the ten richest, is a cyberlord. The economic powers of cyberlords are immense, and these powers are increasingly being felt in the political and diplomatic arena. Among U.S. negotiators, for instance, IPR—the mechanism which gives software cyberlords their power—is invariably a non-negotiable item in their agenda. It is the partnership among the information cyberlords, industrial cyberlords, and Finance capitalists which is at the core, the third wave of Globalisation.

TO SUM UP

An information economy is one information sector which has become the main source of wealth, eclipsing the earlier and still dominating criteal industrial and agricultural sectors. The products of industrial and agricultural economies are material goods; the products of an information economy, however, are non-material goods. The reproduction cost of information goods is very low. This has led to the widespread social practice of freely sharing and exchanging information. On the other hand, it also promises extremely high profit margins, if the seller can monopolize information. Information monopolies have become the main form of ownership in the information sector. The high profit margins that they realize have led to a continuous movement of investment capital towards the information sector, eventually making it the most dominant sector of the economy and transforming the economy into an information economy. The products of this information economy spread worldwide, as people freely share and exchange information goods.

Thus as information economy needs a global system for enforcing its monopolies as well as for gathering information materials, tapping intellectuals and, of course, collecting payments worldwide. This leads to the Globalisation of the information economy and is the engine of the third wave of Globalisation. The main propertied classes within the information cyber lords, who control information content, are industrial cyber lords, who control information infrastructures, and finance capitalists, who control investment funds.

The present situation of economic imbalance is generally due to evolution of institutions, which are one-sided because these institutions had been the brain child of developed countries. The developed countries, because of their edge over the developing nations, played an important role in international scene. The countries situated in the South were kept at a low profile as they were considered late comers on the international fora. Realising the situation, therefore, the developing countries have pertinently asked for a New Economic Order as only a new order could satisfy the needs and wants of developing countries.

Economic Darwinism is both a new form of international order and a threat to the poor nations. What we call Darwinism is nearer to Galbraith's 'Second Imperialism' which deals with the core nations' behaviour *vis-à-vis* others. The will to national independence according to him, is the most powerful force in modern times. Therefore, its antithesis is not mere imperialism but, to use Kautsky's phrase, 'Ultra Imperialism'. If the national leadership is strong, effective and well regarded, it will not tolerate foreign domination. If the leadership is weak, ineffective, unpopular, corrupt and oppressive, it may accept foreign guidance, support and a measure of domination, to be ultimately marginalised. But then it may not be tolerated by its own people. This is the eroding effect of new imperialism.

Notes and Refences

1. Hirst, Paul and Grahame Thompson, Globalisation in Question: The International Economy and the Possibilities of Governance (Cambridge: Polity Press), 1996, pp. 7-16
2. http://www.cpim.org/marxist/200102_marxist_eco_ppatnaik.htm.
3. Barbara Lee and John Nellis, "Enterprise Reform and Privatisation in Socialist Economies", World Bank Discussion Paper 104, p. 3.
4. Mehta, Sanat, "Effect of New Industrial Policy on Labour", *Financial Express*, 7 November, 1991.
5. Roy, A., Power Politics (Cambridge: South End Press), 2001, p. 43.
6. *World Affairs*, Vol. 5, No. 1, New Delhi, India, p. 30,
7. Soros, G., The Alchemy of Finance, Reading the Mind of the Market (New York: Little Brown and Company), 1987.
8. Stiglitz, Joseph, Globalisation and Its Discontents (Allen Lane: Penguin Press), 2002, p. 9
9. Bhagwati, Jagdish, In Defense of Globalisation (New Delhi: Oxford Press), 2004, p. 3.
10. Chakravarthi, Raghavan, "South May be Trapped into New WTO Round", *Nai Azadi Udghosh*, Vol. 8, No. 1, January-Feburary, 2001, pp. 20-27.
11. World Commission on the Social Dimension of Globalisation, A Fair Globalisation: Creating Opportunities for All (Geneva: International Labour Office), 2004, p. x.
12. Stigliz, Joseph, E., Making Globalisation Work (Allen Lane: Penguin Books), 2006, p. 9
13. Srivastava, Aseem, "Impact of Globalisation: Stagflation and Food Price Rise, *Nai Azadi Udgosh* (Allahabad), Vol. 17, Nos. 6-7, June-July, 2008, pp. 5-12
14. Oliver de Schutter, UN Rapporteur on Food, Interview to Le Monde, May 2, 2008.

15. ILO, A Fair Globalisation: Creating Opportunities for All, Report of the World Commission on the Social Dimension of Globalisation, Geneva, 2004, p. 42.
16. Deaton, Angus and Dreze, Jean, "Poverty and Inequality in India: A Re-examination", *Economic and Political Weekly*, 2003, Vol. 35, No. 45.
17. Soros, G., The Alchemy of Finance, Reading the Mind of the Market, *op. cit.*
18. *Ibid.*
19. *Ibid.*
20. Quoted in P.K. Vausudeva, World Trade Organisation (Delhi: Pearson Education), 2005.
21. World Bank Report, 2000.
22. Chakravarthi, Raghavan, "Hazardous Obsession with Global Integration", *Nai Azadi Udghosh*, Vol. 6, Nos. 3-4, May-April, 2001, p. 11.
23. *Ibid.*, p. 12.
24. *Ibid.*
25. Verzola, Roberto, "Globalisation: Its Third Wave", *Nai Azadi Udghosh*, Vol. 8, No. 1, September-October-November-December, 2003, pp. 4-8.

4

Repercussions of Corporate Sector

THE BEGINNING

East India Company laid the foundation of British colonialisation of India after the Battle of Plassey in 1757 and Industrial Revolution in Britain in the 19th Century. East India Company's loot of India facilitated Industrial Revolution to certain degree and consolidated a long spell of colonial exploitation, as a result of which the once prosperous and sustainable Indian economy—agriculture, industry and commerce was destroyed, and extensive plundering of Indian treasure took place for almost 200 years till India gained independence in 1947 from the British yoke. The British, in Indian eyes, shall forever remain brigands, bandits and thugs! However, the newly gained independence was not to bloom fully. The North, in desperate effort to sustain its high consumption life style, armed with technological superiority and financial military strength, embarked upon recolonisation of the south. "Gun Boat Policy" of the erstwhile colonial powers is now replaced by more sophisticated weapons of debts and aids. Once again, "Free Trade" is their main slogan. It was so in the case of East India Company when in 1813, the British parliament granted it a charter of "Free Trade." Free trade is not, in fact, a late 20th century phenomenon; it is the reemergence of what East India Company and its mentor in England preached in the 18th and 19th centuries. The core content and impact of free trade today is exactly the same as what it was in the 18th century. A horrendous fact should be recalled here. As a result of the erstwhile free trade under British rule in India, had to pay the price of 1.3 million starvation deaths. In the name of free trade, the MNCs, with the help of IMF/WB and WTO, are extending their reach across the planet like a cancer, colonising ever more of the planets living spaces, destroying livelihoods, displacing people, rendering impotent democratic institutions and feeding on life in an insatiable quest of money. In the words of American human rights leader, Mr. Jackson: "Now they do not use gun and rope. They use WB/ IMF."[1]

THE INVISIBLE RULE OF CORPORATIONS

Apparently, we are a democratic nation; we are not yet being ruled by the people's representatives. The corporations have a powerful but silent sway. Behind the scenes, it is they who decide which political parties will come to power, and what policies are to be pursued. The corporations have influence over the state. They have stripped the central government of the decision-making powers and are holding the common man in a state of confusion regarding the causes of their distress. The regulatory bodies, the corporations, tend to dominate these bodies. An active propaganda machinery controlled by the largest corporations constantly reassure us that free trade, liberalisation and globalisation are the only paths to development, consumerism is the only goal to be cherished, and that democratic control over markets are the causes of our distress.

According to the Indian Constitution, Rajya Sabha represents the interests of the states in the Union. An entry into the Rajya Sabha offers a soft option to the corporate world.

There is yet another reason why the corporate bosses want to get into parliament. Money is not enough. They want public glory and hence the quest for the power and the prestige that go with membership of parliament. Ordinarily, they would find it difficult to get an appointment with a minister or even a joint secretary in the government. As MPs, ministers cannot refuse to meet them and bureaucrats would dare do so at their own peril. Revenue intelligence officials, the enforcement directorate and the police would think twice before raiding an MP or questioning him.

CHART 4.1

(Pestle Analysis)

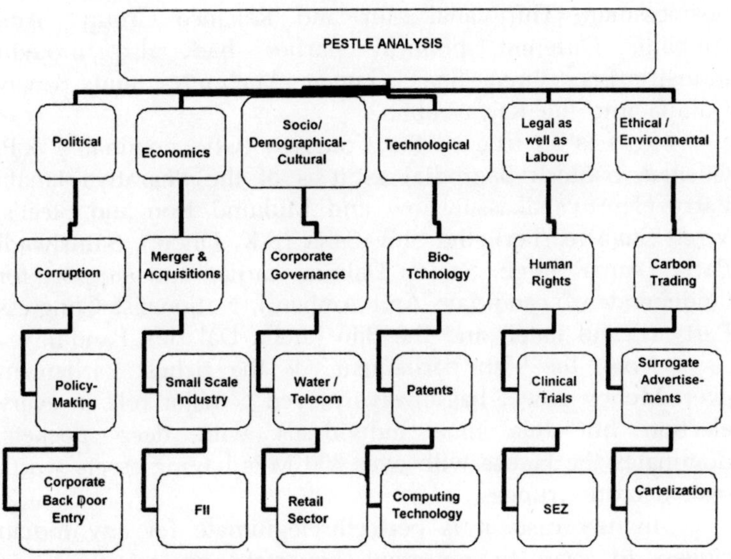

(The PESTEL Analysis (Political, Economic, Social, Technological, Legal and Environmental) factors makes it clear how or and to what degree, corporate sector intervenes in the economy).

Several captains of industry in India have also opted to take the high road to politics through this road to Upper House in India. There were overtly political families like that of the Birlas who traditionally played a role in politics. Neither Ghanshyamdas Birla nor K.K. Birla ever made any bones about their support to the Congress. K.K. Birla served a long and productive tenure in the Rajya Sabha—as an independent for a brief while and then later as a Congress member of parliament. R.P. Goenka has been a long-time Congress supporter and the party has rewarded him with a Rajya Sabha seat.

However, of late, the list of businessmen already in the Upper House or trying to join it has lengthened somewhat—liquor baron, Vijay Mallya, hotelier, Lalit Suri, businessman, Jay Panda, jute and tea baron, Santosh Bagrodia, Videocon's R.K. Dhoot, industrialist, Premchand Gupta, pharma-king, Mahendra Prasad, newspaper barons, Vijay Darda and Girish Sanghi, industrialist, Amar Singh, bidi-king, Praful Patel, businessman, Thiruvanakassur and Reliance Group's Anil Ambani. Different political parties had also brought industrialists, Viren Shah, Jayant Malhoutra and Sanjay Dalmia into the Rajya Sabha.

This is as true of the Congress (who nominated R.P. Goenka, Santosh Bagrodia) as it is of the Bharatiya Janata Party (Thiruvanakassur now and Mukund Iron and Steel's, Viren Shah, earlier), the Shiv Sena (R.K. Dhoot), Samajwadi Party (Amar Singh, Sanjay Dalmia, earlier and support for "independent" candidate Anil Ambani), Nationalist Congress Party (Praful Patel) and the Bjiu Janata Dal (Jay Panda).

Now, the 15th parliament is the richest Parliament ever. Money power has always played a major role in every election but this time individuals with deep pockets, dominates the House with over 300 MPs having assets worth over a crore rupees.

In any case, it is perfectly legitimate for any Indian citizen to seek to represent his state or participate in elections—direct or indirect. If journalists and film stars can get into the Upper House, why should one get worried if some corporate bosses do the same? However, we need to understand the reasons why political parties are nominating rank outsiders, from the corporate sector, to parliament.[2]

It is also a well-known fact that corporate contributions have been coming into the coffers of our political parties. They are made to influence policies and decisions of the government of the day. The big change now is that, while earlier the captains of industry sought to lobby with the government indirectly, now they want to do so directly.

Earlier, the influence of the corporate sector in lobbying for policies could be checked by parliament. All the MPs could not be presumed to be corporate lobbyists. This mechanism has been eroded over time and with the direct presence of the corporate sector in parliament, it is likely to be further weakened. Consider the following hypothetical situation—there is a securities scam and a 15-member joint parliamentary committee—five members from the Rajya Sabha and ten from the Lok Sabha—is set-up to look into it. Of the five members from the Upper House, three are industrialists, the fourth a lobbyist for an industrial house that has nearly 200 front companies playing the market. This lobby then needs to win over only four MPs from the Lok Sabha to command a majority in the JPC—not an insurmountable task at all. What the findings of such a JPC would be is best left to the imagination.[3]

They have taken over the agenda of nation building from people and. Political parties have been silenced by huge amounts of black money. Visible political collapse in our country started during the last two decades when political leaders silently abdicated their responsibilities in favour of the MNCs be suppressing the voice of sizeable dissenters, adopted SAP, liberalisation, globalisation and whatever else was taught to them by the WB/IMF and WTO. With the help of this trio, the MNCs have indeed usurped the programmes of social transformation, and acquired effective control over the reigns and resources of the developing countries.

What is of deep concern to us is that this conglomerate of neo colonists is powerful enough to overthrow legitimate political regimes which do not fall in line with their diktat. History of the third world is full of ghastly incidents of political bribery and murders committed by these neo colonists.

US-BACKED FASCIST COUP IN CHILE

It is pertinent to recall the role of certain corporate interests in the overthrow of the Allende government.[4] In 1970, Salvador Allende had just been elected president. He had won the election in the face of the economic might of US corporations and the government of Richard Nixon which had funded Allende's opponent.

Soon after, in Washington, Nixon received a personal phone call from Donald Kendall, Chairman of PepsiCo. Kendal was an associate of Nixon when Nixon was PepsiCo's corporate attorney. From that phone call, Kendall organised a meeting between the owner of Pepsi's bottling operation in Chile and US National Security Advisor, Henry Kissinger, and soon after that Nixon called in the head of the CIA, Richard Helms. According to Helms's hand written notes, Nixon ordered the CIA to prevent Allende's inauguration as president. The message to the CIA chief of operations in Santiago said that it was "the firm and continuing policy" of the US administration "that Allende be overthrown in a coup." The CIA was to "review all your present and possibly new activities to include propaganda" and "the surfacing of intelligence or disinformation, personal contacts..." The attempted 1970 coup failed, mainly because the CIA found it difficult to sway enough high ranking officers in the Chilean army. Of course, Pepsi and other major corporations such as ITT (now AT&T) and mining interests, with the Nixon administration's cooperation, persisted and in 1973, the US engineered another coup attempt, with General Augusto Pinochet at the helm and Kissinger pulling the strings behind the scenes. The result was a brutal fascist dictatorship that carried out the slaughter, torture and imprisonment of tens of thousands of people

THE ENTRY OF MULTINATIONALS IN INDIA

Coca-Cola and Pepsi, the multinational cola companies, the two quintessential United States-based multinationals' operations in India in the last three decades represent a case study of how India's industrial policy and regulations have been first dodged, then flouted and finally bent, to shape them according to the fancies of these companies.

Although Coca-Cola has been in India for a longer period than its rival Pepsi, it has had a chequered history in the country. Unwilling to accept the regulations governing the extent of operations of foreign companies in India, as prescribed by the now-defunct Foreign Exchange Regulation Act (FERA), it exited from India in 1977. Interestingly, Defence Minister, George Fernandes, then a Minister in the Janata Party government at the Centre, played a key role in the development. Coke's refusal to comply with the stipulated norm that it dilute its equity stake in its Indian subsidiary to 40 per cent resulted in its exit.

Years later, the policy regime entered a more liberal mode. In 1985, the Rajiv Gandhi government delicensed the soft drinks sector. The same year, in May, Pepsi submitted a proposal to enter the Indian market. Pepsi's bid was rejected then, but three years later it made its entry in Punjab. The resulting political furore forced the government to impose several conditions. The government defended itself by saying that Pepsi's foray into agro-processing in terrorism-troubled Punjab would result in more jobs and economic development. But Pepsi's subsequent track record has been one of non-compliance with regulations and the commitments it made to the Indian government.

Meanwhile, Coca-Cola re-entered India in 1997. It too made commitments, and flouted them. Critics of the liberal policy environment have argued that the inability of successive governments to bring the two multinationals to book is closely linked to the control the companies exert on Indian industrial policy.

In July 1996, the United Front Government headed by H.D. Deve Gowda approved a proposal by Coca-Cola South Asia Holding Inc. to establish two subsidiaries in India. The company envisaged an investment of $700 million over a 10-year-period. It also sought the establishment of a wholly owned subsidiary in Gujarat for bottling operations, entailing an investment of $40 million. The company claimed that apart from its flagship products of carbonated soft drinks, it would develop new products such as tea and coffee, non-carbonated fruit juices, and other milk-based drinks.

In early 1997, the Cabinet Committee on Foreign Investment approved Coca-Cola's proposal to float two wholly owned subsidiaries, which were to act as its holding companies in India. These two companies were to set-up downstream operations such as bottling plants. Reflecting the politically controversial nature of the agreement, and in keeping with Indian apprehensions about Coca-Cola's operations in India, the government imposed a few conditions on the multinational corporations. The first condition was that it would offload 49 per cent of its equity in its downstream companies (essentially bottling operations) to Indian shareholders. Reflecting the liberal mindset of Indian policy-makers, the company was given "three to five years" to comply with this stipulation. The company was also prohibited from engaging directly in any other manufacturing activity.

Soon after the approval, Coca-Cola established two holding companies in the country for its Indian operations. Each holding company in turn floated two subsidiaries to engage in bottling operations. Later, in 2000, the company merged the two holding companies into a single entity, Hindustan Coca-Cola Holdings Private Ltd. (HCCHL). The four bottling subsidiaries were also merged into a single entity, Hindustan Coca-Cola Beverages Private Ltd. (HCCBL). Although it is not clear what motivated the company to engage in a complex task of first creating and then merging the companies, it has attracted controversy for its failure to comply with its own commitment that HCCHL would offer 49 per cent of its stake in HCCBL to resident Indians. More importantly, the government's recent announcement of its decision to dilute the terms on which the company operates in India has fuelled apprehensions that the policy regime can be changed according to the whims and fancies of the multinational entities.[5]

According to the original foreign collaboration agreement approved by the government, HCCHL was to divest 49 per cent by July 1997. In August 2002, the government extended the deadline to February 28, 2003. In January 2003, in the face of the fast-approaching deadline, the Foreign Investment Promotion Board (FIPB), under the Finance Ministry, gave HCCHL permission to use a sum of Rs. 803 crores, constituting the "unused balance" in HCCBL's "advance against share capital" account of HCCBL. Reports in the media at that time indicated that the Department of Economic Affairs (DEA) of the Ministry of Finance permitted

HCCHL to use these funds on the explicit condition that HCCHL's voting rights in HCCBL, "under any circumstances", should not exceed 51 per cent.

Coca-Cola, which had lobbied aggressively against the stipulation regarding the dilution of its stake, intensified its effort to change the norms. It argued, rather ingeniously, that since the original commitment was only to dilute its stake, specified in percentage terms, it was free to dilute its stake by issuing non-voting shares to Indian shareholders. The company also argued that fresh conditions, relating to voting rights of shareholders, could not be imposed on it. It was evident that the company, by issuing "dud shares", was seeking to fulfil its obligations in letter, while violating with impunity the spirit of the agreement.

On March 13, 2003, at a meeting of the FIPB, the Department of Industrial Policy and Promotion (DIPP)—a department in the Ministry of Commerce and Industry under which the FIPB used to operate earlier—informed that HCCHL had duly completed its divestment by the end of the February 2003 deadline. At the meeting, the DIPP and the Department of Company Affairs under the Union Finance Ministry, favoured Coca-Cola's claim relating to a revision of conditions relating to voting rights.

The position adopted by the various government departments and agencies in March were in sharp contrast to their earlier position. Earlier, in January, the DEA had asserted that at the time the conditions were agreed to by Coca-Cola in 1997—with the active participation of the DIPP—the question of issuing different types of shares to various categories of investors did not exist. In fact, the DEA's position was conveyed in the government's "action taken report" submitted to the Parliamentary Standing Committee of the Finance Ministry.

By March, it became clear that the tide was turning in favour of Coke. The company mounted a high-voltage campaign, alleging that the conditions imposed on it were unfair. In particular, it alleged that Pepsi did not face similar conditions. However, critics of the company point out that Coca-Cola's demand for a "level playing field" only confuses the issues at stake. Pepsi's violations of the Indian regulatory system have taken a different form, they say, but Coca-Cola's refusal to comply with its own commitments reflects the company's unwillingness to come under public and shareholder scrutiny in India.

As the deadline approached, the company also issued thinly veiled threats in the media. It said that if it was compelled to dilute its stake, it might be forced to repatriate out of the country funds to the tune of Rs. 1,600 crores. The company also said that forcing it to dilute its stake would be counterproductive because it would, in any case, delist the shares in Indian bourses, just as more than 50 foreign companies have done in the last couple of years.

As the controversy gathered steam in the face of the fast-approaching deadline, a decision on the matter was left to the Cabinet Committee on Economic Affairs (CCEA). The FIPB prepared a favourable ruling for Coca-Cola by recommending to the CCEA in January that it delete the stipulation, "Under any circumstances, the voting rights of HCCHL shall not exceed 51 per cent in HCCBL, i.e. the Indian shareholders in HCCHL should get at least 49 per cent voting rights at all times." The CCEA, which met in late June, is reported to have approved HCCHL's proposal to divest 49 per cent to Indian shareholders who will enjoy no voting rights.

It is important to recognise that even a 49 per cent dilution (with voting rights) of Coca-Cola's stake in the bottling company would not have meant it would lose control of the latter.

So, why was the company so vehemently opposed to the dilution? Coca-Cola's critics allege that it is neither related to its contention of "depressed conditions" in the stock markets nor to its accumulated losses. They allege that the company's real motive is to avoid scrutiny by the public, the shareholders, governmental agencies, financial institutions and banks, which a public offering would entail.

The tale of Pepsi's foray into India is similar. In 1985, soon after the soft drinks segment was delicensed, Pepsi Foods Ltd. attempted a tie-up with the R.P. Goenka Group for a project to export Indian agro-products and to develop Pepsi's products in India. This project was rejected, but in

1986 the company made a fresh bid, and said its project was one that offered the scope to bring about a horticultural revolution in Punjab. Pepsi claimed that its project offered hope in the campaign against terrorism, which was at its peak in Punjab then. Like most other ventures involving foreign companies then, the nascent years of liberalisation, the company entered into a joint venture with the Punjab government-owned Punjab Agro Industrial Corporation (PAIC) and Voltas India Limited. Pepsi held the dominant stake in the joint venture, formed in 1988.[6]

In the face of apprehension about the role of multinationals in India, the government imposed several conditions. In addition, Pepsi also made several promises. It claimed that the project would create employment for 50,000 people nationally and that at least 25,000 of the jobs would be in Punjab. It also agreed to restrict investment in manufacturing soft drinks to 25 per cent of its total investments in India. Instead, in keeping with its pledge to play a major role in agriculture in Punjab, it agreed that 74 per cent of the total investment would be in food- and agro-processing. Pepsi also promised to bring "advanced technology in food processing", apart from marketing Indian agro products abroad.

Pepsi also agreed to the condition that there would be no outflow of foreign exchange on account of soft drinks manufacturing. In particular, the company accepted the condition that 50 per cent of the value of its output would be exported. Moreover, it accepted the rather stringent norm that for every dollar of outflow in foreign exchange, it would bring into the country five dollars. The company also agreed to establish an agro-research centre in Punjab.

Within a couple of years, it was evident that the Pepsi dream was souring. The company was nowhere near meeting its obligations. In 1991, the government came under attack for it in Parliament. Interestingly, it was George Fernandes who led the Opposition's onslaught on the Rajiv Gandhi government in the Lok Sabha in a half-an-hour discussion on September 4, 1991. Fernandes said that Pepsi had not only failed to meet its export obligations but also not kept its promise of restricting its production of soft drinks to 25 per cent of its total value of output. "Rather," he said, "the company has become a challenge to the government." Mounting an attack on the company, Fernandes said: "What is there in these soft drinks? What is there in Pepsi Cola? The water is taken from our wells, the sugar is manufactured in our factories. Only they add some colour and an ingredient which adds flavour." Fernandes also alleged the company had transferred money overseas by "preparing bogus receipts and indulging in under-invoicing and over-invoicing." In his response, the then Union Minister of State for Food Processing, Giridhar Gomang, said that a team constituted by his Ministry visited Pepsi's plant in December 1990 and found that the company had "made no effort to export 40 per cent of its own manufactured products." He also said that the company had taken "no concrete steps" to establish the promised agro-research centre in Punjab.

By early 1992, the company directly employed a total of 909 persons in its operations in India. Its agro-processing plant in Hoshiarpur district in Punjab, which was to source tomatoes (for which germplasm had been imported by Pepsi) from local farmers, failed to procure it from the farmers even though the company had entered into a contract with them. It was reported that farmers lost Rs. 25 lakhs as a result of Pepsi's failure to buy from them.

Pepsi's promised exports also did not materialise. Instead of exporting its own products, which is what the spirit of its commitment to the Indian government mandated, it was exporting basmati rice, shrimps, tea, glass bottles, leather products and a range of products totally unconnected to its own operations. By 1994, Pepsi, in keeping with the trend of collapsed joint ventures, bought out its partners' stake.

By this time, policy had changed, and adapted to the changed reality that increasing doses of liberalisation entailed. In particular, in 1997, PepsiCo (the parent company) floated a new fully owned entity, PepsiCo India Holdings Private Ltd., to handle business related to its beverages business. Soon, it had overtaken Pepsi Foods in terms of revenues.

The story of the two companies' operations in India indicates that although they may be rivals the world over, in

India they have both managed to twist regulations to suit their ends. More severe critics would allege that the companies made their entry knowing fully well that since the regulatory system was vulnerable to pressure it could be changed later.[7]

Corruption: The Corporate Mantra

In India, mantra means an effective formula which has an almost magical efficacy. Historian Sheridan noted in 17th century that the East India Company "extended the sordid principles of its origin over all successive operations; connecting with its civil policy, the meanness of a peddler and the profligacy of pirates." From the very beginning, East India Company had combined trade with plunder. It was not an organisation of traders, but of adventurers, who Adams and other eminent scholars have preferred to call "pirates" and "buccaneers." Famous economist, J.M. Keynes has a few striking words on the subject. He says, "The booty brought back by Drake in the Golden Hind (estimated at some 6,00,000 sterling pound) may fairly be considered the fountain and origin of British Foreign Investment. Elizebeth paid off out of the proceeds the whole of her foreign debt and invested a part of the balance in the Levant Company. Largely, out of profits of the Levant Company there was formed the East India Company, the profits of which during the 17th and 18th centuries were the main foundation of England's foreign connection."

Naturally, if more profit was to be wrung, corrupt practices were to be adopted. As the company's servants looted the merchants and traders, its masters corrupted the local chiefs. When Siraj-ud-daulah, the nawab of Bengal proved too strong for them, Clive resorted to mean conspiracy. Clive himself noted that Plassey was "a mixture of fighting, tricks, chicanery, intrigues, politics and Lord knows what."[8]

The phenomenon of corruption is as old as the hills, as ancient as greed. And so is corruption in India. When it comes to the country's corporate sector, however, stories about corruption go back almost half-a-century, to the years after India became politically independent. The stories continue. Only the content changes, not the form. The names of the individuals involved change, not the manner in which they manipulate the system or the way the infamous nexus between business, bureaucracy and politics operates

Corruption closer home is in a comfort zone, cosily with its perpetrators who span all levels of society. Corruption is the leading type of fraud in India, finds a recent survey by KPMG. Theft of cash has paled to the second place. At 33 per cent, 'corruption' is more than three times of what 'false financial reporting' scores, and seven times of 'embezzlement'. Not surprising, because India is ranked 70th, along with Brazil and China, amongst 163 countries in the Transparency International (TI) Corruption Perception Index 2006, with a score of 3.3 on a scale of 10.[9]

There's an important difference between India's track record in curbing corporate corruption and the functioning of the criminal justice system in other democracies, including the US. The claim that the law is above no man sounds good in theory. In actual practice, in India and elsewhere, the long arm of the law does indeed tend to favour the rich and the powerful.

All over India, an estimated Rs. 7000 crores is spent for elections to parliamentary and state legislatures in a cycle of five years. This expenditure can be sustained only when the returns are of very high order and the returns can be high only if high levels of corruption are sustained over long periods of time, resulting in institutionalisation of corruption. The Tatas had set-up a trust for political donations to be followed later by the Birlas and others. Companies were legally allowed to contribute political funds. The benign influence of some of these decisions resulted in more than 70 companies donating over Rs. 1 crore in 2007, according to one estimate. The Election Commission figures show such contributions at Rs. 117 crore between 2003 and 2007. But since the late 90s, the circulation of black money during elections has not fallen. If anything, it has increased. Tata Communications chairman Subodh Bhargava said last week that most business people were being hounded for money. Bajaj group chairman, Rahul Bajaj, said that almost 60 per cent of the companies would eventually give black money to politicians.[10] Meanwhile, expenditure on conducting elections and the money spent by political parties and individual leaders on campaigning are increasing.

This year, the budgetary allocation for the Election Commission (EC) to conduct polls is Rs. 850 crore (Rs. 8.5 billion), while according to estimates of political party managers, the combined expenditure on the campaign plus the EC expenses works out to at least six to seven times this amount.

Under the present laws, for the campaign, a candidate can spend Rs. 10 lakh (Rs. 1 million) to Rs. 25 lakh (Rs. 2.5 million) in a parliamentary poll and from Rs. 500,000 to Rs. 10 lakh (one million) in an assembly poll and has to submit detailed accounts for this. The amount varies in different states. The rule, however, is observed more in its breach than in practice.[11]

Public choice theory—which is a central aspect of the orthodox theoretical framework for privatisation—runs aground in presuming the market does away with bureaucratic self-interest. According to the public choice approach, privatisation is necessary because the public sector is staffed by self-interested bureaucrats. However, it is these self-interested bureaucrats who are expected to implement privatisation policy in a non-self-interested way. Privatisation requires an effective public sector and the people who are most threatened by the policy are the ones who are expected to carry it out.[12] Public procurement provides the main interface between the public and private sectors—and is recognised as a major source of corruption. Evidence from within the EU and across the world shows that today's liberalisation agenda underpinned by a shift in the role of the state from provider to enabler, and leading to an increase in the 'contracting out' and privatisation of 'public services', is increasing both the opportunities and the incentives for the payment of bribes by private companies to government organisations.

Organisations such as the EU and the OECD have long recognised that bribes paid by companies to government officials, not only distort markets and competition, but also undermine decision-making and democracy. Indeed, the

OECD's Convention on the Bribery of Foreign Public Officials (1999), which requires members (including all EU member states) to enact legislation that criminalises the act of bribing foreign public officials, reflects these concerns.

However, today there is evidence that economically powerful Multinational Companies (MNCs) are engaging in a new form of corruption—state capture—using bribery to lever control over legislation, regulation and policy-making. Such 'state capture' significantly raises the stakes, increasing the policy imperative to combat corruption.

The challenge of holding companies to account for their corrupt practices, however, should not be underestimated. In the past, companies have escaped penalty through, for example, the conviction of an employee. In 1994, a senior executive of Lyonnaise des Eaux was convicted and sentenced to prison after magistrates found that bribes of FF 19 million had been paid to the Mayor's electoral campaign in return for Grenoble's water privatisation contract. However, Lyonnaise des Eaux continues to tender for public procurement contracts—across the EU and across the world.

Overall, the number of exclusions of companies from public procurement tendering is low. Even the World Bank, which has pledged to ban companies found to be engaged in corrupt practices on World Bank funded projects[13], has so far failed to bar any MNC from tendering for its projects. The outcome of the long-running trial of the Lesotho Highlands Water Project, in which a number of western construction companies are accused of paying bribes, will provide a test of the Bank's resolve.

The Commission's proposals potentially represent a major step forward in curbing corruption. The threat of being excluded from tendering for public procurement contracts across the EU provides a powerful deterrent. However, the extent to which these proposals prevail over the undoubted legal, economic and practical challenges will be determined by—and testimony to—the political will of the member states.

The award of concessions and contracts and hence the process of privatisation is a major source of corruption.[14] The most celebrated case in Africa at present is the Highlands water project in Lesotho where more than a dozen international companies and individuals have been charged with bribing the former top official of the Lesotho Highlands Water Project. In Uganda, privatisation was temporarily halted in August 1998 due to allegations of corruption and the president's brother resigned after his involvement in the sale of the Uganda Commercial Bank caused an outcry

India: Dabhol Power Company: An Epic of Corruption

A single company that could serve as a symbol of international capitalism in the 1990s, Dabhol Power Company would probably be the one. The giant multinational corporation, Enron, grew from being essentially a gas pipeline company in the 1980s, into the world's single largest energy trader, accounting for around 25 per cent of energy trade in both United States and European markets in 2000, Enron was ranked 16th on the Global Fortune 500 and eighth on the U.S. Fortune 500. Enron had grown into a multisector service corporation with five major divisions: Enron 'Transportation Services' specialised in the company's traditional natural gas pipeline operations. Enron 'Energy Services' was the company's retail arm for the sale of natural gas and electricity to both commercial and industrial users. Enron 'Wholesale Services', which is also the main shareholder in the infamous Dabhol Power Company (DPC) in Maharashtra. Enron 'Online Services' is a commodity trading system. It provided the largest eCommerce site in the world, dwarfing all other energy marketing web sites combined. Enron 'Broadband Services' streamlines media applications and "customises" bandwidth solutions on the Internet

Making use of political connections is a key component of corporate strategy for Enron and one which has come under growing scrutiny with George Bush becoming US president. The connections between Bush and Enron Chairman, Kenneth Lay, go back many years to when Bush was governor of Texas. Lay donated $310,500 to the Republican party over 1999/2000 and raised about another $1m from his company and its employees. According to the Centre for Public Integrity, an American watchdog group, Enron gave more money to Bush's campaign than any other corporation[15] and Bush used the Enron corporate jet to fly round the country on the election campaign. It would seem that the donations do not entirely reflect political persuasion as Enron also gave $520,000 to the Gore campaign.

In India, Enron was responsible for the biggest and most controversial—foreign investment project in India. The Dabhol Power Company, 65% owned by Enron, constructed a power plant at the port of Dabhol about 200 km south of Mumbai, the nation's financial capital. The $3.5 bn project was signed in 1993 and the Phase I (740 MW) came into operation in 1999. Phase II (1,444 MW) was due to be commissioned in 2001. From the start, the project was controversial. There were a number of concerns about the scheme: the high cost of power which was to be purchased by the state, allegations of corruption in the setting up of the project, the procedure regarding granting official clearance for the project, lack of consultation of affected people, the allocation and distribution of compensation for those displaced and environmental destruction.[16] The contract was considered to be generous to Enron. The company promised to invest $3bn which would be repaid with a tariff on electricity charges that was set at such a high level that the company would receive $26 bn in return.[17] In 1993, the World Bank concluded that the project was "not economically viable

The heavy measures used by police which were sponsored by Enron to put down protests against the project led to allegations of human rights abuses. Enron has the distinction of being the only company (rather than government) that has been the specific subject of a human rights report by Amnesty International.[18]

Opposition to the arrangement with the Enron company was so strong that the deal was nearly scrapped in 1995. The Shiv Sena-BJP nationalists who came to power in March 1995 had promised to abolish the deal when in opposition but when they came to power found that to do so would mean paying huge amounts of money to Enron. The contract then was renegotiated and a fresh deal was signed in December 1995.[19]

Arundhati Roy Commented on the Renegotiated Contract

"In August 1996, the Government of Maharashtra

signed a fresh contract with Enron on terms that would astound the most hardboiled cynic. The impugned contract had involved annual payments to Enron of US $430 million for phase I of the project, with phase II being optional. The 're-negotiated' Power Purchase Agreement makes phase II of the project mandatory and legally binds the Maharashtra State Electricity Board (MSEB) to pay Enron a sum of US $30 billion! It constitutes the largest contract ever signed in the history of India. In effect, for an increase in installed capacity of 18 per cent, the MSEB has to set aside 70 per cent of its revenue to be able to pay Enron. There is, of course, no record of what mathematical formula was used to compute the 're-negotiated' bribe. Nor any trace of how much trickled up or down or sideways and to whom."[20]

The terms of the Power Purchase Agreement proved crippling for the MSEB. The financial state of the electricity board declined drastically. By 2001, Maharashtra's tariff payments had more than doubled since 1993. Electricity from Dabhol cost more than three times as much as other power in the system, according to state officials. A number of factors have driven up the price. The first phase of the project was fuelled by naphtha, which had become much more expensive because of rising oil prices. The bills were calculated in rupees, but tied to the dollar, so as the rupee lost value, the price in domestic currency increased. In December 2000, Dabhol was selling power to MSEB for 8 rupees per unit and MSEB was selling it on at 2 rupees.[21]

Furthermore, the state's electricity regulatory commission requires the electricity board to buy the cheapest power first, leaving Dabhol at the end of the line. Demand was much lower than the state had forecasted. Ehile MSEB purchased only 10 to 20 percent of the power that Dabhol is capable of generating, while paying the plant's full fixed costs. In Phase II, which is twice as big as Phase I and fuelled by natural gas imported in liquefied form, the state will also have to pay 75 percent of the fuel costs even if it buys no power.

The contract began to fall apart towards the end of 2000 when MSEB could not pay Enron. At the end of May 2001, Enron served a preliminary termination notice on MSEB effectively saying that the company will quit in six months—warning it would move to recoup damages. It was reported that these damages would be in the region of $3.5 bn to $5 bn.[22] In January it was reported that MSEB had defaulted on payments worth 2.6 billion rupees (US $61 m). for October and November 2001 and Enron called in their sovereign guarantee with the government of India. The government has promised to honour payments if the MSEB defaults but said that the money would come out of the budgetary allocation to Maharashtra.[23]

Relations between Enron and the MSEB have continued to deteriorate. Arrears continued to grow and MSEB responded by rescinding the contract which they said was not a threat but a '"legal notice" provoked by Enron's diminishing performance of certain technical functions.'[24] Enron says MSEB does not have the right to rescind the agreement. MSEB stopped taking power from the plant at the end of May which means that in effect the plant stops production.

MSEB says it will not "entertain such an invoice." Dabhol says it is owed $45 m in unpaid bills. The Indian utility insists the power company owes it much more in rebates for failing to meet technical thresholds, such as the time it takes to reach full capacity from a cold start In 2002 the amount the state's electricity board owes will more than quadruple to over $1 billion a year as the huge turbines for the second phase of the project come on line. Under the 20-year contract, the state and central governments have guaranteed that they would pay the money if the electricity board defaults.

The collapse of the project has implications for the national banking system as there is concern that foreign banks may call in Indian banks' guarantees on their loans. Foreign banks have loaned Dabhol about 30 per cent of the $2 bn in debt raised to finance the project. Indian banks' exposure is $1.4 bn, including guarantees of foreign banks' loans. The Indian banks' loans were not protected by guarantees from their government and they stand to lose heavily if banks, such as Credit Suisse First Boston, ABN Amro and Citibank, call in guarantees

Indian and foreign banks have commissioned a report from a US consultancy to review the feasibility of mothballing the plant for a year to allow the dispute to be resolved. Foreign banks were also demanding a firmer expression of support for the project from the Indian government. Relations have continued to deteriorate with complex legal wranglings emerging. At the beginning of June 2001, Enron issued a writ in the Bombay high court challenging the jurisdiction of Maharashtra's electricity industry regulator, after the regulator issued an interim order that stopped DPC from pursuing arbitration proceedings in London, as provided for under the power purchase agreement.[25]

The controversial Dabhol issue did not die with the fall of Enron.It came to the fore once again when an independent arbitration tribunal in the United States ruled unanimously that the interests of equity holders GE and Bechtel in the Dabhol Power Company (DPC) were improperly expropriated by the Indian government. Moreover, the tribunal ordered a binding award of $28.57 million each to GE and Bechtel for claims that they brought against their political risk insurer, the Overseas Private Investment Corporation (OPIC), an agency of the U.S. government.

GE and Bechtel each own 10 per cent equity in the $3-billion, beleaguered DPC. The arbitrators said that the Government of India (GoI) and its agents violated international law through an unlawful taking of GE and Bechtel's investments in the DPC. Meanwhile, OPIC, which has been slapped with the political risk insurance bill, has turned around and asked the GoI to pay the amount because, according to it, the Indian government's political shenanigans have been primarily responsible for the collapse of the project. Anti-Enron activists in India, have, however, pointed out that the dispute was purely commercial and had nothing to do with politics. Hence they say that the claim does not hold good.

Following the order, GE and Bechtel filed an arbitration action against the GoI to recover their investments. The total claim, according to a press release, could amount to $600 million. The action was initiated by the two companies' affiliates, Energy Enterprises (Mauritius) Company and

Capital India Power Mauritius I. The claim was made under the arbitration rules of the United Nations Commission on International Trade Law and the investment agreement between the Republic of Mauritius and GoI.

According to a press release from Bechtel, the tribunal, which was chaired by a former U.S. District Court Judge, found enough evidence to establish that "the Maharashtra State Electricity Board (MSEB), the GoM and GoI violated the Power Purchase Agreement (PPA), the GoM and GoI guarantees, and the State Support Agreements for political reasons and without any legal justification." Furthermore, the tribunal stated that the "Maharashtra Electricity Regulatory Authority (MERC), the MSEB, Indian Financial Institutions and the Indian courts have enjoined and otherwise taken away the claimants' Bechtel and GE. international remedies under the PPA, all in violation of established principles of international law, in disregard of India's commitments under the U.N. Convention as well as the Indian Arbitration Act."

"Everyone knows Enron is a friend of the present U.S government and everyone knows that OPIC is a friend of Enron's," says Pradyumna Kaul, leader of the Enron Virodhi Andolan.[26] "GE and Bechtel are acting as a proxy for Enron. They are just the latest players of Enron attempting to recover money." Questioning the arbitration proceedings, he told, "Why should this 'independent' panel have any relevance to India? The arbitration is part of an agreement reached among GE, Bechtel and OPIC. It has nothing to do with the Indian government." Not only had OPIC, along with the EXIM bank, loaned Enron $600 million towards owning a 65 per cent stake in the Dabhol project, the agency's political risk insurance cover to the three U.S. promoters amounts to almost $200 million.

The Indian lenders' exposure to the Dabhol project has been pinned at a staggering Rs. 6,000 crores. Initially, lenders proposed selling the assets and recovering part of the loan. Later, interested companies were allowed to bid for the project, which, according to an investment banker, is quite a valuable asset. Although due diligence was to be conducted by six companies, it fell through. Meanwhile, the lenders asked the Bombay High Court to appoint a receiver for the care and maintenance of the plant. A consultancy firm appointed by the main lender, the Industrial Development Bank of India (IDBI), is in the process of restructuring the agreement and calling for international bids to buy the plant. Nimbalkar believes that the issue will soon be settled. An MERC official, however, told *Frontline* that he estimated that a settlement will take another two years. He said: "As per the agreement, the MSEB and Enron will have to fight out the problems in an arbitration panel set-up in London. We must understand that the sale of the DPC will not mean the end of Enron."[27]

The action by General Electric and Bechtel reflects the increasing pressure being applied by the project's foreign lenders, which, alarmed by MSEB's deteriorating payments record and the legal tit-for-tat, have stopped disbursing funds for the second stage.

Enron have since said that they would be willing to sell the Dabhol plant. US energy company (AES) was reportedly considering taking over the project.

There are certain similarities between Enron's experiences in California and India. Jeff Skilling, Enron CEO, himself draws parallels between the two, saying, "India is identical to the California situation except that we have a government guarantee for payment."

In India, instances of well-heeled industrialists being jailed for financial misdemeanours are few and far between. When V.P. Singh was Union finance minister in Rajiv Gandhi's government, in 1985 and 1986, a number of prominent businessmen were apprehended for tax evasion and some of them, such as the late Lalit Mohan Thapar, even had to spend a night or two in Tihar Jail. But this was a rather short-lived phase. Many believe that his actions against industrialists was the root cause for V.P. Singh's estrangement from Rajiv Gandhi as well as other Congress leaders who privately held him responsible for trying to cut off their 'lifeline' of funds. After all, it's hardly a secret that majority of Indian politicians are generously funded by businesspersons for conducting election campaigns, among other things. In return, those providing money and resources to politicians expect various kinds of favours as part of a cosy system of *quid-pro-quo.*

During the days of the licence control raj in the 1960s, 1970s and 1980s, the favours would come in the form of quotas and permits. As the bureaucracy gradually let go off its controls over the levers of the economy, the forms of corruption too started changing. Dhirubhai understood this process well. He once told Time magazine that he was not Mother Teresa—but the manner in which he successfully "managed the environment" undoubtedly raised the hackles of his business rivals.

It was not as if Indian politicians had not helped other industrialists in the past. The difference in the business-politics nexus lay in the fact that by the time the Reliance group's fortunes were on the rise, the Indian economy had become more competitive. Thus, it was not enough for those in power to promote the interests of a particular business group. It became "necessary" to simultaneously put down the competition.

Therefore, the fortunes of Swan Mills, the Orkay group headed by Kapal Mehra, not to mention Nusli Wadia's Bombay Dyeing, all had to be 'sacrificed' to facilitate the speedy growth of the Ambani empire. Even Ramnath Goenka's Indian Express chain of newspapers—that had taken on the Ambanis in the mid-1980s—got trifurcated after his demise.

Few could match Dhirubhai's skills in the fine art of 'managing' the interests of politicians and bureaucrats, from the level of a senior secretary to the government of India to a humble peon. He used to say he was willing to 'salaam' anyone and one thing he did not have was an ego. After Dhirubhai's death, his sons fought bitterly. His corporate conglomerate got divided amidst a flurry of allegations of corporate malfeasance. A consequence of the tussle between the Ambani siblings was that a lot of muck came out into the open—from details about how international telephone calls were sought to be disguised as local calls, to the case of how shares were virtually gifted to individuals known to be close to former Union Communications Minister, Pramod Mahajan. The Supreme Court issued notices to the government and its various investigation and vigilance agencies to probe Pramod Mahajan's allegedly dubious permission to Reliance Infocomm to launch its Wireless in Local Loop (WLL) without paying the appropriate license fee. Income-tax officials intrigued that nobody asked them for details, although it is they who investigated Ashish Deora, allegedly a partner of Mahajan's relatives in a company called IOL Broadband Limited. Deora owns several other companies that actually received one crore shares of Reliance Infocomm at a nominal one rupee per share.

The Mukesh Ambani-led RPL was named among the "non-contractual beneficiaries" in the probe report on the oil-for-food programme investigated by the UN-appointed Volcker Committee for being allegedly awarded three crude oil contracts worth 19 million barrels.

In a letter to the Department of Revenue, the Enforcement Directorate said out of these 19 million barrels, a total of 15.78 million barrels were lifted and that a surcharge of $3,574,808.49 was paid to a designated Iraqi account, over and above the price of oil fixed by the UN.

"These contracts were originally allocated by SOMO (State Oil Marketing Organisation), Iraq, to RLP," said the directorate's letter, by the directorate on the Volcker Report had revealed that the oil was allocated to RPL, which did not lift it itself but authorised another firm Alcon Petroleum of Liechtenstein to do so, said the letter.

"Hence the payment of the surcharge amounts (over and above the actual value of the oil) by RPL, or on their behalf, by some other person/entity to the Iraqi authorities, without the permission of the RBI, perhaps, cannot be ruled out", the letter added. The directorate, therefore, proposed to issue letters of request under Foreign Exchange Management Act, the Income Tax Act and the Civil Procedure Code to competent authorities in Iraq, Jordan and Lebanon to obtain "confirmation" and "supporting documents."

"It is, therefore, requested that necessary permission of the competent authority may please be conveyed for issue of these letters of request by the directorate," the letter added.

The Volcker report had said that the surcharge in question was paid to the Iraqi designated account maintained with the Jordan National Bank by certain individuals through wire transfers from accounts maintained in the First National

Bank in Lebanon in the name of Jabal Petroleum and Petrocorp.[28]

The probe was carried out by what is formally known as the Independent Inquiry Committee, headed by the former chairman of the United States Federal Reserve Board, Paul Volcker.

After the initiative to liberalize Indian economy were taken in 1991, the biggest scandal to hit the country's stock markets involving broker Harshad Mehta broke out. During the inquiry by the Joint Parliamentary Committee into the scam, it became clear that the Union finance ministry (then headed by Dr. Manmohan Singh's right-hand man Montek Singh Ahluwalia) had gone rather slow in empowering the Securities and Exchange Board of India that was headed then by an upright bureaucrat G.V. Ramakrishna. In certain senses, the country's financial system did not learn the lessons it should have. Nine years later, another share market scandal (this time involving broker Ketan Mehta) surfaced.

Four decades before Harshad Mehta had become a household name in India, another HM—Haridas Mundhra—had hogged headlines. In the late-1950s and early-1960s, various wings of the Union government had filed over 200 criminal cases against the Kolkata-based businessman. Mundhra had been accused in Parliament by the then Prime Minister Jawaharlal Nehru's son-in-law Feroze Gandhi of manipulating share prices with the help of funds obtained from the Life Insurance Corporation[29]. The then finance minister in Nehru's cabinet, T.T. Krishnamachari, was forced to resign on account of the scandal.

Even during Indira Gandhi's regime, in 1974, Tulmohan Ram had to put in his papers after he was indicted in a corruption case relating to issuance of import licences. Subsequent financial scandals have, however, not resulted in important political personalities getting disgraced even if their not-so-hidden hand could be detected. Many believe the fundamental reason for widespread corporate corruption in the country is the tangential manner in which political donations are made.

Although the Election Commission (EC) has prescribed "tight legal limits" on the amount of money candidates can spend during election campaigns, the EC has itself acknowledged that the spending limits are often circumvented. This is what is stated in the official website of the EC: "Although supporters of a candidate can spend as much as they like to help out with a campaign, they have to get written permission of the candidate and while parties are allowed to spend as much money on campaigns as they want, recent Supreme Court judgments have said that unless a political party can specifically account for money spent during the campaign, it will consider any activities as being funded by the candidates and counting towards their election expenses."

Compared with India, the American system of political donations is more transparent. Much more information has to be made public. Many Indians disagree with much of the US government's policies. Still, there has been one important development that is certainly worthy of emulation.

On January 18, 2007, the US Senate, by a majority of 96 to 2, voted in favour of far-reaching legislation aimed at curbing the influence of lobbyists. The new law bans senators from accepting gifts and junkets (free trips, usually accompanied by lavish hospitality) from individuals and firms and offers of flights on corporate jets at discounted rates. This law was enacted after the Democratic Party regained control over the Senate and the House of Representatives in the wake of the November elections that saw the defeat of many candidates belonging to the ruling Republican Party. It is about time India enacted such a law.

MERGER AND ACQUISITION

In the today's world, there is a lot of pressure on all executives to grow their companies. Companies can grow in one of three ways, market expansion, product expansion and through Merger and Acquisition. The market expansion and product expansion is considered as internal growth and merger and acquisition as external growth

External growth is considered far easier in many industries than internal growth.

Expanding the market for an existing product gets

harder as the industry matures. The market for soda, beer, tobacco, and a large number of other market segments have stabilised in North America and Europe or even started to decline. The most conservative innovations are extending the brand. Trading on existing brand names has been the main thrust of product development in the last few decades. Mountain Dew, Code Red, Bud Ice, X-treme, Jell-O, Snickers Ice Cream, and Tropicana smoothies..

One plus one makes three: this equation is the special alchemy of a merger or an acquisition. The key principle behind buying a company is to create shareholder value over and above that of the sum of the two companies. Two companies together are more valuable than two separate companies—that's the reasoning behind M&A.

The process of mergers and acquisitions has gained substantial importance in today's corporate world. The M&As, by their very nature, reduce the number of firms in the industry as well as in economy. If mergers are horizontal, the number of firms in the corresponding industry falls; if mergers are vertical, then the number of firms involved in the production and distribution of a product falls. For conglomerate mergers, the total number of firms in the economy as a whole declines. The number of firms is one indicator of the degree of competition in the economy. Fewer firms in an industry create stronger tendencies for lower competition within the industry. Fewer firms in the input supply, production, and distribution channels also produce stronger tendencies for a lower degree of competition. The fact is that a higher concentration ratio indicates greater market power in the larger firms. When an industry is dominated by a few large firms, it is characterised as an oligopoly. A distinguishing characteristic of this market structure is the interdependence of firms within industry. Because there are only a few dominant firms, the actions of one firm affects those of the others, *vice versa*.

The U.S. automobile industry had "the Big Three" for some time. Despite the competition from the Asia and Europe, General Motors, Ford and Chrysler had a combined market share of over 70 percent in 1998. The tobacco industry has the Big Three: Philip Morris, RJR Nabisco, and Brown and Williamson. So does the beverages industry: Coca-Cola, Pepsi, and Cadbury Schweppes. The telephone industry has the Big Four: AT&T/TCI, Bell Atlantic/GTE (Verizon), SBC/ Ameritech and MCI WorldCom. The music industry has the Big Five: Universal/PolyGram, Warner Music, Sony Music, EMI Group and BMG Entertainment. With several significant mergers in recent years, the trend seems to be continuing. In 1998 , Citicorp and Travelers Group (Citi) merged to form the No. 1 financial services company in the world, and Exxon and Mobil Corp. merged to create the world's largest oil producer[30]. The world's audit oligopoly is composed of four accounting firms: PricewaterhouseCoopers, KPMG, Ernst and Young, and Deloitte Touche Komatsu (the Big 4).

In an oligopolistic market, firms have the temptation to collude and establish a cartel in an attempt to keep prices high and increase profits by acting as a joint monopoly. A prominent example of a cartel is the Organisation of Petroleum Exporting Countries (OPEC).

This is not something new for Corporate India. Take-overs evens hostile ones have been around for quite some time. In many ways, the take-over era was inaugurated way back in the early eighties, when Swaraj Paul brought his boisterous and street smart ways to shake up the quiet world of Indian board rooms and launched his bid for Escorts and DCM. Many other take-over artistes followed in his footsteps. R.P. Goenka cobbled together an industrial empire by taking over companies like Ceat and CESC. So did Manu Chhabra, buying companies like such as Shaw Wallace and Dunlop. The Ambanis almost succeeded in taking control of Larsen and Toubro (L&T) but were eventually checkmated by the government of the day, which instructed the Financial Institution (FI's) to keep their distance during take-over struggles.

The Indian economic reform since 1991 has opened up a whole lot of challenges both in the domestic and international spheres. The increased competition in the global market has prompted the Indian companies to go for mergers and acquisitions or perish. The opening of economy makes the Indian firms vulnerable to foreign competitors.This was just like an aquarium fish in front of blue whale.

The process of mergers and acquisitions has gained substantial importance in Indian corporate world. Hindustan Lever Limited (HLL) has taken complete control of Lakme-Lever, a joint venture with the Tata's in which it earlier had a 50% stake. Workhardt had bought out the Tata stake in Pharma Company Merind. These have been friendly deals. But there have been hostile ones as well. India Cements did cast its eyes on Raasi Cements after buying out the state of one of the latter's promoters. A potent take over attempt, targeting a 20% stake in Indian Aluminium (INDAL) was made by Sterlite Industries.

Acquisition of foreign companies by the Indian businesses has been the latest trend in the Indian corporate sector. Favourable government policies, buoyancy in economy, additional liquidity in the corporate sector, and dynamic attitudes of the Indian entrepreneurs are the key factors behind the changing trends of mergers and acquisitions in India.

Acquirer	*Target Company*	*Country Targeted*	*Deal value ($ ml.)*	*Industry*
Tata Steel	Corus Group plc Steel	UK	12,000	Hindalco
Novelis	Canada	5,982		Steel
Videocon	Daewoo Electronics Corp.	Korea	729	Electronics
Dr. Reddy's Labs	Betapharm	Germany	597	Pharma-ceutical
Suzlon Energy	Hansen Group	Belgium	565	Energy
HPCL	Kenya Petroleum Refinery Ltd.	Kenya	500	Oil and Gas
Ranbaxy Labs	Terapia SA	Romania	324	Pharma-ceutical
Tata Steel	Natsteel	Singapore	293	Steel
Videocon	Thomson SA	France	290	Electronics
VSNL	Teleglobe	Canada	239	Telecom

These are considered as landmark victories in India's corporate history.[31]

However in case of Ranbaxy, take over the following companies

Homegrown to the Belgium, Ranbaxy Belgium N.V. was earlier known as the Ethimed N.V. It was involved in production of generic pharmaceuticals through Ranbaxy (Netherlands) B.V. Ranbaxy purchased the company at a transaction of $1.58 million (Rs. 69.65 million).

Entire Mundogen Pharma SA aquistion took place through Laboratorios Ranbaxy S.L., Spain, on a transactional value of Euro 4.57 million (Rs. 266.12 million). The aquired company was the generic business of the GlaxoSmithKline (GSK), Spain.

Ranbaxy group aquired the significant part of the unbranded generic business of Allen S.P.A. The said company was the division of GlaxoSmithKline, Italy. The deal clicked on the amount of Euro 8.14 million (428.75 million).

Ranbaxy acquired the Be-Tabs Pharmaceuticals (Pty) Limited ("Be-Tabs"), South Africa on 1 December, 2006 with a total amount of 500 Million ZAR (USD 70 Million).

To ensure a high growth in areas like Biologics and Speciality injectables, Ranbaxy has increased its share of equity from 6.94 per cent to 46.95 per cent in Zenotech Laboratories Ltd., Hyderabad.[32]

In Jupiter Biosciences Limited, Hyderabad Ranbaxy aquired 14.9 per cent stake with the help of equity warrants. The said movemnet helped the Ranbaxy group to excel the booming opportunities in the growing therapeutic segment of Peptides.

On a total amount of $26 million, the Ranbaxy group aquired 13 dermatology products of Bristol Myers Squibb (BMS), USA. But in the last same was acquired by another Multinational Co. Daiichi Sankyo, Japan's No. 3 drug maker.[33]

If we go through the forbes list, Mukesh Ambani-promoted Reliance Industries Limited has ranked 121 position in the Forbes Global 2000 list., is also a Fortune Global 500 company and is the largest private sector company in India. The rest two public sector companies SBI (150 Rank) and ONGC (152 Rank).

SMALL SCALE INDUSTRY

The SSI sector has emerged over five decades as a highly vibrant and dynamic sector of the Indian economy. SSI is the second largest manpower employer in the country next only to the agriculture sector. SSI helps in industrialisation of rural and backward areas and reduce regional imbalance. It can also facilitate effective mobilisation of local resources and skill which might otherwise remain untapped.

The government also supported this sector through various stimulus through its industrial policies. The main item of policy support were reservation of a large number of items for SSI, excise exemption, credit under priority sector lending from banks and financial institutions, marketing support by reserving items of SSI products for Government purchases, providing infrastructure facilities like sheds, plots in industrial estates, technical support, training and entrepreneurship development, etc. Reservation supports to SSIs against competition from medium/large/multinational companies. The policy received statutory backing in 1984 under Section 29B of Industries (Development and Regulation) Act, 1951.[34]

By the end of March 2000, the SSI sector accounts for 95 per cent of the industrial units contributing about 40 per cent of value addition in the manufacturing sector, nearly 80 per cent of manufacturing employment and about 35 per cent of exports (both direct and indirect). More than 32 lakh units (which include both registered and unregistered units) are spread all over the country producing over 7500 items and providing employment to more than 178 lakh persons.

This sector is also facing challenge after the liberalisation wave and WTO trade negotiations. Indian SMEs incapable of developing the right perspective, as they are technologically, financially and organisationally weak compared to global SMEs.

Due to WTO trade negotiation implication,the government started dereservation with the removal of quantitative restrictions on different products from April 2002, the policy of reservation of products for exclusive manufacture of SSI has eventually become redundant.there are now just 239 products reserved for SSI sector which once was 800 products at the peak.

But Due to removal of QRS, many of the SSI units, especially in the consumer goods sector, will find it difficult to survive unless cost and quality improves as more imported products will find easy access to the Indian market. Similarly, the WTO clause of greater transparency of Government purchases, when implemented, will abolish the reserved list of items for purchase from SSI by the Government along with 15 per cent price preference enjoyed by the SSI in Government purchase. Falling demand for their products, globalisation, acute cash crunch and availability of cheap chinese products are crippling medium and small scale industries. The state government lack lusture approach towards SSI is also very damaging. As a result, scores of medium and hundreds of small units have already closed down. According to a survey, conducted by the Department of Industries, Punjab, in Mohali district. Out of the total registered industries in Mohali, 51 per cent have closed shop over the years, including many industries which were set-up way back in the seventies.[35]

Role of Foreign Institutional Investors (FII) in Indian Stock Market

The Indian stock markets have been known for severe manipulations by the owners of companies, financiers and brokers who indulge in insider trading and fixing of prices. It is suspected that the boom has come in handy for such unscrupulous elements to take advantage and raise prices further. Often, owners of companies that are not doing well use this device to manipulate the price of their stocks and make huge sums of monies at the expense of the gullible small investors. The media is cynically used to plant stories. All this has been noticed in the past three stock market booms in the last 16 years.[36]

Why do prices not shoot up like this in the mature economies? The reason is that the Indian markets are rather narrow. The organised sector of the Indian economy is less than 50 per cent of the economy and employs only about six per cent of the work force. If the government is taken out of this, the rest would be the corporate sector which is broadly represented in the stock markets. Thus, the private corporate sector is not more than 30 per cent of the national output and employs only two per cent of the work force. Further, the ownership of this sector rests with less than 0.1 per cent of the population. The public owns only about 10 per cent of the shares of the corporate sector, the vast bulk being held by promoters, FIIs, financial institutions and the like. In fact, a large part of the FII holding also belongs to the friends of the promoters so that no threat of takeover emerges. In companies like WIPRO or Infosys, the number of stockholders is less than a few thousand and the owners and FIIs own around 90 per cent of the equity stock.[37]

This volatility has been visible in the medium and long-term as well. From a low of 2924 on April 5, 2003, the Sensex had risen to 6194 on January 14, 2004, only to fall to 4505 on May 17, before rising to close at a peak of 6679 on January 3, 2005. These wild fluctuations have meant that for those who bought into the market at the right time and exited at the appropriate moment, the average return earned through capital gains was higher in 2003 than 2004, despite the extended bull run in the latter year. The result is small floating stock of shares (especially of the good companies) in the Indian markets and little relationship with the larger economy so that small infusion of funds can cause large price changes. This along with the above mentioned manipulations make the Indian markets volatile. This is compounded by the fact that the return on stocks is largely made up of capital gains and not dividend. Thus, if the market stops rising the expected return becomes very small and then it is not worth investing. In other words, when prices change rapidly, there is no stable resting point for the stock markets. A rapid rise invariably leads to an equally rapid opposite movement. Fluctuating markets do not move with the fundamentals. In fact, most of the time, they are not in sync.

The increase in wealth associated with the stock market boom is notional. It is based on small amount of trades and does not correspond to any real increase in wealth. This causes imbalances in the economy because it is concentrated in the hands of less than 0.1 per cent of the economy and spells danger for the country with vast sections getting marginalised and instability in society rising. It results in devaluation of work and weakening of democracy.

Chart 4.2

Historical Chart of Sensex

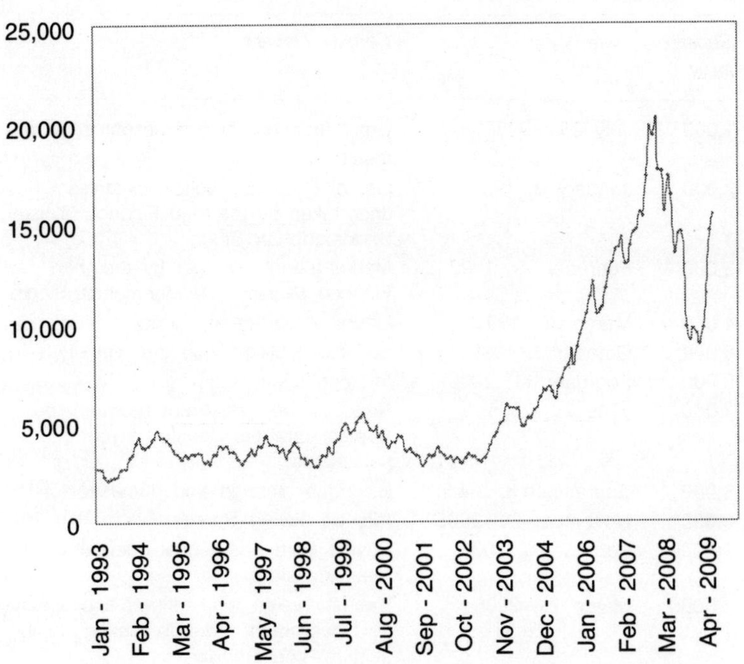

There are two messages that this experience sends out. The first is that, if market expectations can turn so whimsically, the signals or rumours on which they are based must lack any substance since any "fundamentals" on which they could be anchored have not shifted so violently. The second is that there must be some unusually strong force that is determining movements in the market which alone can explain the wild swings it is witnessing.

The combination of these two factors is indeed a disconcerting phenomenon, since if some force has the ability to lead the market and the others can be taken along without much resistance, the market is in essence being subjected to manipulation, even if not always consciously. Not surprisingly, recent market developments have once more focused attention on the volatility that has come to characterise India's stock markets.

Sensex Milestones

Sensex level	*Date*	*Sensex Drivers*
1,000	July 25, 1990	Good monsoon and excellent corporate results.
2,000	January 3, 1992	Liberal economic policy initiatives undertaken by the then Finance Minister, Dr Manmohan Singh.
3,000	February 29, 1992	Market-friendly Budget by the then Finance Minister, Dr Manmohan Singh.
4,000	March 30, 1992	Liberal export-import policy.
5,000	October 8, 1999	BJP-led coalition won the majority.
6,000	February 11, 2000	Infotech boom
7,000	June 20, 2005	News of the settlement between the Ambani brothers boosted investor sentiments
8,000	September 8, 2005	Buying by foreign and domestic funds
9,000	November 28, 2005	FIIs on buying Spree.
10,000	February 6, 2006	Buying from FIIs, Local operators and retail investors
11,000	March 21, 2006	Robust foreign fund inflows and a move by Government towards greater capital account convertibility.
12,000	April 20, 2006	Massive buying from mutual funds around Rs. 3400 cr. in just 19 trading sessions, favourable credit policy. Expectation of robust fourth quarter earnings by corporate and S&P upgrading India's sovereign credit rating from stable to positive
13,000	October 30, 2006	Fund infusion from market players, falling oil prices and strong second quarter results from Technology and Banking companies. Robust growth in infrastructure sector.

14,000	December 5, 2006	Strong FII inflow, healthy corporate earnings and continued strong economic data coupled with slash in petrol and diesel prices fuelled the latest surge on the bourses.
15,000	July 6, 2007	The softening trend in inflation below the five per cent level, indications of interest rates having peaked, strong FII inflows and expectations of good quarterly results.
16,000	September 19, 2007	US fed rate cut by 50 basis points, strong foreign fund inflows, softening trend in inflation below the four per cent level and Good Kharif crop.
17,000	September 26, 2007	Robust FII inflows and positive sentiments across the board.
18,000	October 09, 2007	Strong FII Inflows and short covering due to easing of political tension between LEFT and UPA over the Nuclear Deal.
19,000	October 15, 2007	Strong fund flow and expectation of good quarterly result from companies fuelled this leg of rally.
20,000	October 29, 2007	Strong FII buying coupled with short covering led to sharp up move. Registering of FII and P notes issue clarification has put momentum into Sensex.
21,000	January 08, 2008	Expectation of excellent quarterly result and strong forward momentum played major role.

Movements in the Sensex during the two decades have clearly been driven by the behaviour of foreign institutional investors (FIIs),[38] foreign institutional investors in Sensex companies and their active trading behaviour, their role in determining share price movements is considerable. Indian stock markets are known to be narrow and shallow in the sense that there are few companies whose shares are actively traded. Thus, although there are more than 4700 companies listed on the stock exchange, the BSE Sensex incorporates just 30 companies, trading in whose shares is seen as indicative of market activity. This shallowness would also mean that the effects of FII activity would be exaggerated by the influence

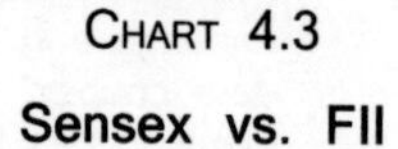

CHART 4.3

Sensex vs. FII

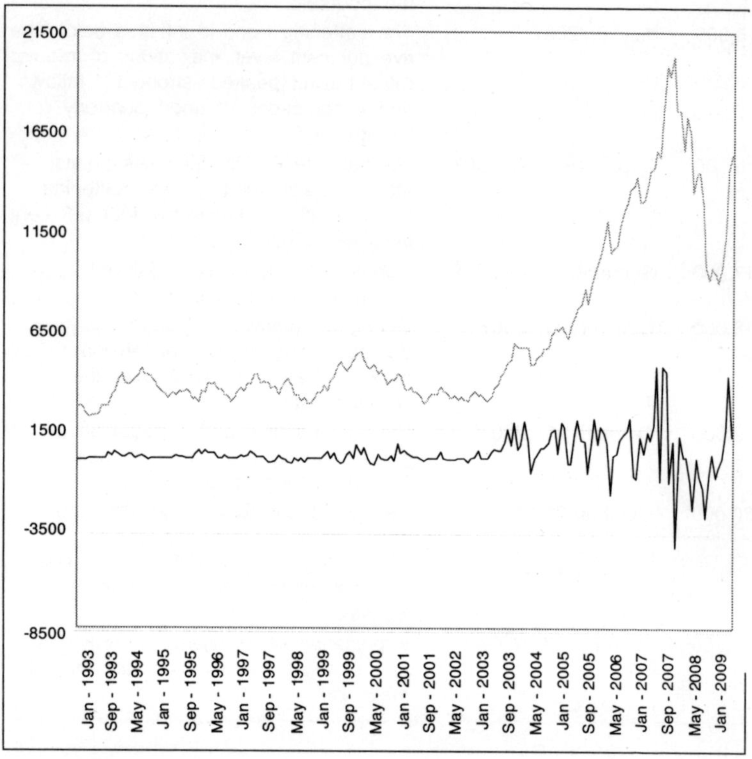

their behaviour has on other retail investors, who, in herd-like fashion tend to follow the FIIs when making their investment decisions.

These features of Indian stock markets induce a high degree of volatility for four reasons. In as much as an increase in investment by FIIs triggers a sharp price increase, it would provide additional incentives for FII investment and in the first instance encourage further purchases, so that there is a tendency for any correction of price increases unwarranted by price earnings ratios to be delayed. And when the correction begins, it would have to be led by an FII pull-out and can take the form of an extremely sharp decline in prices.

Secondly, as and when FIIs are attracted to the market by expectations of a price increase that tends to be automatically realised, the inflow of foreign capital can result in an appreciation of the rupee *vis-à-vis* the dollar (say). This increases the return earned in foreign exchange, when rupee assets are sold and the revenue converted into dollars. As a result, the investments turn even more attractive triggering an investment spiral that would imply a sharper fall when any correction begins.

Thirdly, the growing realisation by the FIIs of the power they wield in what are shallow markets, encourages speculative investment aimed at pushing the market up and choosing an appropriate moment to exit. This implicit manipulation of the market if resorted to often enough would obviously imply a substantial increase in volatility.

Finally, in volatile markets, domestic speculators too attempt to manipulate markets in periods of unusually high prices. Thus, most recently, the SEBI has issued show cause notices to four as-yet-unnamed entities, relating to their activities on around Black Monday, May 17, 2004, when the Sensex recorded a steep decline to a low of 4505 after fall of 565 points.

All this having said, the last two years have been remarkable because even though these features of the stock market imply volatility there have been more months when the market has been on the rise rather than on the decline. This clearly means that FIIs have been bullish on India for much of that time. The problem is that such bullishness is often driven by events outside the country, whether it be the performance of other equity markets or developments in non-equity markets elsewhere in the world. It is to be expected that FIIs would seek out the best returns as well as hedge their investments by maintaining a diversified geographical and market portfolio. The difficulty is that when they make their portfolio adjustments, which may imply small shifts in favour of or against a country like India, the effects it has on host markets are substantial. Those effects can then trigger a speculative spiral for the reasons discussed above, resulting in destabilising tendencies.

These aspects of the market are of significance because

financial liberalisation has meant that developments in equity markets can have major repercussions elsewhere in the system. With banks allowed to play a greater role in equity markets, any slump in those markets can affect the functioning of parts of the banking system. For example, the Nedungadi Bank was merged with Punjab National Bank due to the losses it suffered because of over exposure in the stock market.[39]

On the other hand if FII investments constitute a large share of the equity capital of a financial entity, as seems with the case of HDFC, an FII pull-out, even if driven by development outside the country can have significant implications for the financial health of what is an important institution in the financial sector of this country.

What is bothersome is that we have become in some way a hostage to foreigners, all over again. This time around, it is happening with respect to our capital market which has become the symbol of our economic health and almost every one seems to be rejoicing the fact, quite like many who still nostalgically remember the Raj!

For nearly a decade now, FIIs have dominated. Most see them as God-like institutions, as saviours. The current surge in the market is attributable almost entirely to them. It is hard core truth that FIIs are motivated only by profits. They should not be seen as developmental institutions, with any long-term stake in the Indian economy. Over-dependence on such capital can, therefore, be disastrous, as has been witnessed in several countries. More often than not, FIIs act in tandem and their actions are not always rational. FIIs are also often the first to flee, leading to a snowballing.

PARTICIPATORY NOTES (PNs) are instruments held by entities that are otherwise not allowed to invest in Indian markets by the market regulator, the Securities and Exchange Board of India (SEBI). These instruments confer anonymity on those who hold them. PNs are a class of Offshore Derivative Instruments (ODI) and have been the main avenue for the officially barred hedge funds to enter Indian markets.

Brokerages affiliated to foreign institutional investors (FIIs) buy India-based securities and then issue PNs to foreign investors, which are basically in the form of IOUs.

Even though PN holders do not own the shares directly, they are able to collect dividends or capital gains that accrue from the underlying assets. Moreover, the velocity of circulation of this instrument is enhanced by the fact that it can be traded in international markets, which is why foreign investors find it attractive.

It is a derivative instrument since it "derives" its value from an underlying share or security. It allows investors to build portfolios depending on their preference for individual shares. The instrument is issued through the sub-accounts of registered FIIs operating in Indian markets.

Of the little over 1,000 FIIs registered with SEBI only about 34 are both stockbrokers and institutional investors (in March 2004 there were only 14). These are the entities that issue PNs. Hedge funds are reckoned to be among the main holders of PNs. Merrill Lynch, Morgan Stanley, Credit Lyonnais, Citigroup and Goldman Sachs are among the prime issuers of PNs.

According to SEBI, the notional value of PNs outstanding has shot up ten times between March 2004 and August 2007—from Rs. 31,875 crore to Rs. 3,53,484 crore.

For regulatory agencies PNs are a major irritant because they are opaque instruments belonging to faceless investors. But more importantly, from a wider economic perspective, they amplify the risks associated with volatility in financial markets. For instance, sub-accounts themselves pool the PNs and use them as collateral to raise loans. The scope for such leveraging is amplified when the resulting investments go into other derivative instruments such as futures and options of shares in Indian markets. This kind of leveraging amplifies not only the scope for investing but also the movements of share prices in the markets. The fact that players in the futures market need pay upfront only a small part of the value of the contract as margin money further amplifies the fluctuation in turnover and prices.

The Reserve Bank of India (RBI) has been a consistent opponent of these instruments. In November 2005, it presented a dissenting note to the Finance Ministry's Expert Group on Encouraging FII Flows and Checking the Vulnerability of Capital Markets to Speculative Flows.

The RBI reiterated its "stance that the issue of PNs should not be permitted." It pointed out that its "main concerns" pertained to the regulator's inability to know the identity of the owner of the assets or who are the actual "beneficial owners" of these instruments.

It also pointed out that the instrument encourages "multilayering, which will make it difficult to identify the ultimate holder of PNs." This results from the ability of the original PN holders to sell them to other players, whose identity is also unknown. The central bank always regarded the spiralling trade in these opaque instruments as a serious hazard. It also observed that weeding out these instruments would actually "enhance the reputation of markets and lead to healthy flows."

The RBI has also reiterated its case that the modus operandi of PNs is a gross violation of the know-your-customer norms, which are a basic requirement for any investor participating in any financial market.[40]

In the past two years, there were several proposals to ban PNs. The S.S. Tarapore Committee's report on full capital account convertibility in July 2006 recommended that FIIs be prohibited from investing fresh money through PNs. It recommended that PNs be phased out in a year after providing its holders an exit route.

In fact, a few years ago, under the stewardship of G.N. Bajpai, SEBI itself considered banning PNs. This was based on its investigation of the stock market scam in 2000, orchestrated by the Kolkata-based broker Ketan Parekh. In fact, SEBI admitted, "it is not possible to identify the actual beneficiaries of PNs."

The regulator also found that about $2 billion had been brought in and taken out of the country by Overseas Corporate Bodies (OCBs) registered in Mauritius. Although the RBI subsequently banned OCBs from investing in the stock market, the PN game continued with SEBI and the Finance Ministry looking the other way. The Finance Ministry's logic, driven by its overarching interest in wooing foreign investors at any cost, was that PNs provided an opportunity for unregistered investors to invest in India.

The dangers posed by PNs can be disproportionately

larger than the actual amounts involved in the transactions. For instance, the Joint Parliamentary Committee (JPC) probe into the stock scam of 2000 (popularly known as the Ketan Parekh scandal) revealed that although only four sub-accounts issued PNs (against shares worth Rs. 14,000 crore) involved in the scandal, they were used to rig share prices on a much wider scale, which disrupted the entire system.

Fears have repeatedly been expressed by not only the RBI but also political parties that these opaque instruments pose a serious security hazard. In particular, there is the apprehension that they can be used by drug cartels and terrorist organisations to funnel money into India. While this may be so, the threat perception need not necessarily be based on such fears alone.

For a long time now, PNs have been regarded as a threat to the very integrity of the economic system. Quite apart from the fact they are a prime vehicle for the burgeoning foreign exchange reserves, which has been a worrisome factor for the RBI in the past four years, they pose other systemic risks as well. For one, it is well known that Indian promoters of companies have used PNs to bring in funds parked overseas to fund the creeping acquisition of their companies' stock to guard against takeovers. Tax authorities also fear that Indian money launderers use PNs to ship funds out of the country using the hawala route and then get it back into the country posing as PNs.

Corporate Governance

The head of Indian outsourcing company Satyam Computer Services resigned this year disclosing that profits had been falsely inflated for years thus plunging its shares nearly 80 percent.

India's biggest corporate scandal in memory threatens future foreign investment (FDI) flows into Asia's third-largest economy and casts a cloud over growth in its once-booming outsourcing sector. The news sent Indian equity markets into a tailspin, with Bombay's main benchmark index tumbling 7.3 percent and consequently the Indian rupee fell. The New York Stock Exchange halted trading in Satyam's shares indefinitely, saying it wanted to review the news. Ramalinga

Raju, founder and chairman of India's fourth largest software services exporter, said in a statement that Satyam's profits had been massively inflated over recent years. He added that no other board member was aware of the financial irregularities at the Satyam, Satyam in Sanskrit means "truth."

Raju, who founded Satyam as a family business with his brother and brother-in-law more than two decades ago, said about $1 billion or 94 percent of the cash on the company's books was fictitious.

Raju, 54, came under close scrutiny after the company's botched attempt to buy two construction companies partly owned by its founders, which Raju said on Wednesday was a final attempt to resolve the problem of the fictitious assets. "It was like riding a tiger, not knowing how to get-off without being eaten," Raju, a management graduate from Ohio University, said in his letter, adding he was prepared to face up to the legal consequences.

The startling admission comes as investors across the globe pay more attention to oversight following last month's arrest of Bernard Madoff over charges he swindled clients out of billions of dollars.

"In a bull market, people forgot about it (corporate governance)," said Singapore-based Ashish Goyal, chief investment officer at Prudential Asset Management. "In a bear market chickens are coming home to roost, so it gets highlighted at a time like this."[41]

The company's difficulties multiplied when the World Bank, a major customer, barred Satyam from new business, citing "improper benefits" given to Bank officials.

Satyam rose to prominence in the late 1990s when Raju was among the first to spot outsourcing opportunities in the year 2000 rollover problem, which saw the coming of age of the software outsourcing industry.Just three months ago, Satyam received a Golden Peacock award from a group of Indian directors for excellence in corporate governance.By close of trade, Satyam's share value slumped to about $550 million from around $7 billion as recently as last June 2008. New York-listed Satyam specializes in business software and back-office services for clients such as General Electric and Nestle.

"I think there is no future for this stock. This case for India is similar to what happened to Enron in the U.S.," said Jigar Shah, senior vice-president at Kim Eng Securities. "It will not stop at Satyam. Many more companies will come into scrutiny like that. There is a strong possibility investments in India will be affected."[42]

Telecom Sector

The telecom services have been recognised the world-over as an important tool for socio-economic development for a nation. It is one of the prime support services needed for rapid growth and modernisation of various sectors of the economy. Indian telecommunication sector has undergone a major process of transformation through significant policy reforms, particularly beginning with the announcement of NTP 1994 and was subsequently re-emphasised and carried forward under NTP 1999. Driven by various policy initiatives, the Indian telecom sector witnessed a complete transformation in the last decade. It has achieved a phenomenal growth during the last few years and is poised to take a big leap in the future.

Status of Telecom Sector

The Indian Telecommunications network with 430 million connections (as on March 2009) is the third largest in the world. The sector is growing at a speed of 46-50% during the recent years. This rapid growth is possible due to various proactive and positive decisions of the Government and contribution of both by the public and the private sectors. The rapid strides in the telecom sector have been facilitated by liberal policies of the Government that provides easy market access for telecom equipment and a fair regulatory framework for offering telecom services to the Indian consumers at affordable prices. Presently, all the telecom services have been opened for private participation. The Government has taken following main initiatives for the growth of the Telecom Sector.

LIBERALISATION

The process of liberalisation in the country began in right earnest with the announcement of the New Economic Policy in July, 1991. Telecom equipment manufacturing was delicensed in 1991 and value added services were declared open to the private sector in 1992, following which radio paging, cellular mobile and other value added services were opened gradually to the private sector. This has resulted in large number of manufacturing units set-up in the country. As a result, most of the equipment used in telecom area is being manufactured within the country. A major breakthrough was the clear enunciation of the government's intention of liberalising the telecom sector in the National Telecom Policy resolution of 13th May 1994.

National Telecom Policy, 1994

In 1994, the Government announced the National Telecom Policy which defined certain important objectives, including availability of telephone on demand, provision of world class services at reasonable prices, improving India's competitiveness in global market and promoting exports, attracting FDI and stimulating domestic investment, ensuring India's emergence as major manufacturing/export base of telecom equipment and universal availability of basic telecom services to all villages. It also announced a series of specific targets to be achieved by 1997

Telecom Regulatory Authority of India (TRAI) The entry of private service providers brought with it the inevitable need for independent regulation. The Telecom Regulatory Authority of India (TRAI) was, thus, established with effect from 20th February 1997 by an Act of Parliament, called the Telecom Regulatory Authority of India Act, 1997, to regulate telecom services, including fixation/revision of tariffs for telecom services which were earlier vested in the Central Government.

TRAI's mission is to create and nurture conditions for growth of telecommunications in the country in a manner and at a pace, which will enable India to play a leading role in emerging global information society. One of the main objectives of TRAI is to provide a fair and transparent policy environment, which promotes a level playing field and facilitates fair competition. In pursuance of the above objective, TRAI has issued from time to time a large number of regulations, orders and directives to deal with issues coming before it and provided the required direction to the evolution of Indian telecom market from a Government owned monopoly to a multi operator multi-service open competitive market. The directions, orders and regulations issued cover a wide range of subjects including tariff, interconnection and quality of service as well as governance of the Authority.

The TRAI Act was amended by an ordinance, effective from 24 January 2000, establishing a Telecommunications Dispute Settlement and Appellate Tribunal (TDSAT) to take over the adjudicatory and disputes functions from TRAI. TDSAT was to adjudicate any dispute between a licensor and a licensee, between two or more service providers, between a service provider and a group of consumers, and to hear and dispose of appeals against any direction, decision or order of TRAI.

The most important milestone and instrument of telecom reforms in India is the New Telecom Policy 1999 (NTP-99). The New Telecom Policy, 1999 (NTP-99) was approved on 26th March 1999, to become effective from 1st April 1999. NTP-99 laid down a clear roadmap for future reforms, contemplating the opening up of all the segments of the telecom sector for private sector participation. It clearly recognised the need for strengthening the regulatory regime as well as restructuring the departmental telecom services to that of a public sector corporation so as to separate the licensing and policy functions of the Government from that of being an operator. It also recognised the need for resolving the prevailing problems faced by the operators so as to restore their confidence and improve the investment climate.

National Long Distance Services

National Long Distance services were opened for private participation. The Government announced on 13.08.2000 the guidelines for entry of private sector in

National Long Distance Services without any restriction on the number of operators. The DOT guidelines of license for the National Long Distance operations were also issued.[43]

Highlights–NLD Guidelines

- Unlimited entry for carrying both inter-circle and intra-circle calls.
- Total foreign equity (including equity of NRIs and international funding agencies) must not exceed 74%. Promoters must have a combined net worth of Rs. 25 million.
- Private operators will have to enter into an arrangement with fixed-service providers within a circle for traffic between long-distance and short-distance charging centres.
- Seven years time frame was set for rollout of network, spread over four phases. Any shortfall in network coverage would result in encashment and forfeiture of bank guarantee of that phase.
- Private operators to pay one-time entry fee of Rs. 25 million plus a Financial Bank Guarantee (FBG) of Rs. 200 million. The revenue sharing agreement would be to the extent of 6%.
- Private operators allowed to set-up landing facilities that access submarine cables and use excess bandwidth available.
- Licence period would be for 20 years and extendable by 10 years.

The liberalisation measures post-1990 have changed with foreign investments radically, now portfolio as well as Foreign Direct Investment are not only allowed but also actively encouraged. During the decade of the nineties, the 'ceilings' on FDI in different sectors were progressively raised. In 2001, 100 per cent foreign investments were allowed in several industrial sectors. Also, 100 per cent Foreign Direct Investment is allowed in almost all the infrastructure sectors.

FDI can Enter India through Two Possible Channels

The automatic route under which companies receiving Foreign Direct Investment need to inform the Reserve Bank of India within 30 days of receipt of funds and issuance of shares to the foreign investor.

For sectors that are not covered under the automatic route, prior approval is needed from the Foreign Investment Promotion Board (FIPB).

India's telecom network with about 210 million telephones is now one of the largest in the world and second largest among the emerging economies of Asia. The Indian Telecom sector has witnessed dramatic transformation on almost all the fronts. The share of private sector has increased to more than 66% and the contribution of mobile telephony has gone upto 80%.

However, economic deregulation has forever been a fertile breeding ground for controversy. Periodic eruptions of acrimony are especially likely when the sector is one where profits are reasonably assured and the pace of technological change is rapid. Since the government monopoly in telecommunications was effectively ended by the 1994 policy formulation, a number of commercial groups with potentially conflicting interests have come to flourish in the sector. Some of them have become well entrenched enough to seek or to dictate the course of policy.

When the telecom regulators talked about restricting ownership in telecom sector, one of the most important arguments forwarded for limiting foreign ownership was security of critical telecom infrastructure. Security is considered important as telecom assets are a key target in any hostility and any damage to them can impair the functioning of the country. Telecom networks are seen as nervous system of the country as critical information passes through it.

In today's environment, where global terrorism is seen as the biggest threat and surveillance agencies of developed countries try to subvert the control of local authorities across the world, security on telecom assets needs a closer look. Today, it is not only government controlled surveillance agencies which have access to technologies for surveillance, even terrorists do. General stores sell technology which makes it possible for calls to be tapped.

This is where a window has been opened by the Indian telecom regulator. While the regulator is monitoring the ownership of telecom companies, it has no regulation for passive infrastructure which is being outsourced or shared.

There are two parts of a telecom network: a passive part and the active or electronics and fibre optics part. Companies like Bharti have already outsourced their electronics part of the network, so it is effectively in the hands of foreign companies. Now, while the regulator may be barring ownership in telecom services provider, it has forgotten the critical security concerns, amidst the present euphoria about the rapid telecom sector growth.[44]

If surveillance has to be controlled, clarity on the security protocol followed at the passive infrastructure level is extremely important. Passive infrastructure is basically the physical infrastructure concerned with the provision of power supply required to house various electronics and radio equipment.

Hypothetically, if the enemy wants to destroy the cellular infrastructure it can either attack the telecom hub which is carefully protected or switch-off power for the cell sites across the state.

The cell site is important as it is used by the operator to locate the cell phone owner and for surveillance. For instance, if surveillance needs to be carried out in someone's office or residence and it is difficult to get access to the location due to high security there, the next best thing is to use the cell site as a location.

A cell site already has so much radio equipment installed on it that any anti-surveillance sweeping device will not be noticed as its radio frequency will get clubbed with the existing equipment. Anti-surveillance equipment looks for signature of radio frequency to detect snooping devices. The issue raises concerns especially if it is being done by a foreign agency or party.

While the government is concerned about foreign investors, it does not seem to be concerned about telecom infrastructure. Indian telecom regulation insists that even the top management in a telecom company must be from local citizens. But, there seems to be no concern regarding funds which are getting invested directly into infrastructure. These funds may be controlled by foreign agencies and may end up owning a crucial piece of India's infrastructure.

Around 200 m cell sites will map out the total Indian terrain and a lot of these cell sites will come up near sensitive defence locations. Till now the government has not been too concerned about the proximity of these cell sites to defence locations. Maybe there needs to be some diligence applied in this area as these cell sites can be used for surveillance due to the high powered radio equipment they already carry.

Another area which regulations have to address is the health hazards which arise from the high-powered radio equipment. Several buildings have multiple radio transmission equipments on their terrace. Direct exposure to such high frequency radio equipment is harmful. While prolonged use of cell phones causing damage to the brain or heart are overblown, the real concern is cell sites radiating strong radio frequency-waves through multiple sites on a building and direct exposure to them.

In a recent study on the impact of the electromagnetic radiation of cellphones, conducted by Panjab University, on eggs is an indication, this modern-day wonder could be doing considerable damage to all of us. The eggs, kept between four working cellphones, were cooked hard-boiled.

The study shows that cellphone radiation could well also be responsible for chirping sparrows in their vanishing act in Chandigarh.[45]

While scientists across the world are trying to find a reason for the extinction of a common bird such as a house sparrow and have linked it with the excessive radiation of EM (electromagnetic) waves in our environment, a team of researchers from Panjab University has proved it that the waves adversely affect even the tiniest of insects, mustard seeds, wheat grains and even eggs of hen.

These rays (same as those in a microwave oven) generate heat and adversely affect seed germination in plants and impair cell expansion.

It is pertinent to mention here that as per this study,

which was started in 2005, there were a total 199 mobile towers in Chandigarh alone and the electromagnetic radiation released by these towers were far more than the prescribed limit (as per a petition filed in the Supreme Court).

According to Dr S. Vijayan, Director of the Salim Ali Centre for Ornithology and Natural History (SACON), "A number of studies has been conducted to find out the relationship between the increase in electromagnetic waves and the decrease in the number of sparrows. A positive correlation has been found between them."

A study was initiated earlier this year in London by the British Trust for Ornithology to investigate whether the explosion of electromagnetic waves from portable handsets is wiping out sparrows in London. The British study involves 30,000 birdwatchers who will examine the urban sparrow population near cell-phone masts, where electromagnetic fields are most concentrated.

London has witnessed a steep fall in its sparrow population—a 75 per cent fall since 1994, which coincides with the emergence of the cell-phone.

Electromagnetic waves travel through the air to the cell-phone masts . located above tall buildings in the cities. These waves then travel to and fro between the handset and the tower while one is using the handset, and this results in increased electromagnetic contamination in the air.

The rapidly increasing number of cell-phone subscribers is resulting in higher concentration level of electromagnetic waves in the air which clashes with the earth's electromagnetic field.

"These are all circumstantial evidences. it probably affects their central nervous system. increased exposure to electromagnetic waves can affect small animals. For example, in rats, it is found that the sperm count has decreased while in the case of chicken embryonic, mortality has become very high.[46]

Though, these radio waves are not the ionising kinds like X-rays and do not get fully absorbed by the human body, they still pose health hazards. Every country in the world has important regulations in place to protect its citizens from exposure to these radiations. US ECC, Australia, New

Zealand all have specific regulations for preventing health damage due to exposure to radio equipment at cell sites. While India is busy touting its telecom revolution and the penetration rates, these vital issues have largely been ignored.

Allocation of Spectrum

Allocation of spectrum is the biggest scam in the history of Independent India. The perpetrator of the scam, Union minister for telecommunications and information technology Andimuthu Raja is trying to brazen it out protesting his innocence. He says he has played by the rule book and that the Cabinet and the ministry of finance have approved his decisions. His mentor, DMK supreme, Muthuvel Karunanidhi, claims he is being victimised because he is a Dalit. But facts tell a diametrically different story.[47]

The exchequer has lost roughly Rs. 80,000 crore because of the flawed manner in which electro-magnetic spectrum, used for mobile telecommunications, has been allotted. Spectrum is a scarce national resource. The government is supposed to act as a custodian of the people. But the manner in which a clutch of private companies have gained, at the expense of the country, is nothing short of being scandalous. These acts of crony capitalism comprise the underbelly of the telecom revolution that has swept India in recent years.

Two recent transactions, the first involving Swan Telecom (earlier associated with the Reliance Anil Dhirubhai Ambani Group) and Etilasat (or Emirates Telecommunications Corporation, the main telecom operator in the United Arab Emirates), and the other between a division of Unitech Ltd, United Wireless, and Telenor (of Norway), confirm the view that the nation lost no less than Rs. 60,000 crore because of the methodology that was adopted by the Department of Telecommunications (DoT) while allotting spectrum.

If one adds to this figure the amount lost due to excess spectrum being allotted to existing telecom operators like Bharti, Vodafone and Idea—the same so-called cartel that Mr. Raja alleges has been working against him without naming them—besides Reliance Communications (RComm) and Tata Teleservices, the total loss figure would rise by roughly Rs. 20,000 crore. In other words, the scam is in the region of Rs. 80,000 crore or more than what the Central government spends in a year on healthcare.

Mr. Raja has steadfastly refused to allot spectrum through an open public auction and instead chose the first-come-first-served (FCFS) route that was not merely opaque but also discriminatory. Thus, second generation (2G) spectrum for all-India mobile telephony was allotted to individual private companies, for Rs. 1,651 crore each (this price was determined seven years earlier) against a current market price that was at least six times higher.

Mr. Raja replaced Dayanidhi Maran as communications minister in May 2007. On October 19, 2007, the DoT had changed its policy by issuing a press note. The same evening, RComm was ready with a demand draft of Rs. 1,651 crore and was conferred the status of a GSM (general system of mobile communications) licensee by virtue of the original licence it had been holding. The company had earlier been primarily using the competing CDMA (code division multiple access) technology.

RComm was able to jump the queue ahead of 46 corporate entities/groups that had placed 575 applications with the DoT, none of which had at that time received letters of intent despite the fact that some (such as ByCell, Idea and Spice) had been waiting for over a year-and-a-half. In the queue were all kinds of firms, including realtors and retailers, none of which had any experience in telecom, who later received licences and with it, spectrum. After RComm, Tata Tele became the next beneficiary and were thereafter followed by others.

The ministry of finance has, in an internal note, claimed that the government should have obtained Rs. 31,453 crore for the 120 licences given to nine corporate entities with start-up spectrum in the first quarter of 2008 instead of Rs. 8,987 crore actually obtained (as these are based on 2001-02 prices arrived at through a public auction). The two industry lobbies (divided into GSM and CDMA technology users) have been at loggerheads for a while now. RComm and its supporter Amar Singh of the Samajwadi Party have accused old GSM operators (led by Bharti and Vodafone) of hoarding spectrum worth Rs. 20,000 crore.[48]

Privatising of Water

Recent developments in the water sector presage a new direction in international policy. The largest water corporations are acknowledging that they cannot make money from the poor, and therefore that they can't provide them services. The international institutions' reliance on these multinational corporations to deliver water services to developing countries is becoming less and less tenable. Suez's experience has taught the company that its previous profits model for water privatisation in developing countries is not sustainable. SAUR had already come to the same conclusion, and Vivendi is also restricting its investments. The requirements set out by Suez for its future investments in developing countries are extremely demanding. The company is requiring unequivocal guarantees for its investments against all forms of risk, and requiring all of its operations—not just future contracts—to generate cash for all investments.

This is a commercial impossibility for the poor, and so the companies are effectively demanding subsidies and guarantees from the development banks as a pre-condition for attempting to connect the poor. This is contrary to the rhetoric which Suez, especially, has employed in the past, that the companies can connect the poor. It also challenges the very reasons for involving the private sector in such an essential public service—the capacity to take on risk, to bring in their own capital and to provide the 'benefits' of competition. As it turns out, these multinationals are unable to do any of these.

The cases of Thames in Izmit and IWL in Tallinn reinforce this message. A guarantee to multinational's is a country's risk, which can be translated into a huge financial burden at an unexpected moment. The connection with corruption is also obvious.

The most basic lesson is for governments, development banks, donors and community organisations concerned with water to recognize these facts. It is not credible for the World Bank to continue making policy on the assumptions of the 1990s, when the flagship concessions of Buenos Aires and Manila are collapsing, and Suez says it will 'prepare to depart'. It is no longer 'business as usual' with the water multinationals. The water multinationals are now clearly prepared to abandon concession contracts which do not meet the new demand for security for their investments. Communities, governments and public authorities, where there are existing concessions with the multinationals, especially to Suez, should themselves initiate a review of the concessions and identify best options from the local perspective.

In India, the World Bank has committed to fund $150 million for capacity building in the water sector for 13 towns in Karnataka. A part of this fund will go towards awarding management contracts with the new regional utilities through international bids. In addition, the Asian Development Bank has given the Karnataka government a grant of $175 million to develop the water sector in coastal towns. The changes envisaged in the water policy would require substantial amendment of the KUWSBD Act, the BWSSB Act, 1964, and the Karnataka Municipalities Act. The corporatisation process of the two boards, while recommended in the draft water policy, was taking shape on a parallel track.[49]

Water being a fundamental need of life, the privatisation of this sector involves issues that are different from the privatisation of the energy or telecommunications sectors. The state or a strong regulatory body must ensure its delivery to the poor and disadvantaged sections. The poor already pay a disproportionately high price for water, and a high water tariff imposed by private companies will push the poor out of a protected water system. So, the service obligation in the water sector has implications for tariffs and subsidies. Secondly, the health and sanitation aspects of water supply have to be regulated carefully and cannot be left entirely to private operators. Britain, which in 1989 went in for the outright privatisation of its water sector, had to pay a price when water providers reneged on their commitments to provide potable water. In the case of water, unlike energy or telecom, the costs lie in transmission and distribution and not in the cost of initial production or storage.

In June 1997, the Karnataka government decided that it would invite private sector participation on a BOOT basis for the implementation of the Cauvery Water Supply Scheme

Stage 1V Phase II and Stage V for a total quantity of 500 MLD of water. The total project size was estimated at around Rs. 1,500 crores then. The BWSSB was asked to invite global tenders. In a controversial move, the J.H. Patel government signed a memorandum of understanding with the Malaysia-based firm Biwater. Not unlike the model for private participation in the energy sector, the BWSSB would have had to lift all the water supplied by Biwater at a fixed tariff with a built-in rate of return. In June 1998, Biwater had stipulated that the tariff would be Rs. 26 a kilolitre. The latest tariff offered by Biwater is believed to be just under Rs. 23 a kilolitre. The Board's current water tariff is between Rs. 17 and Rs. 18. The Congress(I), while in Opposition, raised stiff objections to the Biwater agreement in the State legislature on the grounds that it could land the State government in a Dabhol-like financial bind. When the S.M. Krishna government came to power, the MoU with Biwater went into cold storage.

RETAIL SECTOR

India is a land of retail democracy—hundreds of thousands of weekly haats and bazaars are located across the length and breadth of our country by people's own self-organisational capacities. Our streets are bazaars—lively, vibrant, safe and the source of livelihood for millions. According to a Confederation of Indian Industry—McKinsey report, India has the highest number of retail outlets per capita in the world at 5.5 per 1,000 people. It is through this multitude of small retailers that India's fast moving consumer goods (FMCG) giants built up their empires.[50]

This does not include the village haats.

Our retail democracy is characterised by:

1. High levels of livelihoods in retail with nearly 40 million employed which accounts for 8% of the employment and 4% of the entire population.
2. High levels of self-organisation.
3. Low capital-input.
4. High levels of decentralisation.

Now, Giant corporations like Wal-Mart[51] and Reliance have started to try and take over the Indian retail sector. The entry of the giant corporate retail in India's food market will have direct impact on India's 650 million farmers and 40 million people employed in tiny retail. More than 6600 mega stores are planned with Rs. 40,000 crore by 2011. Currently the value of the retail market is estimated at around $ 270 billion with a growth rate of 5.7 per cent per annum according to the Indian retail report. The size of small retail is big, the size of big retail is small, a mere Rs. 250 billion in 2004 or 3% and Rs. 485 billion or 4.7% per cent of the retail market in 2006. However, the large scale corporate retail is projected to grow at the rate of 28% to 30% per annum, reaching Rs. 1000 billion or $ 70 billion by 2010 from the current size of US $ 8.7 billion. The tenfold increase in corporate retail will be at the cost of small scale retail, which employs nearly 10% of India's population. A number of cultural categories and policy instruments are being used to make corporate retail grow. Wal-Mart is the biggest player in retail. In a report "Oligopoly Inc. 2005", the ETC Group has shown that consolidation, cut throat competition and aggressive global expansion are the driving forces in the food retail sector. In 2004, the top 10 global food retailers accounted for combined sales of $840 billion, 24% of the estimated $3.5 trillion global market. This was up from $ 513.7 billion in 2001. If Wal-Mart and other retail chains get a foothold in India, it will mean displacement of small retailers and farmers.

Till now Reliance has planned to make the biggest investment in this sector in India. They plan to invest Rs. 25,000 crore in coming four years. The company that is floated for this purpose is known as Reliance Retail Limited and it would be owned totally by Reliance Industries Limited. The Reliance Fresh has been averaging a sale of Rs. 3.5 to Rs. 4 lakh per day per shop. A study done by RFSTE/ Navdanya exposed two myths of Reliance Retail. Firstly, contrary to the "Farm to Fork" projection of buying directly from farmers, Reliance Fresh is buying from existing mandis. This also exposes the myth that existing retail is "unorganised", and corporate retail is "organised."[52]

Corporate retail is using the organisational capacities of our wholesale and retail systems to hijack retail. The second myth is that corporate retail will have no impact on tiny retailers, hawkers and shopkeepers. As per nearly 90% small retailers have been negatively impacted within a few months of a Reliance Fresh store coming up in their neighbourhood and 87% said Reliance has taken away their business. 66% small vendors said that they would have to close their shops because of declining business. Corporate Retail is clearly growing at the cost of small retail. Food retail in India has clearly become an important part of global trade wars. But this is about more than trade. For the people of India it is about culture and ecology, about employment and food security.[53]

The corporate control of food and agriculture, from seed to retail, is a recipe for disaster in our context of more than 650 million farmers and millions involved in retail at the tiny scale.With the livelihoods of small traders and hawkers in threat due to the corporate entry in retail.

BIOTECHNOLOGY RULES THE WORLD

Food has long been a political tool in US foreign policy. Twenty-five years ago USDA Secretary Earl Butz told the 1974 World Food Conference in Rome that food was a weapon, calling it 'one of the principal tools in our negotiating kit'. As far back as 1957 US Vice-President Hubert Humphrey told a US audience, 'If you are looking for a way to get people to lean on you and to be dependent on you in terms of their cooperation with you, it seems to me that food dependence would be terrific'.[54]

The business of genetically engineered agricultural products is closely interwoven with the so-called "life sciences" business, After several decades of mergers and acquisitions, the top five "Gene Giants" (Astra-Zeneca, DuPont, Monsanto, Novartis, and Aventis) have built their strategic monopolies incorporating dominant positions in the seed, agrochemicals, pharmaceuticals and related markets. They account for nearly two-thirds of the global pesticide market, almost one-quarter of the commercial seed market, and virtually 100 percent of the transgenic seed market.

Now source of the food stream, basic to human life, is being diverted through the advocacy of genetic engineering and the patenting of living organisms to serve the priorities of the transnational corporations, many of those corporations are larger in economic terms than countries, yet they are private bodies whose recent evolution into global giants has been extremely rapid. The biotech companies are not among the largest in the world, but their ability to change our lives arguably places them among the most powerful, since their work involves bypassing the process of evolution and changing genomes irrevocably. The colonisation of indigenous agriculture through the green revolution has destroyed farming systems and eliminated locally adapted varieties and knowledge, undermining the agricultural diversity that has been nurtured over millennia. Each farmer variety that is lost means the loss of germplasm and knowledge painstakingly selected, built up, exchanged and passed on down the generations. Such wealth is irreplaceable. These systems are being replaced by crops that depend on inputs and farming systems that depend on agribusiness, while farmers are being displaced to expanding cities. All this has intensified cycles of dependence and struck at the roots of self-reliance. A system of commerce based on perpetual growth requires an unquestioning mass consumer culture in order to thrive. This provides the perfect context for the operations of the large corporations. Genetic engineering will intensify this process and GM contamination has already penetrated Mexico, the centre of origin for maize, transformed by farmers over thousands of years from a plant of little food value to a world staple Financial markets have been liberated over the last 20 years, enabling corporations to move their capital freely and change their focus at will. This has greatly facilitated the growth of corporate power. The World Trade Organisation's agreements are designed to give corporations freedom to operate wherever profits can be maximised. Many countries in the South lack national rules on monopolies, and there is currently no way to tackle global monopolies. Governments with the largest number of corporations—in the US, Europe and Japan—have become increasingly complicit in corporate interests. Politicians and corporate executives regularly swap places in a flurry of revolving doors, especially in the US. All this is facilitating the entry of private corporations into areas of public interest which were formerly the preserve of local communities or governments. The extension of patents to cover living organisms from 1980 was vital to the biotechnology industry, enabling it to raise capital on the markets and to construct systems of exclusive monopoly control. It is not surprising that the corporations have invested so much energy in securing intellectual property rights legislation such as TRIPs and the European Directive on the Protection of Biotechnological Inventions. Now they seek a harmonised global patent regime. The effort to develop a genetic engineering technology to prevent the germination of seed and to control the expression of traits (Terminator and Traitor technologies) was initially a collaboration between the US government and a US company. It aimed to increase profits and create an incentive for corporations by preventing.[55]

Pulling Strings in Pakistan

Under current WTO regulations, the TRIPs agreement obliges countries to implement law to protect intellectual property rights. Currently a major struggle is over the fact that countries are allowed to make an exception for plants and animals, although micro-organisms are part of the regime. In Pakistan, an official with the Ministry of Food and Agriculture told IPS news service that Monsanto was lobbying the government aggressively to implement patenting law. He said that 'Monsanto is pulling powerful strings to influence the legislative process in its favour, sending letters to government officials, holding meetings with politicians.'[56] Monsanto was concerned that the legislation could favour farmers' rights over those of TNCs. According to Dr Shahid Zia, an NGO representative and research fellow with the Sustainable Policy Development Unit (SDPI), 'The proposed law would allow farmers to save, retain and exchange seeds. It requires a genetically modified or transgenic plant to clear tough environmental impact and biosafety assessments before being given protection'.[57] The law was unacceptable to Monsanto. In a letter to the government's Seed Certification

Department, Monsanto's Managing Director in Pakistan went on the offensive: In the presence of this clause, anybody from the public can sue us and ask for compensation for hazards and damages which are kind of openended risks. Hence, take out this clause.... Again I repeat that this clause is not acceptable to any multinational companyy and it should not be different than any non-transgenic variety.[58]

Farmers from freely saving and breeding seed, forcing them to purchase it anew each year. The level of control delivered by the technology is formidable, since it covers both the product and the intellectual property invested in the product. Nowhere else has the naked intent of the biotech industry been so clearly revealed. Research is being profoundly affected by a creeping corporate takeover. The obsession with obtaining patents is restricting the free exchange of information and limiting access to information and technology. The quest for rapid returns on investment is distorting the sciences; the hunt for profitable applications risks turning the pursuit of knowledge into a race for technological fixes. Increasingly, technology is driving social development and this is particularly true of biotechnology, where technological optimism is endangering the principle of scientific scepticism. Governments have been complicit here too, hoping for technological solutions to problems that require political commitment. Genetic engineering technologies feed this longing very aptly and the industry has not held back, ably assisted by a burgeoning and rapidly consolidating public relations industry that is full of clever ideas about how to present GM biotechnology as benign. Since so much of the current excitement rests on projections of future possibilities, the painting of dream pictures is made even easier. The increased vertical and horizontal integration of the biotech industry means that ten companies control almost 33 per cent of the commercial seed market; five control 75 per cent of the vegetable seed market, while four control almost 100 per cent of the GM seed market. Two companies control 34 per cent of the global agrochemical market and ten control 85 per cent. Currently, Monsanto traits can be found in 91 per cent of GM crops grown worldwide. Recent mergers and acquisitions (such as the creation of Bayer CropScience and Syngenta) have been approved without building in any capacity for addressing the issue of global monopolies. Meanwhile, public interest research is being increasingly hijacked by corporate priorities and corporations are gaining access to public funding and publicly funded institutions such as universities and agricultural research centres.The British East India Company began as a group of traders and ended up ruling India: Yet an empire of trade unexpectedly became an empire of conquest. From 1740, interventions in local politics and the deployment of increasingly effective armed forces gave company employees the confidence and capacity to impose their will on annexed territories in northern India. The transformation from trader to sovereign was swift, brutal and decisive. By the 1770s, a company state had been created in Bengal, and further expansion was sustained by the formation of a large army of Indian sepoys financed through the collection of land revenues. From a limited body of merchants, the east India Company have become the 'Arbiters of the East'. Today, there is the serious risk of being ruled by corporations far more completely and powerfully than the East India Company ever ruled India. They are busy recolonising every space that has experienced colonisation before, and a multitude of new spaces that could not previously be colonised either because the technology or the legal rights were not available—our bodies, our brains, the products of collective and traditional human experience and creativity.[59]

There are no of examples the current generation of GM crops are beginning to show signs of failure. Evidence shows that yields are not as good as promised. Pests and weeds are developing resistance to pesticides and herbicides. It is often the case that new technologies reveal only their positive side at first. Whatever the impact on the farmer, it was all good business for the companies. Moreover, chronically dependent customers, whoever they may be, are ideal fodder for generating profits. If those customers are tied up by debt and vanishing profit margins, all the better. The corporations are already promising new generations of GM crops designed to tolerate salt and drought. They do not mention that there are already farmer varieties of crops worldwide that are able to do the same thing. They do not publicise the fact that all over the world people are maintaining, rebuilding and creating ways of producing food that thrives on diversity instead of monoculture, and that work with soil, climate, ecology and other species, instead of treating them as obstacles. In Cuba, where the collapse of the former Soviet Union left the country short of inputs and petroleum, they are developing organic food gardens; in Argentina, following the collapse of the economy, people are turning to their own resources to do the same thing. In Africa, where most farmers still save and breed their own seed, many are *de facto* organic or use very low levels of inputs.

The crisis in Indian agriculture is evident from farmers' suicides in every corner of the country and since 1995 more than 25,000 farmers brethren have committed suicides all over the country. This is because of the cascading effect of the capital-intensive, corporate agribusiness-driven, export-oriented, peasant-insensitive domestic policies coupled with the subsidised import surge due to withdrawal of Quantitative Restrictions, which has led to depression in the domestic farmgate commodity prices. The burden of the agrarian distress has fallen on the small and marginal farmers in India. This is a direct result of the WTO's Agreement on Agriculture that protects subsidies in the developed countries and allows them to dump cheap commodities in countries such as India.

When Monsanto first introduced Bt Cotton in 2002, the farmers lost 1 billion rupees due to crop failure. Instead of 1,500 kilos per acre as promised by the company, the harvest was as low as 200 kilos per acre. Instead of incomes of 10,000 rupees an acre, farmers ran into losses of 6,400 rupees an acre. In the state of Bihar, when farm-saved corn seed was displaced by Monsanto's hybrid corn, the entire crop failed, creating 4 billion rupees in losses and increased poverty for desperately poor farmers. Poor peasants of the South cannot survive seed monopolies. The rigged prices of globally traded agriculture commodities steal from poor peasants of the South. The crisis of suicides shows how the survival of small farmers is incompatible with the seed monopolies of global corporations.

Patents

Colonialism in its day was furnished with an ideology no matter how abominable it may look now. In contrast, globalisation, notwithstanding its broad sweep and power, is bereft of any serious theoretical underpinning. There is no philosophical basis for it beyond current economic interests. Enforcement of globalisation seems to be its only legitimation. The foremost task today is developing a cross-cultural civilisational perspective on those aspects of globalisation that deal with food and healthcare and which consequently are literally matters of life and death for many countries. In particular, questions pertaining to intellectual property rights associated with traditional knowledge should not be addressed by individual countries in a knee-jerk fashion. Rather, attempts should be made to develop a global ethical framework which should be binding on all major players.

When patent laws at international level were first introduced, they dealt with tangible things, applied to a small part of the world, and had the benefit of actual practice over four centuries at local levels. In contrast, intellectual property laws pertaining to biotechnology and impinging on such civilisationally basic areas as food and health are being framed at the outset itself, when there is neither any ethical framework to interpret them nor benefit of actual practice to fall back upon.

Today when we talk of globally applicable laws, no national laws can serve as a role model. This is so because so far laws have been made to safeguard national or local interests. Global laws require fresh thinking. When the world was Euro-centric, it was easy to define what was new. If Europe did not know of it, it did not exist before. In 1738 William Champion was granted a patent in his capacity as "the first European to produce metallic zinc," even though the process was known to have been brought from Asia. However, 100 years previously, in 1608, when Hans Lipperhey applied for a patent on telescope, he was turned down "on the ground that it is evident that several others have knowledge of the invention." By the same logic, if the knowledge is available anywhere in the world today, it should not be possible to patent it.[60]

The onus of protecting traditional knowledge should not rest on individual countries. (Much of it transcends current political boundaries). Traditional knowledge in its entirety should be treated as common heritage of humankind. If it is incorporated into modern scientific mainstream with a view to deriving commercial benefit, then royalty should be paid into a global fund specially created for the purpose. This fund in turn should be used for the good of the repositories of traditional knowledge.

Latin American farmers now buy seeds made in labs in the North from genetic material they donated in the 1970s, just as South American nations imported British goods manufactured from their wool and leather in the 19th century.

That trend has not just continued. It has taken on huge proportions. For example, more than half the known plant species in Brazil, one of the countries with the richest biodiversity in the world, have already been patented by large transnationals.

At the First Latin American and Caribbean Indigenous Seminar, held sometime back in Mexico, participants charged that several international labouratories have patented in Europe and the United States the medicinal properties of 5,000 of the 13,000 plants used in traditional indigenous medicine in the region.

Tropical America is still a land of promise, according to experts in genetic resources, who cite the case of Zea diplorernnis, a variety of corn that is resistant to four out of the seven known illnesses that affect the plant.

This plant was not found growing in the forest. Scientists found it in 1997 being cultivated on a two-hectare plot in Western Mexico's Manatlan Mountains by an indigenous family who had been producing it for generations, and using it along with common maize as food for their animals during the dry season.

The potential value of this corn species, from a genetic standpoint, is in the region of billions of dollars.

The Green Revolution, spearheaded after World War II by the United States and TNCs linked to agriculture, hinged on the improvement of soils and the intensive use of industrial seeds and pesticides in most parts of the world.

It was often the same companies that provided the seeds, the fertilizers and pesticides. This monopoly generated huge profits and enormous accumulation of capital. Since then, these companies have been investing part of their profits in the development of biotechnology and genetic engineering.

The new production pattern, called agriculture and sustainable development—the name is drawn from the environmentalist terminology now in vogue—is based on the widespread, almost exclusive use of genetically manipulated seeds produced in the labouratories of TNCs.

Through patenting, these companies ensure that they will have a monopoly in global agricultural production.

Transgenetic—genetically modified—seeds can be immune to certain herbicides, resistant to drastic climate change, mature more rapidly or more slowly and produce vegetables that are bigger, smaller, or have different nutritional values than the original ones.

In order to make the huge investments required to produce these seeds, several major transnationals have been merging, the big race now is between two U.S. companies: Monsanto and DuPont, both of which aim to create an oligopoly.

In the past few months, DuPont has invested 4.8 billion dollars buying out or buying into various big companies, he says. At the same time, Monsanto has been doing the same thing in another part of the market and its investments have amounted to 5.2 billion dollars.

Biotechnology is going through a moment in history in which humanity needs to reflect on its destiny. These corporations can create plants, animals, small and large beings manipulate genes until something comes out.

The colonisation is unethical for a few corporates to dominate the production of food on the planet and to own life.

Do they have the right to create beings that are going to serve their interests? Can they go into a country, take over its biodiversity, extract the raw material and register it in their names?

According to statistics from the International Council

for Plant Genetic Resources (ICPGR), the 1974-85 period saw the heaviest traffic in genetic resources, with developing nations donating 91 percent of the samples analysed and industrialised in other countries.[61]

On the other hand, the industrialised countries received 42.3 percent of the donated germ plasm through the ICPGR(International Council for Plant Genetic Resources), while the countries of the South received only 14.5 percent.

In an article included in a book titled 'Biotechnology: After the Green Revolution', Canadian author, Pat Mooney, argues that by 1982, the Organisation for Cooperation and Economic Development (OCED) was reporting that developing countries contributed some 500 million dollars each year to the value of the U.S. wheat harvest.

According to Mooney, this means the real contribution made by developing countries is greatly undervalued. If all the important harvests in North America were included in the calculation, the contribution would be in the region of billions of dollars each year. Developing countries also make such contributions to Europe and Australia.

Their contribution is in the form of germ plasm, the genetic characteristics added to new crop varieties throughout the world. The North may be rich in grains, but the South is rich in genes, the expert says.

Mooney concludes that the South donated this genetic material believing that its botanical treasures would become part of the common inheritance of humanity, but the North has patented the products of this legacy and now sells its seeds throughout the world, making enormous profits.

Patents are nothing but biopiracy, where seeds such as the Basmati seed, the aromatic rice from India, which we have grown for centuries, is being claimed as novel invention by RiceTec.

Neem, which have been used for millennia for pest control, for medicine, which is documented in every one of our texts, have used for everyday functions in the home, for protecting grain, for protecting silks and woolens, for pest control, is treated as invention held by Grace, the chemical company.

This epidemic of piracy is very much like the epidemic

of piracy which was named colonialism 500 years ago. It will soon need to name this round of piracy through patents as recolonialisation as a new colonialisation which differs from the old only in this—the old colonialisation only took over land, the new colonialisation is taking over life itself.

The third world is that part of the world which became the colonies in the last colonialisation. It wasn't an impoverished world then, in fact the reason it was colonialised is because it had the wealth. Columbus set sail to get control of the spice trade from India, it's just that he landed on the wrong continent and named the original inhabitants of this land Indian thinking he had arrived in India. Latin America was colonialised because of the gold it had. None of these countries was impoverished. Today they are called the poorer part of the world because the wealth has been drained out.

People have survived in the third world because in spite of the wealth that has been taken from them, in spite of their gold and their land having been taken from them, they still have biodiversity. They still have that last resource in the form of seed, medicinal plants, fodder, which allowed them access to production. It allowed them to meet their needs of health and nutrition. Now this last resource of the poor, who had been left deprived by the last round of colonialisation is also being taken over through patenting. And seeds which peasants have freely saved, exchanged, used, are being treated as the property of corporations. New legal property formations are being shaped as intellectual property rights treaties, through the World Trade Organisation, trying to prevent peasants of the third world from having free access to their own seed, to have free exchange of their own seed. So that all peasants, all farmers around the world would be buying seed every year thus creating a new market for the global seed industry.

80 percent of India takes care of its health needs through medicinal plants that grow around in back yards, that grow in the fields, in the forests, which people freely collect. No one has had to pay a price for the gifts of nature. Today, everyone of those medicines has been patented and within five, ten years down the line, we could easily have a

situation in which the same pharmaceutical industry that has created such serious health damages and is now shifting to safe health products in the form of medicinal plant-based drugs, Chinese medicine, aromatic medicine from India, will prevent the use. They don't even have to come and make it illegal because long before they have to take that step, they take over the resource base, they take over the plants, they take over the supply, they take over the markets, and leave people absolutely deprived of access.

The situation in which the third world, which has been the main supplier of biodiversity, the main producer of food in the world, where the majority of people are engaged in food production, is being attempted to be converted into a consumer society. But one can't have a consumer society with poor people and, therefore, what you will have is deprivation, destitution, disease, hunger, epidemics, hunger, malnutrition, famine and civil war. What is being sown is the greed of the corporations of stealing the last resources of the poor. It really is seeds of uncontrollable violence and decay of societies on a very large scale.

When a seed is planted, there's a very simple prayer that every peasant in India says: "Let the seed be exhaustless, let it never get exhausted, let it bring forth seed next year." Farmers have such pride in saying "this is the tenth generation seeds that I'm planting," "this is the fifth generation seed that I'm planting." Just the other day, I had a seed exchange fair in my valley and a farmer brought Basmati aromatic rice seed and he said "this is five generations we've been planting this in our family." So far human beings have treated it as their duty to save seed and ensure its continuity. But that prayer to let the seed be exhaustless seems to be changing into the prayer, "let this seed get terminated so that I can make profits every year" which is the prayer that Monsanto is speaking through the terminator technology—a technology whose aim is merely to prevent seed from germinating so that they don't have to spend on policing.

Patents are also a way to prevent farmers from saving seed. The corporations which have patents will have to do policing, they have to mobilize detectives to ensure that farmers aren't saving seeds. The terminator is an extremely secure technology for corporations like Monsanto because neither do they have to do the policing, nor do they have to worry whether some segregation works, now you just basically terminate. But this is not just a violence against farmers whose basic right is seed saving. A farmer's duty is protecting the earth, maintaining it's fertility, and maintaining the fertility of seed. That is part of being a farmer. The real definition of a farmer is a person who relates to the land and relates to the seed and keeps it for future generations, keeps renewing it, and maintaining fertility.

First of all, when farmers have been selecting they have been selecting between two boundaries and limits that they set for themselves. The first is the ecosystem limit. Farmers select crops according to the ecosystems in which they produce. No farmer in the world has done seed selection sitting in tropical Africa and trying to grow crops in temperate Sweden. Africans have bred crops for Africa, and Swedish farmers have evolved crops for Sweden.

The second is related to the fact that they have always worked within the limits set by intra-species breeding. One have to work with rice to evolve new rice plants. You work with wheat to evolve new wheat plants. You do not try and cross the species boundaries. In fact, even conventional breeding which was not farmers' breeding which had already been taken over by scientists and industry and violated the ecosystem boundary because it tried to breed beyond ecosystem adaptation—it did still respect the species boundary.

Genetic engineering is violating both boundaries. It's violating the ecosystem boundary. It is generating crops to be planted on millions of acres because there's no point in having patents on a particular Bt cotton if you are then only going to grow it in twenty acres where it suits that particularly variety. But for Monsanto, there is market around the world to maximize the return on your patents, your revenues, etc. This means you have to grow it everywhere. You have to violate ecosystem boundaries.

But more important than that, for the first time, genetic engineering is doing something different from what conventional breeders have done. And no matter how many times they tell this lie, it doesn't make it a truth. Transgenic organisms are not equivalent to farmers breeding or conventional breeding because transgenic by its very definition means something which has crossed species boundaries, something in which an alien gene has been introduced into a plant. In the case of Bt., it is the toxic bacteria gene. In the case of other crops it will be antibiotic genes

SOFTWARE GIANT MICROSOFT CORPORATION

The company's operating systems run an estimated 80 per cent of the world's 200 million-plus personal computers. After years of offering also—ran word-processors and spreadsheets, the Microsoft Office package has 80 per cent of the sales in this hot product category. For more than two decades, Microsoft has engaged in a carefully designed and extremely successful campaign to protect and extend its monopolies. Microsoft has repeatedly made market allocation proposals to its competitors and has used a broad range of other anticompetitive and unlawful tactics to eliminate potential rivals, including tying, predatory product design, and intentional deception.

Microsoft owns several monopoly products, including its Windows operating system and Office suite of productivity applications These monopolies are extremely lucrative: Microsoft generates more than $60 billion each year, largely from Windows and Office.[62] It has profit margins of 77% and 65% for these two monopoly products. Over the years, Microsoft has carefully cultivated and expanded the barriers to entry protecting these monopolies.

That barrier—the "applications barrier to entry"—stems from two characteristics of the software market: (1) most consumers prefer operating systems for which a large number of applications have already been written; and (2) most developers prefer to write for operating systems that already have a substantial consumer base. This "chicken-and-egg" situation ensures that applications will continue to be written for the already dominant Windows, which in turn ensures that consumers will continue to prefer it over other operating systems. Indeed, Microsoft originally gained its Office monopoly for the express purpose of strengthening the applications barrier that protects Windows.

Microsoft recognised, however, that owning Office and other applications would not alone be sufficient. In particular, Microsoft saw a serious potential threat in the form of so-called "middleware" products. Middleware products are software products that, like Windows, expose application programming interfaces ("APIs") that software developers can use in writing other applications. Microsoft recognised that, if any middleware product gained widespread popularity, "developers might begin to rely upon APIs exposed by the middleware for basic routines rather than relying upon the API set included in Windows."[63] Microsoft has therefore crushed middleware threats, such as Netscape's web browser.

Although Microsoft has paid many multimillion-dollar settlements for its antitrust violations over the years, these settlements have proven a small price for such a large ongoing revenue stream. Microsoft's past conduct demonstrates its ability and willingness to engage in In the early 1980s, Microsoft purchased an early version of a standard disk operating system ("DOS") that became known as MS-DOS. At the time, a number of rival operating systems offered features, such as the ability to run multiple programs at the same time, that Microsoft's operating systems would not offer until years later. At the time, operating systems were just beginning to move from a command-based interface to a graphical user interface. Microsoft developed a graphical user interface known as Windows. Early versions of Windows did not actually "run" the computer—rather, they were a shell surroundding the underlying DOS program, which in turn ran the computer. Initially, Windows embraced the DOS standard, which meant that Windows would run on top of any DOS, including DR-DOS, Microsoft's principal rival in the DOS market.

Most operating systems are purchased by original equipment manufacturers ("OEMs"), such as Dell and HP. OEMs preinstall operating systems on the computers they manufacture before selling the computers to consumers. In the late 1980s, Microsoft began requiring OEMs to pay Microsoft a "per processor license fee" for each computer they shipped, regardless of whether they installed Windows on the computer. This arrangement gave OEMs a powerful incentive not to pay for and install competing operating systems. In 1994, the U.S. department of Justice ("DOJ") filed an antitrust suit against Microsoft challenging this conduct, resulting in a consent decree under which Microsoft agreed to stop using per processor license fees.[64] But the anticompetitive practice had already been quite effective in reducing competitors' share, particularly when combined with Microsoft's other actions directed against DR-DOS. The DOJ consent decree also sought to impose some

IBM

IBM was a major customer of Microsoft's. Microsoft retaliated against IBM for developing competing software products by charging IBM discriminatorily high license prices for Windows, delaying licensing negotiations with IBM for Windows 95, and withholding technical support. Microsoft informed IBM executives that it would only stop treating IBM less favourably than other OEMs when IBM ceased competing with Microsoft's software offerings. This resulted in $180 million in lost revenue for IBM, and other damages. IBM eventually brought suit against Microsoft and Microsoft settled the claim for $775 million.[65]

INTEL

Microsoft used a similar approach in 1995, when it forced Intel to drop development of Native Signal Processing ("NSP"), a set of instructions that would have allowed a computer's processor to directly support audio, video, and 3D graphics. Intel is a manufacturer of microprocessor chips that are purchased by OEMs to use in the computers they manufacture. With NSP, Intel hoped to create a platform for multimedia applications that would run on any operating system, not just Windows. Microsoft thus viewed NSP as a serious threat to its Windows monopoly. In order to extinguish NSP, Microsoft told Intel that it would make Windows incompatible with Intel chips if Intel did not abandon the technology, and Microsoft forced its OEM customers into a collective boycott of Intel's microprocessor chips.[66]

WordPerfect

Beginning in 1994, Microsoft launched an anticompetitive campaign to extinguish WordPerfect, an office productivity application owned by Novell and competing with Microsoft's Office suite. Office productivity applications (including word processing, spreadsheet, and presentation applications) are one of the most important groups of applications and contribute substantially to the applications barrier to entry protecting Microsoft's operating system monopoly. When Microsoft began this campaign, WordPerfect enjoyed widespread popularity. In order to eliminate its competitor, Microsoft withheld crucial technical information about Windows, going so far as to extend the Windows API, the set of commands a program uses to communicate with the operating system, to ensure that WordPerfect did not work smoothly with Microsoft's monopoly operating system.[67] Microsoft also used its monopoly power to control industry standards, thus requiring WordPerfect to implement proprietary technology or risk incompatibility with Windows. It excluded WordPerfect from the major channels of distribution for office productivity applications. For example, Microsoft forbade OEMs from pre-installing Novell products and gave discounts for refusing to sell other developers' office productivity applications. As part of Microsoft's strategy to eliminate Novell Microsoft extinguished WordPerfect and gained a monopoly in office productivity application suites, accomplishing its goal of "dramatically widening the moat" protecting its lucrative Windows monopoly

UNIX

Microsoft chose initially "to invest in interoperating" with UNIX, by promoting its Windows Interface Source Environment ("WISE"), a program that purportedly allowed developers to write software to Windows APIs and run the resulting programs on Macintosh and UNIX systems.[68]

Microsoft's plan was successful. By 1996 Microsoft had captured a large share of the corporate market. Microsoft then took the next step in its standard "embrace, extend, extinguish" playbook and extended the Windows API without copying its changes to the WISE program. This meant that developers could no longer smoothly port applications to UNIX and Macintosh. In public, however, Microsoft continued to lead developers into believing that this software was still fully cross-platform. Microsoft had successfully extinguished the cross-platform threat to its operating system monopoly. In a subsequent antitrust suit, a district court called this move "a classic 'bait-and-switch' tactic."

Netscape

In 1996, Microsoft began a series of steps to eliminate a threat to its operating system, monopoly from Netscape's web browser. Web browsers are "middleware" products, meaning that they expose APIs that developers can use in writing other applications. Microsoft recognised that if developers began using the APIs in Netscape's browser rather than the APIs in Windows, consumers might eventually have access to the applications they needed from any computer with Netscape's browser installed and would not be locked into computers running. Windows Microsoft first sought to deal with this threat through a direct market allocation proposal:

Microsoft told Netscape that if Netscape would agree to stop exposing APIs, Microsoft would provide Netscape with special help in developing "value-added" software applications that relied on Microsoft's proprietary technologies. Netscape rejected Microsoft's proposal.[69] Microsoft then responded by taking steps to "cut-off Netscape's air supply." It developed its own web browser, Internet Explorer, and then technologically and contractually tied Internet Explorer to its monopoly Windows operating system. To ensure that only Internet Explorer ran well on Windows, Microsoft designed Windows, as its then Vice-President Brad Chase wrote, to make "running any other browser a jolting experience."[70] To ensure that Internet Explorer had exclusive access to the primary browser distribution channels, Microsoft also used an extensive set of exclusive-dealing contracts with OEMs, independent software vendors ("ISVs"), Apple, and others. Microsoft was very aggressive in its campaign to shut Netscape out of all major distribution channels.

For example, when Apple resisted distributing Microsoft's Internet Explorer web browser with its Mac OS operating system, Microsoft threatened to stop supplying Microsoft Office for Mac OS.65 As the district court found, "ninety percent of Mac OS users running a suite of office productivity applications used. Microsoft's Mac Office. In 1997, Apple's business was in steep decline.... Had Microsoft announced in the midst of this atmosphere that it was ceasing to develop new versions of Mac Office, a great number of ISVs, customers, developers, and investors would have interpreted the announcement as Apple's death notice

The importance of Office to Apple did not go unnoticed by Microsoft. As Microsoft's then-program manager for Windows, Ben Waldman, explained in an email to Bill Gates and then-CFO Greg Maffei: "The threat to cancel Mac Office 97 is certainly the strongest bargaining point we have, as doing so will do a great deal of harm to Apple immediately." Or, as one Microsoft Vice-President put it in an email to Ben Waldman, "MacOffice is the perfect club to use" to persuade Apple to "materially disadvantage Netscape."[71] Apple capitulated and began pre-installing Internet Explorer as the default browser on Mac machines. Once Microsoft had achieved wide distribution for its own browser through these tactics, it then moved to "extend" industry standards for HyperText Markup Language ("HTML") and Cascading StyleSheets ("CSS") to ensure that users would become reliant on Microsoft's own web browser.[72] Microsoft also introduced its ActiveX technology extensions, which allowed software written much like traditional computer programs to run in the Internet Explorer browser, but that only worked on Microsoft's monopoly operating system. Unfortunately, however, the U.S. browser case was settled with a consent decree that has been wholly ineffective in restoring competition to the state that prevailed prior to Microsoft's unlawful actions.

Sun Microsystems

In 1996, Microsoft turned its attention to Sun Microsystems' Java middleware

technologies as another nascent threat to its operating system monopoly. Sun Microsystems was at the time promoting its Java technologies with the slogan, "Write-once-run-anywhere" to illustrate the cross-platform benefits of writing Java applications.[73] Microsoft immediately recognised Java as middleware and moved to eliminate this threat. As usual, Microsoft first embraced Java by licensing the technology from Sun Microsystems and investing in building its own Java-related developer tools. Microsoft then extended its Java developer tools with its own proprietary technology. Microsoft threatened Intel that if it did not stop aiding Sun on the multimedia front, then Microsoft would refuse to distribute Intel technologies bundled with Windows."[74] Intel capitulated, and dropped its support for Java. Microsoft's overall plan to neutralize Java as a middleware threat was extremely successful. As the Fourth Circuit explained in a subsequent private suit brought by Sun Microsystems: First, Microsoft "embraced" the Java technology by licensing from Sun the right to use its Java Technology to develop and distribute compatible Products. Second, Microsoft "extended" the Java platform by developing strategic incompatibilities into its Java runtime and development tools products.... Third, Microsoft used its distribution channels to flood the market with its version of the Java Technology in an attempt to "hijack the Java Technology and transform it into a Microsoft proprietary programming and runtime environment."[75]

Media Players Real Networks

In 1997, Microsoft recognised that media players also represented a nascent threat to its profitable operating system monopoly. Like web browsers, media players are middleware products that expose APIs to software developers. Fearing that media players might come to support multimedia applications on any operating system, Microsoft took action to eliminate the threat. Consistent with its previous tactics, Microsoft first embraced the leading media player software, designed by Real Networks, announcing an agreement to collaborate in streaming media.[76] The agreement encouraged RealNetworks to make its media player Windowsdependent in return for compensation from Microsoft. When RealNetworks continued to compete against Microsoft, Microsoft became increasingly aggressive in its actions. Microsoft tied its own media player to Windows.[77]

APPLE

In 1997, Microsoft targeted Apple's QuickTime media authoring software, another threat to Microsoft's operating system monopoly. Like RealNetworks' multimedia player, Apple's multimedia technology ran on several platforms and exposed APIs to content developers. Microsoft saw the Apple product as a particularly serious threat to the applications barrier to entry in light of Apple's expertise in the operating system market. Microsoft thus reverted to its standard playbook, first attempting to allocate the market with Apple by offering not to enter the authoring business if Apple stopped developing a Windows 95 version of QuickTime. When Apple refused to participate in Microsoft's illegal scheme, Microsoft threatened to make its products incompatible with Apple's products if Apple did not abort its work on its new QuickTime product.

When Microsoft first began bundling Windows Media Player with its monopoly operating system, Microsoft also released a version of its media player for apple's Mac operating system. During the period when Windows Media Player was competing with RealPlayer and Apple QuickTime, Microsoft frequently released new versions of its product for the Mac. By 2003, however, Microsoft had gained the upper hand, capturing more users than RealNetworks and Apple.

In the mid to late 1990s, computer networks were growing in speed and Microsoft sensed a threat to its core operating system monopoly from more centralised, server-based computing. Determined to head-off any potential competition, Microsoft decided that it needed to add server operating systems to the "moat" surrounding its Windows operating system monopoly. To gain inroads into this market, Microsoft embraced industry standards for file-and-print sharing, user management, and identity verification so that its products would be compatible with the then-prominent Unix server operating systems. But as Microsoft's server systems started to gain a foothold in the market, Microsoft quietly started to "extend" support for industry standard protocols in its Windows operating system so that Windows clients would have a better experience when connected to Microsoft's servers.[78] Eventually, by changing its Windows personal computer operating system so that Windows computers could not fully connect to any server that did not use Microsoft's proprietary extensions unless the users installed special software on their machines, Microsoft established and reinforced its dominance in the work group server operating system market, where Microsoft maintains a share of approximately 77%.

Microsoft's conduct eventually drew scrutiny from the European Commission, which condemned Microsoft's refusal to release information that would allow other server operating systems to connect to personal computers running Microsoft's Windows operating system. In a 2004 decision, the European Commission found that if Microsoft succeeded in eliminating other server operating systems as competitive threats, then innovation would be severely limited. And, in fact, after releasing Windows Server 2003 to lukewarm reviews,[79] Microsoft failed to release a new server version of Windows until 2008. Even then, many reviewers noted that, despite aggressive marketing to small- and midsize-business users and a special edition of the server operating system just for these users, Microsoft had done very little to address their needs, and instead had essentially re-packaged a scaled-down version of an existing enterprise-level product.

In 2003, the DOJ discovered that Microsoft had built a feature into Windows that invoked Microsoft's Internet Explorer browser, rather than the user's chosen default browser, contrary to the clear obligations of the Final Judgment. Similarly, in 2004, Microsoft attempted to require licensees of its middleware offering, the NET Framework, to obtain Microsoft's prior consent before publishing any benchmark testing results for the software. In 2005, Microsoft demanded that manufacturers of portable music players sign exclusive deals if they wanted integration with Microsoft's Windows Media Player.In 2007, Microsoft made changes to allow consumers limited choice of desktop search products in Windows Vista only following an extensive government investigation and pressure from a number of U.S. States. While Microsoft eventually made changes to its conduct in each of these instances, these incidents all demonstrate Microsoft's willingness to use its monopoly products aggressively first and make changes later only when confronted about its behaviour. This is particularly striking coming, as it does, within the very limited range of issues covered by the Final Judgment. Despite international scrutiny of Microsoft's anticompetitive conduct, Microsoft has continued to take similar unlawful actions to eliminate potential competitive

The open source Linux operating system is the principal rival to Microsoft Windows. Linux has been taken up by both corporate customers and, increasingly, by private individuals for home use. In response to other competitive threats, Microsoft has used unfair and anti-competitive tactics to try and slow the uptake of Linux. In particular, Microsoft has made and continues to make broad, unsubstantiated claims that software developers distributing Linux or other open source software, as well as their customers, are infringing Microsoft's patents.

MICROSOFT'S MONOPOLIES HAVE HARMED CONSUMERS

Microsoft's conduct has allowed it to protect its monopolies, which has led to a lack of choice, higher prices, and less innovation than would otherwise have prevailed in a competitive marketplace. The barriers to entry surrounding Microsoft's core monopolies remain very high, and Microsoft's market shares and profit margins in desktop operating systems, office productivity suites, and browsers have continued to reflect its overwhelming monopoly power in these markets. In short, Microsoft's misconduct has harmed and continues to harm consumers significantly.

Microsoft's Office Monopoly has Harmed Consumers

Microsoft's Office suite likewise maintains a 95% market share. The standard Office suite includes Word (word processing software), Excel (spreadsheets), PowerPoint (presentations), and Outlook (desktop email client), Microsoft has more than 500 million Office users. The business division at Microsoft, which includes Office, operated on a profit margin of 65% and brought in almost $19 billion in revenue in 2008.[80] Microsoft's monopoly power in office productivity applications has, likewise, bred complacency that is harmful to consumers. Even Microsoft's founder and former Chief Software Architect, Bill Gates, asserts that the only real competitive pressure on Microsoft to improve Office today is that consumers might not upgrade to the next version. Between 1997 and 2007, Microsoft released only three new versions of Microsoft Office, a very slow pace by software industry standards, and reviewers noted that each release offered only small improvements over the previous ones. It was not until 2007, with the advent of competing online office productivity applications, that Microsoft redesigned the Office user interface and, not coincidentally, introduced new, incompatible file formats. Microsoft's conduct over the last two decades has demonstrated Microsoft's willingness and ability to engage in unlawful conduct to protect and extend its core monopolies. This conduct has caused real harm to consumers, who continue to pay high prices and use lower quality products than would have prevailed in a competitive market.

Human Rights Violations by Corporate Sector

Corporations carry out some of the most horrific human rights abuses of modern times, but it is increasingly difficult to hold them to account. Economic globalisation and the rise of transnational corporate power have created a favourable climate for corporate human rights abusers, which are governed principally by the codes of supply and demand and show genuine loyalty only to their stockholders. The world's worst corporate abusers to illustrate that on issues as diverse as assassination, torture, kidnapping, environmental degradation, abusing public funds, violently repressing political rights, releasing toxins into pristine environments, destroying homes, discrimination, and causing widespread health problems, familiar companies like Dow Chemical, Coca Cola, Caterpillar, Lockheed, Philip Morris, and Wal-Mart play a big role

CATERPILLAR

Contracting with known violators of human rights, enabling house demolition, supplying equipment that kills Palestinian civilians and American peace activists

For years, the Caterpillar Company has provided Israel with the bulldozers used to destroy Palestinian homes. Despite worldwide condemnation, Caterpillar has refused to end their corporate participation—house demolition—by cutting-off sales of specially modified D-9 and D-10 bulldozers to the Israeli military.

Israel seeks to portray the destruction of homes as necessary to its self-defense, but nothing could be farther from the truth. As the Israeli Committee Against Home Demolitions has rigorously documented, house destruction is part of Israel's intention to turn the annexation of East Jerusalem and other occupied areas into a concrete fact.

In a letter to Caterpillar CEO, James Owens, the Office of the UN High Commissioner on Human Rights said: "allowing the delivery of your. . . bulldozers to the Israeli army. . . in the certain knowledge that they are being used for such action, might involve complicity or acceptance on the part of your company to actual and potential violations of human rights..."

Peace activist, Rachel Corrie, was killed by a Caterpillar, D-9, military bulldozer in 2003. She was run over while attempting to block the destruction of a family's home in Gaza. Her family filed suit against Caterpillar in March 2005 charging that Caterpillar knowingly sold machines used to violate human rights. Since Rachel's death, at least three more Palestinians have been killed in their homes by Israeli bulldozer demolitions.

CHEVRON

The petrochemical company Chevron is guilty of some

of the worst environmental and human rights abuses in the world. From 1964 to 1992, Texaco (which transferred operations to Chevron after being bought out in 2001) unleashed a toxic "Rainforest Chernobyl" in Ecuador by leaving more than 600 unlined oil pits in pristine northern Amazon rainforest and dumping 18 billion gallons of toxic production water into rivers used as bathing water. The toxic crude oil and formation water seeped into the subsoil, contaminating surrounding freshwater and farmland. As a result, local communities have suffered severe health effects, including cancer, skin lesions, birth defects, and spontaneous abortions. Indigenous communities have been dispossessed of their lands, and millions of hectares of rainforest have been destroyed to make way for the company's pipelines and oil wells.

Chevron is also responsible for the violent repression of nonviolent opposition to oil extraction. In Nigeria, Chevron had collaborated with the Nigerian police and military who have opened fire on peaceful protestors who opposed oil extraction in the Niger Delta. In 1998, two indigenous Ilaje activists were killed by Nigerian military officers flown in by the company while the former were protesting at an oil platform in Ondo state. In 1999, two people from Opia village were killed by military personnel paid by Chevron, after soliciting a meeting to complain about the company's harmful effects on local fishing. And in 2005, Nigerian soldiers fired upon protestors at Escravos oil terminal, leaving one protestor dead.

Additionally, Chevron is responsible for widespread health problems in Richmond, California, where one of Chevron's largest refineries is located. Processing 350,000 barrels of oil a day, the Richmond refinery produces oil flares and toxic waste in the Richmond area. As a result, local residents suffer from high rates of lupus, skin rashes, rheumatic fever, liver problems, kidney problems, tumors, cancer, asthma, and eye problems.

In December 2004, the Unocal Corporation, which recently became a subsidiary of Chevron, settled a lawsuit filed by 15 Burmese villagers, in which the villagers alleged Unocal's complicity in a range of human rights violations in

Burma, including rape, summary execution, torture, forced labour and forced migration. Despite the settlement, human rights abuses continue along the oil pipeline in Burma, which is still "secured" by the Burmese military. Chevron is responsible for the risks associated with this pipeline.

COCA-COLA

Coca-Cola Company is perhaps the most widely recognised corporate symbol on the planet. The company also leads in the abuse of workers' rights, assassinations, water privatisation, and worker discrimination. Between 1989 and 2002, eight union leaders from Coca-Cola bottling plants in Colombia were killed after they protested the company's labour practices. Hundreds of other Coca-Cola workers who have joined or considered joining the Colombian union SINALTRAINAL have been kidnapped, tortured, and detained by paramilitaries who intimidate workers to prevent them from unionising. In Turkey, 14 Coca-Cola truck drivers and their families were beaten severely by Turkish police hired by the company, while protesting a layoff of 1,000 workers from a local bottling plant in 2005.

In India, Coca-Cola destroys local agriculture by privatising the country's water resources. In Plachimada, Kerala, Coca-Cola extracted 1.5 million liters of deep well water, which they bottled and sold under the names Dasani and BonAqua. The groundwater was severely depleted, affecting thousands of communities with water shortages and destroying agricultural activity. As a result, the remaining water became contaminated with high chloride and bacteria levels, leading to scabs, eye problems, and stomach aches in the local population. Water shortages have occurred in Varanasi, Thane, and Tamil Nadu as well. The company is also guilty of reselling its plants' industrial waste to farmers as fertilizers, despite its containing hazardous lead and cadmium.

Coca-Cola is one of the most discriminatory employers in the world. In the year 2000, 2,000 African-American employees in the U.S. sued the company for race-based disparities in pay and promotions. In México, Coca-Cola FEMSA, the largest Coca-Cola bottler in Latin America, fired a senior bottling manager for being gay. Finally, by regularly denying health insurance to employees and their families, Coca Cola has failed to help stop the spread of AIDS in Africa. The company is one of the continent's largest private employers, yet only partially covers expensive medicines, while not covering generic medicines at all.

DOW CHEMICAL

Creation of chemical weapons, marketing poisonous chemicals, illegal dumping of toxins into populated areas, environmental destruction, health problems, death.

Dow Chemical has been destroying lives and poisoning the planet for decades. The company is best known for the ravages and health disaster for millions of Vietnamese and U.S. Veterans caused by its lethal Vietnam War defoliant, Agent Orange. Dow's "invent first, ask questions later" standard of business led the multinational company to develop and perfect Napalm, a brutal chemical weapon that burned many innocents to death in Vietnam and other wars. In 1988, Dow provided pesticides to Saddam Hussein despite warnings that they could be used to produce chemical weapons.

In 2001, Dow inherited the toxic legacy of the worst peacetime chemical disaster in history when it acquired Union Carbide Corporation (UCC) and its outstanding liabilities in Bhopal, India. As the Students for Bhopal website recount. "On December 3rd, 1984, thousands of people in Bhopal, India were gassed to death after a catastrophic chemical leak at a UCC pesticide plant. More than 150,000 people were left severely disabled-of whom 22,000 have since died of their injuries-in a disaster now widely acknowledged as the world's worst ever."

Dow refuses to address its liabilities in Bhopal or even admit its existence, continuing in Union Carbide's tradition of profiting from extreme corporate irresponsibility. In India, Dow's subsidiary faces manslaughter charges and is considered a fugitive from justice for a pending criminal case related to the 1984 chemical explosion. Dow and UCC's lack of accountability in the disaster continue to affect the lives in Bhopal to this day.

World-wide, Dow is involved in human rights abuses: environmental destruction, water and ground contamination, health violations, chemical poisoning, and chemical warfare. Dow Chemical's impact is felt globally from their Midland, Michigan headquarters to New Plymouth, New Zealand. In Midland, Dow has been producing chlorinated chemicals and burning and burying its waste including chemicals that make up Agent Orange. In New Plymouth, New Zealand, 500,000 gallons of Agent Orange were produced and thousands of tons of dioxin-laced waste was dumped in agricultural fields. Dow's toxic legacies of human rights abuses traverse to agricultural fields in Central America where Dow exported EPA-banned pesticide DBCP for use on banana and pineapple crops. As a result, thousands of banana workers were exposed to DBCP and became sterile. In retail markets across the world Dow's dangerous chemicals are present as common household solvents, plastics, paints and pharmaceuticals.

DYNCORP/CSC

Causing health problems, environmental devastation and death; endangering lives; physically abusing individuals; sex trafficking—Private security contractors have become the fastest-growing sector of the global economy during the last decade—a $100-billion-a-year, nearly unregulated industry. DynCorp, one of the providers of these mercenary services, demonstrates the industry's power and potential to abuse human rights. While guarding Afghani statesmen and African oil fields, training Iraqi police forces, eradicating Colombian coca plants, and protecting business interests in hurricane-devastated New Orleans. These hired guns bolster the security of governments and organisations at the expense of many people's human rights.

DynCorp's fumigation of coca crops along the Colombian-Ecuadorian border led Ecuadorian peasants to sue DynCorp in 2001. Plaintiffs argued that DynCorp knew—or should have known—that the herbicides were highly toxic, and should, therefore, be held accountable for health problems and death among local people and widespread environmental damage to their subsistence agriculture. A

Colombian newsweekly called DynCorp—which also sprays herbicides in Peru and Bolivia—"lawless Rambos."

DynCorp's questionable actions in Haiti include its training of the national police force after the first coup against President Aristide, paving the way for Tonton Macaoutes to return to power.

In 2001, a mechanic with DynCorp blew the whistle on DynCorp employees in Bosnia for rape and trading girls as young as 12 into sex slavery. According to a lawsuit filed by the mechanic, "employees and supervisors were engaging in perverse, illegal and inhumane behaviour and. were purchasing illegal weapons, women, and. forged passports." The mechanic observed DynCorp employees buying and selling women and bragging about the ages and talents of their female slaves. DynCorp fired the whistleblower, who later claimed that "DynCorp is just as immoral and elite as possible, and any rule they can break they do." The company transferred the employees accused of sex trading out of the country, eventually firing some. None were prosecuted though.

FORD MOTOR COMPANY

The US automobile industry is fueling America's addiction to oil. Automobiles are the single largest consumer of oil in the US, a country that constitutes less than five percent of the world's population but consumes 25 percent of its oil. The US addiction to oil is linked with a host of human rights and environmental problems, including human rights abuses in countries such as Nigeria, Ecuador, Sudan, South Africa and Indonesia. The US oil addiction has prompted the US government to cozy up to human rights violating governments such as that of Saudi Arabia. It has pushed indigenous people off their land and destroyed hundreds of thousands of acres of rainforests, which were home to half the planet and animal species on the planet. It has fueled wars for oil, such as the war in Iraq, which has so far caused the deaths of more than 2,100 US troops and an estimated 27,000 to 100,000 Iraqis. It has polluted cities, endangering the health of millions of people who live in high-ozone communities and leading to hundreds of thousands of cases of childhood asthma. And, by being a major contributor to global warming, has increased the likelihood of extreme weather events like Hurricane Katrina, which killed at least 1,289 people.

Among automakers, Ford Motor Company is the worst. Every year, since 1999, the US Environmental Protection Agency has ranked Ford cars, trucks and SUVs as having the worst overall fuel economy of any American automaker. Ford's current car and truck fleet has a lower average fuel efficiency than the original Ford Model-T.

Ford is also in last place when it comes to vehicle greenhouse gas emissions. According to a recent report by the Union of Concerned Scientists, Ford has "the absolute worst heat-trapping gas emissions performance of all the Big Six automakers." In fact, if Ford were a country, it would be the 10th largest global warming polluter worldwide, behind Italy.

Amazingly, despite the company's recent greenwashing PR campaign, its record has actually worsened. According to Ford's own sustainability report, between 2003 and 2004, the company's US fleet-wide fuel economy decreased and its CO2 emissions went up. Ford is also lobbying to prevent the U.S. and state governments from improving the situation: the company has lobbied against law-makers' efforts to increase fuel economy standards at the national level and is also involved in a lawsuit against California's fuel economy standards.

KBR (KELLOGG, BROWN, AND ROOT): A SUBSIDIARY OF HALLIBURTON CORPORATION

They are engaged in overcharging and providing unnecessary services on taxpayer's dollar, bribery, exploiting third country nationals .

KBR is a private company that provides military support services. Notorious for its questionable book-keeping, dishonest billing practices, and no-bid contracts, KBR has violated human rights on the U.S. dollar.

KBR provides key logistical support for war, occupation and unlawful detention. The company provides the critical support services US troops need to be able to continue their occupation of Iraq. KBR also constructed the detention facility in Guantanamo Bay, where hundreds of detainees have languished for more than three years, many of whom have suffered abuse and torture.

KBR's dubious accounting in Iraq came to light in December 2003 when Pentagon auditors questioned possible overcharges for imported gasoline. Former employees have testified about KBR's billing for $100 laundry bags and $45 cases of soda; failing to provide simple mechanical parts such as oil filters, feeding soldiers outdated rations, and charging for meals never served. In June 2005, a previously secret Pentagon audit criticised $1.4 billion in "questioned" and "unsupported" expenditures.

However, given KBR's history, this is no surprise. In 2002, the company paid $2 million to settle a Justice Department lawsuit that accused KBR of inflating contract prices at Fort Ord, California. In 2000, the GAO scrutinised KBR for overcharging and providing unnecessary services in the Balkans. Bribes to local officials (such as in Nigeria) or sub-contractors also appear to be part of KBR's modus operandi.

Many third-country national (TCN) labourers have been hired by KBR to "rebuild" Iraq. Generally hailing from impoverished Asian countries, they have unexpectedly become part of the largest civilian workforce ever hired in support of a U.S. war.

An intricate network of sub-contractors who recruit and employ most TCNs lowers the prime contractors' costs and hinders any oversight by contract auditors. The labourers often take out usurious loans to pay a finder's fee for the overseas jobs. Once abroad, the workers find themselves with few protections and uncertain legal status. TCNs often sleep in crowded trailers and wait outside in scorching heat to eat "slop." Many lack adequate medical care and put in hard labour seven days a week, 10 hours or more a day. Few receive proper workplace safety equipment or adequate protection from incoming mortars and rockets.

KBR is now accused of perpetuating the same system in areas destroyed or damaged by Hurricane Katrina. Reports have surfaced about KBR's sub-contractors exploiting TCN's (this time, Latinos), many of whom are unpaid, unfed, living in squalid conditions and suffering from untreated ailments.

LOCKHEED MARTIN

Lockheed Martin is the world's largest military contractor. In 2003, the year of the Iraq invasion, the company held $21.9 billion in Pentagon contracts. Providing satellites, planes, missiles, and other lethal high tech items to the Pentagon keeps the profits rolling in. Since 2000, the year Bush was elected, the company's stock value has tripled.

A large company like Lockheed Martin has the ability to shape the business environment, and marketing war is very beneficial to the bottom line. As the Centre for Corporate Policy (www.corporatepolicy.org) notes, it is no coincidence that Lockheed's VP, Bruce Jackson, who helped draft the Republican foreign policy platform in 2000—is a key player at the Project for a New American Century, the intellectual incubator of the Iraq war.

Lockheed Martin is not the only defense contractor that goes behind the scenes to influence public policy, but it is one of the worst. Stephen J. Hadley, who now has Condoleeza Rice's old job as Assistant to the President for National Security Affairs, was formerly a partner in a big DC law firm representing Lockheed Martin. He is only one of the beneficiaries of the so-called revolving door between the military industries and the "civilian" national security apparatus. These war profiteers—the makers of the Trident missile; aircraft like the F-16 Fighting Falcon and the F/A-22 and the C-130 Hercules, as well as high tech space based military components like the DSCS-3 satellite—have a profound and illegitimate influence on our country's international policy decisions.

MONSANTO

Monsanto is, by far, the largest producer of genetically engineered seeds in the world, dominating 70% to 100% of the market for crops such as soy, cotton, wheat, and corn. The company is also one of the most egregious abusers of the human rights of food sovereignty, access to land, and health.[81]

Monsanto promotes mono-culture—the practice of covering large swaths of land with a single crop. This practice pushes out subsistence farms and destroys arable land by drastically decreasing soil and water quality for years, draining soil of key nutrients. The company also undercuts food prices by flooding countries like Mexico, India, and Brazil with cheap, genetically modified foods, resulting in the displacement of millions of farm workers, who are forced to migrate to cities or work as landless peasants or share croppers.

Monsanto is the world's leading producer of the herbicide glyphosate, marketed as "Roundup." Roundup is sold to small farmers as a pesticide, yet harms crops in the long run as the toxins accumulate in the soil. Plants eventually become infertile, forcing farmers to purchase genetically modified Roundup Ready Seed, a seed that resists the herbicide. This creates a cycle of dependency on Monsanto for both the weed killer and the only seed that can resist it. Both products are patented, and sold at inflated prices.

Roundup Ultra, a version of the pesticide that is unavailable on the commercial market, is regularly employed in fumigation of areas of illicit crop production. However, as it destroys fields of drug plants, it also destroys subsistence crops like banana, palm heart, and coffee. Exposure to the pesticide is documented to cause cancers, skin disorders, spontaneous abortions, premature births, and damage to the gastrointestinal and nervous systems.

According to the India Committee of the Netherlands and the International Labour Rights Fund, Monsanto also employs child labour. In India, an estimated 12,375 children work in cottonseed production for farmers paid by Indian and multinational seed companies, including Monsanto. A number of children have died or became seriously ill due to exposure to pesticides.

NESTLÉ

Abusive child labour, repression of worker rights, aggressive marketing of harmful products, violation of national health and environmental laws

There's a secret in the chocolate industry, and once people find out about it, their chocolate doesn't taste as sweet any more: Much of the chocolate eaten all over the world is made of cocoa beans that have been harvested by illegal child labour, including child slave labour.

The problem of illegal and forced child labour is rampant in the chocolate industry, because more than forty percent of the world's cocoa supply comes from the Ivory Coast, a country that the US State Department estimates had approximately 109,000 child labourers working in hazardous conditions on cocoa farms in what's been described as the worst form of child labour. In 2001, Save the Children Canada reported that 15,000 children between 9 and 12 years old, many from impoverished Mali, had been tricked or sold into slavery on West African cocoa farms, many for just $30 each. Just this summer, the International Labour Rights Fund and a Birmingham law firm filed a class-action lawsuit against Nestlé and several of its suppliers on behalf of former child slaves.

Nestlé is the target of this lawsuit and is singled out by corporate campaigners, because it is the third largest buyer of cocoa from the Ivory Coast, has processing, storage and export facilities there, and is well aware of the tragically unjust labour practices taking place on the farms with which it continues to do business. Nestlé and other chocolate manufacturers agreed to end the use of abusive and forced child labour on cocoa farms by July 1, 2005, but they failed to do so.

Nestlé is also notorious for its aggressive marketing of infant formula in poor countries in the 1980s, which may have led to the deaths of countless children who did not receive the nutrients that would have been present in breast milk. Because of this practice, Nestlé is still one of the most boycotted corporations in the world, and its infant formula is still controversial. In 2005 in Italy, police seized more than two million liters of Nestlé infant formula that was contaminated with the chemical isopropylthioxanthone (ITX), a component in the packaging's ink. It turned out that the company knew about the contamination for months, but did not recall the formula.

Additionally, violations of labour rights are reported from Nestlé factories in numerous countries. In Colombia, Nestlé replaced the entire factory staff with lower-wage workers and did not renew the collective employment contract. In Cabuyao Laguna, Philippines, a 3-year strike against Nestlé was partially precipitated by Nestlé's refusal to include the retirement benefits of the workers in the collective bargaining agreement, despite the Supreme Court's ruling in favour of the workers. The company has brutally attempted to break the strike; this year, two unionists, including prominent labour leader Diośdado Fortuna, have been murdered.

PHILIP MORRIS USA and PHILIP MORRIS INTERNATIONAL (a.k.a. the Altria Group Inc.)

According to the World Health Organisation, tobacco is the second major cause of preventable death in the world. Nearly five million lives per year are claimed by the tobacco industry, whose products result in premature death for half the people who use them. Among tobacco companies, Philip Morris is notorious. Now called Altria, it is the world's largest and most profitable cigarette corporation and maker of Marlboro, Virginia Slims, Parliament, Basic and many other brands of cigarettes. Philip Morris is also a leader in pushing smoking with young people around the world.

Philip Morris has consistently misled consumers about the dangers of its products. Documents uncovered in a lawsuit filed against the tobacco industry by the state of Minnesota showed that Philip Morris and other leading tobacco corporations knew very well of the dangers of tobacco products and the addictiveness of nicotine, yet they continued to deny these realities in public until the internal company documents were brought to light. To this day, Philip Morris deceives consumers about the harm of its products by offering light, mild and low-tar cigarettes that give consumers the illusion that these brands are "healthier" than traditional cigarettes.

Philip Morris has actively targeted the world's youth by researching smoking patterns and attitudes and targeting youth as potential customers. Marlboro cigarettes are the top brand for youth in the United States. Although the company says it doesn't want kids to smoke, it spends millions of dollars every day marketing and promoting cigarettes to youth. Overseas, it has even hired underage Marlboro girls to distribute free cigarettes to other children and sponsored concerts where cigarettes were handed out to minors.

As anti-tobacco campaigns and government regulations are slowing tobacco use in Western countries, Philip Morris has aggressively moved into developing country markets, where smoking and smoking-related deaths are on the rise. According to a study by the Harvard School of Public Health, tobacco's killing fields are shifting to the developing world and Eastern Europe, where most of the world's smokers now live. Preliminary numbers released by the World Health Organisation predict global deaths due to smoking-related illnesses will nearly double by 2020, with more than three-quarters of those deaths in the developing world.

Meanwhile, Philip Morris' profits continue to grow. In the third quarter of 2005 alone, Altria's net revenue was $25 billion, up from 2004 in large part due to the high performance of Philip Morris USA and Philip Morris International.

PFIZER

Pfizer is one of the largest and most profitable pharmaceutical companies in the world with revenues of $52.5 billion in 2004. In addition to Viagra, Zoloft, Zithromax, and Norvasc. Pfizer produces the HIV/AIDS-related drugs Rescriptor, Viracept and Diflucan (fluconazole). Like other drug companies, they sell these drugs at prices poor people cannot afford and aggressively fight efforts to make it easier for generic drugs to enter the market. They have even cut off drug shipments to Canadian pharmacies that sold Pfizer drugs to patients in the United States for costs more affordable than those offered in US pharmacies.

To ensure its profits, Pfizer invests heavily in US campaign contributions. Though it can't seem to afford to offer life-saving drugs at affordable prices, it was able to scrounge up $544,900 for mostly Republican candidates in election cycle 2006 and $1,630,556 in the 2004 election cycle.

Drug companies' refusal to put human beings' health ahead of their own greed and profits is especially deadly for people with HIV/AIDS. AIDS killed 3.1 million people in 2004, a shocking death rate that could be greatly reduced if treatment was made available to people who right now cannot afford it. Pfizer and other drug companies have refused to grant generic licenses for HIV/AIDS drugs to countries like Brazil, South Africa, and the Dominican Republic, where patients are forced to pay $20 per weekly pill for drugs like fluconazole, though the average national wage is only $120 per month.[82]

Instead of helping eradicate the world's worst pandemic in history, the World Trade Organisation has made matters worse. Beginning in 1995, the agreement on Trade-Related Aspects of Intellectual Property Rights (TRIPS) protected companies by stopping WTO member countries from making generic versions of their drugs. Because of public pressure, the WTO announced a new agreement in 2003 to allow poor countries to access cheap generic antiretroviral drugs, but in practice, the drugs are just as inaccessible to poor countries as they were before.

SUEZ-LYONNAISE DES EAUX (SLDE)

The privatisation of water has had a disastrous impact on the human right to clean water, and the French company Suez is the worst perpetrator of this abuse. The company's billions of dollars in profit come at the expense of poor people living in countries where thousands lack access to potable water, and, because of private water contracts, are also facing skyrocketing water prices.

Suez goes by many names around the world—Ondeo, SITA, and others—to mask its worldwide net of controversial activities. But no sleight of hand can hide the fact that Suez, which is one of the largest water companies in the world, has been a leader in turning the human right to water into an unaffordable luxury. According to Public Citizen, Suez has raised water rates, cut off the water of people unable to pay, refused to extend services to poverty-stricken neighbourhoods, and then threatened legal action when contracts are terminated.

For example, in Manila, Philippines, after seven years of water privatisation under a Suez company (Maynilad Water) contract, studies showed that water rates increased in some neighbourhoods by 400 to 700 percent. These studies also showed that the negligence of the company resulted in outbreaks of cholera and gastroenteritis that killed six people and severely sickened 725 in Manila's Tondo district.

In Argentina, Suez mixed companies have refused to make promised investments in the water infrastructure, which has resulted in serious water pollution problems. They also charge high consumer rates and cut off water access for citizens unable to pay, leaving those most in need without access to a life-sustaining natural resource.

In Bolivia, a Suez company (Aguas de Illimani) left 200,000 people without access to water and caused a revolt when it tried to charge between $335 and $445 to connect a private home to the water supply. Countless people were unable to afford this charge in a country whose yearly per capita GDP is $915.

Unfortunately, the IMF and World Bank are playing a key role in pushing water privatisation all over the world. Many countries have been required to open up their water supply to private companies as a condition for receiving IMF loans, and the World Bank has approved millions of dollars in loans for the privatisation of water systems.

WAL-MART

Wal-Mart is the biggest corporation in the world. It owns 5,100 stores worldwide and employs 1.3 million workers in the United States and 400,000 abroad, as well as a millions more in the factories of its suppliers. Because of the company's enormity, its business model has a huge influence on workers and businesses around the world; so far Wal-Mart has used that influence to ruthlessly drive down costs as a means of making profit, violating a vast array of human rights and labour rights along the way.

Many people have heard of the way that Wal-Mart steamrolls its way into every possible town, destroying local supermarkets and countless small businesses. We have also heard about Wal-Mart's long track record of worker abuse, from forced overtime to sex discrimination to illegal child labour to relentless union busting. Wal-Mart also notoriously fails to provide health insurance to over half of its employees, who are then left to rely on themselves or taxpayers, who provide for a portion of their healthcare needs through government Medicaid.

Less well known is the fact that Wal-Mart maintains its

low price level by allowing substandard labour conditions at the overseas factories producing most of its goods. The company continually demands lower prices from its suppliers, who, in turn, make more outrageous and abusive demands on their workers in order to meet Wal-Mart's requirements. In September 2005, the International Labour Rights Fund filed a lawsuit on behalf of Wal-Mart supplier sweatshop workers in China, Indonesia, Bangladesh, Nicaragua and Swaziland. The workers were denied minimum wages, forced to work overtime without compensation, and were denied legally mandated health care. Other worker rights violations that have been found in foreign factories that produce goods for Wal-Mart include locked bathrooms, starvation wages, pregnancy tests, denial of access to health care, and workers being fired and blacklisted if they try to defend their rights.

Additionally, nearly 70% of Wal-Mart's goods are made in factories in China, a country where garment workers are often kept under 24-hour-a-day surveillance and can be fired for even discussing factory conditions. The Chinese government does not allow independent human rights groups to exist, and all attempts to form independent unions have been crushed. Wal-Mart refuses to reveal its Chinese contractors and will not allow independent, unannounced inspections of its contractors' facilities.

Clinical Trials by Pharma Companies

The last 10 years have been witness to an increasing number of clinical trials conducted in India. Indian pharmaceutical companies are investing higher amounts in R & D as they nurture global ambitions. Significantly, many multinational pharmaceutical companies are eyeing the opportunities available in India to augment their R & D productivity. The result has been an exponential growth in the number of clinical trials conducted in India. This growth is mirrored in large measure by the increase in the debate on the ethics of such trials in India. The Mashelkar Committee recommends that phase I clinical trials of new drugs of foreign origin may take place concurrently in this country and abroad. It's after a drug clears labouratory tests on animals that it enters the phase I trial stage, wherein it is tested on a small group of human volunteers for health safety routine practice and the doctor's team is expected to spend much more time with the patient than in routine practice. The premise of any clinical trial is the "principle of essentiality" elucidated by the Indian Council of Medical Research. A clinical trial is done, simply because, it needs to be done. If other methods were available to evaluate new medicines, scientists and governments would be more than happy to use those for evaluation of new agents. A number of commentators, in India and abroad have alluded to the participation of Indians in clinical trials as the "guinea pig syndrome." 49 babies out of 4,142 died in clinical trials conducted by a foreign pharmaceutical company in India. This implies two things. One that the babies died due to the drugs tested and two, those foreign pharmaceutical companies are exploiting us. A clinical trial, simply put, is an experiment conducted to study if a new medication is safe and effective in the treatment of a particular medical condition. Because not much is known about the new medication at the time of a clinical trial, doctors are required to follow a rigorous schedule to oversee patient's safety. Patients may be required to follow-up with the doctor more often than in routine. However, even though a number of initiatives are being explored to reduce the number of patients exposed to new clinical trials, the fact remains that the clinical trial remains the most robust way to evaluate new agents today. It's also important to appreciate that modern medicine, though highly evolved, is yet an imperfect science. Most medicines used today offer significant alleviation of suffering in relative terms but in absolution, modern drug suffer from safety and efficacy issues. Scientists and doctors over the world continue the search to understand which treatments are safer and better for their patients. So, when a doctor offers to enroll a patient into a clinical trial, he's really requesting the patient's collaboration in an experiment to further the understanding of medicine. The objective is to allow patients access to better medicines in the future to come. The medical world went into shock and awe when the world's biggest pharmaceutical company, Pfizer, announced in December 2006 that it was terminating clinical trials of its new cholesterol-reduction drug Torcetrapib.[83]

It had reportedly spent $800 million on these trials. The reason for stopping the trials was the high death rate among the 15,000 trial subjects spread over three continents. No damages could be claimed as participants had agreed to waive such rights before joining the trial.

Pfizer's situation is by no means unique. In recent years, there has been a spate of failures of clinical trials with many of the top pharma companies being forced to withdraw drugs after adverse reports. While Bristol-Myers Squibb terminated a new diabetes drug, AstraZeneca halted work on a new drug for stroke patients.

What is more ominous is that there are several cases now of a drug being put on the market only to be pulled out after discovering that it has caused irreversible damage to patients.

GlaxoSmithkline had to withdraw its anti-depressant Seroxat and issue warnings about its diabetes drug Avandia, which was found to increase limb fractures. Merck called back its painkiller Vioxx, that had earned the company $2.5 billion, after it was shown that it caused increased heart attacks.

Several factors are contributing to this increased failure rate. Patents of several blockbuster drugs, like Pfizer's cholesterol lowering Lipitor, are due to expire, but the pipeline of new drugs is drying up. The US Food and Drug Agency (FDA), which grants permission for trials and marketing of new drugs, approved only 20 drugs in 2005, down from 36 in 2004. Faced with the increasing costs of clinical trials and a shortage of willing participants, western drug companies are looking at off-shoring the trials to the third world.

India is seen as a prime location for such trials because it has the world's largest patient pool. Moreover, Indian patients are largely 'treatment-naove', that is most have not been taking any other medicine. The main consideration is costs—industry watchers say drug companies may save up to 50% of the costs of new drug development by conducting trials in India.

Small wonder that many clinical research organisations (CROs) have sprouted up in India offering to carry out such trials. Industry sources say that Indian CROs are getting business worth up to $120 million a year, nearly two-thirds of which is for clinical trials. It is expected that nearly $2 billion worth of clinical trials will end up in India by 2010. The government has made changes in laws and regulations to accommodate the clinical trial boom. Apart from changes in patent laws which will protect data confidentiality, initial or phase 1 trials are also permitted.

A Framework for Good Clinical Practices has also been announced. In the budget for 2007-08, the service tax on clinical trials was done away with. However, India's top regulatory body, the Drug Controller General-India (DCGI), is still preparing itself to deal with the influx, and there are doubts whether it is technically equipped to handle the challenge.

Currently, over 226 FDA-approved clinical trials are in progress in India, many of which are sponsored by top drug companies like Pfizer, BristolMyers Squibb, GlaxoSmithkline, Eli Lilly, etc.

Big cities are favourite spots for these trials, with Delhi having 76 trials, Mumbai 86, Chennai 50 and Bangalore 64. However, the lax regulatory regime, susceptibility of patients who are needy and ignorant of their rights, and unscrupulous operators contribute to making this an arena fraught with serious risks.

Several cases of botched trials or violations by sponsors in India underline the risk. Trials on Johnson and Johnson's anti-psychotic drug, Risperdal, were among several suspect trials mentioned in a recent BBC report.

In 2003, Letrozole, an anticancer drug, was tested on more than 430 young women at a dozen private clinics to find out whether it promoted ovulation. In 2002, two new chemical entities discovered in US were tested on 26 patients with oral cancer at the government-run Regional Cancer Centre in Kerala.[84]

In 2004, two Indian drug companies, Shantha Biotech in Hyderabad and Biocon in Bangalore, came under scrutiny for conducting illegal clinical trials that led to eight deaths. Shantha Biotech failed to obtain proper consent from patients while testing a drug meant to treat heart attacks. Biocon tested a genetically modified form of insulin without the proper approval from the DCGI.

In the same year, unqualified researchers in private clinics formulated "vaginal pellets" of erythromycin and tried them as contraceptive agents on more than 790 illiterate women in West Bengal. All these trials took place without regulatory approval.

Dr. K. Srinath Reddy of the Public Health Foundation of India points out, "the ethical question of carrying out trials of drugs that will be too expensive for the subjects to ever buy also needs to be confronted."[85]

SEZ

Indian Economy is Agrarian economy. Till today, two thirds of the population depends on agriculture. Hence while acquiring the land for the SEZ, due care should be taken that those who get displaced should get employment opportunities and share in the units which are going to be established in the SEZ. SEZ policy will encourage the corporate to relocate their units in SEZ which offers many tax benefits besides other concessions. This will lead to concentration of the units in a particular area which will create a lop-sided development. Hence this matter should be viewed in the context of the balanced, equilibrium development of the different regions. Especially underdeveloped region. This will be in line with our country's social and economic objectives to provide opportunities for the people by generating adequate employment opportunities which will help to improvise their standard of living. If we look at International SEZ experience, especially with reference to China, one noteworthy thing is that majority SEZs are in coastal areas and owned by the Government. The goods produced can be easily transported through well developed supply chain linkages. To a certain extent, it has tried to sort out poverty, employment and government priority related issues from the country's best interest. This has encouraged the unbalanced, lop-sided economic development which is really very costly in the long run. Hence International experience of SEZ should be viewed and aligned with our country's existing priorities and agenda. Hence, labour standards, working conditions in the SEZ units should be justified and should not be totally in favour of the corporate/developer in the name of export, foreign direct investment and foreign exchange earnings nor should it be in favour of the labourer. International experience regarding SEZ can only be justified if it could be able to focus on the national priorities and it's interest. Only efficient organisation which has a export potential and follows the best management practices should only be encouraged. It is proven fact that the corporate which stand in competition, redesign and reformulate their strategies according to the need of the Market, they only proved to the test of time. Hence SEZ policy should not discourage the efficient units which are doing well and discharging the social responsibilities well. Rather bureaucratic red tapism, single window clearance and speedy execution of the project should be encouraged.

The corporate malpractices had aggravated tension between two key ministries of the UPA government, finance and commerce, the former initiated a probe on the SEZ units indulging in tax evasion by diverting goods and services in the Domestic Tariff Area (DTA).

The Central Board of Excise and Customs (CBEC), an arm of the finance ministry, issued a circular for its field formations to conduct an immediate survey to identify SEZ units that have been evading taxes by providing services outside the special zones.

Interestingly, the CBEC order came on a day when a section of the media published the contents of a letter written by commerce minister, Kamal Nath, to PM, Manmohan Singh, seeking his intervention to restrain the finance ministry.

The commerce ministry favours a blanket tax waiver on all units set-up in the SEZs, Nath in his letter to the PM, said that it had become difficult to meet export targets as the finance ministry was blocking a number of his proposals. Nath reportedly said that lack of cooperation would make it difficult to implement measures for boosting industrial growth.

The CBEC, however, cites a Comptroller and Auditor General (CAG) report on diversion of services and goods by SEZ units in DTA as one of the reasons behind the survey order. The probe has to be completed by October 20.

The circular has clarified that "service tax is applicable on taxable services provided by SEZ units", except for a few exempted categories. The "field formations should ensure that units providing taxable services to any person for consumption in the DTA discharge their service tax liability", it stated.

The CAG, in its report released early this year, had asked the government to review its SEZ policy as the present provisions in the policy guidelines were leading to diversion of goods in the DTA causing huge loss to the exchequer. The country's top auditor had found that many of these units were achieving the net foreign exchange (NFE) earning targets, set by the government as part of the SEZ policy, by indulging in domestic sales. The prime objective of the government to promote exports through these tax havens had thus been defeated, the report pointed out.

Customs duty to the extent of Rs. 1,043 crore was foregone on imports by these units, the CAG report said in a sample study conducted on 550 units. Quoting a major case, the CAG said its "scrutiny of records of Nokia's unit in Chennai SEZ revealed that the unit had cleared mobile phones with a value of Rs. 4,855 crore in 2006 and 2007 in the domestic market without payment of any duty."[86]

CARBON TRADING–BIG CORPORATES GAME WITH ENVIRONMENT

The Kyoto Protocol is the firm example of corporate colonialism which demonstrates business power over politics, and when profit scores over the planet, the political will to address climate change will be in short supply.

It is the stark reality that the rich countries of the North, with less than 20 per cent of the world's population, bear a 75 per cent responsibility for having already filled up the atmospheric dumping space for carbon dioxide so much that far too little is left for the poorer countries of the South as they step up to climb the conventional development path charted for them by the rich. India and China put together are responsible for less than 10 per cent of historic emissions, while the U.S. and the E.U. together account for 42 per cent.

On a per person basis the disparity is even more stark even when the atmosphere, a common good, belongs to all equally. An average American emitted 40 times as much as an average Indian in fossil fuel emissions of the last century.

Gases such as carbon dioxide, methane, nitrous oxide, and refrigerants create a greenhouse effect by trapping heat in the lower atmosphere. This makes the Earth warmer because the sun's rays are allowed into the lower atmosphere but the heat from these rays isn't able to escape.

In 1995, 2,500 scientists prepared a report called the Second Assessment of the Intergovernmental Panel on Climate Change (IPCC). The IPCC reports that global warming and climate change is a reality, and that human emissions of greenhouse gases are a culprit. There are several harmful impacts that result from a global warming trend. Impacts from global warming include sea level rise, more extreme weather events including heat waves, frosts, droughts, storms, extinction of species, loss of entire forests, and glacial retreat. 1998 was the hottest year since accurate records began in the 1840s, and 10 of the hottest years have occurred during the last 15 years. By examining growth rings from trees and ice cores drilled in Antarctica, scientists have determined that the past decade was the warmest in more than four centuries, and that the current rate of warming is probably unprecedented in at least 10,000 years. The damage to our environment has already started. For example, sea level has risen by 10-25 centimeters and will continue to rise for centuries even if we stop all global warming emissions immediately. As the world warms, the outlook for all life forms looks bleak, unless we can turn down the heat by reducing concentrations of greenhouse gases in the atmosphere.

The Kyoto Protocol to the United Nations Framework Convention on Climate Change was adopted by over 160 nations on December 11, 1997. On November 12, 1998, the United States signed the Protocol in Buenos Aires. As of mid-January, 1999, 71 countries had signed the treaty, including the European Union and most of its members, Canada, Japan, China and a range of developing countries. The great majority international agreement linked to the United Nations

Framework Convention on Climate Change. The major feature of the Kyoto Protocol is that it sets binding targets for 37 industrialised countries and the European community for reducing greenhouse gas (GHG) emissions. These amount to an average of five per cent against 1990 levels over the five-year period 2008-12. Recognising that developed countries are principally responsible for the current high levels of GHG emissions in the atmosphere as a result of more than 150 years of industrial activity, the Protocol places a heavier burden on developed nations under the principle of "common but differentiated responsibilities." The Kyoto mechanisms Under the Treaty, countries must meet their targets primarily through national measures. However, the Kyoto Protocol offers them an additional means of meeting their targets by way of three market-based mechanism

These carbon credits are with the large manufacturing companies who are adopting UNFCCC norms. It is bad enough that carbon trading allows northern corporations to pollute as heavily as ever (and sell excess credits to other emitters). It is worse that the credits are calculated and verified by agencies firmly embedded in the corporate world and devoted to it. The credits are based on imaginary or speculative estimates of the difference between what the emission levels might have been had a certain CDM project not been undertaken, and the level following the project's completion. Powerful southern governments and companies are exploiting carbon trading to make profits, but accept no obligation to cut emissions.

In South Asia, millions of people will find their lands and homes inundated, according to a draft report of the Intergovernmental Panel on Climate Change. It lays out in explicit detail what lies ahead for India and the rest of Asia. It also presents an opportunity for the country to take the lead in defining a more secure and sustainable future for itself.

Here are some of the devastating consequences detailed in the provisional February 16, 2007, IPCC report on Asia: Sea levels will rise by at least 40 cm by 2100, inundating vast areas on the coastline, including some of the most densely populated cities whose populations will be forced to migrate inland or build dykes—both requiring a financial and logistical challenge that will be unprecedented. In the South Asian region as a whole, millions of people will find their lands and homes inundated. Up to 88 per cent of all of Asia's coral reefs, termed the "rainforests of the ocean" because of the critical habitat they provide to sea creatures, may be lost as a result of warming ocean temperatures.[87]

The Ganga, Brahmaputra, and Indus will become seasonal rivers, dry between monsoon rains as Himalayan glaciers will continue their retreat, vanishing entirely by 2035, if not sooner. Water tables will continue to fall and the gross per capita water availability in India will decline by over one-third by 2050 as rivers dry up, water tables fall or grow more saline. Water scarcity will in turn affect the health of vast populations, with a rise in water-borne diseases such as cholera. Other diseases such as dengue fever and malaria are also expected to rise.

Crop productivity will fall, especially in non-irrigated land, as temperatures rise for all of South Asia by as much as 1.2 degrees C on average by 2040, and even greater crop loss of over 25 per cent as temperatures rise up to 5.4 degrees Celsius by the end of the century. This means an even lower calorie intake for India's vast rural population, already pushed to the limit, with the possibility of starvation in many rural areas dependent on rainfall for their crops. Even those areas that rely on irrigation will find a growing crisis in adequate water availability.

Mortality due to heat-related deaths will climb, with the poor, the elderly and daily wage earners and agricultural workers suffering a rise in heat-related deaths.

This grim future awaits India in the coming century. The irony is that much of this damage will be self-inflicted, unless the country is prepared to make a radical, enlightened change in its energy and transportation strategies.

The path that India has taken thus far, of waiting until wealthy countries take action on global warming, is understandable if viewed in isolation. The U.S., the U.K., and other countries in the wealthy North, have developed their economies largely thanks to fossil fuels. It is only fair that India be allowed to attain the same standard of living before curbing its emissions.

But as the IPCC report makes clear, while it may be "fair" to do so, it is also suicidal for India to pursue any strategy but the least carbon-intensive path toward its own development. Wealthy, less populous countries in the North are very likely and very unfairly going to suffer fewer devastating blows to their economies, and may actually benefit with extended growing seasons, while India and other South Asian nations will dramatically and painfully suffer if action is not taken now.

Today, much of India's energy comes from coal, most of it mined in the rural areas of Orissa, Jharkhand, and Bihar with devastating consequences. Tribals and small and marginal peasants are being forced to resettle as these mines grow wider by the day. Inadequate resettlement plans mean more migration of landless populations to urban slums. The environment is being destroyed by these mines and their waste products—among them fly ash laced with heavy metals and other toxic materials. But the biggest irony of this boom in coal-fired power is that much of the power is going to be export-oriented, energy-intensive industry. At Orissa's coal belt, one can find a plethora of foreign-owned and Indian aluminium smelters, steel mills, and sponge iron factories all burning India's coal, at a heavy cost to local populations then exporting a good share of the final product to China, the U.S. or other foreign markets.

India is one of the top destinations globally in the growing carbon market. In exchange for carbon trade projects in India, wealthy polluters in the North are able to avoid restrictions on their own emissions. Rather than financing "clean development" projects as promised, many of these trades are cheap, dirty, and harmful to the rural poor. Fast-growing eucalyptus plantations are displacing farmers from their land and tribals from their forests. Sponge-iron factories are garnering more money from carbon trades earned by capturing "waste heat" than from the production of the raw material itself. Toxic fly ash from coal-fired power plants is being turned into bricks, and the carbon that would have been released from traditional clay-fired brick kilns, is now an invisible commodity that can be sold as carbon credits. These carbon trades are not helping finance clean energy and development for India's rural poor.

Global warming will tighten this growing squeeze to a noose, as huge areas of Bangladesh go underwater and environmental refugees flood across India's borders. IPCC report shows that Bangladesh is slated to lose the largest amount of land globally approximately 1000 square km of cultivated land due to sea level rise. Where will all of those hungry, thirsty, landless millions go?[88]

Surrogate Advertisements

"Surrogate advertising", duplicating the brand image of one product extensively to promote another product of the same brand, has become commonplace. As a reaction to the directive of Government, the liquor and tobacco majors sought other ways of endorsing their products. They have found an alternative path of advertising through which they can keep on reminding their liquor brands to their customers. They have introduced various other products with the same brand name. Launching new products with common brand name is known as brand extension, which can be carried out for related products (eg: Tata Salt and Tata Tea) or unrelated products (eg: Tata Tea and Tata Indica). *Prima facie*, there is nothing wrong with brand extension. The problem occurs when brand extension is carried out in response to the ban on advertisement of one product category. In this case, the companies launch other products with the same brand name for the purpose of reminding their old customers. Heavy advertising is done so that the customers do not forget their liquor and tobacco brands, for which advertisements are banned. The advertisements for such new products are placed under the category of "Surrogate Advertisements." Their only objective is to compensate the losses arising out of the ban on advertisements of one particular product (i.e. liquor).[89] According to dictionary—surrogate means substitute. Many of us have come across this word in connection with surrogate motherhood. This time, it has come in a new avataar—"Surrogate Advertisement." This is a loophole challenging the Government's action. However, the companies can claim that the order is being implemented and advertisements of liquor are banned, but the objective of the Government behind imposing the ban is not fulfiled

The liquor industry is a prominent player in this game. Few surrogate advertisements shown in print, electronic and outdoor media are—Bagpiper soda and cassettes and CDs, Haywards soda, Derby special soda, Gilbey green aqua, Royal Challenge golf accessories and mineral water, Kingfisher mineral water, White Mischief holidays, Smirnoff cassettes and CDs, Imperial Blue cassettes and CDs, Teacher's achievement awards, etc.[90] These products bear exactly the same brand name and logo, which we had seen earlier in liquor advertisements. It was little surprising to know that liquor giants like McDowell's and Seagram's have entered into new segments like cassettes and CDs, mineral water, sports accessories, etc. Later, it was found that the basic aim of these surrogate advertisements was to promote their liquor brands like beer, wine, vodka, etc. This brand extension is an act of bypassing the advertisement ban.

A similar trend is followed by companies making Cigarettes, Paan Masala and Gutkha. A few examples of surrogate advertisements in this category are—Red and White bravery awards, Wills lifestyle, Four Square white water rafting, Manikchand awards, etc. Though a ban has been imposed on advertisements endorsing tobacco products, this industry resorted to surrogate advertising a few years ago. The Health Ministry has recently implemented the tobacco control legislation which will imply a complete ban on advertisements and all direct and indirect promotional campaigns for tobacco products. In 2001, Indian Tobacco Company (ITC) had voluntarily withdrawn the Wills Sports sponsorship of the Indian cricket team when the Government had first proposed a ban on advertising through legislation.

THE CORPORATE STANDPOINT

The industry segment has its own standpoint in defense. The liquor lobby claims that everything is in accordance with the Government regulations. "If a brand has equity, why shouldn't it be allowed to advertise? Also, brand extension is an industry practice adopted by different product categories," comments Alok Gupta of UB group. "When we advertise our products, we follow all the guidelines," declares president, sales and marketing, Radico Khaitan. They clarify that they have stopped showing liquor advertisements and they are free to use the brand name for any other products. Even the Confederation of Indian Alcoholic Beverages Companies (CIABC) advertising code maintains that advertisement of products (real brand extensions) by the liquor industry must be allowed.

From a layman's point of view, their claims seem to be justified. But this is a clear example of taking advantage of the loopholes. There is a point to ponder. When they have stopped showing liquor advertisements, why the same brand name and logo is used to promote products like cassettes and CDs or mineral water? They could have assigned different brand names. It seems they have a hidden agenda of highlighting the liquor or tobacco brand.

A similar tussle over the issue of surrogate advertisements in politics was raised in April 2004 on the eve of Lok Sabha elections. Complaints of slanderous and offensive advertisements were raised by two major political parties—BJP and Congress against each other. The issue became so serious that the Supreme Court had to interfere in this affair. Finally, on 13th April 2004, the Court gave a verdict to curb smear advertisements on electronic media. By appointing Election Commission as referee, the court has tried to put an end to surrogate advertising in politics.

According to the Cable Act under the ministry of information and broadcasting,—"no broadcaster is permitted to show an advertisement which promotes directly or indirectly, sale or consumption of cigarettes, tobacco products, wine, alcohol, liquor or other intoxicants..." Now a new clause has been added under the act stating that "any advertisement for a product that uses a brand name which is also used for cigarette, tobacco product, wine, alcohol, liquor or any other intoxicant will not be permitted." Finally, in April 2005, the ministry resorted to a ban on surrogate advertisements of liquor and tobacco products on television.[91]

Western companies including Nestlé and Danone are accused today of breaching an internationally agreed code on the promotion of baby milk in the developing world, which is contributing to the deaths of thousands of children.

Every 30 seconds, campaigners claim, a baby dies from

unsafe bottle feeding. Yet despite the marketing code and an international boycott of the companies involved over more than 20 years, the trade continues.

The latest evidence comes from a survey conducted in Togo and Burkina Faso in West Africa, where companies were found to be routinely flouting the code agreed by 118 countries in 1981. The code was drawn up to ensure that any woman who wished to breast feed would not be dissuaded by promotions undermining the message that breast is best.

One of the major problems facing health workers in the developing world is that breast feeding is seen as backward, and bottle feeding is regarded as more modern and sophisticated, a result of the successful marketing of breast milk substitutes. Breast feeding has long been known to be the safest way of raising infants, providing them with the nutrition they need and protecting them from infection at a crucial stage of development. Bottle feeding carries greater risks from contaminated water used to make up the feed and unsterilised equipment.

Researchers from Helen Keller International, a charity based in New York, found that free samples of infant formula were given to health clinics for distribution to mothers, in contravention of the code. A mother who gives up breast feeding will not start again. Leaflets advertising the products failed to emphasise the advantages of breast feeding or explain how the bottle feeds were to be made up safely.

The breast milk substitutes and similar products including fruit juices and infant cereals were promoted with pictures and drawings idealising their use as the modern way to raise children. Forty products were identified which were in breach of the labelling standards set down in the code 21 made by Danone, 11 by Nestlé and eight by other manufacturers.

The survey was conducted by Victor Aguayo and colleagues, and published in the *British Medical Journal*. As per their recommendations, that urgent action is needed to ensure families get objective information on child feeding "at a time when it can mean the difference between life and death."

They add: "Infant mortality in Togo and Burkina Faso

is among the highest in the world. Every year, sub-optimal breast feeding is the underlying cause of an estimated 3,300 infant deaths in Togo (25 per cent of all-cause infant mortality) and over 6,200 infant deaths in Burkina Faso (11 per cent of all-cause infant mortality)."[92]

Corporate Cartels

Cartels, in simple terms, are the result of a collusive, unethical and illegal action by firms in the same line of products getting together to fix prices, limit production, and divide territories and/or customers. Collusion by traders to maximise their profits is as old a phenomenon as trade itself, going back to when people began exchanging goods for cash.[93]

In India, the history about cartels began as early as in 400 BC, when Kautilya, in his monumental political economy treatise, Arthashastra, had prescribed norms for such anti-competitive behaviour. Cartels were recognised—and prohibited—in the days of the Eastern Roman Empire (Byzantium). For instance, the Constitution of Zeno in 483 AD punished price-fixing in clothes, fish, sea urchins, and other goods with perpetual exile, usually to Britain, then a Roman colony.

Under Section 10 of the MRTP Act, 1969, cartelisation in any industry is prohibited and is defined as a "restrictive trade practice" as it imposes unjustified burden on consumers

Cartelisation is termed as the most egregious form of anti-competitive practice by the competition community, through artificial increase in prices. Take, for example, a cement bag being sold at Rs. 200 before cartelisation took place; and, say, after cartelisation, the prices shoot to Rs. 250 per bag. If the cost of cement in a building were 10 per cent of the total construction cost, it would go up by 10.25 per cent. For a consumer, it may be marginal, but to the builder, if the cost of all cement in a project were Rs. 10 crore, then his costs go up to Rs. 10.25 crore, or an extra cost of Rs. 25 lakh. The builder passes on the increased costs to the consumers. There are myriad such cartels in many goods and services, and one can imagine the increase in consumer cost as a whole. It can be quite high

The OPEC (Organisation of Petroleum Exporting Countries) accused of operating as a cartel restricting output thus keeping prices artificially high—legitimate because it is treated as sovereign function of states that own the oil reserves. This too has been challenged in the US, but has not progressed because of the jurisdiction problem. The oil cartel is blamed for the high crude prices—the all-time high of $147 a barrel, from a price of $35 about two years ago. Not long ago, the former Petroleum Minister of India, Mr. Mani Shankar Aiyer, floated the idea of forming a buyers' cartel of net consuming countries, but that did not move far[94]. Indeed, it did succeed in setting the price of crude during the 1970s and the first half of the '80s. But, with increased futures trading and contracts, the control of crude pricing has moved from Opec to banks and markets that deal with futures trading and contracts.

The most common form of cartels is 'price-fixing,' which is treated as a criminal act in the US; many other jurisdictions, including the EU (European Union), have started adopting the same treatment.

Price-fixing is a term that is generically applied to a wide variety of concerted actions taken by competitors having a direct effect on price. The simplest form is an agreement on the price or prices to be charged on some or all customers.

Next on the list are cartel agreements that divide markets by territory or by customers among competitors. If anything, such arrangements are even more restrictive than the most formal price-fixing agreement since they leave no room for competition of any kind and, hence, are often held illegal *per se* by competition laws around the world.

Under the third category of cartel behaviour is output restriction, when companies producing/supplying the same products/services agree to limit their supplies to a lower proportion of their previous sales. The ultimate objective of limiting supplies is to create scarcity in the market and subsequently raise prices of products/services. The fourth type, bid rigging, involves coordinated actions by firms on tenders and auctions. Bid rigging, as all other cartel-type behaviour, can be hard to spot and prosecute.

Cartelist behaviour is difficult to detect, and even when

detected, might be countered by various defences. To make matters worse, cartels can occur in almost any industry and can involve goods or services at any level along the value chain.

Of course, the government can take action against illegal cartels by implementing suitable competition or antitrust laws, such as the MRTPA. The only problem with busting cartels is collecting incontrovertible evidence against such cartels, because of their secretive nature. Most cartels exist only on verbal agreements, and colluders take care to never record their understanding.

Yet, cartels are being busted every other day in the western countries due to suitable legal provisions in their competition laws. It is mainly due to amnesty provisions, which are used by one of the colluding firms to spill the beans against their partners in crime.

Definitely, because, quite often, cartels operate in the intermediate goods and services sector, such as in the animal feed additives business, so consumers do not feel the pain—they remain ignorant of the fact that such artificial price increases lead to a higher price of finished goods which they buy/consume.

The direct costs of a cartel to consumers are increases in the cost price of the product if the cartel is successful, fewer product choices (if the geographical markets are allocated among producers), and a slower rate of product innovation and technological change. To ensure that a cartel survives, cartels may engage in activities that block or slow the entry by producers that are not members of the cartel.

This is major challenge, this is, for the new competition authority in India, apart from the other major challenge of abuse of dominance. Many experts consider anti-cartel activity the most important function of a competition agency. They feel that because cartels cause the greatest harm to consumers, finding and prosecuting the concerned name in these agreements should be a top priority of competition officials.

Prosecuting cartels may be the most difficult of the tasks assigned to competition authorities as cartels are conceived and carried out in secret. Cartel operators, knowing that their conduct is unlawful, do not willingly cooperate with competition officials in the course of investigations. Thus obtaining evidence to prove the existence of cartel agreements requires adequate legal provisions, special investigative tools and skills.

Under the MRTPA, the Commission had tried to prosecute two international cartels: one in soda ash and the other in float-glass, both of which are not consumer goods. But, while it succeeded in passing good orders, the Supreme Court turned them down on two grounds: first, that the MRTPC does not have extra-territorial jurisdiction; and second, that cartels are not properly defined in the MRTPA. The new Competition Act of 2007 has taken care of both these points by providing for jurisdiction on any anti-competitive practice that takes place outside the territory but having an impact on India; also cartels are clearly defined

Over the last century, in particular, there was a global resurgence of international cartels, which became evident, thanks to the numerous efforts to uncover them by the competition authorities. It is believed that the US and the EU authorities have prosecuted about 100 international cartels in the given time period. They have had effective competition regimes for many years, which have been refined over time.

Both the US and EU are capitalist economies and firmly believe in the private sector as the most important component of their economy. Yet, they are very tough on collusive activities such as cartels because they sap the economy. The record, sadly, has been much poorer in the developing world—not because cartels are less common here but because the law enforcement agencies are less well equipped to deal with them.

Thus, there is a strong case for strengthening the enforcement activity of competition authorities in developing countries *vis-a-vis* cartels. This continues to be hampered by inadequate legal frameworks or tools, information asymmetries, or worse, human resource handicaps. Such is the situation in countries like India.

India has the Competition Act, 2002, amended in 2007, and this has provisions for amnesty for any firm that blows the whistle on the others in the cartel. The law is yet to be notified in full and made operational, but it is on its way. We hope that the new law will be operational soon and we can see effective action against such cartels.

In a very recent case of cartelisation against five elevator manufacturers in Austria, ThyssenKrupp, as the first party who blew the whistle, got away without any fine, while Otis Elevator received a 50 per cent remission in fines for active cooperation in the enquiry. The others in the cartels who were fined a total of 75 million Euros, included Kone, Schindler, Doppelmayr and Haushahn. Some of these operate in India too. Among cartels, one of the most pathological ones is the cement industry, unless there is a state monopoly as had existed in a few socialist countries.

In 1994, the European Commission (EC) levied fines to the extent of 248 million Euros on six companies and the cement manufacturers' association. In judicial appeals, finally decided in January 2004, the fine was brought down by 140 million Euros, and the fine on the trade association was nullified. These six included Lafarge and Holcim. Lafarge was fined with 187 million Euros by the EC in 2003 for participating in another cartel, the third largest fine ever levied for being a habitual offender.

In Taiwan, in December 2005, a fine of $6.3 million was imposed on Cemex, one of 11 manufacturers along with 10 distributors.

In Korea, in September 2003, the competition authority levied surcharges (fixed fines) of $22 million on seven companies in addition to $428,000 on the Korea Cement Manufacturers' Association. In Argentina, five cement companies operated a cartel during 1981-99, until caught and fined a whopping $107 million, the largest fine levied by the country's competition regulator.

In Romania, in 2005, three cement companies—Lafarge Romcim, Holcim and Heidelburg's subsidiary Carpatcement—were fined 27 million Euros or six per cent of their turnover. These three companies shared 98 per cent of Romania's cement market. The probe found that they had inflated prices by as much as 38 per cent. The list is endless.

Let's now take a look at countries where there is no effective competition law, and how cement cartels behave. In

December 2002, the price of cement had fallen to an exceptionally low E£125 a tonne in Egypt. The drop had caused serious worry among the cement producers. In response, almost all local cement producers met and set a price range for cement between E£167 and E£176 a tonne. There was an outcry, but no action could be taken, as Egypt did not have a competition law then. It has one, now, in spite of strong business opposition, but the same is yet to become fully operational.

In Pakistan, which had a law similar to our own MRTPA, the authority did take action against cement cartels in October 1998. Cement manufacturers raised the price of cement in a collective action from Rs. 135 a bag to Rs. 235 a bag. Enquiry by the Monopoly Control Authority found that none of the input costs had gone up. The authority passed orders for reversion to the old prices and levied a fine. The order was stayed by the High Court. The Ministry of Commerce intervened and persuaded the MCA, despite the theoretical independence, to close the case. Now, even Pakistan has a new competition law.[95]

Research in Philippines, which has no competition law, has shown that the cement industry has grown under heavy government protection. The market leader, a state enterprise, Philippines Cement Corporation decides which company produces how much and where it can sell. Collective price action has been seen for a long time. Analyses of cost structures show that in spite of differences, the selling price is uniform. Research in Malaysia shows that the local cement producers may be indirectly affected by Lafarge's international cartel arrangements.

If we look closer at the cement industry in India, it is the second largest in the world with total capacity of 151.2 mt, and growing. All major international cement companies are here. There are some significant domestic players too, but they are closely linked to the foreign players through cross-holdings, which is why we need an effective competition law.[96]

Hitting out at the cement and steel manufacturers, the Union Finance Minister, Mr. P. Chidambaram, said in the Lok Sabha that "I have no hesitation in repeating that cement manufacturers are behaving like a cartel. There are signs that even steel manufacturers are behaving like a cartel...If they do not understand the gravity of the situation and behave responsibly, Government will not hesitate to take tough administrative measures."

P. Chidambaram, the finance minister of India,said that the steel makers' contention that steel prices rise due to increase in prices of gas and iron ore was creating a "logjam" and that somewhere this "logjam" had to be broken.[97]

"While many commodities will indeed reflect international prices, the capacity to exploit excess demand in the economy must indeed be addressed by fiscal, monetary and administrative measures. We have taken fiscal (reduction in excise duty, removal of customs duties) and monetary measures. But we cannot rely entirely on fiscal and monetary measures. We have to take such administrative measures that restrain the proclivity of producers to increase prices simply because the situation allows them to exploit", he said.

Monopolies and Restrictive Trade Practices Commission (MRTPC) has issued a notice of enquiry against Bharti Airtel, Vodafone Essar and Idea Cellular for allegedly forming a cartel to distort competition by increasing tariffs simultaneously. The case was taken up by MRTPC after the three companies announced similar tariff hike on a specific plan in August 2007. While local call charge was increased from Re 1 to Rs. 1.20 per minute, STD rates were increased by 10 per cent on a few pre-paid plans.

The notice from MRTPC comes after its investigative wing, the Director General of Investigations and Registrations (DGIR) report said that the three GSM operators, by colluding, have simultaneously increased the price. The report stated that despite having different cost factors, structures and profits, they all fixed the tariff of their local call at Rs. 1.20 a minute.[98]

Towards end-2007, the Monopolies and Restrictive Trade Practices Commission (MRTPC) had stated that the cement industry and its association have been colluding for over 17 years. The Tamil Nadu Government even threatened to take over the sector. But the MRTP Commission passed only cease and desist orders, which have had no penal impact. When the government allowed imports from Pakistan, the cement lobby raised the issue of Pakistani factories not having ISI licence.

Another sector which the MRTP Commission has also tried to bridle is the tyre industry but with equal ineffectiveness. When the truckers' strike hit the nation in late 2008, the Road Transport Ministry issued half-page advertisements telling the public as to how wrong the strike was. One grouse of the All India Motor Transport Congress was the high prices of tyres due to cartelisation. In the ad, the Ministry advised the truckers to approach the MRTP Commission (now Competition Act) with evidence to deal with the collusive behaviour.[99]

The New Corporate Colonialism

After the debt crisis of the early eighties, there was very little private investment into the Third World and the new money provided by the multinational development banks served above all to enable debtor countries to continue paying interest on loans contracted with the private banks.

In the early nineteen nineties, all this changed. Private investment in the Third World increased by leaps and bounds and went up to something like $400 billion a year, about half of which represented long-term investments—the other half being short-term speculative funds. This dwarfed the World Bank's until-now determinant contribution of about $29 billion per year, and has triggered-off stock-exchange booms in the so-called 'emergent markets', though admittedly these have been interspersed with crashes, such as that which recently occurred in Mexico.

This massive increase in private investment has occurred partly because of the mismatch between the vast sums of money in the US and other industrial countries looking for investment outlets and the availability of such outlets in the industrialised world; also, because conditions have now been created world-wide that could not be more favourable to the interests of transnational corporations. Not only have they been provided throughout the world with an abundant unskilled labour force, but also with highly skilled technical and managerial staff at an insignificant fraction of what they would cost in the industrial world, but in addition they also now have access to whatever finance they require and to the latest computer-based technology and management methods.

Also, as a result of the GATT Agreement, Third World countries are under an obligation to: (i) accept all investments from abroad; (ii) give 'national treatment' to any foreign corporation that establishes itself within its borders, whether it is involved in agriculture, mining, manufacturing or the service industries; (iii) eliminate tariffs and import quotas on all goods, including agricultural produce; (iv) and abolish 'non-tariff barriers' to trade, such as regulations to protect labour, health or the environment, that might conceivably increase corporate costs.[100]

Conditions more favourable to the immediate interests of TNCs could scarcely be imagined. Many of them were imposed during the GATT negotiations by the American delegation, and the delegations of other industrial powers, who presumably believed that the vast bulk of the TNCs were located in such countries, and always would be.

However, it seems more and more that this may change. Even strong governments are no longer able to exert any sort of control over transnational corporations. If a country passes a law that they regard as a hindrance to their further expansion, they merely threaten to leave and establish themselves elsewhere, which, under the new conditions, they can do at the drop of a hat. Indeed, they are now free to scour the globe and establish themselves wherever labour is the cheapest, environmental laws are the laxest, fiscal regimes are the least onerous and subsidies are the most generous. As a result, they need no longer identify with or allow their policies to be swayed by any sentimental attachment to any nation state.

Already Volvo, one of the leading Swedish corporations, is now Swedish in name only, having transferred nearly all of its operations abroad. What, we might ask, is to prevent General Motors or IBM from becoming German, Chinese, or merely from shifting their headquarters from one country to another as and when it becomes advantageous for them to do so? Also, as they become increasingly global, what is to prevent them from becoming even bigger, more powerful and even less controllable than they already are?

Consider that a monopoly is usually defined as a situation in which more than 40 per cent of the market for a particular commodity is controlled by less than four or five corporations. This is already the case for most of the commodities traded in the world market today—a state of affairs that can only become more pronounced as there is no way in which a national government can impose anti-trust legislation on stateless TNCs, nor can the World Trade Organisation, that they effectively control, be counted upon to do so.

As a few giant TNCs consolidate their respective monopolies in the world-wide sale of a particular commodity or set of commodities, so it is likely to become even less advantageous to them to compete with each other. Competition mainly reduces profit margins; cooperation, on the other hand, must enable them to increase their hold over governments, and to deal with the veritable opposition from populist and nationalist movements and others who might seek to restrict their power and influence.

Already, TNCs are resorting to more and more vertical integration and thereby coming to control virtually every step in the economic process in their respective fields; for instance, from the mining of minerals, to the construction of factories, to the production of goods, to their storage, their shipping to subsidiaries in other countries, and their wholeselling and retailing to local consumers. In this way, they are effectively insulating themselves from market forces, and assuring that it is they themselves, rather than competition from their rivals, that determine, at each step, the prices that are to be charged.

Already, somewhere between 20 per cent and 30 per cent of world trade is between TNCs and their subsidiaries. Rather than being real trade, this is really but a facet of corporate central planning on a global scale. For Paul Ekins, the British ecological economist, TNCs are becoming "giant areas of bureaucratic planning in an otherwise market economy." He sees "a fundamental similarity between giant corporations and state enterprises. Both use hierarchical command structures to allocate resources within their organisational boundaries rather than the competitive market."[101]

What, one might ask, is to prevent 50 per cent, 60 per cent or even 80 per cent of world trade from eventually occurring within such 'organisational boundaries'? At present, very little, and as one moves relentlessly in this direction, so may one be entering a new era of global corporate central planning—one that will be geared to a new type of colonialism: global corporate colonialism.

The new colonial powers have no responsibility for, nor accountability to anybody but their shareholders. They are little more than machines geared to the single goal of increasing their immediate profitability. What is more they will now have the power to force national governments to defend their interests whenever these are in conflict with those of the people the governments have been elected to protect.

The new corporate colonialism is thus likely to be more cynical and more ruthless than anything we have seen so far. It is likely to dispossess, impoverish, and marginalise more people, destroy more cultures, and cause more environmental devastation than either the colonialism of old or the development of the last 50 years. The only question is how long can it last? In my opinion, for a few years perhaps—a decade at most, for an economy of a sort that creates misery on such a scale is both aberrant and necessarily short-lived

Six billion people now live in a world exposed to escalating crises, further wars and corporate greed.

Any country can now be invaded and its people forced to live under conditions that they did not choose voluntarily. The world is no longer governed by national colonial powers. These colonial mechanisms have been replaced by corporate colonialism and the greed of globally operating investment groups and their political stakeholders. In both cases, the suffering for the people of the world is the same.[102]

Cultural Imperialism/Invasion

Cultural imperialism is the systematic penetration and domination of the cultural life of the popular classes by powerful sections from elsewhere, in order to reorder the values, behaviour, institutions and identity of the weak to conform to the interests of the "imperial classes."

United States' cultural imperialism has two major goals, one economic and the other political. Its goals are; to capture markets for its cultural commodities and to establish hegemony by shaping popular consciousness.

The export of entertainment commodities is one of the most important sources of capital accumulation and global profits, displacing manufacturing exports.

In the political sphere, cultural imperialism plays a major role in dissociating people from their cultural roots and traditions of solidarity, and replacing them with media created "needs", which change with every publicity campaign. The political effect is to alienate people from traditional class and community bonds, atomise and separate individuals from each other. Cultural imperialism emphasizes the segmentation of the working class; stable workers are encouraged to dissociate themselves from temporary workers, who, in turn, separate themselves from the unemployed, who are further segmented among themselves within the "underground economy."

Contemporary cultural colonialism is distinct from past practices in several ways:

Notes and References

1. Kavin Danaher, "50 years are not enough: the case against World Bank and International Monetaey Fund" (ed.) South End Press (1994), pp. 6-7.
2. Bharat Bhushan, "House of Lords", *The Telegraph*, Opinion, Calcutta, Monday, June 21, 2004
3. *Ibid.*
4. David Skidmore, "Contested social orders and international politics", Vanderbilt University Press, Nashville TN, USA, 1997, p. 222.
5. V. Sridhar, "Playing with Regulations" *The Frontline*, Volume 20, Issue 19, September 13-26, 2003.
6. Aimin Yan, Yadong Luo, "International joint ventures: theory and practice", M.E. Sharpe Inc., New York, 2001, 287.
7. *Ibid.*
8. Harris, R.W., "England in the eighteenth century, 1689-1793; A Balanced Constitution and New Horizons Humanities Press, New York, 1968, pp. 10-11.

9. http://www.thehindubusinessline.com/2007/04/19/stories/2007041902330900.htm
10. http://www.dawn.com/wps/wcm/connect/dawn-content-library/dawn/the-newspaper/columnists/jawed-naqvi-obscurantism-black-money
11. http://www.thaindian.com/newsportal/politics/state-funding-of-polls-still-a-far-cry_100166898.html
12. Hirschmann, D., Development Management *versus* Third World Bureaucracies: A Brief History of Conflicting Interests, *Development and Change*, 1999, pp. 287-305.
13. http://www.worldbank.org/html/opr/procure/debarr.html.
14. Hall, D., "Privatisation, multinationals and corruption. Development in Practice", The Corner House, 2000, pp. 539-56.
15. http://www.apfn.org/apfn/enron_republican.htm
16. Loren Fox, "Enron: The Rise and Fall", Wiley.
17. Nick Cohen, "Without Prejudice: U-turns in the U-bend, *The Observer*, U.K, 6-6-1999.
18. India: The "Enron project" in Maharashtra—protests suppressed in the name of Development Report by Amnesty International, 17/7/97 www.amnesty.org
19. "Indian state to renegotiate Enron power project", France Presse agency, 20-12-2000.
20. Arundhati, Roy, "Power Politics: The Reincarnation of Rumpelstiltskin", D.C. Books, 2001, p. 26.
21. Agence France Presse, December 20, 2000, Indian state to renegotiate Enron power project.
22. Earle, Julie, "Enron may seek damages over India project", *Financial Times*, by Julie Earle, May 22, 2001.
23. Dugger, Celia W., "High-Stakes Showdown: Enron's Fight Over Power Plant Reverberates Beyond India", *The New York Times*, March 20, 2001.
24. Merchant, Khozem, "Enron's India contract annulled", *Financial Times*, May 24, 2001.
25. Merchant Khozem, "Enron plant may be mothballed", *Financial Times*, June 7, 2001.
26. Katakam, Anupama, "The issue of arbitration", *The Frontline*, Volume 20, Issue 20, September 27-October 10, 2003.
27. *Ibid.*
28. http://www.headlinesindia.com/business-news/petroleum-and-natural-gas/key-papers-sought-on-reliance-petroleum-role-in-iraqi-oil-deal-7737.html
29. Panchal Komalkirti, "50 years of scams and scandals", *Business India*, August 11-24, 1997, pp. 16-20.
30. DePamphilis Donald, "Mergers, Acquisitions, and Other Restructuring Activities", Second Edition, Academic Press, 2002, London, p. 105.

31. Gathani Batuk, "Acquisition Was A Matter Of Pride", *Business Line*, Thursday, Feb 01, 2007
32. http://www.indianindustry.com/trade-information/acquisition-of-ranbaxy.html
33. "Daiichi Sankyo completes Ranbaxy takeover", *The Financial Express*, Friday, Nov 07, 2008.
34. http://exim.indiamart.com/ssi-regulations/idr-act.html
35. Sethi, K. Chitleen, "50 Pc Of Mohali Units Have Closed Down", *The Tribune*, Chandigarh, Friday, 26-12-2003.
36. Kumar, Arun, "Thwarting National Policy Making", *The Tribune*, Chandigarh, Monday, October 29, 2007.
37. Arun Kumar, "Share Market Gyrations", *Mainstream*, Vol. XLV, No. 50, New Delhi, 3 December 2007.
38. http://en.wikipedia.org/wiki/BSE_Sensex#Sensex_milestones
39. Bansal, Vinay, "Objective Banking and Finace", Upkar Prakashan, Agra, 2006, pp. 27.
40. Sridhar, V., "All about PNs", *Frontline*, Volume 24, Issue 22, Nov. 03-16, 2007.
41. http://www.financialweek.com/apps/pbcs.dll/article?AID=/20090107/REG/901079993/1002/ACCOUNTING
42. http://www.businessworld.in/index.php/Corporate/Reactions-To.html
43. http://www.dot.gov.in/osp/Brochure/Brochure.htm
44. "Security Concerns For Telecom", *The Times of India*, New Delhi, 22 May, 2006
45. Sharma, Smriti, "Cellphone radiation boils egg in 80 min. Think what it can do to your head", *Chandigarh Tribune*, Wednesday, October 8, 2008,
46. Mukherjee, Ambarish, "More mobiles, and sparrows take flight", *Business Line*, Monday, Dec. 01, 2003.
47. Thakurta, Paranjoy Guha, "Spectrum allocation row has cost India Rs. 80,000 crore", *The Asian Age*, Delhi, Tuesday, 16 June, 2009, p. 6.
48. *Ibid.*
49. "Water Supply Parvathi Menon: Cautious Corporatisation", *Frontline*, (Volume 18, Issue 13), Jun. 23-Jul. 06, 2001, pp. 44-47.
50. Sachitanand, N.N., "Will These Goliaths Oust The Davids?, *The Hindu*, Opinion, Friday, Jul. 15, 2005.
51. D. Brunn Stalley, Wal-Mart World: The World's Biggest Corporation In The Global Economy, CRC Press, 2006, pp. 121-22.
52. www.navdanya.org/corporate/research.pdf.
53. *Ibid.*
54. Christopher Stevens, Food aid and the developing world: Four African case studies, Vincent P. Gutschick Publisher: London, Croom Helm, in association with the Overseas Development Institute (1979) pp. 16.
55. Huw Bowen, 'Imperial Adventurers', *Guardian*, 12 January, 2002.

56. Muddassir Rizvi, 'Monsanto Fiddles with Plant Protection Act', Inter Press Service, 31 August 1999.
    http://www.twnside.org.sg/title/fiddle-cn.htm
57. *Ibid.*
58. Letter from Dr. A. Rehman Khan to Chief of the Seed Certification Department, 6 August 1999, quoted in *ibid.*
59. http://www2.essex.ac.uk/ces/ResearchProgrammes/safewexecsummfinalreport.htm
60. Kochhar, Rajesh, "Towards A Global Perspective On Globalisation", *The Hindu,* Tuesday, Dec. 16, 2003.
61. http://www.hartford-hwp.com/archives/40/139.html
62. Microsoft Corp., Annual Report (Form 10-K), at 20, 23, 26 (Jul. 31, 2008), http://idea.sec.gov/Archives/edgar/data/789019/000119312508162768/d10k.htm.
63. Herbert Hovenkamp, Mark D. Janis, Mark A. Lemley, "IP and Antitrust: An Analysis of Antitrust Principles Applied to Intellectual Property Law (Vol. one) Aspen Law and Business Publishers, Herbert (USA), 2002, pp. 132-35.
64. Final Judgment, United States *v.* Microsoft Corp., No. 94-1564, 1995 U.S. Dist. LEXIS 20533, at *8 (D.D.C. Aug. 21, 1995), http://www.usdoj.gov/atr/cases/f0000/0047.htm.
65. http://www.microsoft.com/presspass/press/2005/jul05/07-01msibmsettlepr.mspx.
66. http://www.usdoj.gov/atr/cases/exhibits/276.pdf.
67. Novell, Inc. *v.* Microsoft Corp., No. JFM-05-1087, 2005, U.S. Dist. LEXIS 11520 (D. Md. June 10, 2005).
68. http://www.theregister.co.uk/1999/07/18/analysis_how_ms_used
69. "Netscape Says Microsoft Sought 20% Stake", *The New York Times,* September 28, 1995.
70. Herbert Hovenkamp, Mark D. Janis, Mark A. Lemley, "IP and antitrust: an analysis of antitrust principles applied to Intellectual Property Law", Volume 1, ASPEN Publishers, Frederick, MD, 2007, pp. 140-42.
71. http://www.usdoj.gov/atr/cases/exhibits/268.pdf.
72. Paul, Festa, "IE 5.5 angers Web standards advocates", CNET NEWS, July 13, 2000 http://news.cnet.com/2100-1023-243144.html
73. http://www.allbusiness.com/technology/software-services-applications/7190655-1.html.
74. United States *v.* Microsoft Corp., 253 F.3d 34, 77 (D.C. Cir. 2001) (quoting Findings of Fact, *supra* note 20, 404–05).
75. *In re* Microsoft Corp. Antitrust Litig., 333 F.3d 517, 523 (4th Cir. 2003).
76. http://biz.yahoo.com/msft/p10.html
77. http://www.microsoft.com/presspass/press/2005/oct05/10-11MSRealPR.mspx.
78. http://www.microsoft.com/technet/archive/winntas/deploy/ntunxint.mspx?mfr=true.

79. http://www.crn.com/it-channel/18822436
80. http://idea.sec.gov/Archives/edgar/data/789019/000119312508162768/d10k.htm
81. http://www.globalexchange.org/getInvolved/corporateHRviolators.html
82. http://www.globalexchange.org/getInvolved/corporateHRviolators.html
83. Subodh Varma, "India A Hotbed For Clinical Trials", *The Times of India*, New Delhi, 18 March 2007.
84. *Ibid.*
85. *Ibid.*
86. Thakur, Pradeep, "FinMin wants list of SEZ units evading taxes", *The Times of India*, 17 Sep 2008.
87. Sethi Aman, "Bali road map", *The Frontline*, Volume 25, Issue 01, Jan. 05-18, 2008.
88. Daphne Wysham and Smitu Kothari, "Climate change will devastate India", *The Hindu*, April 9, 2007.
89. Mehta, S., Pradeep, S., "Surrogate advertising—Needed, a spirited attack", *Business Line*, Friday, May 23, 2003.
90. http://www.123eng.com/forum/viewtopic.php?t=16132
91. Sharma, K. Jitendra, "Tobacco ads likely to be stubbed out by Jan-end", *Hindustan Times*, New Delhi, 22 January, 2004.
92. Jeremy, Laurance, "Nestlé breaking code on baby milk for Third World", http://www.independent.co.uk/news/world/politics/nestle acute-breaking-code-on-baby-milk-for-third-world-601941.html
93. http://www.competition-commission-india.nic.in/advocacy/Articles_in_press/CCIWebArticlesCompilationText29042008new.pdf
94. Murali, D., "Cartelist behaviour is difficult to detect", *The Hindu*, Saturday, December 22, 2007.
95. Mehta S. Pradeep, "Cement cartels: flavour of the day", *The Financial Express*, Sunday, June 10, 2007.
96. *Ibid.*
97. "Govt Warns of Stern Steps to Break Cement, Steel Cartels", *Business Line*, Thursday, April 17, 2008.
98. "MRTPC issues notice to Airtel, Vodafone and Idea Cellular", *The Business Line*, Friday, April 04, 2008.
99. Mehta, S. Pradeep, "When economy slows, cartelisation grows", *The Business Line*, Tuesday, April 28, 2009.
100. Arora, Anil, International Trade (New Delhi: Deep and Deep Publications), 2007, pp. 166-75.
101. http://www.edwardgoldsmith.com/page49.html
102. Tamás Szentes, Transformation of the world economy: new directions and new interest", Zed Books Ltd., London, 1989, pp. 62-66.

5

Gandhian Alternative

The evolution of India's development policy over the past several years is a unique illustration of change with continuity. This vast country has had many problems; the nature of problems has varied from region to region and their effects have been different for different social and economic groups within the population. And all of these have changed with changing times. The specific policies adopted by different governments at both the Centre and the States have also been varied. They have been influenced by the varying strengths of different interest groups, and also by the political dominance of the different levels of leadership. It is easy to get bogged down in the details and lose sight of the very significant element of uniformity in the basic character of these problems of development policy that has centered around a general consensus on the objectives of development.

The shapers of Independent India, both during the period of our national movement for Independence and when formulating our national policies after it, always associated political freedom with economic freedom, which went much beyond raising the growth rate of the Gross National Product (GNP). For the nation as a whole, it meant the freedom to follow its own policies without in any way compromising its sovereignty. For the individuals who constituted the nation, it meant gaining control over their destiny. There is no denying the fact that the material model of economic development so widely followed, has not come to grip with unevenness in growth, the growing inequality, income distribution and the problems of coordination of different sections of the economy.[1] In the present model, one find that all that comes across in terms of trade, commerce, financial arrangements and human attitudes are attempts to continue with the past practices of short-term gains of limited groups or communities. These attitudes, structures and arrangements do not provide long-term solution to the problems of mankind.

It is in this background that Gandhian model to economic development can be shown to have its relevance in solution of the basic problems of mankind. It is because of this that economic and social policies, attitudes and structures are being revised in almost all countries of the world to make the efforts of economic development more meaningful. Although the Gandhian economic model had been found by his very disciple, Nehru too slow and too idealistic and dumped by him but now. It has almost been universally realised that the Gandhian model to economic development is the real solution to the problems with which the world economy is concerned. The relevance of Gandhian ideas becomes once more important in the sense that his ideas provide a key to the dilemma of the growth process of the contemporary world economy.

He did not spin his theories in the cloistered atmosphere of his study, they grew and developed in the crucible of experience, in the course of his attempt to wrest freedom for his country and to solve the various practical problems as they emerged in the course of his ling struggle against foreign domination. For a proper appreciation of the economic ideas of Gandhi, it is necessary to bear in mind that he was not an economist in the conventional sense of the term as J.B. Kripalani puts it: "If ever there was a planner without elaborate blue prints, Gandhi was one."[2] Gandhi was not a theorist but primarily he was an actionist. He himself admitted: "I am not built for academic writings. Action is my domain. What I understand according to my lights, to be my duty and what comes my way I do."[3]

THE BASIC GANDHIAN PRECEPTS

First, Gandhi did not believe in the basic postulate of all modern theories that some trade is better than no trade or that more trade means more welfare. This, or any other kind of absolutism, was alien to Gandhi even if it could be true in more cases than those in which it would be proved false. It is wrong to give a theory or a principle and the character of absoluteness even if it satisfies the scientific principles of falsification.

The imports of ex-colonial countries today contain a much lower share, of consumables than earlier. However, this has occurred mainly because domestic capital-intensive activities have taken over in the consumer goods sector. The net impact has been that domestic handicrafts are now being replaced by domestic manufactures of capital-intensive type.

The profits of export industries are by and large proving insufficient to sustain the sky-rocketing capital requirements of export industries, so that resources drawn from less capital intensive sectors are being pumped into the capital-intensive export industries.

Once again, therefore, the same structural anomalies which characterised colonial trade patterns have been reduplicated in post-colonial trade patterns. The exports of poor economies are still on average more capital-intensive than, the average for their home economies. The exports of rich countries continue to be on average more labour-intensive than the average for their economies. This famous Leontief anomaly simply means that the trade pattern is still such that it generates net employment in the richer economies and net employment destruction in the poorer ones.

A Gandhian analysis of post-colonial trade will indicate another surprising fact. This is that what used to be a single level exploitation of poor economies has become a two-level exploitation: (i) of the poorer part of poor economies by its more developed part, and (ii) of the developed part of the poorer economies by the developed nations. This was something Gandhi had noticed emerging as early as in the 1920's.[4]

Evidently, argued Gandhi, as far as the destruction of

employment opportunities is concerned, it does not matter much whether the manufacturing unit (which destroys the handicraft units) is located in Lancashire or in Ahmedabad. The effect on the rural economy is identical. The only change is that instead of going to a city in a foreign country, the fruits of this exploitation go to a city in the same countries. Since, however, there is no net flow of resources back from, domestic city sector to the village sector, the net result is impoverisation of the village sector to the same degree as before.

Nor does this transfer ultimately add to the prosperity of the cities. These are once again constrained to import capital goods so as to establish their own industries. Also, a large part of the surpluses earned are siphoned-off in the consumption of foreign luxuries. The net benefit remaining to the country is negligible. Thus 'domestic industry' represents only a substation in the flow of exploitative profits and employment potential from the poor to the rich countries.[5]

Consequently, there are no gains from trade as far as participation by poor countries in the present system of world trade is concerned. Even the inconveniences of autarchy are preferable to the continual bleeding of resources and employment opportunities represented by the colonial and post-colonial patterns of foreign trade.

Gandhi denounced a lot of the then prevailing system of trade for a variety of reasons, sometimes leaving the impression that he may have been totally against foreign trade but he was not. In his own words: "I have no difficulty, we do not want to cut-off our trade from the whole world. We will have a free interchange with all nations, but the present forced interchange has to go. We do not want to be exploited neither do we want to exploit any other nation."[6] This is a clear statement that trade based on unequal exchange has the embedded element of force. A free trade is not possible under the policies of equal exchange between unequals. He even implies acceptance of one of the basic premises of the conventional doctrine of international trade: international disparity in the endowment of productive resources. Yet Gandhi would not accept an international economic order based solely on the principle of comparative advantage. To him, such a system is vulnerable to unfair competition and economic exploitation; it tends to be much more responsive to reciprocal demand than to mutual need.

Second, Gandhi denounced free trade theory. Although all nations control and manage trade, they all swear by moving towards the goal of free trade. In a system of nations having different productivities, bargaining powers, income levels, and resources endowments, free trade can only produce more inequalities, monopolies, and even ruin weaker economies. Gandhi drew attention to this fact a world divided into nations of different sizes and development stages and strategies. He wrote: "Each country has its own economics. German textbooks are different from the English. Free trade may be England's salvation. It spells our ruin. We have to formulate a system of Indian economics."[7]

Trade ceased to remain a free trade. Old Mercan-tilism appeared in a new garb and a war of restrictions is going on in spite of the U.N.A., International Monetary Fund, World Bank and International Agreements. The story of internal. trade is not much different. Artificial barriers on the movement of goods within a country are also raised under pretext of zonal system, rationing and price control, rationalisation and scientific management, licensing system, planning, etc. The troubled man, who willy-nilly surrendered his rights to the State under the able guidance of the all knowing economist is amazed alarmed and much more unhappy than what he used to be. The remedy has been worse than the disease itself. The poor man has also surrendered his liberty to the State who now refuses to return it back.

The debacle of mighty U.S.S.R., the sole super power U.S.A., with the help of WTO, U.N.O. and its allied agencies is trying to dominate the economies of other countries. This love for money may now lead to economic imperialism.

Let us now turn to the Eastern prescription which Gandhi wanted to administer.

Gandhi wanted to reduce the size of markets of essential consumption goods by decreasing their supply and demand. He, therefore, pleaded that the size of plants should be small[8] and only those machines should be used which will serve as a servant.[9] His production pattern and insistence on decentralisation very clearly give this idea.[10] In such a set-up, the scope for mass production is mainly through masses,[11] and not machines. Gandhi also held that multiplicity of wants beyond a minimum limit would not promote happiness.[12] He, therefore, preached the law of simplicity.[13] The outcome of small production units and minimum wants win give regional self-sufficiency though not individual self-sufficiency. To quote Gandhi:

> "... We have to concentrate on the villages being self-contained, manufacturing mainly for use.... "[14]
>
> "... My idea of village Swaraj is that it is a complete republic, independent of its neighbours for its vital wants, and yet interdependent for many others in which dependence is necessary."[15]
>
> "... What is necessary is to make the village self-sufficient and self-reliant. But mind you, my idea of self-sufficiency is not a narrow one; there is no scope for selfishness and arrogance in my self-sufficiency."[16]
>
> "... Villages collectively, not the villager individually, will become self-contained so far as their clothing requirements are concerned...."[17]

And according to S.N. Agarwal, "the regional unit of economic self-sufficiency will differ with different commodities."[18] But Gandhi's idea of self-sufficiency in basic requirements does not mean isolation.

> "... I am 'not preaching isolation', we have (to) be humble as the dust for the fulfilment of our cause. We have to mix with people even as sugar mixes itself with milk."[19]
>
> "That a man ought to be able to satisfy most of his essential needs himself is obvious, but it is no less obvious to me that when self-sufficiency is carried to the length of isolating oneself from society it almost amounts to sin."[20]

But where does 'self-dependence' end and

'inter-dependence' start? Gandhi wanted to apply the criterion of self-respect to determine their respective spheres. "Self-dependence is a necessary ideal so long as and to the extent that it is an aid to one's self-respect and spiritual discipline. It becomes an obsession and a hindrance when it is pushed beyond that limit. On the other hand inter-dependence when it is not inconsistent with one's self-respect is necessary."[21]

Thus, in Gandhian set-up the size of a market of essential consumption goods will be very small, generally coinciding with a village or a group of villages within a short radius. However, the markets for other commodities might be of a bigger size, they may be even international. To quote Gandhi: "Then every village of India will almost be a self-supporting and self-contained unit exchanging only such necessary commodities with other villages where they are not locally producible."[22] In Gandhian life, the preference to purchase or sell things will be strictly on a priority basis. Immediate neighbours will get priority over the distant ones. Defining Swadeshi, Gandhi wrote: "It follows that Swadeshi, was that spirit which dictated man to serve his next door neighbour to the exclusion of any other. The condition ... was that the neighbour thus served had in his turn to serve his own neighbour...."[23] Again, "In that of economics I should use only things that are produced by my immediate neighbours .... "[24] And if things are not available within the country, Gandhi will not hesitate to purchase them from abroad. "I buy from every part of the world what is needed for my growth."[25] "To reject foreign manufactures mainly because they are foreign and to go on wasting national time and money to provide manufacturers in one's country for without a theory, axioms, or guidelines for public choice, the decision of a modern business organisation, whether in the private sector or in the public sector, there can be no assurance for optimisation and efficient allocation, against market failure, selfishness, and exploitation. The invisible which it is not suited would be criminal folly and a negation of Swadeshi spirit."[26]

Third, a fundamental trading principle is that to buy in the cheapest market adds to welfare, both of the individual and the nation. Such a principle, if not constrained by employment, production of consumption goods by the masses, and styles of life can debase both individuals and societies. Gandhi denounced this principle in no uncertain terms. To a question, "Is the economic law that man must buy in the best and the cheapest market wrong," Gandhi replied, "It is one of the most inhuman among the maxims laid down by modern economists. Nor do we always regulate human relations by any such sordid considerations."[27]

Economists have built their theories on the basis of the behaviour of the markets and not on the basis of the behaviour of the man. In this way, the economic theory was simplified but it got divorced from the increasing complexity of human behaviour. Few economists have succeeded in clarifying the role of human factor in economic behaviour, let alone the market behaviour. Human behaviour has a built in process of learning, Kenneth bounding commented: 'Once we attempt that utility of betterment functions of learning, neo-classical economists, especially welfare economists, fall apart at an alarming rate."[28]

George Katonia wrote an excellent book entitled 'Psycho-logical Analysis of Economic Behaviour' and asked "what difference does it make if we study economic behaviour of men rather than the behaviour of the market?" he found the difference that a result of twenty five years of research in psychological economics, it was found that the" traditional information about economic relations between economic variables are inconsistent with some time greater changing images ... we must give up the notion of establishing laws that are generally followed ... at all times and at all places."[29] Gandhi rejected all universalised economic theories.

Fourth, Gandhi certainly rejected Ricardo's theory of international trade. Even if England had a comparative advantage in the production of cloth and India in the production of cotton, he would call the whole exercise false because conditions of production could change both through economies of scale and through technology. He thought it 'hideously wrong' to send raw materials for processing to other countries and take them back in the form of manu-factured goods, because the consequences of this kind of an approach for the rest of the economy and the society could prove disastrous. The theory of comparative advantage started as a normative principle and was abstracted from reality but on the way it became a theory of exploitation.

Fifth, Gandhi believed that production and distribution are not autonomous activities. They are influenced by the value system of a society and the way of life which people accept or force upon the production system or the latter forces upon them. Therefore, he asserted that favourable or unfavourable balance of trade itself cannot be accepted as determinant of trade and certainly not of other policies. How trade affects domestic distribution is as important as how it influences production. In a country where incomes are low, what is the guarantee that the sophisticated technology would produce low income consumer goods? Besides, how could there really be a true concept of mass production without the involvement of the masses and equal distribution? Gandhi said: "Without simultaneous distribution on any equally mass scale, mass production can result only in a great world tragedy. This was the lesson of the Great Depression."

According to E.F. Schumacher: If you ask an economic expert to ad vise you on the structure of freight rate—the charges to be levied by the Railways, Inland Water Transport, and so forth-he may be inclined to advise that the rates per ton/mile should "taper-off" so that they are the lower, the longer the haul. He may suggest that this is simply the "right" system, because it encourages long distance transport, promote large-scale, specialised production, and thus leads to an optimum use of resources. He may beyond the point of human integrity, the growth of a rootless proletariat, in short, a most undesirable and uneconomic way of life." Do you see that economics does not stand on its own feet?[30]

At the end of the 1920s, India had a favourable balance of trade. Some foreigners asked Gandhi to reconcile his statement about the growing poverty of India with this favourable balance of trade. Gandhi tried to answer the question in the following words and this gives us an insight into his theory of international trade. He said that there was the societal aspect of the problem and therefore a country having a favourable balance of trade is not necessarily in a happier or a better position. This would be accepted by non-Gandhian economists for different reasons.

He said: "suppose that a country whose government had slaveholders and who compelled all the slaves to grow food grains and other articles of value for the world which in turn paid them inadequately so that they could keep the wolf from the door. The slaveholders made enormous profits out of the grains grown and exported. On the other hand, imports were less than the exports to make favourable balance of trade." Gandhi said that this would be 'no test of the prosperity of its people in general, it would exist side by side with the growing poverty and degradation of the slaves, the position of India was not far removed from the slave ridden country imagined?"[31]

In support of his theory, Gandhi cited Dadabhai Naoroji who said that "favourable 'balance of trade' represents the continually bleeding process which is central in order to sustain the role which is based not upon the goodwill of people but upon a show of force which is kept up at an extra-ordinary expense of which a large part goes out of India." The last point deserves special mention. A country having a favourable balance of trade may not enjoy its fruits because it may have to pay for other expenses from that trade: for, it may not be free to decide for itself or may be obliged to buy technologies, management services, insurance, called invisibles, from outside.

Schumacher also remarks: Or you ask an economic expert what the country should do in order to avoid foreign exchange point to the experience of the United States, the United Kingdom, Germany, etc.—all "Advanced" countries employing just the 'tapering device.' Do you see that in doing so he would be recommending one particular way of life—the way of materialism? An "economic expert" steeped in Gandhian Economics would undoubtedly give very different encouragement; but long hauls should be discouraged because they would promote urbanisation, difficulties. Now one expert may advocate the maximum development of exports—to gain all the advantages of the international diffusion of labour. Another expert may advocate certain restrictions on imports—so that the country should not be at the mercy of all sorts of unpredictable disturbances in world markets. These two experts may argue with each other. But do you see that they are not arguing about economics but about a way of life? And so I could multiply examples.[32]

Sixth, another argument in favour of trade expansion is that it enlarges production and even promotes mass production by exploiting resources to the maximum. The added argument is that such a trade enhances total welfare even if its distribution is unequal. However, the problem of distribution may bounce back to distort and even destroy production possibilities in weaker nations thus mass production, without taking distributive aspects into account explicitly., can lead to trade cycle, recession, growth instability, and, above all, to subjugation, Gandhi explicitly stated. Without entering upon an elaborate argument I would categorically state my conviction that the mania for mass production is responsible for the world crises. Granting for the moment that the machinery (technology) may supply all the needs of humanity, still it would concentrate production in particular areas, so that you would have to go in a round about way to regular distribution: Whereas, if there is production and distribution both in the respective areas where things are required, it is automatically regulated, and there is less chance for fraud, none for speculation.[33]

These days we hear slogans such as "export-led growth" or "growth-led export." In a sense, although they seem to be two different principles. In fact, it is not so. For an export-led growth, it seems quite acceptable but one will have to be sure that the growth itself is not based on other imports for growth. If that is so, then the two principles are different. We know this is not so.

Seventh, according to the principle of comparative advantage, the nations of the world must enter into free trade to maximise their economic gains. Gandhian holistic economics rejects the doctrine of the trade on the basis of the principle of Swadeshi. The rejection follows from the Gandhian definition of human welfare in holistic terms in contrast to that by modern economics in terms of maximisation of consumption goods.

Now, purely on economic grounds, trade in the conventional sense among unequal partners, when one country is under-developed and the other is developed, will ultimately harm the interest of the poor country. Import of industrial products leads to the extinction of the handicrafts and the small-scale home industries in the under-developed countries due to their economic inability to stand competition. Consequently, there is a big drain on primary products, raw materials and non-renewable resources in order to meet the demand of the foreign countries. The under-developed country, therefore, gradually becomes more and more impoverished. The natural home economy is shattered without any hope for future. There is large-scale unemployment, and people become poor, degraded and lusterless. The rich country exploits the poor country by offering poor terms of trade and pocketing the major share of the gains. According to J.C. Kumarappa, if any society its necessities on foreign countries, the degree of its exploitation are in direct proportion to the amount of goods imported. Moreover, "Consumption of foreign goods is definitely baited for the foreigners to occupy the country."[34] He has further suggested that trade should be restricted only to surplus commodities in order to give no occasion to exploitation.

Gandhiji, deeply pained by the process of exploitation due to foreign trade, had expressed, "Economics that permit one country to prey upon another are immoral. It is sinful to buy and use articles made by sweated labour. It is sinful to have American wheat and let my neighbour, the grain-dealer, starve for want of custom. Similarly, it is sinful for me to wear the latest finery of Regent Street, when I know that if I had but worn the things woven by the neighbouring spinners and weavers, that would have clothed me, and fed and clothed them."[35] Gandhiji was of the confirmed view that India lost her political and economic independence because her people succumbed to the pressure of greed for gains from trade.

Gandhian pragmatic approach, however, was not for a total rejection of foreign trade. The country must be self-reliant as far as food, cloth and other basic necessities are concerned. Village crafts and industries which can be revived with some effort for their intrinsic merit and their other useful aspects must be given protection. However, goods which are important from people's welfare point of view and which cannot be produced at home may be imported. As he says, "I have never been an advocate of prohibition of all things foreign because they are foreign. My economic creed is a complete taboo in respect of all foreign commodities whose importation is likely to prove harmful to our indigenous interest. This means that we may not in any circumstance import a commodity that can be adequately supplied from our own country."[36] Thus, holistic welfare is the supreme consideration and trade must be subservient to it.

We know Swadeshi was the central principle of Gandhi's Philosophy. He did not believe that self-reliance could be achieved through international trade. He firmly believed that a country has to be self-supporting and self-reliant in all those areas where it could do so without the help of trade and then look for trade with others pursuing the same principles in areas in which self-support was not paramount. Trade and self-reliance had to go together and there could be self-reliance on such fancy principles as export promotion, import substitution, and technology transfer. Only in this sense, a self-reliant economy entering into trade will not get exploited. It is wrong to dub Swadeshi as autarky. The above quote from Gandhi is quite clearly against autarky. But if the choice is between exploitation and autarky, then the choice is explicit. It is like a choice between cowardice and violence.

Gandhi defines Swadeshi as the: "Spirit which dictates man to serve his next door neighbour to the exclusion of any other."[37] He further states that: "The neighbour thus served had in his turn to serve his own neighbour."[38]

In this sense Swadeshi is never exclusive. It recognizes the scientific limitations of human capacity for service. It might appear that by defining Swadeshi as the spirit which restricts us to the use and service of our immediate surroundings and one who serves his immediate neighbour serve the world as a whole. Further Gandhi writes: Our capacity for service has obvious limits. We can serve even our neighbours with some difficulty. If everyone of us duly performed his duty to his neighbour, no one in the world who needed assistance would be left unattended to. In this way one who serves his neighbours sees all the world."[39]

In Gandhi's own words: "A votary of Swadeshi will carefully study his environment, and try to help his neighbour wherever possible, by giving preference to local manufactures, even if they are of an inferior grade or dearer in price than things manufactured .elsewhere."[40] In another context, he put it more forcefully: "It is sinful to eat American wheat and let my neighbour, the grain-dealer, starve for want of customers."[41]

It is obvious that in advocating the Doctrine of Swadeshi, Gandhi is rejecting the Principle of Comparative Advantage. From intuition and observation, Gandhi was convinced that trade and other forms of international economic activity based purely on the principles of comparative advantage and international division of labour could easily degenerate into instruments of exploitation of one nation by another, of the poor by the rich, of the weak by the strong. It is interesting to note that the negative welfare aspects of international economic relations based purely on comparative advantage have been recognised by professional economists who have very little to do with Gandhian economics. These writers have seriously questioned the existence of equity in the distribution of gains from trade and investment among nations.[42]

In a typical pattern of trade between a dominant industrial economy and a dependent under-developed economy, Gandhi saw two forms of exploitation: (a) exploitation of one nation by another nation, and (b) exploitation of the rural poor by the urban elite in the dependent country. Gandhi derived this insight from his observation of the pattern of trade between 'England and India.'

The Gandhian Doctrine of Swadeshi, with its strong emphasis on self-reliance, even self-sufficiency, may be construed as a "negative doctrine of international trade. If every nation vigorously and effectively pursues this doctrine, it may be argued, the channels of world trade-will simply dry up and the benefits of mutually gainful trade will totally disappear. Such arguments will make any sense only if one interprets the Doctrine of Swadeshi very narrowly and very rigidly. Gandhi anticipated such misinterpretation of his doctrine and he wrote: "Even Swadeshi, like any other good thing, can be ridden to death if it is made a fetish. That is a danger which must be guarded against. To reject foreign manufacture merely because they are foreign and to go on wasting national time and in the promotion in one's country of manufacture for which it is no suited, would be criminal folly and a negation of the Swadeshi spirit."[43] His idea of self-sufficiency was that villages must be self-sufficient in regard to food, cloth and other basic necessities. But he stressed that to be self-sufficient was not to be altogether self-contained. He was realistic enough to admit that under no circumstances would one country be able to produce all the things needed. And he wrote: "So, though our aim is complete self-sufficiency, we shall have to get from outside the villages what we cannot produce in the villages. We shall have to produce more of what we can in order thereby to obtain in exchange what we are unable to produce."[44]

Despite the emphasis on self-sufficiency, to the extent it is possible, as suggested by the Doctrine of Swadeshi, a positive doctrine of trade from the Gandhian perspective does indeed emerge out of the mixture of Gandhian idealism and Gandhian pragmatism.

The following distinctive features of the doctrine may be noted as follows:

(a) It accepts the logic of the principle of comparative advantage but rejects it as the sole basis for trade among nations.
(b) It accepts reciprocal need rather than reciprocal demand as the determinant of terms of trade among nations.
(c) It postulates an international economic order based on international cooperation and understanding of mutual need, rather than on market force and competition.
(d) It is guided by a purpose higher than the purpose of pure economic gain. That is the moral purpose

embodied in the notion of service to govern the flow of trade among nations. It suggests an international economic policy which is the antithesis of "beggar-my-neighbour" policy, well-known in modern international economics.

(e) It is an economic doctrine into which is infused the philosophical principle of "Ahimsa" or Non-violence and non-exploitation.

(f) It offers maximum protection against unequal distribution of gains from trade among nations in sharp contrast with the conventional doctrine of international trade.[45]

The principle of Swadeshi demands that person must give preference to local manufacturers even if they are of inferior quality or more costly than articles of foreign make. They should try to search remedy for these defects but not give-up the use of those things. This is true Swadeshi, is thus very helpful. There is no room for hatred for the foreign made things. Gandhi did not reject a foreign made things simply because of its being foreign, he gladly used foreign made things but only when there were no Indian substitute for them and it would have been a criminal waste of time and energy to try to produce them locally, for such Swadeshi some times Gandhi used old Swadeshi and new Swadeshi, i.e. in old Swadeshi goods must be produced in India and village and cottage industries must produce alternative goods for foreign goods is new Swadeshi. Gandhi used the term real Swadeshi for Swadeshi which is 100 per cent Indian.

He did not insist upon the exclusion of such foreign made commodities whose import was harmful to indigenous industries for example, foreign cloth. It may be added that in advocating the complete boycott of foreign cloth, Gandhi bore no ill-will or malice towards the mill owners or labours of Lancashire. He had great love for them and wanted to wean them from what he deemed to be great vice. For him Swadeshi was not a cult of hatred, it was rather a doctrine of selfless service that has its roots in the purest Ahimsa, or love.[46]

In 1926 he wrote: "1 have never considered the

exclusion of everything foreign under every conceivable circumstance as a part of Swadeshi. The broad definition of Swadeshi is the use of all home made things to the exclusion of foreign things, insofar as such use is necessary for the protection of home industry, more especially those industries without which India will become pauperised. In my opinion, therefore, Swadeshi which exclude the use of everything foreign no matter how beneficent it may be is a narrow interpretation of Swadeshi."[47]

Indeed, absence of exploitation, self-reliance, and absence of violence and aggression in economic relations including trade are important considerations in Gandhian general theory, whether they can be quantified or not. There would be no Gandhian theory of trade if it does not take into account all these factors. Gandhi said: "When India becomes self-supporting, self reliant and proof against temptations and exploitation, she will cease to be the object of greedy attraction for any power in the West or the East and will then feel secure without having to carry the burden of extensive armaments. Here internal economy will be India's strongest bulwark against aggression."[48] Gandhi clearly saw the relations between trade in goods and trade in weapons.

Gandhi himself stressed that Swadeshi was not to be seen simply as a political expedient designed to weaken the hold of Lancashire on the Indian market for textiles and thereby embarrass the British rulers. It had to be justified in terms of fundamental moral principles. The principle that he invoked most often for this purpose was that of neighbourhood. Gandhi defined Swadeshi as a principle which is broken when one professes to serve those who are more remote in preference to those who are near. A teaching that is shared by all mankind, states Gandhi, and one that is common to all religions alike, is that one must be kind and attentive to one's neighbours. The duty of helping one's neighbours is the core of the ethics of Swadeshi. Thus again emphasising on the Principles of Swadeshi. Gandhi believed that the necessary determination and fervour could be marshaled only on the basis of a patriotic commitment. Given a commitment to the principle that national economic self-determination is as important as national political self-determination. Gandhi believed that the peoples of the poor nations will be willing to undertake the sacrifices involved in applying the principle of Swadeshi.

The logic of Swadeshi thus is as follows: (a) if there is any product presently imported of which a domestic substitute could be developed, that, substitute must be developed; (b) the domestic substitute developed must be of the labour-intensive type; and (c) if there is no intensive domestic-substitute possible, the product must simply be dispensed with. This means at once that, the pattern of elitist consumption will become much more restricted and the employment created in order to produce the basket of widely consumed, commodities will become much larger. The feasibility of Swadeshi then, depends on the willingness to accept a fairly massive equalisations of the pattern of consumption.

Once the capacity to run a Swadeshi economy is established, one can visualize its gradual relaxation in many ways:

> Manufactured consumption goods surpluses may be exchanged against consumption goods which are not feasible to be produced within the domestic economy. Technological capital goods suitable for mass-employment industries may be imported, as well as other types of such goods sold to other countries. Surplus capacity in the core sector of the economy may be utilised in the service of a wider region than the domestic economy.

All this, however, only after the domestic capacity for survival with autarchy has been established. Unless an economy has always the option of return-to-autarchy open; it cannot possibly avoid being exploited.

Since certain forms of heavy industry will (as we have seen) prove essential even for the development of the mass-employment sectors, Swadeshi economics involves a stress on the build-up of such necessary large-scale industries. Thus, curiously enough, the proponents of the capital-goods-building strategy of development may find a congenial and receptive background in the Gandhian theory of Swadeshi. It is worth-noting that the much-maligned Mahalanobis model (on which the Second Five Year Plan was based[49]) suggested that investment should be concentrated in the capital goods producing industries while consumption needs should be covered by light/small-scale industries. The Gandhian 'Swadeshi Strategy' involves the same two ideas, only with inversion of stress. Consumption goods should be produced (as far as feasible) by labour-intensive methods and modern sector industries should be those which are necessary for the support of mass-employment activities.

The growth tactics of a poor economy employing the Swadeshi strategy can, therefore, be described in terms of the following paradigm. First, there must be a decision to abjure the consumption of any commodity not producible by labour-intensive methods. Second, there must be a plan to build up labour-intensive mass-employment to supply adequate level of goods to the consumption basket. Third, there must be a simultaneous attempt to build up capital/intermediate goods capacity but only to the extent required by the planned pattern of growth of the mass-employment industries. Fourth, any existing unavoidable import will be gradually dispensed, with as domestic output grows. Fifth, as the economy gradually approaches self-reliance trade will be gradually reopened in the form of exports of mass-employment goods surpluses and purchases of manufactures non-producible within the domestic economy.[50]

The Swadeshi strategy is, of course, in close correspondence with the economic reconstruction strategy earlier visualised. However, politically, it is not so much the elimination of domestic poverty which motivates the Swadeshi program, as the patriotic drive for self-reliance which makes possible the sacrifices (on the part of the elite) which are necessary for the anti-poverty program. Gandhi noted the fact that elite accepts sacrifices only under the pressure of national and patriotic motivations. He therefore made the principle of 'Swadeshi' the major motivational basis of the entire program and the call for 'Swaraj' the political slogan under which his economic reconstruction program would sweep the country. History has repeatedly shown that an abstract desire for the betterment of the poor is not a strong enough motivation for the sacrifices necessary for securing the betterment of the poor. On the contrary, the patriotic motivation and the collective self-identification that this generates, prepares people for the necessary sacrifices. One of the fundamental reasons why post-colonial regimes in poor economies have failed in their tasks of popular mobilisation is their failure to keep the patriotic spirit alive.

Swadeshi, then, represents the politico-economic ideology which provides the energy for the implementation of the Gandhian strategy and for creating a milieu in which the conversion of the elite into trustees is made possible by the transmuting force of nationalism. While a commitment to Swadeshi is indispensable, it is not by itself enough. There is the problem of distinguishing between true and false Swadeshi. False Swadeshi is involved in imagining that the mere substitution of an import by a domestic product is enough. The newly emerging domestic industry must fit into the overall scheme of economic reconstruction. It must be either a mass-employment activity or an activity supplying capital goods/intermediates to the mass employment sectors. Otherwise, it will merely strengthen, what has been described earlier as the post-colonial exploitation pattern.

Eight, Gandhi was also against the so-called general theory of interdependence. If a nation is drained-off of its vital nutrients and then in return gets drugs to cure diseases which are produced by the absence of those nutrients, it is a kind of interdependence which Gandhi denounced and said that this is what was the main characteristic of the modern international trade. In those days a lot of food was exported from poor countries including India resulting in considerable malnutrition. He said that "the story of India's exports is the story of our impotence and destruction of well-being of the people.[51]

Thus Gandhi would largely reject modern LDC Trade which made them a principal exporter of raw materials and importers of manufacturers. In this respect, he was against India exporting cotton, food. Oilseeds, hides and skins, and metals and ores. These, he said, could be used in India, "If we have skill and capital enough to put into them or if we had a government that would regard it as a bounden duty to give us the necessary skill and to find out the necessary capital." Gandhi proved himself right by saying that mere political independence would not guarantee these things. The struggle for economic independence will go on even after getting political independence through the struggle for economic self-reliance against the kind of trade that was then being imposed on India. This today is the dilemma and the crisis of the entire. Third world which Gandhi anticipated and warned against. The crisis is blowing at our faces because we opted for the wrong strategy of development, even though export promotion was rejected in the early decades. Somehow import substitution seemed right. It was not because the Indian import substitution model had built into it export substitution. It was rather because the economy was externally trapped.

Finally, as mentioned earlier, today the most powerful of all factors determining economic power is technology. Technology, Science, and R&D are controlled by multinationals, as is the large part of the trade.

Technology beyond human control is one of the gravest dangers faced by the human race. In restructuring the world economic order, the need to reassess technology is imperative. If there are too many clever machines we will have too many stupid people. Gandhi said: "If the craze for the machinery method continuous, it is highly likely that a time may come when we shall be so incapacitated and weak that we will begin to curse ourselves for having forgotten the use of living machines given to us by God. Millions cannot keep themselves fit by games and athletics. And why should they exchange the useful, productive, hardy occupations for the useless, unproductive and expensive games and exercise."[52]

The purpose of industrial advancement is maximisation of consumption now or in future. However, economic growth attributed to industrialisation of this nature is not without its ill-effects. Large scale, capital-intensive, mechanised production ultimately adversely affects the life of man, his relationships and the environment in which he lives. Gandhiji who advocated optimum level of consumption took serious view of the ill-effects of industrialisation. He has spoken and written at length on the evils of machinery and industrialisation. In 'Hind Swaraj', he said, "Machinery is like a snake-hole which may contain from one to hundred snakes."[53] However, he never expressed unqualified opposition to machinery and industrialisation. He favoured machinery within limits and advocated labour intensive small scale industries, village handicrafts and cottage industries. He also did not completely rule out the large-scale, heavy, capital-intensive industries in the national interest, provided they are kept strictly under public control.

'Technology or 'Machinery' in Gandhian terminology used for the purpose of unlimited economic growth leads to the fast depletion of the non-renewable world resources, pollution and problems of ecology. There are limits to which the natural process can replenish then. Nature can not cope up with unlimited industrialisation and technological advancement; the process if unchecked will ultimately lead to the collapse of the world economic system. According to Schumacher, "Modern industrial system with all its intellectual sophistication, consumes the very basis on which it has been erected."[54]

Gandhian Holistic Economics suggests an economy of perma-nence. Industrialisation and technological progress must be carried out within limits so that the natural processes are not disturbed. Non-renewable resources must not be recklessly wasted. They must be used only if they are indispensable. An economy of permanence requires that we must return to nature what we receive from her. Not only that industrialisation and technology must be within limits, the scale of operations must also be small. Advocating small-scale operations, Schumacher has said, "Small-scale operations, no matter how numerous, are always less likely to be harmful to the natural environment than large-scale ones, simply because their individual force is small in relation to the recuperative forces of nature."[55]

Machinery leads to human debasement physically, mentally and morally. The baneful influence of machinery on man has been recognised by Adam Smith, David Ricardo, Karl Marx and other noted economists. It kills initiative, freedom and creativity of the individual. Men are turned into machine minders with little freedom to exercise their own creative faculties. The big organisation due to the large-scale application of technology leading to urbanisation alienates man from nature, his fellow beings, work and his product. Work becomes completely joyless and, therefore, in their leisure hours the workers simply become passive consumers of mechanised goods and entertainment. Schumacher, who advocated appropriate technology or technology with a human face, has remarked: "Modern technology has deprived man of the kind of work that he enjoys most, creative useful work with hands and brains and given him plenty of work of fragmented kind most of which he does not enjoy at all."[56] The application of large-scale technology to industry has either turned man into an exploiter giving full vent to selfishness, envy and violence lying dormant within him or has led him to become the exploited, always living in fear, insecurity, depression and frustration. According to Gandhiji, development of science and technology without spiritual advancement always leads to dehumanisation of man, degradation and destruction. He, therefore, advocated limits to be imposed on machinery, favouring small-scale production and organisation of life ill small communities so that the essential human link between man and nature, his work and product, employer and the employed, producer and consumer is not broken. Modern sociology also upholds the principle that man is happiest when living ill small communities.

Gandhian principle of bread labour also requires that machinery must be kept within limits. Everybody must do some physical labour to deserve the food that one eats in order to maintain the body. This is the sacred law expounded in the Gila and the Bible. The breach of the principle amounts to theft according to the Gita, "If one eats fruits of the earth, rendering to kindly Heaven no gift of toil that thief steals from his world."[57] If this sacred law of bread labour is followed by all, the use of machinery would automatically fall within its proper limits.

Excessive use of machinery leads to decay of human body due to lack of proper use and required exercise. Gandhiji observed, "We are destroying the matchless living machines, viz., our own bodies, by leaving them to rust and trying to substitute lifeless machinery for them."[58]

Gandhi distinguished between tools and implements and large-scale machines; between technology that increases the productivity of individuals and groups, and technology that leads to concentration of power and exhaustion of non-renewable sources of energy. The one leads to peace, co-operation, and universal fellow feeling, and the other leads to violence, concentration of power in the hands of the few, irresponsibility, utter hopelessness and helplessness, aggression and exploitation. He desired to give new direction to technological developments through the symbol of the spinning wheel.[59]

Gandhi rejected all of that technology which produced monopolies. Monopolies would not exist without exploitation. To a question "so you are opposed to machinery only because and when it concentrates production and distribution in the hands of the few," he said: "You are right. I hate privilege and monopoly. Whatever cannot be shared with the masses is taboo to me. That is all." Even if he could show that trade yields advantages, it would still require rejection if controlled by multinationals.

Modern large-scale technology is rapidly replacing out-dated techniques in almost all sectors the world over. But Gandhi admitted large scale technology in his model only in those sectors where it was unavoidable. He wanted the use of machine to be subject to several important constraints. It should not destroy village crafts. It should not increase economic inequality and above all it should not displace Manual labour.[60] Gandhi visualised: "Electricity, ship-building, iron works, machine-making and the like existing side by side village handicrafts .... Hitherto industrialisation has been so planned as to destroy the villages and village crafts. In the state of the future it will subserve the villages and their crafts."[61] He further held: "I can have no consideration for machinery which is meant either to enrich the few at the expense of many, or without cause to displace the useful labour of many."[62] "I am aiming not at eradicating all machinery but its limitation .... The prime consideration is man."[63]

Man should not be made subservient to machine but machine should be subservient or slave to man.[64] Seeing the development of Gandhi's view on machine, some scholars ruminate on the idea that if Gandhi would have been alive in the post-modern technology age, he would have welcomed the latest technology—'the chips and its containers' not as labour saving devices but as clean, decentralised home-bound, clean environment promoting machine.

Gandhi realised that technology was not neutral and Western technology by its very nature was concentrating power in the hands of a few. Accumulation of wealth and political power in the hands of a minority was its natural result. It was expensive, capital-research-intensive, exploitative of natural resources and highly pollutive. The Centre-Periphery nexus at the global level was but a mere extensive reflection of the same phenomenon.[65]

Gandhi understood that large-scale technology was bound to enlarge the power of those who wielded it. He, therefore, opted for small-scale technology making village the primary, basic unit as the seat of that technology providing labour-intensive employment and obviating city's pressure from the top crushing those at the bottom. Such a village economy was to be self-sufficient in meeting its basic needs, but interdependent in other spheres.

As technological innovations take place with the advance of industrialisation, wealth gets concentrated in the hands of a few, sharp inequalities of income accrue, and society gets sharply polarised giving rise to a dualistic nature of economy. The concentration of economic power becomes a cumulative process like a snowball gathering more and more snow, due to more and more technological innovations. The process feeds upon exploitation, the 'haves' exploiting the 'have-nots' at various levels of life. Gandhiji's holistic outlook sharply noticed that machinery leads to the exploitation of the poor by the rich, the employed by the employer, labour by capital, and village by the city. At the international level, the developed countries exploit the under-developed countries. The so-called transfer of technology from developed countries to under-developed countries these days has also become a source of exploitation. The rich countries dump their obsolete and harmful technologies in the poor countries. These technologies make the rich more rich and the poor, more poor.

Professor Galbraith in his writings has laid bare the exploitation carried out by the giant business corporations arising as a result of modern industrial system. He has held that they tend to reduce the state to a subservient position. They exploit the third world countries; control the media, the education system, and the market through advertisements and propaganda, ultimately proving that it is the producer who is the sovereign and not the consumer. Reacting sharply to the evils of machinery, Gandhiji said, "I will not have the enrichment of a few at the expense of the community. At present, the machine is helping a small minority to live on the exploitation of the masses."[66] He further positively asserted, "I want the concentration of wealth, not in the hands of a few, but in the hands of all. Today machinery merely helps a few to ride on the backs of millions.[67]

The views of economists like Schumpeter, Joan Robinson and Marx bear close similarity to those of Gandhiji's as far as the evils of technology are concerned. Innovations and technological progress lead to monopolistic exploitation, unemployment and a capitalist class thriving upon 'surplus value' arising from the exploitation of labour. As Marx sharply commented on the process of industrialisation, "Along with the constantly diminishing number of the magnets of capital, who usurp and monopolise all advantages of this process of transformation, grows the mass of misery, oppression, slavery, degradation, exploitation."[68] Gandhiji who considered exploitation to be the essence of all violence, therefore, emphatically declared, "I am a determined foe of all machinery that is designed for exploitation of people."[69] On being questioned whether he was opposed to machinery only because and when it concentrated production and distribution in the hands of the few, he had pointedly replied, "Whatever cannot be shared with the masses is taboo to me."[70]

Gandhiji's central point of opposition to machinery was that in a country abundant with labour, machinery inevitably leads to unemployment. According to modern economics, the use of technology is warranted because it saves labour and hence helps in the reduction of cost. Displacement of labour is labour saving in an economy having shortage of labour; however in an economy where labour is abundant, displacement of labour swells the rank of the unemployed. Gandhiji for whom full employment was one of the major goals of a non-violent economy, therefore, argued, "Mechanisation is good when the hands are too few for the work intended to be accomplished. It is an evil when there are more hands than required for the work, as is the case in India.... The problem with us is not how to find leisure for the teeming millions inhabiting our villages. The problem is how to utilize their idle hours, which are equal to the working days of six months in the year."[71] Criticising the craze for machinery which is introduced in the name of labour-saving but which eventually leads to unemployment, Gandhiji commented, "Men go on 'saving labour' till thousands are without work and thrown on the open streets to die of starvation. I want to save time and labour not for a fraction of mankind, but for all."[72] Gandhiji was profoundly moved when be saw that machinery creates unemployment, leading to poverty, malnutrition, starvation, hunger and death; he, therefore, wrote poignantly, "Dead machinery must not be pitted against the millions of living machines."[73]

The Gandhian views sharply depart from the modernist view over the chain causation between science and technology on the one hand and development on the other. To Gandhi it was development, its pattern and structure that should and must engender technological development. The modernist view, which lies behind the whole scheme of technology transfer, is that backwardness of the LDCs can be removed only by the technologies that come from the developed world. The modernist view has been the reigning philosophy so far. But the numerous distributions and indeed the end of the very process of development in the LDCs as been partly due to the fact that the import of technologies has set a pattern of development which has proved its own antithesis."[74]

The central point of the Gandhian paradigm is the very definition of economics. In Gandhi's own words: "Economics is untrue which disregards moral values. The extension of the law of nonviolence in the domain of economics means nothing less than the introduction of moral values."[75] If moral element is to be as important as any other, then the entire concept of progress, economic growth, and gains from trade will have to be so redefined as will not to be determined by the compulsion of technology, consumerism, exploitation, and an overall loss of human dignity.

Modern philosophers, who consider equality as a moral ideal, interpret it in practical terms as not that everyone should have equal resources but less should have enough. Trade competition then is immoral because it neither defines nor allows what is enough. Trade provides more than enough to some when there is not enough for everyone. A lot of trade would disappear if the moral principle of "enough" is accepted.

It is neither necessary nor possible to get into the entire alternative of a Gandhian development strategy. A Gandhian development strategy and trade theory would consist of five elements. First, instead of growth rate being the target rate, it will be of full employment around which other variables will resolve. There will be other priorities but what is to be remembered it that the growth rate would be derived from, and will not be the determinant of, other priorities, particularly employment. However, it is easily said than done because such an approach would require complete throwing away of the mainstream planning models, particularly of the kind which India and the other Third World countries have adopted. Technology, production, distribution, and consumption would all be directly subject to employment.

An employment strategy would not succeed unless it is accompanied by a shift from production of mass consumption goods by machines to production of such goods by the masses. Such a shift would mean the relative strengthened integration of the manufacturing sector from the tiny to the small to the medium and, in the end, to the large. Each sector will become comparative within its own sphere. The big will certainly not be allowed to compete in any other sector. There big will certainly not be allowed to compete in any other sector. There would be upgrading of technologies which is consistent with other values so that the whole industrial sector will move up.

It is not difficult to say that in this reverse hierarchy of production, there will be several sectors which will .not require imports but they may enjoy the possibilities of exports. If they do not, the new production structure will remain intact nevertheless.

The second strategy would be to achieve self-reliance in respect of capital goods as well in the production of basic needs: It may not be easy in the former area but, for the latter, the effort will be entirely domestic. As mentioned earlier, a country's autonomy and self-reliance are a function of its capability to provide basic needs domestically. Even if production is made with less sophisticated technology, LDCs which are importing food, clothing, matches, soaps, etc. will completely ban the import of these commodities. It might sound strange to radical economists but Gandhi would insist the banning of the imports of basic needs even before the banning of all those commodities, which middle classes considered as necessary because there would not be enough resources for the production of both. Of course, imports of all luxury items will also be banned. Import of luxuries is very harmful but the import of basic needs is even more so because it destroys the self-reliance of a society.

There is no-question that all luxuries will have to go and they will not go unless the whole policies of import substitution, to which the production of imports of these luxuries are tied, also go. We have witnessed how in the last forty years we have been talking about the banning of import of luxury items but they are either being imported or produced by imported inputs. Indirect import of such goods is caused by import substitution channels. The point is often missed that the dominant character of import substitution has neither been for the production of capital goods not for the mass consumption goods but for the goods of consumption for middle and upper classes.

In other words, we would have to identify the area of not 'trading goods, the production of which will be consistent with the development strategy'. The problem of the production of non-trading goods has always cast dark shadow on all trade theories. Carried by their logic, the mainstream trade theories would point towards complete specialisation of at least one commodity in one country as a necessary condition. But, by the same logic, this would stop the process of factor cost equalisation permanently. The only way to resolve the dilemma is to accept the proposition that there will always be non-traded goods, which would neither be imported nor exported. This limitation was sought to be removed by assuming that non-traded goods can never enter into trade and hence can be treated as an autonomous economic sub-system. Once the assumption is made about the non-traded goods, the Gandhian trade theories can move in to show that for reasons other than those suggested by the trade theories, the area of the non-trade goods will have to be demarcated as autonomous and as prime determinant. By definition, goods of basic needs will not be traded with few exceptions. The trade will be determined by other considerations.

Gandhi philosophy is complete in itself but to reach it one will have to go through a very difficult path The path will be narrow, living would be austere, and difficulties would have to be faced. These difficulties would be recognised and removed step by step. These problems have been defined very well by Schumacher:

> "The New Economics, of which we stand in need, would be based on the recognition—that economic progress is healthy only "up to a point." That the complication of life is permissible only up to a point: that the pursuit of efficiency is good only up to a point: that the use of non-renewable resources is wise only up to a point; that the substitution of scientific method for commonsense is bearable only up to a point; and so on and so forth, never forgetting that all these "Points" lie far lower on the scale than most people dare to think."[76]

The world has come to face many ecological disasters. Eco-balance is no longer a mere problem of adjusting of economic strategy. It has become a problem of the survival of human civilisation, even more serious than the problem of nuclear weapons. The central focus of Gandhi's development strategy would remain on renewable resources and building a new economic structure. Such a structure would require the limits of growth, the rejection of want and gadget-oriented society, cooperation rather than competition between nations, and, above all, non-exploitation. Nothing will be imported or exported which harms the ecosystem. Once again to quote Schumacher:

> "Next in importance comes the distinction between renew-able and non-renewable resources. A civilisation built on renewable resources, such as the products of forestry and agriculture, is by this fact alone superior to one built on non-renewable resources, such as oil, coal, metal, etc., that is because the former can last, while the latter cannot last. The former cooperates with nature, while the latter robs Nature. The former bears the sign of life, while the latter bears the sign of death. It is already certain beyond any possibility of doubt that the Oil Coal Metal Economics cannot be anything else but a short abnormality in the history of mankind—because they are based on non-renewable resources and because, being purely materialist, they recognize no limit."[77]

It is not necessary to go into the absolutist concept like "small is beautiful." One may arrive at the same conclusion by putting the moral constraints on the coercion of the economic and technological systems. Whatever be the production structure, it will have to be consistent with ethics, just distribution, and full employment. No one should eat if he does not work, except those who are unemployed or unable to work. In order to avoid greed and exploitation, it will never be allowed that goods should become more important than people and consumption more important than creativity and trade more important than self-reliance and autonomy.

Comparisons between standards of life in one country and another will exercise a tremendous pressure on the poor countries when they try to limit their wants. It is not the dumb masses who will be putting pressure on them but minority classes which control wealth, power, and status. This is also true of the ruling class. Only a formidable self-denial on the part of the ruling elites of the poor countries can accomplish something. Even when right priorities are followed and masses do get their basic needs satisfied, their life has to be made worth living for which some comforts will have to be made all the more so and completely allowed to go berserk by the high pressure of salesmanship of modern consumption. Therefore, as Galbraith has pointed out: The individual who buys the importance production to satisfy these wants is precisely in the position of the onlooker who applauds the effort of the squirrel to keep abreast of the wheel that is propelled by his own effort.[78] Clearly, the technology of mass production is inherently violent, alternating ecologically damaging and hence has to be gradually eliminated not only from trade but also from production in order to remove domination.

Similarly, he will allow the disposal of the country's surplus goods in foreign countries.

Gandhi was not a follower of Adam Smith in international trade. He was a believer of protective trade. "Free trade may be good for England which dumps down her manufactures among helpless people and wishes her wants to be supplied from outside at the cheapest rate. But free trade has ruined India's peasantry.... Moreover, no new trade can compete with foreign trade without protection."[79] Gandhi wanted protective trade not out of ill-will or hatred: "I would not countenance the boycott of a single foreign article out of ill-will or a feeling of hatred."[80] It was because of the well known infant industry argument that he wanted protective trade. "To talk of no discrimination between Indian interest and English or European is to perpetuate Indian heritage. What is equality of rights between a giant and a dwarf? Before one can think of equality between unequals, the dwarf must be raised to the height of the giant.[81] Thus, protective trade is not a permanent policy with Gandhi.

Gandhi did, not try to give 'an exhaustive catalogue' of articles which can be imported in his scheme of things.[82] He only laid down a general principle, "I buy from every part of the world that is needed for my growth. I refuse to buy from any body anything however nice or beautiful, if it interferes with my growth or injures those whom Nature has made my first care."[83] Again, "My economic creed is a complete taboo in respect of foreign commodities whose importation is likely to prove harmful to our indigenous interests."[84]

Thus, Gandhi will not import or purchase a thing from his neighbour, whether of his own country or of outside, simply because the product is cheap or best. "The rule of the best and the cheapest is not always true. Just as we do not give up our country for one with a better climate but Endeavour to improve our own, so also may we not discard Swadeshi for better or cheaper things."[85]

Obviously, these ideas of Gandhi on trade are more dynamic than those of either Adam Smith or Fedric List or Mercantilists or Neo-Mercantilists, because Gandhi wanted protective trade only so long as the country was not able to stand the vice of dumping.[86] He did neither want exchange control. He wanted the trade to be simple, limited and for mutual gain. However, this trade will not be left to the sole discretion of individuals. According to the known Gandhian Economist, S.N. Agarwal, "Just as individual or a village community should be the agent for internal trade so a nation should be the agent for international trade."[87]

This should not give the idea that Gandhi was against middlemen and wanted to liquidate them. Replying to Shri Jetha Lal Govind, Gandhi wrote, "... He has set before him an ambitious ideal that did not obtain in our country probably at any time even in the past. The cultivator had always to depend for certain necessaries of life on the middleman and it seems to me that this is just as it should be."[88] Gandhi did "not want to take away from the middleman his occupation, but only to give a new orientation to it and to change his mental outlook."[89] Gandhi hoped to do it with his new socio-politico-economic set-up.

When the size of markets for the necessary consumption goods will be small, when different regions of the country will mainly be confined to luxury or comfort articles or the capital goods produced by the State for the welfare of the people, when trade will not be based on "cheapness" but on "growth" principles, when the mass production will be through masses and not labour-saving devices and large size plants, when wants will be minimum and the goal will be 'to live and let others live happily', then the importance of money will automatically go down. It will cease to be the master, the controller of the destinies of the millions. It will nor be the sole measurement of value. "Money has its use as much as labour. After all money is a token of exchange.... The moment labour recognizes its own dignity, money will find its rightful place, and, i.e. it will be held in trust for labour. For labour is more than money."[90] Even taxes will not be necessarily paid in cash. "I have always held that whatever may be said in favour of cash payment of taxes, its introduction injured the nation to the extent that the system of stocking grain in the village was disturbed."[91] Wages will also be paid partly in cash and partly in kind.[92] The importance of capital will be negligible as very little capital will be required and it will be realised that labour is capital and there is no conflict between the two.[93] With the changed importance of money and the limitation of the size of markets in the way that production and consumption are carried out in the same area, price fluctuations will no longer remain a problem. "There is no question of high or low prices when a nation's economics are put on a sound basis ...."[94] This is because the law of supply and demand is replaced with the law by manufacturing enough for the supply[95] on a national scale, demand and supply is aggregated contributing to the Gross National Product which is ultimately a measure of our success as a nation. The business theorists saw an opportunity here. They stepped into this setting and figured that if demand is such a good thing, then they can help both create the desire, and provide the purchasing power, creating the ideal consumer. So, the marketing specialists create images and packaging to make us desire a whole range of goods and services that are probably not normally required. The accounting and finance specialists follow and provide us with various loans and instalment purchase schemes to supply the purchasing power. So, both demand and purchasing power can be created. And, thus, the economy goes around, at least the capitalist version of it! Along the way, the economists and the business theorists have convinced us that consumption is the foundation of human happiness. Our economies are built on consumption, and the collapse of the Soviet controlled economy model has shown that competition and free markets is the only viable alternative for an efficient economy.

Gandhi has an uncanny sense and a discerning eye to find out the germinating roots of the malady and then launch a massive humane-ethical alternative, indeed a very difficult proposition in those hey days of colonialism and perhaps more so today. Yet the Gandhian project has that inevitable spirit and prowess which makes it revive itself repeatedly whenever one of those apocalyptic hallucinations threatens life.

The idea of sustainable environment and sustainable consumption is popular these days. A cynic would argue that the developed world suddenly woke up to the notion of sustainability when they began seeing the poorer nations begin to develop and aspire to the same levels of consumption. When Gandhiji was asked if India would reach Britain's standard of living after Independence, he is said to have remarked, "It took Britain half the resources of the planet to achieve its prosperity; how many planets will a country like India require!"[96]

"Gandhian model is the best and next best alternative to the whole world", opined by Alvin Toffler, the author of 'Future Shocks' and 'Third Wave'.[97] He mentions three waves. One is the wave of capitalism; another is Marxian wave and third is the Gandhian wave. The first wave came through Adam Smith's "Wealth of Nation." The second wave came through Karl Marx, "Das Capital" and the idealistic third wave, Gandhi's, "*Hind Swaraj.*" Gandhian wave builds a desirable ideal society, in which social change is possible through non-violence accomplishment. In capitalist model, there is a place for exploitation and in Marxian model; there is a place for violence and conflict. In Gandhian model, there is a creative conflict which is meant to construct and to liberate. It helps to lead harmonious life. Without violence, social change is possible. It provides better quality of life.

Gandhian model has to be accepted in to in order to have better quality of life.

NOTES AND REFERENCES

1. John, K. Galbraith, "The Public Purpose of Economics", *The American Review*, March 1974, pp. 52-53.
2. Kripalani, J.B., Gandhi: His Life and Thought (Calcutta: Orient Longman), 1961, p. 252.
3. *Harijan*, A Journal of Applied Gandhism, 1933-55 (New York: Garland Publishing Inc.), 1973, January 3, 1946, p. 28.
4. Gandhi, M.K., *Hind Swaraj* (Ahmedabad: Navajivan Publishing House).
5.. *Young India*, 03-09-1926.
6. *Harijan*, 12-02-1938, p. 2.
7. Gandhi, M.K., To the Students (Ahmedabad: Navajivan Publishing House), 1940, p. 152.
8. Kumarrappa, J.E., Gandhian Economic Thought, p. 211.
9. *Ibid.*
10. *Ibid.*
11. *Harijan*, November 2, 1934, "It is mass production, but mass production in people's own homes. If you multiply individual production to millions of times, would it not give you mass production on a tremendous scale."
12. Sharma, J.N., Alternative Economics (New Delhi: Deep and Deep), 2005, p. 20.
13. *Ibid.*
14. *Harijan*, August 29, 1936.
15. *Ibid.*, July 26, 1942.
16. *Hind Swaraj*, December 6, 1944.
17. *Young India*, April 25, 1925.
18. Agarwal, S.N., Gandhian Plan, p. 93.
19. *Young India*, April 25, 1925.
20. *Ibid.*, March 21, 1929.
21. *Ibid.*
22. Gandhi, M.K., Economic and Industrial Life and Relations, Vol. II, p. 69.
23. *Ibid.*, p. 57.
24. *Ibid.*, p. 64.
25. *Ibid.* p. 78.
26. *Young India*, June 18, 1931, *vide*, S.N. Agarwal, The Gandhian Plan, p. 97.
27. Gandhi, M.K., Cent Per Cent Swadeshi (Ahmedabad: Navajivan Publishing House),

28. Boulding, Kenneth, "Human Betterment and Quality of Life," in B. Strumple.
29. J.N. Morgan, and E. Zhan, eds., The Human Behaviour in Economic Affairs. Pfuff, Martin (ed.), Frontier and Social Thought (New York: Columbia University Press), p. 28.
30. Schumacher, E.F., Roots of Economic Growth (Varanasi: Gandhian Institute of Studies), 1962, pp. 5-6.
31. *Young India*, 2-7-1920, p. 125.
32. Schumacher, E.F., Roots of Economic Growth, *op. cit.*, p. 6.
33. Pyarelal, Towards New Horizon (Ahmedabad: Navajivan Publishing House), 1959, pp. 100-101.
34. Bipin Behari, Gandhian Economic Philosophy (Bombay: Vora and Co., Publishers), 1963, p. 95.
35. *Young India*, 13-10-1921.
36. *Ibid.*, 15-11-1928.
37. *Harijan*, A Journal of Applied Gandhism, 1933-55 (New York: Garland Publishing Inc.), 1973, March 23, 1947, p. 320
38. *Ibid.*
39. The Collected Works of Mahatma Gandhi (hereafter used as CWMG) (New Delhi: Publications Division, Ministry of Information and Broadcasting, Government of India), 1961, Vol. XIII, p. 219.
40. Gandhi, M.K., in S. Narayan (ed.) The Selected Works of Mahatma Candhi, 5th Volumes (Ahmedabad: Navajivan Publishing House), 1968.
41. *CWMC*, Vol. VI, 1958, p. 321.
42. Singer, H.W, International Development: Growth and Change (New York: McGraw Hill), 1964, p. 230.
43. Narayan, Shrirnan, Relevance of Gandhian Economics (Ahmedabad: Navajivan Publishing House), 1970, p. 338.
44. *Ibid.*, p. 348.
45. Huq, A.M., "Economics of Growth and Employment: The Gandhian Approach," New Dimensions and Perspectives in Gandhism, pp. 220-30.
46. Narayan, Shriman, Relevance of Gandhian Economics, *op. cit.*, pp. 223-25
47. *Young India*, 1919-31 (Ahmedabad: Navajivan Publishing House), February 17, 1926, p. 213.
48. *Young India*, 2-07-1931, pp. 161-66.
49. Mahalanobis, P.C, *Semkhve*, 1958.
50. *Harijan*, 02-02-1940.
51. *Young India*, 28-03-1929, pp. 100-101.
52. Mathur, I.S., Essays on Gandhian Economics (Allahabad: Chaitanya Publishing House), 1959, pp. 488-89.
53. Gandhi, M.K., *Hind Swaraj*, *op. cit.*, p. 96.
54. Schumacher, E.F., Small is Beautiful (New Delhi: Radha Krishna), 1977, p. 17.

55. *Ibid.*, p. 31.
56. *Ibid.*, p. 140.
57. The Gita, 3.12.
58. *CWMC*, Vol. 25, 1967, p. 562.
59. *Ibid.*, pp. 485-90.
60. Jai Narain, Economic Thought of Mahatma Gandhi (New Delhi: Sehgal Publishers), 1992, p. 47.
61. Bose, N.K., Studies in Gandhism (Calcutta: Indian Associated Publishing Co.), 1947, pp. 48-60.
62. *Young India*, November 13, 1924, pp. 378-79.
63. *Ibid.*
64. Lewis, W.A., The Theory of Economic Growth (London: George Allen and Unwin), 1955, p. 356.
65. Deutsch, Karl W., The Analysis of International Relations (New Jersey: Prentice-Hall International), 1988, p, 300.
66. Gandhi, M.K., Economic and Industrial Life and Relations, Vol. II, camp. V.B. Kher (Ahmedabad: Navajivan Publishing House), 1957, p. 34.
67. *Ibid.*, p. 38.
68. Capra Fritjof, The Turning Point (London: Fontana Peperbacks), 1982, p. 214.
69. Gandhi, M.K., Economic and Industrial Life and Relations, Vol. II, camp, V.B. Kher, *op. cit.*, p. 33.
70. *Ibid.*, p. 173.
71. *CWMG*, Vol. 59, 1974, p. 356.
72. Gandhi, M.K., Economic and Industrial Life and Relations, Vol. II, camp. V.B. Kher, *op. cit.*, p, 38.
73. *CWMC*, Vol. 61, 1975, p. 416.
74. Das, Amritananda, Foundations of Gandhian Economics (Calcutta: Allied Publishers), 1979, p. 8.
75. Sethi, J.D., Gandhi Today (New Delhi: Vikas Publishing House), 1978, pp, 109-10.
76. Bose, N.K., Selections From Gandhi (Ahmedabad: Navajivan Publishing House), 1948, p. 41.
77. Huq, A.M., "Economics of Growth and Employment: The Gandhian Approach," New Dimensions and Perspectives in Gandhism, pp. 220-21.
78. Schumacher, E.F., Roots of Economic Growth, *op. cit.*, pp. 7-8
79. Galbraith, Civilisation, Editorial, Vol. 25, 1975.
80. *Young India*, May 15, 1924.
81. *Ibid.*, November 15, 1928.
82. *Ibid.*, March 26, 1931.
83. Gandhi, M.K., Economic and Industrial Life and Relations, Vol. 11, *op. cit.*, p. 70.
84. *Ibid.*, p. 78.

85. *Young India*, March 23, 1929.
86. *Ibid.*, p. 84.
87. Gandhi advised his American friends not to resort to dumping because it is neither in their own interest nor of others. If they are able to produce surplus, they should gift if out to the needy ones. Vide Tendulkar, *Mahatma*, Vol. (New Delhi: Publications Division, Ministry of Information and Broadcasting, Government of India), pp. 168-69.
88. Agarwal, S.N., The Gandhian Plan, p. 97.
89. *Young India*, March 21, 1929.
90. *Ibid.*
91. *Harijan*, October 16, 1945, Gandhi was impressed by the scheme of Yarn currency tried at Gopuri (Wardha), *Harijan*, March 23, 1942; vide S.N. Agarwal, A Gandhian Plan, p. 102.
92. Jha, S.N., Gandhian Economic Thought, p. 216.
93. Gandhi, M.K., Economic and Industrial Life and Relations, Vol. II, p. 140; also see N.K. Bose, Selection from Gandhi, Sec. 259.
94. *Harijan*, December 28, 1947.
95. Gandhi, M.K., Economic and Industrial Life and Relations, Vol. II, *op. cit.*, p. 99.
96. *The Economist*, Volume 364, 2002, p. 5.
97. Toffler, Alvin, Third Wave (New York: A National Journal Company), 1975, pp. 107, 340-55.

Conclusion

1. Corporations define success in two fundamental ways: by the growth of assets and the rate of profit. These two goals take precedence over concerns of the community or nation in which the corporation does business. There is a strong tension between the corporation's desire for profits and the demands of workers for a decent living wage. The growth imperative also spurs the relentless consumption of finite natural resources. There is a clear and growing gap between the needs of private corporations for economic growth and the planet's need for environmental stewardship.

2. Successfully climbing the corporate ladder means being both aggressive and competitive. Colleagues compete fiercely with each other for promotions; workers are encouraged to compete with each other through special awards (eg. top assembly-line operator of the month) in order to increase productivity and profits. The Japanese labour-management approach of 'teamwork' in the plant merely shifts competition from individual workers to groups of workers. This urge to compete is now seen as basic human nature; so much so that values needed to make the world more just and compassionate, like cooperation and sharing, are fast fading.

3. Decision-making within a corporation is ruled by the

bottom line. In practice this means the interests of the corporation and the interests of the community only overlap when it serves the corporation's purpose. A company may sponsor a baseball team, donate money to a hospital or underwrite a community orchestra. But corporate altruism is usually more public relations than community spirit. The fight to make corporations socially reponsible will always be an uphill battle since corporations are inherently selfish. Their essential responsibility is to their own financial survival, not to the welfare of the public.

4. The organisational structure of the corporate world is based on a strict pecking-order. There is a hierarchy of command and control that extends from the Board of Directors and Chief Executive Officer at the top to the lowliest workers at the bottom. Your place in the pecking-order determines your power, your rewards and your privileges. Orders flow from the top down as they do in other large institutions that use a strict hierarchy—like the military and the government. Notions of hierarchy and status within the corporate world tend to reinforce the idea that inequality and conformity are natural: the world is made of leaders and followers and there is little we can do to change this fact of life.

5. The modern corporation is both a creature and a captive of technology. Companies are engaged in a restless search for technological innovation in order to boost efficiency (i.e. to increase production with less labour and capital). The result is that all technologies are considered benign and objective. In fact modern technologies are biased towards the technocratic worldview that produces them. This is essentially a materialist view based on linear thinking and the tendency to segment and quantify problems. Because corporations are fascinated by technology they have a hard time dealing with non-material values. Old-growth forests are so many board-feet of lumber. Toxic wastes are subject to cost-benefit analysis. Workers fighting for improved working conditions are seen as threats to profitability.

6. Corporations view the world as one big market; social relationships are defined in terms of buying and selling and human activity is seen as a straightforward battle to gain

advantage over your neighbour. The result of this market vision is that human happiness and satisfaction are defined in terms of what we buy. Multinational corporations have been remarkably successful in spreading their attitudes and values around the globe. Television, advertising and films carry the corporate market view everywhere, steamrollering local culture in the process. This growing homogenisation destroys opposition to the 'consumer society', obliterates cultural diversity and accelerates the destruction of natural resources.

7. Corporations have no allegiance to the present because they are riveted on the future and the need to grow. This consuming passion effectively removes them from the day-to-day concerns of the local community. With their eyes fixed firmly on tomorrow, corporations have little commitment to solving the mundane problems of everyday life. Staying flexible in order to be profitable means multinationals can and do pack up and move at the drop of a hat. Inside the corporation life is highly-structured and geared to the clock. Yet corporations can be strangely ephemeral. The future is possibility; the present merely a viewpoint; and the past irrelevant: this operating principle undercuts the search for social stability.

8. Despite the attempt by corporate management to jump on the environmental bandwagon, it's not easy for corporations to be green. That's because corporate activities and the natural world are fundamentally at odds. Manufacturing goods to be bought and sold in the marketplace is essentially a process of transforming raw materials extracted from nature into commodities. This exploitation of the environment is ingrained in corporate behaviour; even service and financial corporations depend indirectly on the conquest of nature. As consumerism spreads around the globe, the search for raw materials accelerates and the ravaging of nature quickens. In an attempt to absorb criticism from environmentalists, multinationals have wrapped themselves in green. Yet any serious attempt to challenge the underlying consumerist credo is still dismissed as subversive—which in essence it is

Economic Globalisation involves arguably the most fundamental re-design of the planet's political and economic arrangements since at least the Industrial Revolution. Yet the profound implications of these fundamental changes have barely been exposed to serious public scrutiny or debate. Despite the scale of the global reordering, neither our elected officials nor our educational institutions nor the mass media have made a credible effort to describe what is being formulated or to explain its root philosophies.

The occasional descriptions or predictions about the global economy that are found in the media usually come from the leading advocates and beneficiaries of this new order: corporate leaders, their allies in government, and a newly powerful centralised global trade bureaucracy. The visions they offer us are unfailingly positive, even utopian: Globalisation will be a panacea for our ills.

Shockingly enough, the euphoria they express is based on their freedom to deploy, at a global level through the new global free-trade rules, and through deregulation and economic restructuring regimes, large-scale versions of the economic theories, strategies and policies that have proven spectacularly unsuccessful over the past several decades wherever they've been applied. In fact, these are the very ideas that have brought us to the grim situation of the moment: the spreading disintegration of the social order and the increase of poverty, landlessness, homelessness, violence, alienation and, deep within the hearts of many people, extreme anxiety about the future. Equally important, these are the practices that have led us to the near breakdown of the natural world, as evidenced by such symptoms as global climate change, ozone depletion, massive species loss, and near maximum levels of air, soil and water pollution.

Ninety percent of the media are owned by big corporations that therefore dominate public discussion and debate; these corporations determine what people will talk about and the limits of the public discussion. The elected government is controlled by corporations through campaign contributions (which are required because expensive media exposure is the key to election); the people are made insecure, discouraged and disengaged largely because of corporate policies and practices (downsising, wage cuts, forced give-backs, overseas flight, union busting—or simply the fear that any of these tactics will be used). Corporations control government; government greases the skids for increasing corporate control. People are disrespected and cut out of the decision-making loop. Democracy is hollowed out —the democratic forms remain, but the substance is missing.

In the present world politicians and corporations use terms that leave us suffering from "hypocognition."[1] Hypocognition results when a term is used to conjure up all-positive images to prevent us from understanding what is really going on. For example, hypocognition makes it hard for the public to believe there can be anything wrong with "globalism" or "free trade," which sound like the apple pie and motherhood of the 21st century. It is easy for the press to portray those who protest against "free trade" as fringe lunatics.

Primitive marketism is a market driven solely by the logic of highest return to existing wealth. It is an arbitrary premise that concentrates wealth and excludes millions of poor from the market altogether. It is based on the simplistic notion that if the market is left to its own devices, it will create beneficial outcomes for us all. The term "primitive marketism" is more appropriate name for what has become the accepted standard of world trade over the last 20 years—that the single principle of highest return to existing wealth is the sole driver of the world-wide system of production and exchange, that leaves cultural integrity, human rights, environmental protection, and even the ability of people to feed themselves as inconsequential to multinational corporations reaching around the world for opportunities for the highest return to existing wealth.[2]

As much as the term "primitive marketism" helps to identify problems inherent in the way global trade is structured today, it takes a bit of bending of the mind and tongue to use it. With the inherent weakness of the government, rampant corruption among its officials and technological backwardness, the present nexus of Multinational Corporation and world trade leaves no room for hypocognition—that is heading towards "corporate colonialism."

Colonialism as "The system or policy by which a

nation seeks to extend or retain its authority over other peoples or territories. Such political colonialism of one nation over another fell by the wayside in the 20th century.

Corporate colonialism requires no armies, weapons, or even threats of violence to reap all the benefits of a colonial power. Whereas 19th-century empire builders sent navies half way around the world to secure their colonial power, 21st-century corporations secure their colonial power through financial contributions to political allies and promise that everyone will get rich if corporations are allowed to work their "magic" around the world.

The reality that world free trade means, multinational corporations exporting production and associated jobs to wherever labour can be secured most cheaply and environmental regulations are least restrictive. One is just beginning to realize that the great-sounding, theoretical idea that goods and services are best produced where they can be produced at the greatest competitive advantage translates into large-scale loss of employment and community disruption as much as it translates into greater profits for the corporate bottom line. It is sobering to realize that the corporate colonialists will exploit "developed" countries as readily as "undeveloped" countries—it takes more money and propaganda in a rich country, but the payoffs are greater.

Nowhere are the disastrous consequences of corporate colonialism felt more than in global food trade. The corporations force the countries to open their markets to cheap, subsidised, industrially-produced food from abroad can eliminate markets for local subsistence farmers, driving them off the land and into the ranks of the hungry. The winners are agribusiness monopolies that ship, trade, and process food. The losers are farmers who lose their livelihood, rural communities that lose their population, and countries that lose food security as they become dependent on imports.

The recent uprising by farmers from around the world at the WTO talks in Cancun may be the beginning of such a revolution. But, judging from the scant US corporate media coverage, which generally reported the collapse of trade talks as a failed opportunity for the world's poor, creating the acute hypocognition.[3]

The passage of the Uruguay Round of GATT (the General Agreement on Tariffs and Trade) with its associated WTO (World Trade Organisation) was celebrated by the world's political leadership and transnational corporations as a sort of global messianic rebirth. They claim that these new arrangements will bring on a global economic order that can produce a $250 billion expansion of world economic activity in a very short time, with the benefits "trickling down" to all. The dominant political-economic homily is "the new rising tide will lift all boats."

Indeed, the global economy is new, but less so in form than in scale: the new global rules by which it now operates; the technologically enhanced speed up of global development and commerce that it facilitates; and the abrupt shift in global political power that it introduces. It is also new that the world's democratic countries voted to suppress their own democratically enacted laws in order to conform to the rules of the new central global bureaucracy. Also new is the elimination of most regulatory control over global corporate activity and the liberation of currency from national controls, which lead in turn to the casino economy, ruled by currency speculators.[4]

But the deep ideological principles underlying the global economy are not so new: they are the very principles that have brought us to the social, economic and environmental impasse we are in. They include the primacy of economic growth; the need for free trade to stimulate the growth; the unrestricted "free market"; the absence of government regulation; and voracious consumerism combined with an aggressive advocacy of a uniform worldwide development model that faithfully reflects the Western corporate vision and serves corporate interests. The principles also include the idea that all countries—even those whose cultures have been as diverse as, say, Indonesia, Japan, Kenya, Sweden, Brazil and India—must sign on the same global economic model and row their (rising) boats in unison. The net result is monoculture—the global homogenisation of culture, lifestyle, and level of technological immersion, with the corresponding dismantling of local traditions and economies. Globalisation of the economy is a new kind of corporate colonialism, visited upon poor countries and the poor in rich countries.

The present economic system will be disastrous for the poor nations. The promised economic expansion of GATT in the last will be translated in favour of developed nations. If peeped in the future, how long the resources, the energy, the wood, the minerals, the water—come from to feed the increased growth. and how long this earth can bear the dumping of the effluents of the process—the solids and the toxics. In future, the ecological results will be more dangerous than the fear of getting of nuclear technology by militant groups. How long the ever-increasing consumption be sustained forever? What will happen if all the forests sacrificed on the name of development?

It is very difficult to get the possible benefit from a system that destroys local and regional governments while handing real power to faceless corporate bureaucracies in Geneva, Tokyo and Brussels. The German economic philosopher, Wolfgang Sachs, argues in his book, "The Development Dictionary" that the only thing worse than the failure of this massive global development experiment would be its success. For, even at its optimum performance level, the long-term benefits go only to a tiny minority of people who sit at the hub of the process and to a slightly larger minority that can retain an economic connection to it, while the rest of humanity is left groping for fewer jobs and less land, living in violent societies on a ravaged planet. The only boats that will be lifted are those of the owners and managers of the process, the rest of us will be on the beach, facing the rising tide.[5]

Our society has been massively launched on to a path to one-knows-not-where, and the people in the media who are supposed to shed light on events that affect us have neglected to do so.

From time to time, the mass media do report on some major problem of globalisation, but the reporting rarely conveys the connections between the specific crises they describe and the root causes in globalisation itself. In the area of environment, for example, one reads of changes in global climate and occasionally of their long-term consequences, such as the melting polar ice caps, the expected staggering impacts to agriculture and food supply, or the destruction of habitat.

One reads too of the ozone layer depletion, the pollution of the oceans, or the wars over resources such as oil and, perhaps soon, water. But few of these matters are linked directly to the imperatives of global economic expansion, the increase of global transport, the overuse of raw materials, or the commodity intensive lifestyle that corporations are selling worldwide via the culturally homogenising technology of television and its parent, advertising. Obfuscation is the net result.

Some publications have carried stories about "corporate greed" as expressed by the firing of thousands of workers while corporate profits soared and top executive salaries were being raised to unheard-of levels. Even these stories, however, rarely mentioned the crucial point that the new corporate restructuring is directly hooked to the imperatives of globalisation and that it is happening all over the world. Obfuscation yet again.

The media also report daily about the immigration crises, about masses of people trying to cross borders in search of jobs, only to be greeted by xenophobia, violence, and demagoguery in high places. The present examples of such violence are daily reported in media of attacking of Indians in Australia. But the role that international trade agreements play in making life impossible for people in their countries of origin is not visible in such reports. The North American Free Trade Agreement (NAFTA), for example, was a virtual knockout blow to the largely self-sufficient, small, corn-farming economy of Mexico's indigenous peoples—as the Zapatista rebels tried to illuminate in 1994—making indigenous lands vulnerable to corporate buyouts and foreign competition from the United States.[6]

Meanwhile, in India, Africa and South America, similar World Bank development schemes over the past few decades have deliberately displaced whole populations of relatively prosperous peoples, including small scale self-sufficient farmers, to make way for giant dams and other mega development schemes. The result of such "development" is that millions of small farmers are turned into landless refugees seeking nonexistent urban jobs.

On the food shortages, rarely is the connection drawn between hunger and the increased control of the world's food supply by a small number of giant (subsidised) corporations, notably Cargill, which effectively determines where food will grow, under which conditions it will grow and what ultimate price consumers will pay. The food, rather than being eaten by local people who grow it, is now typically shipped thousands of miles (at great environmental cost) to be eaten by the already well fed.

Horrible new disease outbreaks are very thoroughly reported with ghoulish relish in the Western press. The part that is omitted, however, is the connection between these outbreaks and the destruction of rainforest and other habitats. As economic expansionism proceeds, previously uncontacted organisms hitch ride on new vectors for new territory.

One also reads stories about the "last indigenous tribes" in the Amazon, Borneo, Africa or the Philippines; stories that lament the inevitability that native people, even against their clearly articulated wishes, even against the resistance of arrows and spears, must be drawn into the Western economic model to benefit from our development plans. Insufficiently reported are the root causes of this: the demands of economic growth for more water or forest resources; the desperate need for new lands for beef cattle, coffee or timber plantations; the equally desperate need to convert previously self-sufficient peoples into consumer clones. This is not to mention the far deeper need to destroy the "other" for the psychological threat they represent and for their example of viability in an entirely alternative context.[7]

As for the role of technology, the powers that be continue to speak of each new generation of technological innovation in the same utopian terms they used to describe each preceding generation, going back to the private automobile, plastics and "clean nuclear energy", each introduced as panaceas for society. Now we have global computer networks that are said to "empower" communities and individuals, when the exact opposite is the case. The global computer-satellite linkup, besides offering a spectacular new tool for financial speculation, empowers the global corporation's ability to keep its thousand-armed global enterprise in constant touch, making instantaneous adjustments at the striking of a key. Computer technology may actually be the most centralising technology ever invented, at least in terms of economic and political power. This much is certain: The global corporation of today could not exist without computers. The technology makes globalisation possible by conferring a degree of control beyond anything ever seen before.

Meanwhile, new technologies such as biotechnology bring the development framework to entirely new terrain by enabling the enclosure and commercialisation of the internal wilderness of the gene structure, the building blocks of life itself. The invention and patenting of new life forms, from cells to insects to animals to humans, will have profound effects on Third World agriculture, ecology and human rights.

The point is this: all of the subjects are treated by the media, government officials and corporations alike as if they were totally unrelated. This is not helpful to an insecure public that is attempting to grasp what's happening and what might be done about it. The media do not help us to understand that each of these issues—overcrowded cities, unusual new weather patterns, the growth of global poverty, the lowering of wages while stock prices soar, the elimination of local social services, the destruction of wilderness, even the disappearance of songbirds—are the products of the same global policies. They are all of one piece, a fabric of connections that are ecological, social and political in nature. They are reactions to the world's economic-political restructuring in the name of accelerated global development. This restructuring has been designed by economists and corporations and encouraged by subservient governments; soon it will be made mandatory by international bureaucrats, who are beyond democratic control.

In such a scenario, the Gandhian alternative discussed in chapter V becomes more relevant and urgent.

Notes and References

1. Frances Moore Lappe and Anna Lappe, "Hope's Edge: The Next Diet for a Small Planet", Weider Publications, Boca Raton FL 33431, 2002, pp. 123-45.
2. http://www.foodandsocietyfellows.org/publications.cfm?refID=79259
3. Biju Raghavan Mootheril, "Good Governance and administrative practices, Mittal Publication, New Delhi, 2007, p. 178.
4. http://www.resurgence.org/contributions/contrb_l_m.htm#mander
5. Sachs, Wolfgang (ed.), The development dictionary: a guide to knowledge as power, Zed Books [U.A.], London:, 1992, pp. 334-35.
6. Pasricha, Ashu, WTO, Self-Reliance And Globalisation, Deep & Deep Publications, New Delhi, 2004, pp. 35-36.
7. Mander, Jerry (ed.), The Case Against Global Economy, Sierra Club Books, San Francisco, 2007, pp. 131-45.

Bibliography

Agrawal, Pradeep, Economic Restructuring in East Asia and India: Lessons in Policy Reform, London: Macmillan, 1995.

Ahluwalia, Isher J. and Little, I.M.D. (eds.), India's Economic Reforms and Development for Manmohan Singh (New Delhi: Oxford University Press), 1998.

Ahluwalia, Isher J., Productivity and Growth in Indian Manufacturing (New Delhi: Oxford Press), 1991.

Aimin Yan, Yadong Luo, International joint ventures: theory and practice, New York, M.E. Sharpe Inc, 2001.

Aiyangar, K.V. Rangaswami, Aspects of Ancient Economic Thought (Varanasi, Banaras Hindu University), 1965.

Alavi, Hamaza, *et. al.*, Capitalism and Colonial Production (London: Oxford University Press), 1982,

Amjad, R. (ed.), To the Gulf and Back: Studies on the Economic Impact of Asian Labour Migration, ILO/ ARTEP and UNDP, New Delhi, 1989.

Anesty, Vera, The Economic Development of India, New York, Arno Press, 1977.

Angus Maddison, Monitoring the World Economy, Paris: OECD Publications, 1995.

Arora, Anil, International Trade (New Delhi: Deep and Deep Publications), 2007

Arundhati Roy, Power Politics: The Reincarnation of Rumpelstiltskin, Kottayam, D.C. Books, 2001.

B. Sheikh Ali, H.V. Sreenivasa Murthy, Essays on Indian history and culture: Felicitation volume in honour of Professor B. Sheik Ali; 1st edition, New Delhi, Mittal Publications (1990).

Bagchi, A.K., Private Investment in India, (1900-1939), Cambridge, Cambridge University Press, 1972.

Bailey, David, Harte George, Sugden Rogerl, Transnational and Governments: Recent Policy in Japan, France, Germany, the United States and Britain, London, Rutledge, 1994.

Bansal, Vinay, Objective banking and finace, Agra, Upkar Prakashan, 2006.

Barnett, R.J. and Cavanagh, J., Global Dreams, New York: Simon and Schuster, 1994.

Barro, R.J., and X. Sala-i-Martin, Economic Growth, New York: McGraw-Hill, 1995.

Barro, R.J., Determinants of Economic Growth, Cambridge : MIT Press, 1997.

Bates, Robert H. and Anne O. Krueger, Political and Economic Interactions in Economic Policy Reform: Evidence from Eight Countries, Oxford, Blackwell, 1993.

Beer, G.L., The Old Colonial System (1660-1754), New York, Bibliov Bazaar, 1912.

Bhagwati, Jagdish, In Defense of Globalisation (New Delhi: Oxford Press), 2004.

Bhattacharya, Sabyasachi, The Mahatma and the Poet (New Delhi: National Book Trust), 1977.

Biju Raghavan Mootheril, Good Governance and Administrative Practices, New Delhi, Mittal Publication, 2007.

Blackwell, T. and J. Seabrook, The Revolt Against Change: Towards a Conserving Radicalism, London: Vintage, 1993.

Brahmananda, P.R. and Panchamukhi, V.R., The Development Process of the Indian Economy, Bombay, Himalaya Publishing House, 1987.

Brailsford, Hen Noel, Rebel India (London: Victor Gollancy Ltd.), 1931.

Chakravarthi, Raghuvan, South May be Trapped into New WTO Round, *Nai Azadi Udghosh*, Vol. 8, No. 1, January-Feburary, 2001.

Chakravarty, Development of Development Thinking in R. R. Kale Memorial Lecture delievered at the Gokhakle Institute of Politics and Economics, Pune, reprinted in Selected Economic Writings (Delhi: Oxford University Press), 1989.

Chandra, Bipan, Essays on Colonialism, Hyderabad, Orient Longman, 2000.

Chandra, Bipan, India's Struggle for Independence, 1857-1947, New Delhi, Viking, 1988.

Chandra, Bipan, Nationalism and Colonialism in Modern India, New Delhi, Orient Longman, 1979.

Chandra, Bipan, The Rise and Growth of Economic Nationalism in India: Economic Policies of Indian National Leadership, 1880-1905, New Delhi, People's Pub. House, 1966.

Chandra, Bipin, Sociological Theories: Race and Colonialism, Paris: UNESCO, 1980.

Chase-Dunn, C., Global Formation, Oxford: Basil Blackwell, 1989.

Chaudhuri, Pramit, The Indian Economy: Poverty and Development, London, Crosby Lockwood Staples, 1978.

Christopher Stevens, Food aid and the developing world: Four African case studies, Vincent P. Gutschick Publisher: London, Croom Helm, in association with the Overseas Development Institute (1979).

Collected Works of Mahatma Gandhi, New Delhi, Publications Division, Ministry of Information and Broadcasting, Govt. of India, 1969.

Cook, Paul and Frederick I. Nixson (eds.), The Move to the Market? Trade and Industry Policy Reform in Transitional Economies, London: Macmillan, 1995.

Crafts, N.F.R. and G. Toniolo, Economic Growth in Europe Since 1945, Cambridge: Cambridge University Press, 1996.

Datt and Sundharam, Indian Economy, New Delhi : Niraj Prakashan, 1969.

David Skidmore, Contested social orders and international politics, Nashville, T.N., USA, Vanderbilt University Press, 1997.

Davis, Kingsley, The Population of India and Pakistan, Princeton, Princeton University Press, 1951.

DePamphilis Donald, Mergers, Acquisitions, and Other Restructuring Activities, Second Edition, London, Academic Press, 2002.

Dhawan, Gopi Nath, The Political Philosophy of Mahatma Gandhi (Ahmedabad, Navajivan Publishing House), 1951.

Diamond, Larry and Marc F. Plattner, Economic Reform and Democracy, Baltimore, Johns Hopkins University Press, 1995.

Diamond, Larry and Marc, F. Plattner, Economic Reform and Democracy, Baltimore, Johns Hopkins University Press, 1995.

Dicken Peter, Global Shift, London, Paul Chapman Publishing Ltd., 1998.

Dunning, J.H., Globalisation: The Challenge for National Economic Regimes, Dublin: The Economic and Social Research Council, 1994.

Dunning, J.H., Multinational Enterprises and the Global Economy, Wokingham, Berkshin, Addison Wesley, 1993.

Dunning, J.H., Multinational Enterprises and the Global Economy, Wokingham, Berkshin, Addison Wesley, 1993.

Dunning, J.H., The Globalising of Business, London and New York: Rutledge, 1993.

Earle, Julie, Enron may seek damages over India project, *Financial Times,* by Julie, Earle, May 22, 2001, *Economic and Political Weekly*, Volume 21, 1986.

Economic Polities of Indian National Leadership, 1880-1905, New Delhi, 1966.

Encyclopedia Britanica (London: Encyclopaedia Britanica Inc.), 2002.

Evans, Peter B., Embedded Autonomy: States and Industrial Transformation, Princeton, Princeton University Press, 1995.

Farooqi, I.H., Macro Structure of Public Enterprises in India (Bombay: Asia Publishing House), 1979.

Furnivall, J.S., Colonial Policy and Practice, New York University Press, (New York), 1956.

Gandhi, M.K., An Autobiography or The Story of My Experiments with Truth (Ahmedabad: Navajivan Publishing House), 1988.

Gandhi, M.K., Economics of_Khadi (Ahmedabad: Navajivan Publishing House), 1941.

Gandhi, M.K., From Yervada Mandir (Ahmedabad, Navajivan Publishing House), 1957.

Gandhi, M.K., *Sarvodaya* (Ahmedabad: Navajivan Publishing House), 1954.

Gandhi, M.K., *Sarvodaya* (Ahmedabad: Navajivan Trust), January 1954.

Gandhi, M.K., The Collected Works, Vols. 1-100, New Delhi.

Gandhi, M.K., The Collected Works, Vols. 1-100, New Delhi.

Gathani Batuk, Acquisition, 'Was A Matter Of Pride', *Business Line,* Thursday, Feb. 01, 2007.

Govt. Warns Of Stern Steps To Break Cement, Steel Cartels, *Business Line,* Thursday, Apr 17, 2008.

Grover, B.L., and Sethi, R.R., A New Look on Modern Indian History (New Delhi: S. Chand and Co.), 1970.

Gupta, K.L., Bharat Men Loghudyog, Navyug Sahitya Sadan (Agra), 1984,

Gus Liebenow African politics: Crises and challenges, Indiana University Press, Indiana, 1986.

Habib, Ifran, Relationship of Capitalism and Colonial Accumulation: The Indian case, Department of History, Aligarh Muslim University, Aligarh, 1988.

Haggard, Stephan and Robert, R. Kaufman (eds.), The Politics of Economic Adjustment: International Constraints, Distributive Conflict and the State, Princeton, Princeton University Press, 1992.

Hall, D., Privatisation, multinationals and corruption, Development in Practice The Corner House, 2000.

Hanson, A. H., Public Enterprises and Economic Development (London: Routledge and Kegan Paul Ltd.), 1960.

Hanson, A.H., Public Enterprises and Economic Development.

Haq, A.M., Welfare Criteria in Gandhian Economics, *Gandhi Marg,* Vol. 11, No. 5, August 1981.

Harijan, 12.2.1938.

Harijan, 23-1.1939.

Harijan, 25.2.1939.

Harijan, A Journal of Applied Gandhism, 1933-55 (New York: Garland Publishing Inc.), 1973, January 3, 1946.

Harris, R.W., England in the eighteenth century, 1689-1793; A Balanced Constitution And New Horizons, Humanities Press, New York, 1968.

Henderson, J., The Globalisation of High Technology Production, London, Roultedge, 1989.

Herbert Hovenkamp, Mark D. Janis, Mark A. Lemley, Ip and Antitrust: An Analysis of Antitrust Principles Applied to Intellectual Property Law (Vol. one), Herbert (USA) Aspen Law and Business Publishers, 2002.

Hersch, Jacques, The USA and the Rise of East Asia Since 1945, London: Macmillan, 1993.

Hingorani, Anand, K. (ed.), The Gospel of Swadeshi (Bombay: Bhartiya Vidya Bhawan), 1976.

Hirst, Paul and Grahame Thompson, Globalisation in Question: The International Economy and the Possibilities of Governance, Cambridge, Polity Press, 1996.

http://www.twnside.org.sg/title/fiddle-cn.htm

Ian Cummins, Marx, Engels, and National Movements, Redwood Burn Ltd., London, 1980.

ILO, A Fair Globalisation: Creating Opportunities for All, Report of the World Commission on the Social Dimension of Globalisation, Geneva, 2004.

Inkeless, Alex, Making Men Modern: Interactions, On the Causes and Consequences of Individual Change in Six Developing Countries, New York: Basic Books, 1964.

Iyer, Raghavan, N., The Moral and Political Thought of Mahatma Gandhi (Delhi: Oxford University Press), 1973.

James Mahoney, A Comparative Historical Analysis, Polity Press, Cambridge, 1986.

John, K. Galbraith, The Public Purpose of Economics, *The American Review,* March 1974, Johnson, Chalmers, MITI and the Japanese Miracle: The Growth of Industrial Policy, 1925-75, Stanford University, Stanford, CA.

Johnson, Chalmers, MITI and the Japanese Miracle: The Growth of Industrial Policy, 1925-75, Stanford, CA, Stanford University Press, 1982.

Kanter, Rosabeth Moss, World Class: Thriving Locally in the Global Economy, New York, Simon and Schuster, 1995.

Katakam, Anupama, The issue of arbitration, *The Frontline*, Volume 20, Issue 20, September 27-October 10, 2003.

Kavin, Danaher, 50 years are not enough: the case against World Bank and International Monetaey Fund (ed.) South End Press (1994).

Kennedy, Paul, The Rise and Fall of Great Powers: Economic Change and Military Conflict from 1500 to 2000, London, Unwin Hyman, 1988.

Kenney, M. and Florida, R., Beyond Mass Production, Oxford and New York: Oxford University Press, 1993.

Kher, V.B. (ed.), Gandhi: Economic and Industrial Life and Relations (Ahmedabad: Navajivan Publishing House), 1957, Vol. II.

Kidron, Michael, Foreign Investments in India, London, 1965.

Kingsley, Mary, West African Studies (London: Oxford Press), 1901, Chaps. XII to XV.

Kochhar, Rajesh, Towards A Global Perspective On Globalisation, *The Hindu*, Tuesday, Dec. 16, 2003.

Koontz, Harold and O'Donnell Cyril, Essentials of Management (New Delhi: Tata Mc-Graw Hill), 1978.

Krasner, Stephen D. (ed.), International Regimes, Ithaca, New York, Cornell University Press, 1983.

Kripalani, J.B., Gandhi: His Life and Thought (Calcutta: Orient Longman), 1961.

Kriplani, J.B., The Meaning of Swadeshi, *Gandhi Marg*, Vol. 2, No. 3, July 1967.

Krishnaji, N., Halfway House (New York: New York Press), 1980.

Kumar, Arun, Thwarting National Policy-making, *The Tribune*, Chandigarh, Monday, October 29, 2007.

Kumar, Dharma, ed., The Cambridge Economic History of India, Vol. 2, New Delhi, 1999.

Kuttner, R., The End of Laissez Faire, New York: A.A. Knopf, 1991.

Lash, S. and Urry, J. Economics of Signs and Spaces, Macmillan, London, 1993.

Lee, W. Barbara and Nellis, John, Enterprise Reform and Privatisation in Socialist Economies, Washington, World Bank Discussion Paper, 1990.

Lenin, V.I., Imperialism: The Highest State of Capitalism, New York, International Publishers, 1974.

Letter from Dr. A. Rehman Khan to Chief of the Seed Certification Department, 6 August 1999, quoted in *ibid*.

Levkovsky, A.I., Capitalism in India, New Delhi, 1966.

Lewis, W.A., The Evolution of the International Economic Order, Princeton, NJ: Princeton University Press, 1978.

Lindblom, Charles E., Politics and Markets, The World's Political Economic Systems, Basic Books, New York, 1977.

Lipset, Seymour Martin, Kyoung-Ryung Seong and John Charles Torres, A Comparative Analysis of the Social Requisites of Democracy, *International Social Science Journal*, Vol. 45, 1993.

Lipset, Symour Martin, The Encyclopedia of Democracy (London: Roultege), Vol. I, 1995.

Lipsey, R.E., Global Change and Economic Policy, Simon Frazer University, mimeo, Vancouver: 1990.

Lundell, Krister, Contextual determinants of electoral system choice: a macro, Abo Akademis forlag (Michigan), 2005.

Lyer, Raghvan N., The Moral and Political Thought of Mahatma Gandhi (Delhi: Oxford University Press), 1973.

Maddison, A., Monitoring the World Economy: 1820-92, Paris: OECD Development Centre Studies, 1995.

Maddison, A., Phases of Capitalist Development, Oxford University Press, Oxford, 1982.

Maddison, Angus, Class Structure and Economic Growth: India and Pakistan Since the Moghuls, London, 1976.

Mallya, M.N., Public Enterprise in India (New Delhi: National Publishing House), 1971.

Mander, Jerry (ed.), The Case Against Global Economy: Sierra Club Books, San Francisco, 2007.

Manorma Year Book (Kerela: Manorama Publishing House), 1982.

Maratha, 15 March, 1896.

Marie-Bénédicte Dembour, Recalling the Belgian Congo: Conversations and Introspection, Berghahn Books; 2nd edition, 2001.

Martin Carnoy *et al.*, The New Global Economy in the Information Age, Penn State University Press, 1993.

Marx, Karl and Engels, Communist Manifesto, Foreign Languages Publishing House, Moscow, 1962.

Marx, Karl and F. Engels, Collected Works (Moscow), Vol. 6, 1976.

McKenzie, R.B. and Lee, D.R., Quicksilver Capital, New York: The Free Press, 1991.

Mehta, S. Pradeep, Cement cartels: flavour of the day, *The Financial Express,* Sunday, June 10, 2007.

Mehta, S. Pradeep, Surrogate advertising—Needed a spirited attack, *Business Line,* Friday, May 23, 2003.

Mehta, S. Pradeep, When economy slows, cartelisation grows *The Business Line,* Tuesday, Apr. 28, 2009.

Mehta, Sanat, Effect of New Industrial Policy on Labour, *Financial Express,* 7 November 1991.

Merchant Khozem, Enron plant may be mothballed, *Financial Times,* June 7, 2001.

Microsoft Corp., Annual Report (Form 10-K), at 20, 23, 26 (Jul. 31, 2008).

Miliband Ralph, The State in Capitalist Society, Oxford University Press (London), 1969.

Miliband, R. and J. Saville, moving on (ed.), Socialist Register, London, 1976

Mittelman, James H. (ed.), Globalisations, Boulder Co., Lynne Rienner, 1995.

Mohammad Ghosh, Poverty Structural Change and the Indian Constitution, in M. Mehmood (ed.), Social Justice and Social Process in India.

MRTPC issues notice to Airtel, Vodafone and Idea Cellular, *The Business Line,* Friday, Apr. 04, 2008.

Muddassir Rizvi, 'Monsanto Fiddles with Plant Protection Act', Inter Press Service, 31 August, 1999.

Mukherjee, Ambarish, More mobiles and sparrows take flight, *Business Line,* Monday, Dec. 01, 2003.

Mukherjee, Ramakrishna, The Rise and Fall of the East India Company, Berlin, 1955.

Murali, D., Cartelist behaviour is difficult to detect, *The Hindu,* Saturday, December 22, 2007.

Muratori, Relations des missions du Paraguai, (French trans) J. Marmaduke (Paris), 1759.

Naisbitt, J., Global Paradox, New York: William Morrow, 1994.

Naoroji, Dadabhai, Poverty and Un-British Rule in India (New Delh: Publications Division, Ministry of Information and Broadcasting, Governement of India), 1996.

Nayar, Baldev Raj, Globalisation and Nationalism: The Changing Balance in India's Economic Policy, 1950-2000, New Delhi, Sage Publications, 2001.

Nehru, Jawaharlal, The State's Role in Industrialisation, Inaugural address to the U.N. Seminar on Management of Public Industrial Enterprises in the ECAFE region, in Jawaharlal Nehru's Speeches, 1957-63 (New Delhi: Publications Division, Government of India), 1959.

Netscape Says, Microsoft Sought 20% Stake, *The New York Times,* September 28, 1995.

New Standards Encyclopedia (Chicago: Standard Educational Corporation), Vol. 3, New York: Basic Books, 1964.

Nick Cohen, Without Prejudice: U-turns in the U-bend, *The Observer,* U.K., 6-6-1999.

Novell, Inc. *v.* Microsoft Corp., No. JFM-05-1087, 2005, U.S. Dist. LEXIS 11520 (D. Md., June 10, 2005).

O'Rourke, K.H., and J.G. Williamson, Globalisation and History: The Evolution of a 19th Century Atlantic Economy, Cambridge, MA: MIT Press, 1998.

OECD, Technology and the Economy, Paris: OECD, 1992.

Ohmac, K., The Borderless world. New York: Harper Business, 1990.

Oliver de Schutter, UN Rapporteur on Food, Interview to Le Monde, May 2, 2008.

Oman, C., Globalisation and Regionalisation: The Challenge for Developing Countries, Paris: OECO Development Centre, 1994.

Osterhammel, J., Colonialism: A Theoretical Overview (New Jersy: M. Wiener), 1997.

Panchal Komalkirti, 50 years of scams and scandals, *Business India*, August 11-24, 1997.

Parvathi Menon, Water Supply: Cautious Corporatisation, *Frontline*, (Volume 18, Issue 13), Jun. 23-Jul. 06, 2001.

Pasenberg, N., Exploring the Black Box, Cambridge: Cambridge University Press, 1988.

Pasricha, Ashu, WTO, Self-Reliance and Globalisation, Deep & Deep Publications, New Delhi, 2004.

Patel, I.G., A Self-Generating Economy, Problems in the Third Plan: A Critical Miscellany (New Delhi: Publications Division, Government of India), 1961.

Patnaik, Prabhat, A Synoptic View of Underdevelopment, Review of The Political Economy of Underdevelopment, by A.K. Bagchi, *Economic and Political Weekly*, Vol. 19, No. 28, 14 July 1984.

Paul Festa, I.E. 5.5 angers Web standards advocates CNET NEWS, July 13, 2000 http://news.cnet.com/2100-1023-243144.html

Pauling Linus, World Encyclopedia of Peace (Oxford: Pergamon Press), Vol. 1.

Performance of Indian Public Enterprises: *Scope*, New Delhi, 1978, Quoted in P.K. Vausudeva, World Trade Organisation (Delhi: Pearson Education), 2005.

Peter Stalker, The Work of Strangers, ILO, Geneva.

Piore, M. and Sabel, C., The Second Industrial Divide: Possibilities for Prosperity, New York: Basic Books, 1984.

Polanyi, Karl, The Great Trasformation, New York, Rinehart, 1957.

Raj Kumar, Essays on Modern India?, Discovery Publishing House, New Delhi 2003.

Rajagopalachari, C. and Kumarappa, J.C., The Nation's Voice (Ahmedabad, Navajivan Publishing House), 1957,

Ram Gopal, How India Struggled for Freedom (Bombay: The Book Centre Pvt. Ltd.), 1967.

Ramanadham, V.V., The Stucture of Public Enterprises in India.

Ranade, M.G., Essays in Indian Economics (Madras: G.A. Natesan & Co.), 1906.

Rao, V.K.R.V., The Public Sector in Indian Socialism, Indian Economic Development and Policy, P.R. Brahmananda and Others (eds.), 1979.

Reinhard, W., Kleine Geschichte des Kolonialismus (trns.) (Stuttgart : Kroner), 1996.

René Maunier, The sociology of colonies: an introduction to the study of race contact, Part 1, Routledge, 2002, London.

Report of the Study Team on Public Sector Undetakings, 1967.

Rost, W.W., The Stages of Economic Growth: A Non-communist Manifesto, Cambridge University, 1960.

Roy, A., Power Politics (Cambridge: South End Press), 2001.

Ruigrok, W. and Van Tulder, R., The Logic of International Restructuring, London and New York, Routledge, 1995.

Sachitanand, N.N., Will These Goliaths Oust The Davids? *The Hindu*, Opinion, Friday, July 15, 2005.

Sachs, Wolfgang, The Development Dictionary, Baba Barkha Natha Printer, 2000,

Saletor, B.A., Ancient Indian Political Thought (Bombay: Asia Publishing House), 1968.

Sarkar, Sumit, The Swadeshi Movement in Bengal: 1903-08 (New Delhi: People's Publishing House), 1994.

Sassen, S., Cities in a World Economy, Thousands Oaks, CA, Pine Forge/Sage, 1994.

Sassen, S., The Global City, Princeton, NJ, Princeton University Press, 1991.

Schumpeter, J.A., Capitalism. Socialism and Democracy, New York: Harper and Row, 1947.

Security Concerns For Telecom, *The Times of India*, New Delhi, 22 May, 2006.

Sengupta, Arjun, Reforms, Equity and the IMF: An Economist's World, Har Anand, New Delhi, 2001.

Sethi, Aman, Bali road map, *The Frontline*, Volume 25, Issue 01, Jan. 05-18, 2008.

Sethi, J.D., Gandhi Today (New Delhi: Vikas Publishing House), 1978.

Sethi, J.D., International Economic Disorder (Shimla: Indian Institute of Advanced Study), 1990.

Sethi, K. Chitleen, 50 Pc Of Mohali Units Have Closed Down, *The Tribune*, Chandigarh, Friday, 26-12-2003.

Seymour Martin Lipset, Jason M. Lakin, The Democratic Century, University of Oklahoma Press, Oklahoma, 2004.

Sharma, Jai Narain, Alternative Economics: Economies of Mahatma Gandhi and Globalisation, New Delhi, Deep and Deep, 2003.

Sharma, K. Jitendra, Tobacco ads likely to be stubbed out by Jan.-end, *Hindustan Times*, New Delhi, 22 January 2004.

Sharma, Rashmi, Gandhian Economics: A Humane Approach (New Delhi: Deep and Deep), 1997; Siddharthan, N.S., Industrial Development Issues and Policy Options, *Economic and Political Weekly*, May 11, 1985.

Sharma, Smriti, Cellphone radiation boils egg in 80 min. Think what it can do to your head, *Chandigarh Tribune*, Wednesday, October 8, 2008.

Shashi Tharoor, India: From Midnight to the Millennium, Arcade Publishing, 1997.

Sills, David, L. (ed.), International Encyclopedia of the Social Sciences (London: Collier-Macmillan Publishers), Vols. 3 and 4,

Simpson, John and Edmund Weiner (eds.), Oxford English Dictionary (Oxford: Oxford University Press), 1976.

Singh, K.P.R., Relevance of Public Enterprises in Developing Economics (Bangalore: *Southern Economists*), 1986.

Sir Charles Metclafe quoted by Desai, A.R., in Social Background of Indian Nationalism (Bombay: Popular Prakashan Pvt. Ltd.), 1976.

Sitaramayya, Pattabhi, History of Indian National Congress (S. Chand & Company), 1969, Vol. I.

Smith, Adam, Wealth of Nations, Modern Library, New York 1776.

Smith, Tony, A Comparative Study of French and British De-Colonisation, Comparative Studies in Society and History, Vol. 20, 1978.

So, Alvin Y., Social Change and Development, Modernisation Dependency, and World System Theories,: Sage, London 1990.

Soros, G., The Alchemy of Finance, Reading the Mind of the Market (Little Brown & Company), New York, 1987.

Sridhar, V., All about PNs, *Frontline*, Volume 24, Issue 22, Nov. 03-16, 2007.

Srivastava, Aseem, Impact of Globalisation: Stagflation and Food Price Rise, *Nai Azadi Udgosh* (Allahabad), Vol. 17, Nos. 6-7, June-July, 2008.

Stiglitz, Joseph, Globalisation and Its Discontents (Penguin Press), Allen Lane, 2002.

Stiglitz, Joseph, E., Making Globalisation Work (Penguin Books), Allen Lane, 2006.

Stopford, J. and Strange, S., Rival States, Rival Firms, Cambridge: Cambridge University Press, 1991. Stubbs, Richard and Geoffrey, R.D. Underhill (eds.), Political Economy and the Changing Global Order, Toronto: McClelland and Stewart, 1994. Tausch, Amo with Fred Prager, 1993, Towards a Socio-Liberal Theory of World Development, London: Macmillan. Tilly, Charles (ed.), The Formation of National States in Western Europe, Princeton, Princeton University Press, 1975. Weiss, Linda and John M. Hobson, States and Economic Development: A Comparative Historical Analysis, Cambridge, Polity Prtess, 1998. Weiss, Linda, The .Myth of the Powerless State, Ithaca, New York, Cornell University Press, 2000. Wendt, H., Global Embrace, New York: Harper Business, 1993, Williamson, O.E., The Economic Institutions of Capitalism, New York: Free Press, 1985. Williamson, John (ed.), The Political Economy of Policy Reform, Washington, D.C., Institute for International Economics, 1994. World Bank, Global Economic Prospects and The Developing Countries, Washington: The World Bank, 2002. World Bank, World

Development Report, Oxford, Oxford University Press, 2002. World Bank, The East Asian Miracle, Oxford: Oxford Univresity Press, 2002. Wurfel, David and Bruce Burton (eds.), Political Economy of Regionalism in Southeast Asia in the 1990s, London: Macmillan, 1995.

Stubbs, Richard and Geoffrey, R.D. Underhill (eds.), Political Economy and the Changing Global Order, Toronto: McClelland and Subodh Varma, India: A Hotbed For Clinical Trials, *The Times of India*, New Delhi, 18 March, 2007.

Tamás Szentes, Transformation of the world economy: new directions and new interest, Zed Books Ltd., London, 1989.

Tausch, Amo with Fred Prager, Towards a Socio-Liberal Theory of World Development, Macmillan, London, 1993.

Thakur, Pradeep, FinMin wants list of SEZ units evading taxes, *The Times of India*, 17 Sep., 2008.

Thakurta, Paranjoy Guha, Spectrum allocation row has cost India Rs. 80,000 crore, *The Asian Age*, Delhi, Tuesday, 16 June 2009.

The Collected Works of Mahatma Gandhi (New Delhi: Publications Division, Government of India), Vol. 13.

Thomas Weber, Gandhi as disciple and mentor, Cambridge University Press, 2004.

Tilly, Charles (ed.), The Formation of National States in Western Europe, Princeton University Press, Princeton, 1975.

Toffler, Alvin, Future Shocks (A National Journal Company), New York, 1971.

Toffler, Alvin, Third Wave (A National Journal Company), New York 1975.

United Nations, Measures for Economic Development of Underdeveloped Countries, New York, 1951.

V. Sridhar, Playing with Regulations, *The Frontline*, Volume 20, Issue 19, September 13-26, 2003.

Verzola, Roberto, Globalisation: Its Third Wave, *Nai Azadi Udghosh*, Vol. 8, No. 1, September-October-November-December, 2003.

Visvesvarayya, M., Planned Economy for India (Bangalaore Press), Bangalore, 1934.

Wakefield, Edward Gibbon, A View of the Art of Colonisation in Present Reference to the British Empire in Letters between a Statesman and a Colonist (London: John W. Parker), 1849. (Rpt. by NY: Augustus M. Kelley, 1969).

Weiner, Myron, Empirical Democratic Theory, in Competitive Elections in Developing Countries (ed.) Myron Weiner and Ergun Ozbunduu (N.C.: Duke University Press), Durham, 1987.

Weiss, Linda, The Myth of the Powerless State, Ithaca, Cornell University Press, New York, 2000.

Williamson, John (ed.), The Political Economy of Policy Reform, D.C., Institute for International Economics, Washington, 1994.

World Affairs, Vol. 5, No. 1, New Delhi, India.

World Bank Report, 2000.

World Bank, Global Economic Prospects and the Developing Countries, Washington: The World Bank, 2002.

World Commission on the Social Dimension of Globalisation, A Fair Globalisation: Creating Opportunities for All (Geneva: International Labour Office), 2004.

Wurfel, David and Bruce Burton (eds.), Political Economy of Regionalism in Southeast Asia in the 1990s, London: Macmillan.

Young India, 12-3-1925.

Young India, 14-01-1920.

Young India, 17-2-1926.

Young India, April 2, 1931.

Young, Robert, Post-colonialism: A Historical Introduction (Blackwell), Oxford, 2001.

Articles

Bharat Bhushan, House of Lords, The Telegraph, Opinion, Calcutta, Monday, June 21, 2004.

Chakravarthi, Raghavan, Hazardous Obsession with Global Integration, *Nai Azadi Udghosh*, Vol. 6, No. 3-4, May-April, 2001.

Chaudhri, Sudip, Public Enterprises and Private Purposes, *Economic and Political Weekly*, Vol. XXIX, No. 22, May 28, 1994.

D. Brunn Stalley, Wal-Mart World: The World's Biggest Corporation In The Global Economy, CRC Press, 2006.

Daiichi Sankyo, Completes Ranbaxy Takeover, *The Financial Express*, Friday, Nov. 07, 2008.

Deaton, Angus and Dreze, Jean, Poverty and Inequality in India: A Re-examination, *Economic and Political Weekly*, 2003, Vol. 35.

Dugger Celia, W., High-Stakes Showdown; Enron's Fight Over Power Plant Reverberates Beyond India, *The New York Times*, March 20, 2001.

Huw Bowen, 'Imperial Adventurers', *Guardian*, 12 January 2002.

Wysham Daphne and Smitu Kothari, Climate change will devastate India, *The Hindu*, April 9, 2007.

Websites

"http://afraf.oxfordjournals.org/cgi/reprint/68/272/269.pdf

"http://biz.yahoo.com/msft/p10.html

"http://en.wikipedia.org/wiki/BSE_Sensex#Sensex_milestones

"http://exim.indiamart.com/ssi-regulations/idr-act.html

"http://idea.sec.gov/Archives/edgar/data/789019/000119312508162768/d10k.htm

"http://idea.sec.gov/Archives/edgar/data/789019/000119312508162768/d10k.htm.

"http://plato.stanford.edu/entries/colonialism

"http://www.123eng.com/forum/viewtopic.php?t=16132

"http://www.allbusiness.com/technology/software-services-applications/7190655-1.html.

"http://www.apfn.org/apfn/enron_republican.htm

"http://www.businessworld.in/index.php/Corporate/Reactions-To.html

"http://www.competition-commission-india.nic.in/advocacy/Articles_in_press/CCIWebArticlesCompilationText29042008new.pdf

"http://www.cpim.org/marxist200102_marxist_eco_ppatnaik.htm.

"http://www.crn.com/it-channel/18822436

"http://www.dot.gov.in/osp/Brochure/Brochure.htm

"http://www.edwardgoldsmith.com/page49.html

"http://www.financialweek.com/apps/pbcs.dll/article?AID=/20090107/REG/901079993/1002/ACCOUNTING

"http://www.foodandsocietyfellows.org/publications.cfm?refID=79259

"http://www.globalexchange.org/getInvolved/corporateHRviolators.html

"http://www.globalexchange.org/getInvolved/corporateHRviolators.html

"http://www.hartford-hwp.com/archives/40/139.html

"http://www.headlinesindia.com/business-news/petroleum-and-natural-gas/key-papers-sought-on-reliance-petroleum-role-in-iraqi-oil-deal-7737.html

"http://www.indianindustry.com/trade-information/acquisition-of-ranbaxy.html

"http://www.microsoft.com/presspass/press/2005/jul05/07-01msibmsettlepr.mspx.

"http://www.microsoft.com/presspass/press/2005/oct05/10-11MSRealPR.mspx.

"http://www.microsoft.com/technet/archive/winntas/deploy/ntunxint.mspx?mfr=true.

"http://www.resurgence.org/contributions/contrb_l_m.htm#mander

"http://www.thehindubusinessline.com/2007/04/19/stories/2007041902330900.htm

"http://www.theregister.co.uk/1999/07/18/analysis_how_ms_used

"http://www.usdoj.gov/atr/cases/exhibits/268.pdf.

"http://www.usdoj.gov/atr/cases/exhibits/276.pdf.

"http://www.worldbank.org/html/opr/procure/debarr.html.

"http://www2.essex.ac.uk/ces/ResearchProgrammes/safewexecsummfinalreport.htm

"www.navdanya.org/corporate/research.pdf.

Index